Transnational Muslim Politics

A wide variety of 'translocal' forces – such as diasporic communities, transnational social movements, global cities and information technologies – are challenging the traditional state-centric 'political imaginary' of international relations. Moreover, just as people are translocal, so are their ideas, theories and worldviews. This provocative, ground-breaking book analyses Islam as a form of 'travelling theory' in the context of such contemporary global transformations. Peter Mandaville examines how 'globalisation' is manifested as lived experience through a discussion of debates over the meaning of Muslim identity, political community and the emergence of something like a 'critical Islam'.

After a critique of state-centric thinking in international relations, the book goes on to suggest that more sophisticated treatments of translocal politics can be found in the literatures of anthropology, post-colonial and cultural studies. Mandaville introduces a non-essentialist conception of Islam, and discusses the conditions under which Muslim discourses on the *umma* (the world community of believers) have historically been produced; he also introduces three key theoretical tropes – travelling theory, hybridity and diaspora – as framing devices for understanding translocal politics.

This radical book argues that translocal forces are leading to the emergence of a wider Muslim public sphere. Furthermore, the critical discourses enabled by this translocal space amount to a reconceptualisation and reimagining of the *umma*.

Peter Mandaville is Assistant Professor of Government and Politics at George Mason University, and was formerly Lecturer in International Relations at the University of Kent, Canterbury. Previous publications include a co-edited volume, *The Zen of International Relations*.

Transnationalism
Series editor: Steven Vertovec
University of Oxford

"Transnationalism" broadly refers to multiple ties and interactions linking people or institutions across the borders of nation-states. Today myriad systems of relationship, exchange and mobility function intensively and in real time while being spread across the world. New technologies, especially involving telecommunications, serve to connect such networks. Despite great distances and notwithstanding the presence of international borders (and all the laws, regulations and national narratives they represent), many forms of association have been globally intensified and now take place paradoxically in a planet-spanning yet common arena of activity. In some instances transnational forms and processes serve to speed up or exacerbate historical patterns of activity, in others they represent arguably new forms of human interaction. Transnational practices and their consequent configurations of power are shaping the world of the twenty-first century.

This book forms part of a series of volumes concerned with describing and analysing a range of phenomena surrounding this field. Serving to ground theory and research on "globalization", the Routledge book series on "Transnationalism" offers the latest empirical studies and ground-breaking theoretical works on contemporary socio-economic, political and cultural processes which span international boundaries. Contributions to the series are drawn from Sociology, Economics, Anthropology, Politics, Geography, International Relations, Business Studies and Cultural Studies.

The series is associated with the Transnational Communities Research Programme of the Economic and Social Research Council (see http://www. transcomm.ox.ac.uk).

The series consists of two strands:

Transnationalism aims to address the needs of students and teachers, and these titles will be published in hardback and paperback. Titles include:

Culture and Politics in the Information Age
A new politics?
Edited by Frank Webster

Routledge Research in Transnationalism is a forum for innovative new research intended for a high-level specialist readership, and the titles will be available in hardback only. Titles include:

1 New Transnational Social Spaces
International migration and transnational companies in the early twenty-first century
Edited by Ludger Pries

2 Transnational Muslim Politics
Reimagining the Umma
Peter Mandaville

Transnational Muslim Politics

Reimagining the umma

Peter Mandaville

London and New York

First published 2001
by Routledge

11 New Fetter Lane, London EC4P 4EE
Simultaneously published in the USA and Canada
by Routledge
29 West 35th Street, New York, NY 10001

Routledge is an imprint of the Taylor & Francis Group

© 2001 Peter Mandaville
Sections of Chapter 1 are reprinted with the kind permission of *Millenium:
Journal of International Studies*. Portions of Chapter 5 are reproduced with
the kind permission of Maisonneuve et Larose, Paris

Typeset in Baskerville by Taylor & Francis Books Ltd
Printed and bound in Great Britain by St Edmundsbury Press,
Bury St Edmunds, Suffolk

British Library Cataloguing in Publication Data
A catalogue record for this book is available from the British Library

Library of Congress Cataloging in Publication Data
Transnational Muslim Politics: reimagining the umma. Peter Mandaville
p.cm - (transnationalism)
includes bibliographical references and index
1. Islam and politics 2. Globalization - religous aspects - Islam 3. Islam and
state 4. Umma (Islam) I. Title II. Series

ISBN 0-415-24694-6

For my parents

Contents

A note on style and transliteration

In transliterating Arabic terms, I have adopted the following scheme: at its first appearance, each Arabic term is italicised and transliterated in full following the system used by the *International Journal of Middle East Studies*. Thereafter, repetitions of the same term appear in regular type without any diacritical marks; only the medial hamza is indicated (e.g. Qur'an).

In rendering Muslim names, I have tried as much as possible to use the English forms preferred by the individuals in question.

Preface

This book's earliest antecedents date from at least ten years ago when I moved to the United Kingdom to study after having spent my childhood in a rather different sort of kingdom in the Arab Gulf. Very quickly, something started to puzzle me. The source of this confusion was the intense discrepancy between what I had come to know of Islam and, more specifically, of Muslims, over two decades in the Middle East, and the images and theories of Islam that seemed to populate contemporary Western discourse. To say that these images were merely 'inaccurate' or 'distorted' (which they certainly were) would be a severe under-statement. Very quickly, I came to realise that something far more troubling was afoot. In seeking to know or understand Islam, people seemed to me to be asking entirely the wrong questions. For example, when those claiming Muslim identity planted bombs or vented spleen at the United States (and according to the Western media, Muslims seem to do little else), analysts or observers would attempt to explain these acts by reference to something called Islam. What is this thing called Islam, they would ask. What do its traditions, books and (loudest, most radical) leaders have to tell us? There seemed, in short, to be a belief that existing within this seemingly singular and undifferentiated religion were certain innate features that not only legitimised such activities, but which quite actively encouraged them. Islam came to be a registered trademark of illiberalism – the ideational source of countless malignant practices. In sum, when dealing with Islam, labels and stereotypes are the norm; this by now is almost a truism.

My purpose here is not, however, to offer yet another rant against Western distortions and misrepresentations of Islam. The background offered above is only intended to give some insight into the discursive climate that prompted the ideas, questions and approaches animating this book. My purpose here is rather to offer an understanding of Islam that relies neither on complaint about how the West views and treats Islam, nor on finding alternative readings/interpreta-tions of Islamic tradition which bring it in line with Western expectations or affirm its compatibility with Western norms. I want to focus instead on Islam as a lived experience. What does Islam mean today to those Muslims living under globalising conditions, particularly as minority communities in Western Europe? Furthermore, can a better understanding of Muslim politics accrue not from something called 'Islamic studies', but by reading contemporary Islam through the lens of various global and transnational transformations? How, I ask, can we usefully make a link between changing configurations of political space and Muslim political discourse? To this end, I consciously avoid offering an exegesis of Islam's canonical texts. Rather, I am more interested in the things that Muslims – particularly those of the younger generation – are reading, writing, thinking and doing: in youth groups, on the Internet and in 'transnational space'. I am not in any way claiming that the classical texts tell us nothing useful about Islam. Their importance is beyond doubt. I *am*, however, claiming that we learn very little about Islam as a lived experience by going straight to the books; we learn a great deal, however, if we go to the texts *through the people who read them*. My plea, then, is for less concentration on Islam *per se*, and more on the Muslims who, on a daily basis, negotiate the complex, ambiguous circumstances of their lives through Islam.

This book also, and perhaps over-ambitiously, has a second purpose. My interest in Muslim conceptions of political community (as embodied in, for example, the *umma*) happened to coincide with other questions I was beginning to ask in the context of my own 'disciplinary home', international relations. How is it that a field of study claiming global import had managed to become so narrowly obsessed with a single form of political community, the Western, liberal nation-state? What does this say about the nature and limits of politics as understood by its dominant theorists? Most importantly: how might it be possible to understand transnational and globalising practices as disruptive of this state-centrism – as developments which provide greater space, discursive and otherwise, for the (re)emergence of alternative conceptions of community, identity and the Good? I hardly even scratch the surface of these questions in the present book; where I do, my treatment of them is often constrained by the book's larger framework related to transnationalism and Islam. I very much hope to stay with this line of inquiry in subsequent studies, however. The philosophy of community leads everywhere and beyond…

The book's omissions are many. When the ostensible scope of the study was combined with the realities of cohesive frameworks and word limits, such absences became inevitable. Particularly regretful to me was my inability to include the considerable material relating to Indonesia that I began to collect after the main text was complete. A brief visit to the State Institute for Islamic Studies in Jakarta in April 2000 confirmed to me so much of what I had been thinking about the hybrid nature of travelling theories. Indeed, a reviewer of this manuscript had already by this time pointed out to me that Indonesia would prove a particularly fertile setting in which to study the interface of Islam and globalising modernities. I look forward to continuing this project.

As this book has evolved from confusion to dissertation to book form (without losing any of the confusion!), numerous individuals have offered inspiration, advice, criticism and support. Vivienne Jabri was my first ever tutor in international relations as an undergraduate, later my dissertation supervisor and, eventually, a colleague at the University of Kent. (Makes you feel old, doesn't it, Viv?) It is she who – through her fine example – first taught me to look critically at questions of social and political theory, and for this I will always be grateful. James Piscatori offered the insight of his exemplary scholarship and the goodness of his spirit on various occasions throughout the process of completing this book. Andrew Linklater, another source of inspiration, provided valuable and challenging feedback on the final version of the manuscript. An anonymous reviewer commissioned by Routledge also offered very useful feedback.

I have benefited immensely from comments by and conversations with Dale Eickelman, Debbie Lisle, Bobby Sayyid, Annabelle Sreberny and Annick Wibben, among others. The Department of Politics and International Relations at the University of Kent under the stewardship of A.J.R. Groom has been particularly generous to me over the years, and for this I would like to register my thanks. Two colleagues in particular, Mervyn Frost and Stefan Rossbach, have been important intellectual *provocateurs*. Various friends and colleagues have provided support in ways that are difficult to specify; they are very much part of this book – in particular, Tarak Barkawi, Andrea den Boer, Kathryn Coughlin, Madeleine Demetriou, Ali Mohammadi and Gillian Youngs.

I am also grateful to the various organisations that have taken an interest in this work and provided me with forums for discussion and debate: Dick Douwes and the Institute for the Study of Islam in the Modern World (ISIM) in Leiden, the Felix Meritis Foundation of Amsterdam and the Association of Muslim Researchers in the UK. I would also like to acknowledge the financial support of the British International Studies Association and the University of Kent's Faculty Research Committee.

Of the many Muslims who gave so generously of their time in conversation with me, I would particularly like to acknowledge Sa'ad al-Faqih and Dilwar Hussein: my gratitude and *salaam*.

In preparing the manuscript, Craig Fowlie and Milon Nagi at Routledge offered valuable editorial assistance. On late summer evenings (after ridiculously full days), Alicia Phillips fought her narcoleptic impulses to proofread the final text intently and meticulously, querying my strange, mid-Atlantic syntax throughout.

My final and greatest thanks go to my parents. This book is for them. Over the years they have always and unfailingly trusted in me as I wander and wonder. It is this trust and my desire to live up to it that has often been the greatest inspiration.

Washington, DC
August 2000

Introduction

In the early 1990s, a group of distinguished Muslim scholars met at Chateau Chinon in France to consider the problems faced by Muslim communities in Europe. They decided that Islamic political theory could no longer classify non-Muslim states as *dār al-ḥarb* (the domain of war); instead, the West was to be considered *dār al-'ahd* (the domain of treaty), signifying a willingness towards greater dialogue.[1] In the spring of 1996, Citicorp announced the launching of an Islamic banking unit which would cater to 'investors and businesses requiring special financial services conforming to Islamic law'.[2] They were hoping to tap into the estimated $120 billion currently on deposit in various Islamic banks around the world.

These symbiotic images – the West adjusting its economic practices to account for Islam, and Islam changing the boundaries of its political community to enable dialogue with the West – are, in part, the product of various global sociocultural transformations which are currently modifying conventional conceptions both of world politics and of what it means to 'relate internationally'. Unprecedented global flows of peoples and cultures, transnational social movements, the rise of world cities, supranational political forms and globalising media technologies: all are calling into question the hegemony of national and statist forms of political identity, and also giving rise to discrepant visions of non-Western politics and polities. As one observer notes, 'the networks and circuits in which transnational migrants and refugees are implicated constitute fluidly bounded transnational or globalised social spaces in which new transnational forms of political organization, mobilization, and practice are coming into being'.[3] These developments challenge our conventional conceptions of how and where to locate the political.

This book is therefore motivated by two central concerns. One is to account for and provide better ways of thinking about politics and political identity under the transformative conditions highlighted above. The second is to provide an alternative reading of 'political' Islam, focusing not on militant movements and their struggles against 'the West' and/or various state governments, but rather on the politics which constitute the daily lives of the vast majority of the world's Muslims. The 'debate' between Islam and the West is certainly important, but we have allowed it to so overdetermine our perceptions of Islam that crucial contestations and negotiations *within* Islam go unnoticed. My purpose in this book is to provide, through a discourse of what I call *translocal politics*, an account of the new forms of politics emerging from the Muslim world's experience of globalisation. This line of inquiry, in which Muslim politics are understood as an aspect of 'lived' Islam under globalising conditions, can provide us with a much richer picture of how Muslims come to define and experience their political identities in the contemporary world. Much has been written about manifestations of political Islam in various national, historical and sociopolitical contexts. Several 'grand theories' about Islam's place in a global scheme have also been advanced; sadly, however, too many of these have been fairly crude, essentialising hypotheses of the 'clash of civilisations' variety. What is missing from the literature is any attempt to provide a political sociology of Islam, theoretically informed by wider developments in social theory related to migration, diaspora and translocal politics. What follows can be read as an attempt to offer exactly this.

I begin with a critique of dominant conceptions of the political in international relations and argue that the authority of statist politics is currently under threat from a variety of global sociocultural transformations which serve to disembed political identities from national contexts and also to stretch social relations across time and space. After reviewing the contributions which critical approaches to international theory are making towards accounting for these changes, I suggest that international relations would do well to supplement its discourse by engaging in dialogue with debates and developments in other disciplinary projects – namely, post-colonial studies, cultural studies and, especially, anthropology. These other fields, working as they do with richer conceptions of the linkages between culture and political identity, have been able to provide sophisticated accounts of how post-national, post-territorial and translocal idioms of the political are emerging out of globalising processes.

In the second chapter I argue for a non-essentialist definition of Islam which focuses on the notion of Muslim subjectivity rather than on 'Islam' in the sense of a given culture. This is crucial, I argue, for recognising the multiple articulations of Muslim identity found in translocal space. I then go on to situate contemporary Muslim discourse in the context of debates on modernity, postmodernity and the West, arguing that the same shifting configurations of hegemony which enable Islamist voices to articulate alternative visions of modernity also open spaces for the rearticulation and renegotiation of Islam itself. A key titular trope of the book then comes into play as I examine two historical contexts in which the *umma* (the world community of Muslims) has been elaborated as an 'alternative' political order. The history of the founding community of Muslims under Muhammad in seventh-century Medina helps us to understand the normative vision which motivated early Islam, and the anti-colonial discourses of the nineteenth- and early twentieth-century Pan-Islamic reformers provide us with a political context in which the Muslim world – from North Africa to Southeast Asia – was for the first time in centuries able to mobilise the umma as a discrepant idiom of political community in the face of a common 'other', the West. Both of these periods are important in that they represent key reference points for contemporary translocal Muslim discourse.

I return in Chapter Three to the concept of translocality and outline three theoretical themes which I see as the primary mediators of culture and politics in translocal space. The notion of travelling theory helps us to understand what happens to peoples, cultures and ideas when they move across and between various sociopolitical settings. Hybridity theory, I suggest, offers a conceptual language with which to analyse the innovative cultural intermin-glings which emerge from translocal encounters both between and within particular traditions. I then argue that post-colonial and metropolitan concep-tions of diaspora which celebrate the de-centred, 'free floating' nature of migrant identities assume a certain ironic standpoint which politicised and antagonised identities (e.g. Islam) find difficult to assume. Travelling theory, hybridity and diaspora, I claim, all help us to account for the ways in which translocal identities '[defy] assimilation into conventional political discourses and practices...and challenge conventional modes of interpreting the world within specific territories'.[4]

Chapter Four seeks to provide a detailed case study of the Muslim diaspora in the West, focusing on how Islam 'travels' and on the debates about authority and authenticity which emerge from these translocal processes. While considerable work has been done on Muslim communities in the West, none has so far attempted to situate the Muslim diaspora within a wider framework of post-national, translocal politics. The empirical material is organised according to three themes: debates with the Muslim 'other'; rethinking politics, community and gender in translocality; and transnational diasporic networks. I suggest that diasporic Muslims can be seen to possess a form of interstitial identity which fully participates neither in the politics of the majority non-Muslim society nor in the politics of the country of origin. John Eade puts it well:

> They navigate the disjunctures between different political and cultural formations and attempt to make sense of these differences in ways which do not necessarily conform to a specific tradition. Their journey is largely an imaginative, reflexive movement where they can draw on traditions in other parts of the world and in the process construct their own translation.[5]

Chapter Five examines the ways in which Muslims have been making use of media and information technologies. I first look at how the rise of print tech-nology in the nineteenth century helped to diminish the traditional scholars' monopoly over religious knowledge. I then argue that this process is being further radicalised in the present era by the widespread availability of 'Islamic' CD-ROMs and the Internet in the Muslim diaspora. These resources and forums provide Muslims with new modes of communication and interaction across distance (i.e. 'reimagining the umma'), and new public spheres in which novel forms of authority and 'authentic' Islam are able to emerge. I then look briefly at the 're-localisation' of the Internet in the Arab Gulf states as an example of what happens when these translocal public spheres enter specific sociopolitical contexts. Related to all of these developments has been the rise of a new breed of Islamist intellectual whose political programmes are more likely to be found on an audio cassette or printed in a pamphlet than heard in the mosque. The populist discourse of this new intellectual is often explicitly anti-statist and emanates from spaces and places beyond the reach of institutionalised, formal political power.

In the final chapter, I draw together the two narrative strands of the book – travelling Islam and translocal politics – in order to more explicitly illuminate the relationship between them. I argue that largely under the influence of translo-cality, political Islam – often depicted as a retrograde form of pre-medieval (un)reason – has actually become a far more complex entity in terms of the soci-ology of knowledge. New explorations in what we might term a 'critical Islam' are emerging through a reassessment and re-interpretation of traditional textual sources. Going back to the early traditions is hence not a throwback to 'fundamen-talism', but, in the case of these new Muslim discourses, an attempt to critically re-read the ethical core of the founding texts directly into contemporary contexts without the mediation of centuries of dogmatic theology. The emergence of a new Muslim public sphere has also meant a significant change of personnel in terms of who is authorised to undertake this critical renewal of Islam.

Finally, I outline the three key mechanisms through which translocality is changing the boundaries of Muslim political community. The first of these relates to the disembedding qualities of global sociocultural change which were analysed in the first chapter. In these transformations, Muslims are removed from particular national settings and resettled as minority groups such that their political identities become configured in relation to multiple locales, but also in relation to a discrepant normative vision (all the while inverting traditional conceptions of political community). Second, encounters with the 'Muslim other' in translocality relativise a Muslim's sense of identity and cause him or her to reassess the boundaries of inclusion/exclusion which determine who and what counts as 'authentic' Islam. Third, debates over the political imperatives of translocal Islam – and also over who can legitimately set this agenda – serve to create new Muslim public spheres in which formerly disenfranchised voices (e.g. 'deviants', 'moderates' and women) are empowered to articulate alternative interpretations of Islamic authenticity.

My main argument, therefore, is that under translocality the process of reimagining the umma becomes one of *reconceptualising* the umma. Many Muslims do not see global processes simply as a means by which to bridge the differences and distances between them, but rather as an opportunity to critically engage with the question of who, what, and where Muslim political community can be in the time of translocality. Their efforts can be seen as an example of how one particular set of identities is experiencing globalisation as a new form of transnational grassroots politics. Undoubtedly, as translocality becomes more and more invasive, other discrepant visions of the political will also emerge. International relations needs to account for this.

1 Beyond disciplinary boundaries

International relations and translocal politics

> If the social world…is not entirely defined in terms of repetitive, sedimented prac-
> tices, it is because the social always overflows the institutionalised frameworks of
> 'society', and because social antagonisms show the inherent contingency of those
> frameworks. Thus a dimension of construction and creation is inherent in all
> social practice. The latter do not involve only repetition, but also reconstruction.
>
> (Laclau, *The Making of Political Identities*)

> It is necessary to ask how it has become so easy to believe that movements act
> 'down there' among the locales, among those forms of life that are contained
> within the grander structures 'above'. Social movements that work entirely within
> the modern reification of spatiotemporal relations simply affirm the limits of
> their ambition.
>
> (Walker, 'Social Movements/World Politics')

The aim of this first chapter is to construct the broad theoretical architecture of
the book. I will begin by arguing that the conception of politics found in dominant strains of international relations (IR) theory – and neo-realism in particular
– is incapable of accounting for forms of politics enabled by the current climate
of rapid, global sociocultural change. By locating 'the political' within the state,
conventional IR theory reproduces a set of political structures unsuited to
circumstances in which political identities and processes configure themselves
across and between bounded forms of political community. After reviewing some
of the (infra)structural transformations which have been affecting world politics
in an increasingly globalised – or 'translocal' – era, I go on to look at the
progress which critical approaches to IR theory have made towards compre-
hending alternative notions of the political. I then suggest that IR has much to
gain from engaging with debates going on within other disciplinary projects –
namely post-colonial studies, cultural studies, and, especially, anthropology.
These fields, I argue, have been better placed to anticipate these transformations
and have consequently been able to provide considerably more sophisticated
treatments of these issues. Transnational anthropology, in particular, has begun
to develop various modes for theorising post-statist forms of politics. After a critical review of some of this thinking, I go on to develop a conception of

translocality as an increasingly important form of political space. I see the translocal as an abstract category denoting sociopolitical interaction which falls between bounded communities; that is, translocality is primarily about the ways in which people flow *through* space rather than about how they exist *in* space. It is therefore a quality characterised in terms of *movement*. I will argue that the 'travelling' which takes place in translocality serves to enact forms of politics which challenge sedentary notions of community and identity.

International relations: a limited political imagination?

The majority of international relations theory is effectively blind to a great deal of political activity in the world today. The purpose of this first section is to explain why this is so and also to argue that IR's limited imagination of the political prohibits its appreciation of important new forms of 'international' politics located outside the traditional realm of the state.

There is a strong sense in which IR has been going by the wrong name since its institutional inception in 1919. Whether styled 'international relations', 'international politics' or 'international studies', the implication has been the same, namely that what interests the scholars of these fields are relations between *nations*. A quick glance at the 'classic texts' of the discipline – and even the majority of current research in the field – reveals, however, that the IR envisaged by many of its most eminent students would have more properly been labelled 'inter-*state* politics'. State-centrism, usually identified as a fetish of realist thought, actually predates the latter insofar as the state was already coded as the centre of gravity for international political life well before the disillusionment of the inter-war years that gave rise to what we recognise today as classic realism. The argument that state-centrism in IR is merely a by-product of realism therefore misses the point, for the nexus of state and politics has exercised hegemony over our political imaginations long before anyone thought to theorise IR as an autonomous sphere of activity. It was taken for granted that what we understood by 'international relations' were really relations between state governments which, according to the modern ideal of the nation-state, were supposedly representative of their constitutive nations.

Defining the nation has proved one of the most contentious tasks of the social sciences in recent years, and the present study will not attempt or pretend to make any contribution to this ongoing melee. It will be necessary, however, in developing the post-statist framework in which this book is situated, to make some comments as to the distinction between nation and state. As regards the nature of the nation, I am broadly sympathetic to Benedict Anderson's notion of the 'imagined community'.[1] By his use of the idiom 'imagination', Anderson is not trying to suggest that nations are fictional figments, or somehow 'not real'. Rather, his is a much more complex argument about how people become cognisant of themselves as part of a social collective. In this sense, then, the construction of the nation is first and foremost about understanding the self as part of a greater whole, but one which possesses boundaries – a clear sense of inside and out. Indeed, if we examine the various sociohistorical contexts in which nations have been elaborated, we find many in which the act of creating a nation is as much about saying who one is *not*, as it is about saying who one is. It is therefore an inherently political process in the sense that it constructs boundaries of inclusion and exclusion. Furthermore, the nation exists in more than just space, it also endures in time. It is a life-world which requires reproduction in order to survive. Insofar as the nation is a discursive formation (as opposed to a corporeal construct) it requires reiteration in order to sustain itself. The nation is a story of identity, memory and belonging which needs to be told and told again. It is this dimension of the nation which leads Homi Bhabha to speak of its 'narration'.[2] The nation is hence a living thing: the reification of culture (language, morality, memory, experience, 'forms of life') into an exclusive community.

I understand the contemporary state, on the other hand, more as a technology of governance, a bureaucratic apparatus for the organisation of power and control. Like the nation, the contemporary state is also a historically-constituted, sociocultural construct. People (often in the guise of nations) produce and define state forms. The state is, however, the product of a particular political culture (European modernism) whose hegemony (in the sense of an historical particularity masquerading as the universal) has permitted its political imagination to assume tangible, institutional form. In this regard, the fact that we find a great deal of isomorphism within the modern state system is more a reflection of the history of power relations between its constituent members than a testament to the intrinsic durability of the European state model. And while the state is therefore a product of human – perhaps even of national – agency, it cannot however be denied that state hegemony has also served to structure and define the range of possibilities which we as political agents possess.

My major complaint about dominant theories of international relations such as neo-realism is that they persist in working with a relatively unproblematised understanding of the nation-state despite the veritable upheavals in citizenship, ethical capacity and sovereignty highlighted above. Where these transformations *are* recognised, they tend to be marginalised in favour of an image of IR which reproduces political realism's 'timeless wisdom'. More specifically, traditional modes of theorising IR see the nation-state as the focal point of international politics and, indeed, operate with an understanding of the political as something which only legitimately emanates from the state. In doing so, however, realism and its more recent incarnations effectively ignore the fact that there are many other layers and spaces of politics. Indeed, within the unproblematised nation-state that IR sees as central there are at least three complex political dynamics at work: (1) a politics of inclusion, exclusion and national narration; (2) a politics in which the state attempts to distil national identit(ies) into a (usually singular) 'national interest'; and (3) a meta-politics which seeks to maintain the fusion of nation and state as the most effective logic by which to order the international system.

A critique of IR's state-centric nature is, of course, nothing new. Realism has had its vociferous critics for many years.[3] Other normative visions, from Burton's 'world society' to the World Order Models Project (WOMP) have been voiced.[4] Theorists of complex interdependence have sought to downplay state hegemony.[5] Indeed, many IR theorists today would tell you that we have moved beyond our obsession with the state, citing important work being done in areas such as gender studies, ecology and international political economy in which the state, when present, tends to play the antagonist. The spectre of the state, however, is still very much with us. We tend to slip easily into realist-type language when asked to explain some aspect of contemporary world politics to someone outside the discipline. Indeed, part of IR's problem – as I will argue later – is the image that those outside the discipline hold of it. It is expected that an international relations specialist will have something to say about what the United States is doing in the Balkans, or the intrigues of a vote in the UN Security Council. In short, it is expected that IR should be able to account for inter-state politics. And with good reason. The state is still a very important actor in world politics – one would, I think, be foolish to claim otherwise at the present time. My argument, however, is not simply that we need to ask questions about the existence of other actors in world politics (for I take this as given), but rather that we need to ask questions about the nature and location of the political within what we understand as world politics. By this I mean that theories of international relations have tended to assume that 'proper' politics is something involving particular forms of decision-making by particular actors within specific institutional spaces (e.g. diplomats voting on trade agreements in the GATT). I do not deny that these are important aspects of world politics. However, there are other forms of world politics to which IR theory is effectively blind because it has only been taught to recognise a limited range of shapes and colours as political. In this sense, the question of what IR can and cannot 'see' is central to this book. This line of inquiry becomes all the more important when we begin to realise that the world is undergoing transformations which threaten further alienation in the relationship between world politics and the ways we think about the nature and location of the political. Thus I wholeheartedly agree with Rob Walker when he writes:

> My concern with the limits of the modern political imagination is informed both by a sense of the need for alternative forms of political practice under contemporary conditions and by a sense that fairly profound transformations are currently in progress. But it is also informed by a sense that our understanding of these transformations, and the contours of alternative political practices, remains caught within discursive horizons that express the spatiotemporal configurations of another era.[6]

Before I go any further something needs to be said about the nature of the 'political imagination' which I am attributing to state-centric forms of IR theory. Up to this point I have been speaking of the state as the location of 'the political' and using terms such as politics, political identity and political community without explaining how I understand them. This is particularly important insofar as one of the primary objectives of this book is to explain how certain global transformations currently underway are forcing us to reassess how we think about 'the political'. My major complaint is that the vast majority of international theory has allowed what it understands as 'the political' to be determined by *where* it sites the political. Rather than asking questions about the particular qualities of politics and political relationships (i.e. what makes them 'political'), many theorists have equated politics with those activities which fall within the remit of state structures (i.e. politics = the state). When extra-statist relations are occasionally recognised as political in nature, they tend to be dismissed as insignificant. This is because the dominant discourse sees institutionalised procedures, offices and formal bureaucratic frameworks (e.g. elections, presidents and parliaments) as the only 'real' way to practice politics. In my understanding of the political, however, there are political aspects to countless other daily social practices (e.g. sexuality, employment and religion), and these are not politics which can simply be dismissed as irrelevant. Furthermore, I want to argue that the current globalising climate serves to amplify these practices by disrupting the disciplining mechanisms of state sovereignty (see below) and by opening up new public spaces in which alternative political views can be articulated. Before I get on with the task of theorising these changes in political space, let me first make a short but crucial detour and say something about what I understand the political to be.

Politics is first and foremost a social activity; it is about relationships between people(s). Not all relationships are inherently political, although non-political relationships can at times assume political qualities. So what is the particular quality of a political relationship – or, in other words, what makes it 'political'? On my reading, the political can be characterised by two different sorts of claims: identity claims and ethical claims. I will deal with identity first. Drawing on the work of Ernesto Laclau and Chantal Mouffe, I want to suggest that social *antagonism* is one possible root of the political. Antagonism refers to a condition in which the differentiation of identity – the split between us and them – begins to appear as something more than just difference. In an antagonistic situation, one identity (the 'self') comes to see the other as a force seeking to negate its identity. 'From that moment on', writes Mouffe, 'any form of us/them relationship – whether it be religious, ethnic, economic or other – becomes political'.[7] The example often employed by Laclau and Mouffe is that of the peasant whose use of the land is under threat from a landlord. If the identity of peasant is premised upon working the land, then any force which threatens to remove this capacity also threatens the very existence of peasant identity. Antagonism is therefore the product of a politics of identity. In this sense 'the political' is not a sharply demarcated sphere of activity unto itself, but rather it describes a mode of interaction – one characterised by the negotiation of identity. According to Mouffe:

> Looking at the issue of identity in this way transforms the way we think of the political. The political can no longer be located as present only in a certain type of institution, as representative of a sphere or level of society.

It should rather be understood as a dimension inherent in all human society which stems from our very ontological condition.[8]

The ontological dimension of the political is related to one's assertion of a particular identity because that assertion is, in effect, a claim to 'be' – to exist according to one's construction of a particular identity – and, furthermore, to have that existence recognised by the other. Antagonism arises when this recognition is withheld, or when the other attempts to force a discrepant identity. Without this constitutive recognition, an identity cannot survive, or, at the very least, will always fail to become social in the sense of allowing one to relate to the other in terms of that identity. In this sense the political is primarily a *mode* rather than a description of a specific practice. It is a form of social relationship characterised by contestation.

The second possible manifestation of the political involves ethical claims. Politics is often about the assertion of a particular vision of what constitutes 'the good' in the face of other competing claims. This is a conception of the political which focuses on its normative aspects, the ways in which different political practices reflect particular ethical agendas. Thus the political pertains not only to claims about who we are, but also to claims about what we think is right. That there is a close relationship between these two claims is self-evident. Identity claims will often overlap quite significantly with ethical claims, especially when particular identities are seen to be closely related to certain ethical projects. This emphasis on the ethical component of the political leads me to another important distinction that needs to be made between political identity and politicised identity. I need to elaborate this difference in order to point out that I am not simply conflating politics and political identity. On my reading, a political identity refers to a particular normative vision, a set of beliefs about the nature of 'the good' and how one should go about achieving it. A politi-*cised* identity, on the other hand, is a political identity which has been placed in a situation of antagonism such that its ethical claims are challenged by counter-claims from other political identities. Therefore (to employ an analogy from physics) political identity refers to 'potential' politics, while the politicisation of identity marks a conversion into 'kinetic' form, or the actuality of the political. It is important to make this semantic distinction so that my deployment of the term 'political identity' throughout this book will not be taken to imply the presence of a political relationship. When I speak of political identity, therefore, I am referring to identities possessing particular normative visions. However, I do not want to refer to these various ethical conceptions simply as different 'worldviews', 'values' or 'culture'. As I will argue later, the alternative political spaces of translocality are sites where these different 'cultural' forms – and particularly the conversations between them – fulfil important political functions. This is why it is also crucial to understand the dialectical relationship between political identity and the politicisation of identity. The politicisation of identity is very often the process which constructs (new) political identities. In other words, it is often the encounter with 'the other' that engenders the shifts, negotiations and debates which produce new ethical claims and hence new political identities. Translocal political space emerges as a particularly rich site of both political identities (i.e. different conceptions of 'the good') *and* politicised identities (i.e. dialogue between these differing conceptions).

I need to say something now about what I understand by political community, and this will start us on our return journey to (re)considerations of political space. Taken at face value 'political community' would seem to refer simply to those communities in which a particular form of politics is practised, reflecting a common conception of 'the good'. State institutions and their related structures – from the local council to the dynastic realm – would all, in this sense, constitute forms of political community, as would various religious establishments and their associated organisations. The concept of political community which I intend to develop in this study, however, places its emphasis elsewhere. Rather than identifying political community with institutions representing particular ethical claims – such as churches and states – my understanding of political community concentrates instead on the contestations and counterclaims of those who are on the 'receiving end' of such politics. I am interested in those peoples who are subject to a particular form of politics – or, put another way, those who constitute the objects of a given ethical claim (e.g. the relationship between 'Islam' and 'Muslims'). My emphasis here, then, is on those political identities which inhabit spaces outside formal institutions – thus allowing us to account for important forms of popular politics. This approach facilitates an understanding of the subjectivities of a given political order, those whose lives are mediated by, and who themselves attempt to mediate, the influence of various political actors and hegemonies. Where before those actors have primarily tended to be states, I will be arguing that political communities are increasingly coming to be figured around sources of 'the good' other than the state.

A political community is hence a system composed of a set of ethical claims and its subject constituency, both of which are to some extent predicated on one another. I make this latter point in order to emphasise that neither the nature of these claims (e.g. Islam) nor the identities which populate a political community (e.g. Muslims) are prior to the *political* (i.e. negotiational) processes which constitute them (as per above). A vital component of all political communities, and one which will be emphasised throughout the account of Islam that follows, is the 'public space', or the area where normative interventions are received, mediated and contested by those who are subject to them. This public space, as we will see, can take on many different forms and can exist in varying strengths from context to context, and from culture to culture. The 'public' nature of this discourse is, however, particularly salient in the case of Islam because according to conventional accounts of modernity, religion has been relegated to the domain of the private. By re-asserting itself in public space, Islam is hence disrupting the modernity which lies at the root of the state. To the extent that translocality fosters the presence of Islam in the public sphere – and I will be arguing later that it does – it would appear to challenge the conventional dualism between public and private. In summary, we can say that European modernity has represented political community through a particular configuration of state and society. The hegemony (i.e. universalising tendencies) of this conception is, however, currently under threat from a variety of transformative forces, some of which I detail below. Most important among them is the emergence of new forms of public space whose boundaries do not conform to those of the territorial state. These spaces are translocal in the sense that they refer to activities which occur in the interstices between bounded communities, yet these activities are increasingly immune to the ethical claims of the state. In this sense they represent discrepant forms of political community.

Before I go on to describe the emergence of translocality, however, I need to say something more about the state. It would be impossible to dismiss this form of political community as a mere historical accident born to those with power. The state has acted (and in many respects continues to do so) as the primary subject of international theory and has also fulfilled a number of vital functions as regards territorial governance, the maintenance of order and international justice. Even when seeking to move beyond the state, we must first necessarily pass through it. In particular I want to draw attention to the ways in which the state has acted as the primary bearer of three key aspects of international life – ethical political identity (citizenship); ethical accountability (the state as a legal instrument and a site of the 'good'); and the legitimising principle of political autonomy (state sovereignty) – and how these roles are changing or being challenged in the current era. I will take them in order.

Citizenship provides a framework for political identity, usually envisaged as a mutually constitutive package of rights and obligations defining the legal parameters of the ethical self. The citizen is intrinsically linked to the state insofar as it is only the state which can bestow this status upon an individual. One might argue that the employee of a corporation is usually empowered by a certain legal status. Yet in the sense that all employers are based within the boundaries of the political space of the state and insofar as any claim made by an employee against his or her employer passes through the legal bureaucracy of the state, even the status of 'employee' (if it is to be legally meaningful) must somehow be linked to notions of citizenship – or at least to some 'official' status bestowed by the state. This infrastructure is currently under strain due to a number of forces. One is an increasingly global market which does not respect state borders. Corporations are able to identify and recruit labour from beyond the borders of the state in which their operations are based, yet there is no guarantee that the relevant state will allow 'non-citizens' to participate in its labour market. This phenomenon is prevalent from one end of the employment spectrum to the other, from the 'illegal' Mexican migrant worker in the United States to the information technology specialist in Southeast Asia. The point I want to draw from this is the fact that increasingly today there is a disjuncture between one's legal identity as a citizen and one's political identity as an actor in the public sphere. Benedict Anderson makes the point well when he alludes to the 'counterfeit' quality of passports:

[I]n our age, when everyone is supposed to belong to some one of the United Nations, these documents have high truth claims. But they are also counterfeit in the sense that they are less and less attestations of citizenship, let alone of loyalty to a protective nation-state, than of claims to participate in labor markets. Portuguese and Bangladeshi passports, even when genuine, tell us little about loyalty or habitus, but they tell us a great deal about the relative likelihood of their holders being permitted to seek jobs in Milan or Copenhagen. The segregated queues that all of us experience at airport immigration barricades mark economic status far more than any political attachments.[9]

Traditional conceptions of citizenship are also facing other threats. Experiments with 'supra-national' – and again, it would be more accurate to say 'supra-state' – forms of political community, such as the European Union, are forcing us to rethink citizenship's exclusive relationship with the nation-state. Some theorists have started to work towards envisaging more inclusive forms of citizenship whose criteria for membership are not limited by the spatial extension of the modern state.[10] Particularly important in the present context is the fact that citizenship, at least in its liberal variants, has always implied an implicit universalism – i.e. an assumption that the same rights and obligations should and do apply to all peoples. There is a sense in which this apparent inclusivity is highly democratic. However, there is also a sense in which such 'universalism' can be read as a form of exclusion which, by its assumption of homogeneity, negates difference. This aspect of citizenship was first queried by feminist writers who noticed that the classic conception of the citizen tended to refer to white, property-owning men.[11] Their argument was that citizenship requires the capacity to account and provide for the needs of *specific* identities. Because the nation-state is based on this more traditional conception of the citizen, its integrity is challenged by those groups – genders, sexualities, religions, ethnicities – seeking to devise idioms of citizenship whose inclusivity is not premised on a particular preconception of the citizen-subject.

The state has also traditionally served an important function as the site of the ethical. That is to say, the state has been understood as an apparatus whose core function is to provide protection and social justice for its citizens. Democratic, participatory politics and the right to due legal process have served as the cornerstones of this ethical identity. In traditional communitarian forms of normative theory, the state serves as the *sine qua non* of ethical life, and as the primary institutional context in which individuals are constituted as rights-holders. However, there have been moves by some recent communitarian theorists to reconstitute political community beyond the state within a wider 'global civil society'.[12] This is a response, in part, to the creation of a public sphere beyond the confines of the state, a space populated by a variety of globalised media and a plethora of multinational corporate entities. We also see a wide range of transnational non-governmental actors pursuing particular ethical agendas. These organisations – groups such as Amnesty International, Greenpeace and Médécins Sans

Frontières – see themselves as addressing normative issues which are somehow larger than and *beyond* the state. In fact, their activities are often explicitly critical of state activities such as torture, detainment without trial, nuclear testing and refusal to grant access to those offering humanitarian aid.

The latter issue, refusal by a state to grant access to its territory, brings us to a principle at the very foundation of the international system: state sovereignty. This capacity, which involves the recognition of a particular state identity's control over a spatial extension, has traditionally been seen as the criteria by which one's efficacy as an international political actor (at least legally) is judged; sovereign states are very much the key players in the system. Although we must view it as a historical construct, state sovereignty has in the modern era assumed something of a mythical quality, and is often represented in contemporary international political discourse as the be-all and end-all of international life.[13] It places within the competence of a recognised state the capacity to claim the right of non-interference, to deny the right of any other political actor to intervene within its territorial space. It is the legal embodiment of autonomy and the exercise of self-determination, with a decided emphasis on the self; 'the self' is defined here as the collective state. It is therefore not difficult to understand why tension arises between sovereign states and NGOs seeking to challenge the legitimacy of the state. In the eyes of the latter, state sovereignty is an ethical capacity as well as a politico-legal one. It involves commitment on the part of a state to uphold the 'rule of law' (another problematic notion) within its territory as part and parcel of its sovereign jurisdiction. State sovereignty is currently facing a host of challenges. Borders have been rendered more permeable by non-corporeal expressions of political agency (e.g. satellite television and computer-mediated communication); multinational corporations are increasingly taking on competences usually seen to fall within the remit of the state (e.g. hiring armies); and people live their lives across and between territories rather than within the 'little boxes' of official state space. 'As fissures emerge among local, translocal, and national space', writes one commentator, 'territory as the ground of loyalty and national affect is increasingly divorced from territory as the site of sovereignty and state control'.[14]

Global sociocultural change and the political

So what are these changes which force us to rethink conventional categories of politics and community? Following on from the challenges to state-centric politics alluded to above, I want now to outline the ongoing global sociocultural transformations which I take to be salient to the arguments I will be making in this book about the emergence of translocal spaces. The prominence of political realism in international theory, I have argued, has ensured that the state remains the pre-eminent site of the political and, consequently, that other locations of political discourse – no matter how long they have been with us – stay off our political maps. The flux and transformation of world politics in recent years has, however, occurred with unprecedented velocity and invasiveness. Changes in modes of social (and hence political) organisation have been more rapid and deep-reaching in the present era than ever before. While these processes have existed for several centuries, various sociocultural and technological transformations during the past fifty years – some of which I review below – have sharply boosted its intensity. It is this changing climate, I believe, which requires us to rethink our categories of political analysis.

The sorts of transformations to which I am referring are usually analysed under the rubric of 'globalization'; this term has, however, acquired so much ideological and sensationalist baggage in recent years as to become almost analytically meaningless. I will further clarify my dissatisfaction with the discourse of globalization in a later section, but suffice it to say for the moment that some of the dynamics I have in mind are often much less than global in scope; indeed, many of them are better understood as particularly 'local' phenomena, albeit ones which sometimes operate across vast distances – hence my emphasis on the notion of translocality. So while I may make use of some of the theories and ideas about globalization, I am not convinced that they actually pertain to 'the globe' as a single space. Rather, I am seeking to understand the ways in which changes in how we and our ideas/theories interact between and across social spaces (often separated by great distances) constitute new locations for the construction of political identity and also new spaces of political discourse. Thus I am primarily interested in two sorts of transformation. One concerns changes to the ways in which social relations exist in space (more specifically, the reconfiguration of 'here' and 'there'; see below), while the other pertains to alterations in our understanding and constitution of political identity. There is, however, a motif which runs through the dynamics of both these aspects, that of *movement*. On the one hand I am interested in how movement creates *new political space*, and on the other in those sites (and sorts) of *politics which travel*. By the latter I mean the ways in which competing identity and ethical claims are transformed when they move between sociocultural contexts. Let me go on now to review some of the developments which I see as constitutive of these translocalising processes:

First, there has been a phenomenal growth in **the movement of peoples**: from labour diasporas, guest workers and economic migrants to political exiles and the refugees of humanitarian disasters. Lives (and lifestyles) are increasingly mobile for a variety of reasons. In the latter cases (refugees, exiles, etc.) movement is often a life and death imperative, while in the former situations (e.g. economic transmigrants) movement is usually the result of global labour divisions and transnational capital flows. One analyst, for example, speaks of 'forms of international migration that emphasise contractual relationships, intermittent postings abroad, and *sojourning*, as opposed to permanent settlement and the exclusive adoption of the citizenship of a destination country'.[15] There are clear implications here for our theories about citizenship, and also for how we think about political identity. The configuration of lives and identities across and between multiple political spaces ensures that the construction of the 'political' self will be a much more intricate process than if one existed solely within bounded political space. Even when actual physical travel does not take place, people are increasingly aware of activities and politics in other parts of the world. Popular imaginations travel well today. Media technologies are largely responsible for this development. They permit us to reproduce and sustain forms of communal identity across great distances. While the distinction between 'here' and 'there' may still endure, 'there' is no longer very far away. In the present book, the movement of peoples is crucial in that the 'travelling Muslims' who constitute its object of inquiry are for the most part participants in transnational patterns of labour and migration. The ways in which movement has transformed their ideas about Muslim identity and political space will be examined in depth in Chapter Four.

Second, we have seen the emergence of **transnational social movements** which occupy a particular political space (in the sense of an agenda dealing with gender issues, human rights, religious and/or ethnic identity) but not necessarily a specific *place*. By this I mean that many of these movements operate across borders and without exclusive reference to a specific state, nation or region. Moreover, they often engage in activities which are explicitly critical of state regimes and/or traditional aspects of state sovereignty. Human Rights Watch, for example, monitors and reports the use of violence *within* states (torture, extrajudicial execution, etc.), and a group such as Médécins Sans Frontières questions the inviolability of state borders in times of humanitarian emergency (e.g. environmental disasters, the suffering of civilians during wartime).

It should be noted that we tend to understand the term 'transnational social movement' as referring primarily to Western 'progressive' agendas (e.g. gender, the environment, human rights) – indeed, this is the sense in which the term is used in much of the literature devoted to social movements, especially that dealing with so-called 'new social movements'.[16] However, we also need to recognise the existence of many other such transnational interest groups – ones whose concerns are easily overlooked because they do not fall into the range of activities we usually associate with the political. These are groups whose activities do not address the state, or even explicitly recognise its existence. Many such organisations, of all shapes and sizes, operate across and between bordered spaces. They represent a diverse range of interests, often related to the sustenance/advancement of various ethnic and/or religious identities. One relevant example is the Muslim Jama'at al-Tabligh movement, a group we will look at more closely in a later chapter, whose annual gatherings attract over one million attendees. Its activities are inherently transnational in that it is devoted to Islamic missionary activity on virtually every continent. Movement is hence the group's key dynamic. The Jama'at is also avowedly apolitical in the sense that it refuses to become engaged in debates relating to the activities of states. It does, however, possess a clear normative agenda. Members seek to reform society through the production of devout, ethical individuals, and not through what would be considered conventional political channels (e.g. setting up a political party and contesting state-run elections). So although the group is in one sense 'apolitical', there is another sense in which it is actually taking a very political stand by denying conventional notions and sites of the political. Given that groups such as the Jama'at feature quite heavily in the daily lives of their adherents, they must also be accounted for in our analyses of the ways in which globalising forces are embedded in lived experience. As an eminently mobile community, the Jama'at and other groups like it must be seen as forces which serve to translocalise particular notions of the (a)political. As Walker notes,

> This is not least because whatever they are...social movements are usually designated precisely as social *movements*, as phenomena that are explicitly at odds with the spatial framing of all ontological possibilities, of greater and lesser, higher and lower, inner and outer, that have made it so difficult to envisage any form of politics other than that associated with the modern state and its self-identical subjects.[17]

In this sense we have two different types of social movement here. There are those for whom the state is still the primary object of their politics, despite the fact that they mobilise across its borders. On the other hand there are those such as the Jama'at al-Tabligh – and these are the ones that most interest me – who do their best to ignore the state, or to operate *as if it did not exist*. That is, transnational movements which understand the location and legitimacy of the political and the ethical to be elsewhere. This is a theme which I will develop further below.

Third, experiments with **supranational political forms** – such as the European Union – provide an institutionalised forum for thinking beyond the nation-state. One observer sees the EU as the first 'multiperspectival polity' to emerge in the modern era. For him, 'it is increasingly difficult to visualize the conduct of international politics among community members, and to a considerable measure even domestic politics, as though it took place from a starting point of [fifteen] separate, single, fixed viewpoints'.[18] In this sense, the identity of each member state is in part constituted by the other fourteen. Modes of organisation and interaction increasingly require Europeans to look beyond the particularity of their national identities in order to prosper. In its present form the EU is still very much an intergovernmental (i.e. inter-*state*) organisation. Even if the logic of integration were followed through to its most extreme form, the complete dissolution of all national boundaries, it is very likely that a European federation (which itself still implies the existence of constituent members) would institutionally be nothing more than the state writ large. However, what would be interesting and relevant here would be the social (and necessarily political) processes by which people come to see themselves as part of or in relation to a European identity – e.g. education, polylinguality, trans-European residence, etc. There are also obvious implications here for citizenship, as discussed above, and also for state sovereignty. The politics of supranational membership are in fact often discussed largely in terms of ('losing') the latter. In the context of Islam, the notion of a supranational form has great resonance with the concept of the *umma*, a term which refers to the world community of Muslims. This notion, as we will see in the next chapter, has important political and ethical functions in Islam, representing as it does a 'global' or translocal community of believers in which racial, ethnic or national differences are irrelevant.

Fourth, the rise of **global cities** has meant the emergence of spaces that are particularly rich in transnational significance. The cities in question (London, Hong Kong, Singapore, New York) are often linchpins in the global world economy and hence their inhabitants are often implicated in the transnational labour processes alluded to above. Analysts of global cities have identified the existence of new 'transterritorial economies' and innovations in the spatial expression of capital mobility.[19] These polyglot metropoles also bear witness to extraordinary processes of identity (re)formation and sociocultural melange – as well as providing an abundance of material for the morphology of cultural dynamics. Other writers have emphasised the role global cities play in the disjunctures of national identity and citizenship,[20] and speculated about the role these sites play in the elaboration of new forms of what one author has termed 'transnational grassroots politics'.[21] In addition to the global city, I think we can today meaningfully speak of a second and closely related form of urban space, the **migratory city**. This term refers to those settings which have received large numbers of immigrants, migrant workers and various other groups covered under the generic idiom of 'movement of peoples'. Migratory cities are often also global cities. They share many of the same qualities as regards the intermingling of culture and identity. However, migratory cities do not always necessarily possess the same diversity of transnational flows that might be found in, say, Tokyo or London. Migratory cities are sometimes created by historical labour patterns. The English city of Bradford, for example, received a great influx of immigration from the Indian subcontinent in the years following India's independence. Much of this was due to an increased demand for miners and factory workers. In many ways, migratory and global cities are today the very best example of what is referred to by the notion of 'translocal space', and, as sites in which large numbers of Muslims are settled in Europe, will feature heavily in later chapters.

Finally, phenomenal developments in the **technologies of travel and communication** have played a crucial role in enabling many key features of these transformations. By allowing people to move across distances and to communicate far more easily, they have effectively led to the compression of space and time. Furthermore, our very notions of distance and chronology have been relativised such that we begin to perceive our relationships within space and time differently. This relates again to the sense in which the boundaries between 'here' and 'there' become blurred and eroded. Air travel and various media technologies (telephone, fax, satellite television, e-mail, etc.) are perhaps the most relevant here, facilitating on the one hand very rapid transport and on the other near instantaneous communications. In the context of Islam, these technologies have had important transformative effects on politics in the sense that they have permitted a wider range of voices to enter the public sphere and to articulate different understandings of Islam. Furthermore, they have brought Muslims from different sociocultural backgrounds together within translocal spaces, hence leading to a 'politics of authenticity' centred around the question of who represents 'real' Islam. By bridging distances, these technologies have also led some Muslims to begin reimagining the umma as a renewed form of political community. Both of these developments will be examined more closely in Chapter Five.

These five themes can all be related to my emphasis on the political implications of movement. For example, supranational political forms represent a shift in political space while transnational social movements allow for politics to become mobile. In the same way, a global city can become the site of profound shifts in identity, and new dynamics of migration and diaspora give rise to travelling identities. Technologies of information and travel are obviously implicated across the board. In summary, these changes have brought about two mutually constitutive developments: deterritorialised, mobile forms of political space and displaced, hybridised ('travelling') identities. Travelling identities challenge notions of political space/time while shifts in political space/time allow for the emergence of new forms of identity. It is in this sense, as concurrent and overlapping processes, that these developments need to be seen as mutually constitutive.

It is part of my contention that for the most part international relations has not been very effective in accounting for these various transformations. There are, of course, some exceptions. Certain trends of international theory have recently put the relationship between politics and space under intense scrutiny. This critical literature has been the result of two inter-related phenomena. The first factor which motivates this critical project is an increased awareness of the questions posed by the transformations I have identified above, political forces which are trans-, anti- or post-territorial in nature. How should we account for forms of politics which increasingly transcend (or which never really fit into) the limits of the state in the sense of a bounded, fixed space? Or, to put it another way, how can we escape 'a politics of little boxes'?[22] The second is a growing appreciation of the fact that many of our seemingly natural and unproblematised categories of political thought have been constituted as such only through various processes of discursive hegemony, processes which are themselves deeply political in nature. By abandoning what it regards as the ahistorical essentialism of traditional political analysis, the critical turn in international theory seeks to investigate the sociopolitical and historical contexts which have produced (and reproduced) particular forms of knowledge as 'political theory'.

Problematising the political in international relations

Various figures within mainstream international relations have offered theories, models and explanations of the sorts of changes I mention above. John Ruggie, for example, presents a historical sociology of bounded political space in order to ask whether we might now be moving 'beyond territoriality',[23] while James Rosenau describes these developments as a form of 'turbulence in world politics'.[24] Although these theorists have made significant contributions to this discourse, there is still a sense in which their work fails to engage with the problematic of the political *per se*. What I mean by this is that they seem to work with an unproblematised notion of what (and where) politics is. Rather than seeking to understand how we have come to associate politics with a limited range of activity within a specific location – and by so doing to 'de-naturalise' the state – Ruggie and Rosenau do not move much beyond questioning how current dynamics might effect the state; therefore they also do not question whether the state is the best point of departure from which to understand the political.

Other theorists have been more radical in their analyses. These writers have been contributing to a rapidly growing literature on critical international theory.[25] Borrowing from Habermasian sociology, for example, Andrew Linklater is engaged in a normative project which seeks to map the contours of what he terms a 'post-Westphalian order'.[26] Linklater focuses on the question of citizenship and asserts the need to uncouple this category from those of sovereignty, nationality and territoriality. 'The practical task', he argues, 'is to envisage forms of citizenship which are appropriate to the post-Westphalian condition of multiple political authorities and allegiances'.[27] To this end, he examines new categories of transnational and cosmopolitan citizenship. Modifying citizenship means more than simply loosening the parameters of the term; rather it requires a reconceptualisation of what it means to be a citizen. Given the increasing plurality of political authorities to which Linklater refers, the question surfaces as to what exactly one is a citizen *of*. Wheras before the term tended to bear a connotation of monism (i.e. one's affiliation was to a single state) the new global market for political loyalties is such that it becomes increasingly difficult to think of citizenship in such exclusionary terms. Linklater's understanding of political community is also crucially linked to moral boundaries. Indeed, his vision of politics relates to the boundaries of particular ethical practices. In this regard, his analysis of the post-Westphalian order considers the ways in which the sites and institutions of ethical political practice and accountability (i.e. states) are changing. He has an interest in experiments with supra-national political forms – and the European Union in particular.

The point I want to draw from this is the following. While Linklater does have important things to say about the future of political identity *qua* citizenship, he concentrates primarily on transformations taking place within conventional political spaces (states) and does not give much attention to the plethora of alternative sites – often informal and uninstitutionalised – which are rapidly becoming important loci of political loyalty and activity. I am not seeking to characterise Linklater's work as somehow 'conservative', nor am I accusing him of not going far enough. I believe his project to be immensely valuable in itself, but would like to suggest that a better understanding can accrue by combining it with an examination of alternative spaces and notions of the political. It is at this juncture that I want to turn to the work of two other critical thinkers in international relations, R.B.J. Walker and Warren Magnusson. Their work has raised a number of questions about the efficacy of the modern state and has also begun to recognise the emergence of new alternative political spaces. In a sense, the present book can be read as an attempt to illustrate how IR might go about unpacking their observations within the context of a particular post-statist political community.

Walker's recent work has been motivated by two central concerns. The first of these relates to the reification of political modernity and its concomitant spatiotemporal arrangements. Walker is concerned to understand how it is that political forms (e.g. the state) born of a particular European historical experience have managed to bequeath so strong a legacy to contemporary international relations theory. He seeks to question the neat and tidy order which modernity has sought to fix upon politics, and to challenge prevailing understandings of the relationship between sovereignty and territory. Walker's work is all the more relevant to the present context in that he posits his inquiry against a backdrop of global transformation:

> What is at stake in the interpretation of contemporary transformations is not the eternal presence or imminent absence of states. It is the degree to which the modernist resolution of space-time relations expressed by the principle of state sovereignty offers a plausible account of contemporary political practices...[W]e should expect to experience increasingly disconcerting incongruities between new articulations of power and accounts of political life predicated on the early-modern fiction that temporality can be fixed and tamed within the spatial coordinates of territorial jurisdictions.[28]

Here he alludes to the second of his theoretical concerns, an investigation into how it is that the category we refer to as 'the political' has come to be monopolised by the state and its various apparatuses. Walker believes that the search for wider understandings of politics and political identity/community are hindered by the fact that our conceptual language is so thoroughly permeated with early modern conceptions of space-time and sovereignty.[29] He acknowledges that 'there are good reasons both in our experiences and in our selective memories to be impressed by the resilience of the spatial politics of both *polis* and state', but then goes on to argue that 'it requires a fair degree of historical myopia to give much credit to the claim that these experiences and memories tell us what and where the political *must* be, or even what and where it is now'.[30]

The transformations which Walker identifies are relatively analogous to those I have enumerated above. With respect to the question of political community, he observes three major themes: first, the existence of a complex multitude of global connections in the present era; second, that the existence of these global connections does not necessarily entail some form of universalism; and third, that despite the global nature of these connections, peoples' daily lives are embedded in a myriad of particular locations and circumstances. 'These three themes converge', he argues, 'on a recognition that in the modern world, communities and solidarities have to be grasped as a dialectical moment, as a sense of participation both in large scale global processes *and* in particular circumstances'.[31]

As regards international relations theory, Walker adopts an epistemological position which views IR theory not as an explanation of international relations, but as a constitutive aspect of world politics itself.[32] He is particularly interested in the strong distinction which most political and international theory tends to make between 'domestic' and 'inter-state' levels of analysis – or as Walker styles it, between inside and outside: a 'distinction [which]…continues to inform our understanding of how and where effective and progressive political practice can be advanced'.[33] He notes that we possess a rich variety of language for the description and analysis of political life within state boundaries, but that our lexicons tend to run dry when we seek to characterise relations *between* states. This latter realm (the 'outside') is seen to be somehow profoundly remote, a space in which entirely different rules apply. This symptom is most strongly manifest in those IR theories which read the core dynamic of international political life as anarchy rather than community.[34] Walker, in turn, seeks to read these same theories as 'expressions of an historically specific understanding of the character and location of political life in general'.[35] It is his dissatisfaction with conventional IR theory that leads him to call for a re-orientation of the discipline from international relations – a barren landscape of (largely 'anarchical') interaction between integral, 'sovereign' state identities – to *world politics*. The latter designation is seen to be more capable of rendering the whole planet as a single political space, unencumbered by obsessions with state, sovereignty or cleanly demarcated 'levels of analysis'.

Walker's attempt to locate political spaces other than the state has led him to consider the increasingly important role played by various transnational social movements – a topic touched upon briefly above. His consideration of social movements is closely linked to the questions he asks about the nature and location of the political. Walker argues that social movements are usually treated as relatively insignificant irritants who do no more than throw the occasional spanner into the machinations of the state; in other words, as I have alluded to above, they do not constitute 'real' politics. However, this view only arises from a conception of the political in which the state and state processes remain the central units of analysis. Related to this same discourse is the tendency to understand social movements as merely 'social'; that is, as not truly political either because they tend to be confined to those spaces which the state labels as society, or because they concern themselves with 'social issues'. Walker, on the other hand, insists that '[i]t is futile to try to gauge the importance of social movements without considering the possibility that it is precisely the criteria of significance by which they are to be judged that may be in contention'.[36] Or, as I would want to ask, is the social not also sometimes the political?

Of particular relevance to the present study is the way Walker seeks to emphasise *movement* as a vital aspect of social movements, arguing that it is actually this very quality which lends them their force. Where conventional politics requires its subjects to be pinned down and static (i.e. stat*ist*) – or at least to provide an illusion of inertia, for states themselves are constantly moving – transnational social movements provide both alternative political spaces and alternative conceptions of the political:

It is in this context...that one might begin to read some social movements as practices in search of the political rather than simply as sociological phenomena working within a particular account of what and where the political must be. It is in this context, furthermore, that one might read highly specific local struggles in relation to broader, even global, processes without assuming that one must bow down to the sovereign state as the only intermediary between local and global or here and there.[37]

The present book and Walker's work are both particularly interested in the experiences of social movements outside the European context. He wisely warns against the dangers of applying the criteria of political modernity when attempting to assess the significance of such movements elsewhere. '[T]he experiences of the so-called new social movements or attempts to revitalize the civil societies of modern states do not always translate easily into accounts of what are taken to be social movements elsewhere'.[38] Walker presents a reading of the *Swadhyaya* movement in India, a group which is also very active amongst expatriot communities in the West. He argues that this movement has managed to avoid embroiling itself in the party politics of the Indian state by setting up alternative forms of social organisation – a discrepant idiom of politics which affects the lives of up to four million people.[39] By focusing on non-European perspectives, he suggests, it becomes possible to 'give a reading of the emergence of similarities elsewhere, of the diffusion of ideas or an elaboration of diasporas...but also to become more acutely aware of the specificity of locations and traditions'.[40] Furthermore, it can be argued, such perspectives might provide more inclusive conceptions of the nature and location of politics. The reading of transnational Islam which I will elaborate in later chapters can be seen as attempt to do just this.

A second writer within IR closely linked with Walker is Warren Magnusson. His work has also focused on the problem of modernity and its location of legitimate political activity. His work helps us to begin moving beyond bounded political territory by looking at what goes on in the 'gaps' between societies and states. By doing so, Magnusson seeks to identify forms of 'global popular politics', or what I would want to see as alternative forms of political community:

My claim is that popular politics occurs at the juncture of localities and movements, and that state-centric theories conceal the character of politics by reifying localities and movements as dimensions of the state or of prepolitical civil society...Mine is a worm's-eye view, which focuses on realities at the margin between 'the state' and 'civil society', or between formalised politics and social actions. At first sight, these realities seem far removed from international relations, but in fact they are the presence of popular politics in the global domain.[41]

In Magnusson's reading, many contemporary political scientists and sociologists still view society as an entity defined in relation to, and differentiated from, the state. Politics, for them, is the governmental process through which the reunion, or intercourse, of state and society is achieved – a practice most certainly located, in this conception, within territorial boundaries of the nation-state. In this regard, both disciplines tend to ignore political processes which do not fit into a cybernetic dynamic of state-civil society relations.[42] Like Walker, Magnusson's dissatisfaction with conventional idioms of the political also leads him to consider the role of social movements. He makes the important point that social movements tend to be considered political only when they become institutionalised – that is, when pinned down and made to wear the garb of proper politics. 'This suggests that the collective activities of ordinary people, in working out new understandings of themselves and bringing those understandings into the world, are themselves *prepolitical*. Thus, the creative social activity in which ordinary people are most likely to be engaged appears *beyond or outside politics*'.[43] He goes on to argue that this distorted view of social movements arises from a political imagination constrained by state-centric conceptions of what it means to act politically. 'If we begin with popular political activity', he argues, 'rather than from the enclosure imposed upon it, another dimension of reality emerges'.[44] Magnusson sees social movements as the cutting edge of a creative politics embedded in the minutiae of daily life, and emphasises the important role of localities in providing a socio-cultural context for the elaboration of popular politics:

> Localities are the venues for such politics. They are the places where the various practices of domination meet with the practices of political resistance and invention. Politics as a creative popular activity thus occurs at the junctures of localities and movements. These junctures are obscured by the reification of political community as the state and political theory as the theory of the state. To focus on these junctures is to open two analytic dimensions: first, *locality* as the place where movements arise and where they meet; and, second, *movement* as a mode of action that redefines political community, and hence connects localities to one another. In exploring these dimensions, we become acutely conscious of the fact that the state never fully contains the everyday experience of politics or political community.[45]

It is the fusion of locality and movement that constitutes what I want to call *translocality*. My usage of this term will be elaborated below, as will the arguments I wish to make on its behalf. My claim, in short, is that these interstices, junctures and 'gaps' (i.e. spaces between bounded communities) are replete with international relations but not of a sort which international relations theorists would recognise. Because the state never fully contains the everyday experience of politics or political community, conventional IR theory fails to account for a great deal of political activity. As the relationship between political identity and those categories closely associated with the state (e.g. citizenship and nationality) becomes increasingly tenuous, the conceptual language with which we read and write political identity requires rethinking. '[T]he politics of "patriotism" may', suggests Walker, 'need to be grasped in a rather different way'.[46] This is not to argue, it should be reiterated, that the absence of the state is imminent. Only that political identities are increasingly likely to find themselves 'caught between an affirmation of forms of political life constituted through the principle of state sovereignty…and a recognition of the need to challenge the principles that make those forms of political life possible'.[47]

> Thus in addition to the rearticulation of political space generated largely by global economic and technological processes, it seems reasonable to expect as well a rearticulation generated by struggles to rethink the possibilities of 'local' identity on the basis of novel cultural explorations and community practices.[48]

Within the context of international relations, I want to make the point that what follows is not simply an argument for a different 'level of analysis'. For, as Walker points out, '[t]he brutal chasm between inside and outside is too easily rewritten as an inclusive metaphysics of above and below'.[49] One recent commentator on the levels of analysis debate within IR points out that there has been relatively little work done on the ways in which various levels of analysis are reflected in the standard practice of delineating distinct spheres of political, economic, military and societal activity in IR.[50] He does not seem to recognise, however, that this scheme of classification is itself a highly political activity. It implies, for instance, that we have a set of criteria which tells us what counts as 'political' or 'societal' and international theory, I have argued above, tends to work within predetermined limits of what can legitimately be called politics. Therefore I am not simply putting forward a case for concentrating on 'low' rather than 'high' politics, for to adopt such a scheme would do nothing but reinforce that dichotomy; my aim, rather, is to question the nature of politics and not simply to relocate it in a pre-existing, overdeterminate scheme. In this sense, then, I am interested in finding new idioms of what politics *can* be – or, indeed, *must* be – under conditions of rapid and profound social transformation.

In this section I have argued that conventional international relations theory fails to take account of many forms of politics, community and identity thrown up by the tensions of a turgid late modernity. Intense social transformations – the key features of which I identify above – cause us to problematise our received notions of the political and to recognise new spaces and sites in which politics takes place. Furthermore, the state-centric nature of traditional IR theory has blinded it to any political form which does not conform to the requirements of political science *qua* state science. Even those theorists who do take account of 'alternative' actors in international relations still tend to use the state as a benchmark by which to evaluate the efficacy of these politics. As Yosef Lapid puts it:

> [A]s an 'inter-' type discipline long dominated by political realism, the IR field should have been doubly well prepared to deal with issues of diversity. Instead, recent events have rendered apparent IR's inability to encompass

vastly accelerated and co-occurring dynamics of integration and disintegration at both sub- and supra-state levels. It seems as if IR's fascination with sovereign statehood has greatly decreased its ability to confront complex issues of ethnic nationhood and political otherhood.[51]

I have also argued that certain trends in critical IR theory offer potent analyses of the discipline's failings in this regard. Writers such as Walker and Magnusson, but also figures such as Michael Shapiro, David Campbell, Andrew Linklater and Robert Cox, have challenged the foundations upon which IR constitutes politics and political identity and have begun to investigate forms of 'post-Westphalian', 'post-national', or 'post-international' politics. One of the most sustained attempts to rethink 'the political' in international relations has come from feminist writers. Cynthia Enloe and Christine Sylvester, for example, have both been arguing for several years now that we need to pay more attention to and appreciate the important political function of locations such as factories, rural collectives, and border crossings.[52]

Having recognised the value of the critical turn in IR and taking much of its insight as a departure point, I want now to go on to suggest that an awareness of these developments can and should be supplemented by an examination of various 'translocal' debates going on within other disciplinary projects. Sociology and anthropology have in recent years provided important new ways of thinking about political identity in the wake of globalised structures and processes. Furthermore, it is in these fields that we find the most cogent analyses of transnational identities, new idioms of citizenship and 'travelling cultures'. Where critical IR has mostly identified key problematics, sociology and anthropology have offered wide-ranging theoretical and empirical investigations. My aim in the following section is to survey developments in these fields and to suggest that sociology and anthropology have extremely important things to say about (and *to*) international relations – particularly given the present climate of global sociocultural transformation.

The anthropology of 'relating internationally'

As world structures change, so the disciplinary components of the social sciences also adjust themselves. Nowhere have these transformations been more dramatic – and, I would argue, more productive – than in the field of anthropology. Over the last ten or fifteen years the literature(s) of this discipline have been witnessing an increasing diversification in their ontological and epistemological perspectives. Ontologically, we find that the anthropological world is now concerned to take account of an ever-widening array of peoples, places, processes and 'things'. This phenomenon is in many cases closely related to the global sociocultural transformations alluded to above. In others cases it is also linked to a greater epistemological sophistication in the field, and the posing of new questions about what it means to be, quite literally, 'in the field'. There seems now to be a wider vision as to what counts as anthropological knowledge, and also a greater sense of self-reflexivity in the discipline. Drawing on critical and post-structuralist thought, a number of anthropologists have recently embarked on projects which seek to problematise the self/other and subject/object distinctions which have traditionally served as the discipline's ordering principles. Anthropology has long been concerned with writing difference, that is of constructing the borders that separate an observing (and somehow universal) 'we' from a 'they' dwelling in a particular, local place distant from us in both time and space.

It is particularly interesting in this regard to note that the relationship between anthropology and the state possesses a special heritage. Edward Said, among others, has argued that the origins of the anthropological enterprise were intimately connected with the maintenance of colonial apparatuses.[53] Anthropological knowledge is in this sense representative of a Foucauldian power/knowledge equation in which a colonising state provides patronage for those academic activities which produce forms of knowledge conducive to the subjugation and control of colonised peoples. Even after decolonisation, the argument goes, the methodologies and categories of anthropology continued to bear the markings of its colonial origins. It is therefore not surprising to find that some of the most hard-hitting attacks on classical anthropology come from the environs of post-colonial studies, particularly from those influenced by the many and various forms of critical theory. Aside from these important epistemological critiques, there is also a somewhat more 'organic' logic behind the contemporary transformation of the field. 'Anthropology, as an official discipline', writes Michael Kearney, 'is a constituent of the state, and as the boundaries and construction of the nation-state change so should we expect to find a restructuring of anthropology as a scientific field'.[54] Peoples and cultures are spilling over state borders, and in the process of doing so reconstruct anthropological borders. Locales, as anthropological sites, have become problematic. It has become increasingly difficult – if indeed it was ever possible – to study them as isolated, bounded spaces: people are on the move and therefore anthropology must become mobile. In this sense 'international relations' is becoming a way of life rather than a form of state science.

What, then, we may ask, have students of peoples and students of states had to say to each other? Surprisingly little actually. Instances of interaction between anthropology and international relations have been few and far between. This can be explained to a large extent by the ways in which these disciplines have been represented. International relations is supposedly concerned with the lofty heights and intrigues of intergovernmental forums, that is with various forms of 'important', 'high' politics. Anthropology, on the other hand, functions to provide us with 'academic' accounts of strange and exotic peoples living in far-away villages – places which are somehow *without politics*, where instead we find only kin-groups, rites of passage, and violent rituals. There is actually, however, a great deal of discursive overlap between anthropology and international relations in that they are both fields whose more traditional variants specialise in the construction of 'Others' – exotic cultures in one case, and enemies of the nation-state in the other.

Among the official academic disciplines anthropology is unusual in the degree to which it has been assigned responsibility for articulating differentiation, and thus engaging in the intellectual/symbolic reproduction of differentiation, on a global scale, with respect to 'less developed peoples' as compared with 'us'.[55]

This statement also functions as a remarkably accurate description of what goes on in much of international relations. There is a striking resemblance, for example, between the anthropological categories of 'the home' and 'the field' and IR's construction of 'the domestic' and 'the foreign'. Fieldwork (or the 'diplomatic mission') allows 'us' to venture forth and gain information about 'them'. In a recent book, one feminist anthropologist has suggested that more time should be spent on 'homework' and less on fieldwork.[56] The suggestion here is that anthropologists (and, by extension, foreign ministries) should be willing to engage with and problematise their own positionalities and situatedness before presuming to position and describe others.

Some have argued that in certain contexts anthropology is particularly well-placed to undertake political analysis, functioning as it does with a more holistic understanding of what and where the political is. One of the few writers to encourage dialogue between anthropology and IR, Dale Eickelman, notes that:

[a]nthropologists have a notion of politics more applicable to many Third World situations than those disciplines that identify the 'political' primarily with formal institutions. One strength of anthropology is that the discipline is attuned to discerning the political voices and roles of…'social actors less talkative than the elite', even if their significance is denied, ignored, or suppressed by the state elite or by political leaders. Anthropologists take seriously the views of the non-elite on politics, economic development, state authority, nation, and religion and how these are perceived in the context of ordinary lives and implicitly limit what political leaders can successfully propose and accomplish.[57]

He goes on to emphasise that official policy-making circles prefer to consume forms of knowledge which have been produced as clearly defined, unambiguous 'facts' – even in situations where information is sparse. This is an environment in which the over-riding imperative is to know in order to control. But, of course, 'brief reports are not always sufficient for "thinking the unthinkable" or challenging accepted ways of doing things'.[58] Ambiguity and the need to interpret are to be avoided at all costs. Anthropology is hence useful only in so much as it can provide information about the Other, but loses all utility as soon as it asks us to *consider* the Other.

Eickelman offers some strong criticisms of the ways in which foreign policy makers go about constructing the objects of their policies, but his 'programme' for the incorporation of anthropological perspectives into IR does not go nearly far enough. To some extent we can put this down to the late Cold War context in which he was writing. For example, he suggests that anthropology provides a superior analysis of political dynamics in a country such as Oman. He notes that it is one of the few states to have countered a Communist insurgency and regained popular support. What jars slightly today, however, is his assertion that 'for this reason alone' the country merits further inquiry.[59] Eickelman's account of anthropology and IR also does not touch on the question of how the two disciplines should respond to the rapid increase in globalising and transnational processes. He does not encourage a widening of his own discipline, nor is he sufficiently vocal about the need for a shift of emphasis in international relations. His preference seems to be more for the application of anthropological methods to the categories and spaces of traditional IR. He suggests, for example, that an anthropology of the intelligence community might be undertaken in order to complement more conventional analyses of foreign-policy making.[60] While the projects he proposes are undoubtedly interesting, Eickelman's text does not seem to recognise the many epistemological critiques of the ways in which both anthropology and international relations construct knowledge.

This sort of self-reflexivity was, coincidentally, arriving in anthropology at about the same time Eickelman was writing his piece on anthropology and IR. The seminal book in this regard is undoubtedly James Clifford and George Marcus' edited volume *Writing Culture: The Poetics and Politics of Ethnography*. This project drew together a number of anthropologists (and commentators on ethnography) who for several years had been experimenting with critical and intertextual methodologies in their own work. The essays in *Writing Culture* 'see culture as composed of seriously contested codes and representations; they assume that the poetic and the political are inseparable, that science is in, not above, historical and linguistic processes'.[61] The book seeks to problematise the ways in which peoples are represented through ethnographic activity. The anthropologist is deprived of his Archimedian privilege and re-situated as an active agent (rather than a passive objective observer) in the construction of peoples and cultures.

> There is no longer any place overview (mountaintop) from which to map human ways of life...Mountains are in constant motion. So are islands: for one cannot occupy, unambiguously, a bounded cultural world from which to journey out and analyze other cultures. Human ways of life increasingly influence, dominate, parody, translate, and subvert one another. Cultural analysis is always enmeshed in global movements of difference and power. How [then]...can ethnography – at home or abroad – define its object of study in ways that permit detailed, local, contextual analysis and simultaneously the portrayal of global implicating forces?[62]

I take this to be the central problem of the social sciences at the present time. How can we understand the ways in which particularities stretch and reshape themselves over distances? What happens to culture when it travels? I want to argue that a richer appreciation of these phenomena can be gained by adopting what we might call 'ontologies and epistemologies of unboundedness'. A number of writers in transnational sociology and anthropology have already begun to deploy these modes. Their work is motivated by a recognition of the rapid sociocultural transformations I have outlined above. It is also – and to varying degrees – informed by the insights of critical and textual methodologies, of which *Writing Culture* is but one well-known example. What do these approaches have to offer? Can international relations travel along some of the same routes?

I want now to look more closely at the literatures of sociology and transnational anthropology in order to help us build a picture of how globalising processes are changing the nature and meaning of sociopolitical activity. I will begin the discussion by looking at how several prominent sociologists have theorised globalization. I will suggest that while much of the conceptual language here is useful for thinking about broad globalising themes, the high levels of abstraction involved prevent us from gaining any meaningful sense of globality as a signifier in daily life. I go on to argue that transnational anthropology, by shifting the discourse away from supposedly *global* processes and looking instead at transnational – or *translocal* – forms of life, is better placed to provide us with effective ways of thinking about a world politics marked by profound sociocultural transformation.

The sociology of globalisation: distanciation, globality and glocalisation

Anthony Giddens' sociology of globalisation calls for a rejection of the notion of society as a cleanly demarcated entity, and a reformulation of social theory which instead seeks to analyse the ways in which spatio-temporality orders social life. For him, a key feature of late modernity (an era which he also terms 'post-traditional') is the overbearing presence of the quality of 'time-space distanciation'. This framework, argues Giddens,

> directs our attention to the complex relations between local involvements (circumstances of co-presence) and interaction across distance (the connections of presence and absence). In the modern era, the level of time-space distanciation is much higher than in any previous period, and the relations between local and distant social forms and events become correspondingly 'stretched'...Globalisation can thus be defined as the intensification of worldwide social relations which link distant localities in such a way that local happenings are shaped by events occurring many miles away and vice versa.[63]

Modernity itself, according to Giddens, is an inherently globalising force. Distanciation and the 'disembedding' of subject consciousnesses from local contexts are seen to be its most salient features. A recurrent theme in many sociological accounts of globalisation is that physical presence or proximity is no longer a prerequisite for the practice of community. 'Globalisation concerns the intersection of presence and absence', writes Giddens, 'the interlacing of social events and social relations "at distance" with local contextualities'.[64] Giddens is referring here to the idea that under globalising conditions any 'here' must necessarily take account of a great many 'theres'. In a recent piece on large-scale social organisation and the creation of community, Craig Calhoun identifies similar qualities:

> A world knit together by indirect relationships poses three challenges in the realm of everyday personal existence: to make sense through abstract concepts of forms of social organization for which everyday experience gives us misleading preparation, to establish a sense of personal rootedness and continuity of existence where connections across time are mainly impersonal, and to establish a sense of place and social context when the coordination of action – and the action of our own lives – constantly transcends locality.[65]

The latter two (inter-related) issues have perhaps the most relevance for the present work in the sense that they relate to the tangible experiences of displacement, alienation, and antagonism which characterise the individual's experience of globality. In the present context I want to implicate distanciation in the ability of certain groups to engage in, sustain, or reproduce particular forms of community across great distances and in the face of competing traditions – a phenomenon I wish to call 'distanciated community'. This designation alludes to those groups who make use of the infrastructural trappings of globalisation (e.g. telecommunications, electronic information transfer, and air travel) in order to bypass the geographical barriers to social interaction. Migrants, exiles, and diaspora groups are obvious examples here.

While the idea of distanciation is undoubtedly useful, there are also problems with the ways Giddens theorises the notion of locality. In earlier work on the subject, he defined globalisation as 'the intensification of worldwide social relations which link *distinct localities* in such a way that local happenings are shaped by events occurring miles away and vice versa'.[66] This account fails, however, to address the fact that processes of globalisation, as our anthropologists know only too well, actually render the existence of such a concept as 'distinct localities' almost impossible. In this sense Giddens veers dangerously close to that model of globalisation which posits an inherently Western (or Westernising) project, seeking to nullify any sense of local culture or difference by universalising all societies under the sanitised efficiency of Adam Smith's invisible hand – an approach which has also been termed the 'homogenisation thesis'.[67] Unfortunately, this discourse on globalisation ignores the complex intercultural relations that necessarily arise from the very processes it identifies. The trajectory of globalisation, I want to argue, is not merely a one-way path from the West to the rest, nor does the popular dichotomy local/global carry much analytical weight unless very precisely elaborated within specific contexts. I would suggest, then, that it is pointless to speak of 'distinct localities' with regard to those societies most heavily implicated in the processes of globalisation. This is not due, however, to the logic of homogenisation, in which a universalising Western culture negates any sense of local 'difference'. Rather, those locales most touched by globalisation are by their very natures anything but distinct – in the sense of being culturally homogenous or unique – because they are already imbued with the cultural differences propagated by globalisation. Indeed, it is this very quality which makes them global – or translocal – spaces.

While Giddens does speak of a realm of cultural globalisation which overlays or forms a backdrop for other components (nation-state system, world economy, labour divisions, military orders), he tends to downplay its relevance and confines his comments only to the intervention of global media in the phenomenon of time-space distanciation. Giddens' apparent neglect of sociocultural forces often features heavily in critiques of his work, as does the question of the viability of the rubric 'modernity = distanciation = globalisation'. '[H]e has to make distanciation, disembedding and reflexivity central to modernity in order to protect the thesis that globalisation is a consequence of modernity', argues one critic. 'Yet he obviously cannot say that [these] are entirely unique to modernity'.[68] Furthermore, by neglecting to account explicitly for questions of culture Giddens' theory of globalisation fails to address the core of the issue:

> While [Giddens] may claim that globalisation does not involve the crushing of non-Western cultures he does not seem to realise that such a statement requires him to theorize the issue of 'other cultures'. His suggestion that there is no Other in a globalised world apparently absolves him from undertaking such a task. He fails to understand that it is only in a (minimally) globalised world that a problem of 'the Other' could have arisen. What he apparently doesn't see is that a view of the world as marked by unicity can coexist with a view of the world as a place of others – indeed that such recognition is central to the conceptual mapping of the global circumstance.[69]

Giddens theory of modernity and self-identity does however offer several themes which I believe to be relevant to the thrust of my argument in this book. The 'facilitating conditions' of disembedding and distanciation have particular consequences with regard to the ways in which the modern consciousness situates itself phenomenologically and reflexively. According to Giddens, the increasingly impersonal and remote nature of social relations forces us to rely upon notions of abstract currency (e.g. money, shared symbols) in order to ensure the reproduction and validity of value across space and time. When I travel, for instance, I rely on the fact that someone in, say, Japan will be willing to give me a number of yen equivalent to the value of pounds sterling I wish to exchange. We also count on certain bodies of specialist knowledge, what Giddens terms 'expert systems', in order to provide infrastructures of security which allow us to go about what we view to be our own personalised, individual agendas with the assurance that someone somewhere is regulating and servicing the more mundane aspects of existence such as transportation, nourishment, financial management, etc. According to Giddens, these expert systems also 'extend to social relations themselves and to the intimacies of the self. The doctor, counselor and therapist are as central to the expert systems of modernity as the scientist, technician or engineer'.[70] Interpersonal relations, and especially the translocal, in so complex and unsure a social environment are thus seen to encompass the qualities of *risk* and *trust*.

The condition of globality, I would argue, in turn conditions the self to move instinctively towards whatever system or idiom of identity and association can offer relative coherence, surety, some semblance of the absolute and – most importantly in the case of political Islam – a sense of *authenticity*. In this view, then, late modernity can be seen as a search for epistemological security. I will return to this idea later in the context of my discussion of globalised religion and Islam. In summary, while Giddens provides crucial themes for our understanding of the ways in which personal identities are formed under conditions of amplified distanciation, the thesis fails – as his critics points out – by not continuing into an exploration of cultural mediations of the self. 'Giddens's overall argument...boils down, in spite of some useful insights, to an updated and overly abstract version of the convergence thesis – homogenised "modern man" injected with a special dose of phenomenological reflexivity'.[71] This distinct absence of an understanding of culture would seem to imply Giddens' acceptance of the globalisation-as-homogenisation approach. Globalisation is, however, best understood for the purposes of this study by shifting the axis of our analysis such that its defining features become instead the encounter with difference and the possibility of cultural heterogeneity coming to terms with itself. I mean by this that globality provides not only the conditions under which disparate societies and symbols converge, but also the space in which traditions are forced to hold a mirror up to the difference and diversity contained within their (supposedly immutable) interiors.

The other sociologist whose work I want to consider, Roland Robertson, can probably most legitimately lay claim to the emergence of globalisation as a distinct field of social theory, and it is also perhaps he who has put forward the most comprehensive theory of this phenomenon to date; a special interest in culture and religion makes Robertson's work all the more relevant to the present book.

A central motif running throughout Robertson's work is something which we might read as an attempt to reconcile sociology and international relations. Informed by the legacies of Weber, Parsons, and Simmel, his starting point is a concern with the 'classic' problems of social and political philosophy. The place of the individual *vis-à-vis* society, the state, and the wider system of societies and states is hence the key problematic here. In seeking to understand these relations, Robertson has devised an apparatus which he refers to as the 'global field'. Its component pieces are: the individual self; the national society; the international system of societies; and humankind in general. The mediation of relationships between these elements constitutes the primary problematics of globality. In Robertson's approach to the global field, which might in some respects be seen as a large-scale version of systems theory, the realm of the cultural is held to be the predominant subsystem. Historically, cleavages within this subsystem were seen to prevent its globalisation, the most important of these rifts being the 'religious' – but

> here the focus is not on religious denominations per se but on general views of life and the world in terms of cognition and values; the cleavage is expressed in such distinctions as inner-directedness versus other-directedness, this-worldliness versus other-worldliness, theoreticism versus aestheticism, rationalism versus traditionalism, and linear conceptions of time versus cyclical conceptions...Religion, in the most general meaning of that term, is therefore the critical factor in globalisation.[72]

The contemporary condition of 'globality' therefore provides the most conducive circumstances yet to the overcoming of these cleavages. This assertion, however, should not be read as a defection to the globalisation-as-homogenisation formula. To quote Robertson himself:

> It has also to be said that in speaking of globalisation, in its most general sense as the process whereby the world becomes a single place, I do not mean that globalisation involves in and of itself the crystallization of a cohesive system. Yet I do maintain that globalisation involves the development of something like a global culture – *not as normatively binding, but in the sense of a general mode of discourse about the world as a whole and its variety.*[73]

It is not being claimed, therefore, that globalisation entails universal convergence around a common set of norms, ideals and a shared system of meaning. Rather, globalisation is seen to be a state of mind which comprehends the world as a single social space or system through the recognition of diversity rather than the imposition of similarity. In *Imagined Communities*, Benedict Anderson was concerned with tracing the historical processes which led to the emergence of the national imagination, and in a similar way Robertson seeks to understand the historical developments which have given rise to a global consciousness. It is the emergence of this 'state of mind' which leads Robertson to the term 'globality' – 'defined in the immediate context as consciousness of the (problem of) the world as a single place'.[74] This evolution is seen to have occurred within the framework of a *longue durée* which began approximately six hundred years ago. Robertson identifies five distinct phases in the history of globalisation. The most recent of these began at the close of the 1960s and is termed 'The Uncertainty Phase'; like Giddens and a number of other contemporary sociologists such as Ulrich Beck,[75] Robertson also recognises the social environment of the current age as one characterised by an absence of certitude.

Robertson's recent writing on globalisation has tended to focus on what at face value appears to be the inverse of globalisation, the phenomenon he terms 'glocalisation'. This somewhat contrived merger between 'global' and 'local' is set up as a deliberate counterpoint to the homogenisation thesis which views the global and the local as mutually exclusive in that the latter is there seen to be swallowed by the former. In line with Robertson's own thinking on globalisation, however, the idea of glocalisation shifts the emphasis onto an analysis of the ways in which the universal (or global) is modified and domesticated by the particular (or local) setting which receives it. Rather than perpetuating the tension between the global and the local, the 'glocalisation' approach reveals instead that these seemingly incongruous aspects are in fact two sides of the same coin. In fact, argues Robertson, '[e]ven though we are…likely to continue to use the concept of globalisation, it might well be preferable to replace it for certain purposes with the concept of glocalization'.[76] The central thrust of globalisation theory hence becomes not the eradication of the local by the global, but rather the processes by which global material is tamed, localised, and made relevant to a particular set of sociocultural practices. In a sense, this involves a process of translation in which a system of meaning which originates from the 'outside' is integrated into the symbolic framework of a receiving society. It is at this juncture – the recoding of imported global culture – that *hybridity* becomes an issue (see Chapter Three). For what else is the resulting construction (be it a commodity, slogan, or ideograph) if not hybrid?

Where Robertson's analysis runs into trouble (at least semantically), I believe, is in his distinction between the 'universal' and the 'particular' with the latter denoting the local and the former the global. It is not the substance of his distinction here so much as his choice of words which causes confusion. I do not take Robertson to be asserting that what he calls 'universal' is actually universal in the sense of being embraced by everyone everywhere. On my reading he is referring to that material which enters the global stream and thereby acquires the potential to be received – although not necessarily accepted – universally. If we invest the abstract constructs of cultural production with some form of consciousness then we are speaking at most of those ideas and commodities which *aspire* to universal relevance, but which are actually nothing more than particularisms – albeit ones which have been rendered ubiquitous by the networks of global distribution. Robertson is himself fully aware that what he terms universal is in fact merely another form of the particular. Indeed, his designation 'universal' can be read simply as a shorthand for what he has previously called the 'universalization of particularism'.[77] Robertson's emphasis on glocalisation therefore lends considerable support to those who seek to read globalisation as primarily a process of hybridisation.

In summary, then, part of the difficulty in theorising the concept of globalisation stems from the fact that the processes which it purports to describe often appear to contradict one another. In the homogenisation thesis, for example, the term would seem to imply the global adoption of certain modes of interaction with regard to international politics, business, and law, increased economic interdependence, and the rise of a global culture. Simultaneously, however, the same mechanisms which permit (or demand) this homogeneity of practice also produce a curious inverse side-effect: localising the global can also at times serve to globalise the local. The channels which open spaces of local political community to the global outside can also be appropriated by those communities in order to export their own notions of the particular. As Appadurai puts it:

> The globalisation of culture is not the same as its homogenization, but globalisation involves the use of a variety of instruments of homogenization (armaments, advertising techniques, language hegemonies, clothing styles and the like), which are absorbed into local political and cultural economies, only to be repatriated as heterogeneous dialogues of national sovereignty, free enterprise, fundamentalism, etc.[78]

In the notion of 'heterogeneous dialogues' we find yet another allusion to hybridity. This model questions the common idiom of globalisation which tends to portray the wholesale bulldozing of 'traditional' local cultures by the rampaging juggernaut of late Western capitalism. A claim is not being made here that the exchange of materials is equal in both (or all) directions, only that the popular monoflow paradigm of a globalising Western modernity is a severe misrepresentation. Several sociological treatments of this phenomenon have, fortunately, been far more nuanced in their analyses.[79] Missing from the literature, however, is an extended study of those 'traditions' seeking to appropriate the mechanisms of globalisation to their own ends, and in the process of doing so to articulate an authentic local response to the 'Other' value systems of which the incoming cultural material is the embodiment. To be sure, a great deal of transnational traffic does flow from the West to the Rest. I want to argue, however, that this particular velocity is not altogether hegemonic. Significant exchange also occurs between the Rest and the West and – above all – important processes of globalisation are certainly at work *within* the Rest. Indeed, the very categories 'West' and 'Rest' become almost analytically useless under the condition of globality: the Rest is already in the West, and vice versa. In later chapters I will be illustrating the ways in which globalising processes bring the Rest into the West through an examination of diasporic Muslim communities in Europe and North America.

Globalisation theory therefore makes a far more useful contribution when it is 'interested in accounting for heterogeneity, without reducing it to a new homogeneity'.[80] It is this notion of globalisation as a means by which to understand the global situation which gives rise to 'globality'. My usage here, like Robertson's, is intended to designate a *condition* or state of consciousness rather than a set of processes – a worldview which suggests wider sets of possibilities or the potential for society to stretch itself across space. In my understanding, there is an important connection between the concept of globality and my earlier emphasis on movement. Insofar as globality represents a widening of vision, it also enables movement. I am speaking here of movement not only in the sense of physical displacement, but also conceptual movement. Globality erodes theoretical inertia, causing people to encounter new forms of thought and to reassess their own taken-for-granted categories. In this sense there is also an important link to be made to the concept of 'travelling theory' which will be elaborated in Chapter Three. While we may not have reached a point at which we are all aware of the globe as a single space, we have certainly reached a state of affairs in which we are beginning to conceive of the world as an increasingly compressed space – a notion most popularly captured in Marshall McLuhan's hyperbolic metaphor of the 'global village'. It is within this 'smaller' world that the trope of movement is activated as a political force. Politics no longer happens in one place, but rather across a multitude of spaces. We see, hear, know, believe, emote and reach out to an ever-increasing range of sites and locales. People travel and their political convictions travel with them; but these peoples and their convictions are also mediated by globality and travel. So how is this condition of globality experienced by individuals and the societies in which they go about their daily lives? What impact has globalisation had upon the ways in which people conceive and imagine their senses of community and culture?

It is when we attempt to answer these sorts of questions that the discourse of globalisation leaves me dissatisfied. My major complaint would be that most of the conversation is far too abstract – that globalisation is often rendered in very generalising and/or facile terms. Talk of 'McDonaldisation' or 'Cocacolonisation' tells us very little, and even categories such as 'centre' and 'periphery' become increasingly tenuous. The historical sociologist Janet Abu Lughod argues that we need to transcend this sort of 'global babble'.[81] Her preference is for an approach which '[tries] to capture the ambiguities and nuances of the concrete, as they are embedded in the lives of people'.[82] In other words, how does globalisation manifest itself in our day to day existence? While notions such as 'distanciation' and 'glocalisation' are useful for understanding the dynamics of contemporary globalisation, the theorists who propose them do not make much effort to demonstrate how they manifest themselves. I am not simply speaking here about an absence of empirical corroboration. The high levels of abstraction, particularly in the case of Giddens, unfortunately leave us with the impression that globalisation is something that is taking place 'out there'; we do not come to appreciate the senses in which peoples and cultures are intimately implicated in globalising processes. It is also the case that trying to analyse a 'global' field can create a discursive economy of scale which quickly exceeds from our grasp. Hyperbole easily runs amok. Simply put, many of the things we tend to call globalisation are in actual fact very rarely global in their impact. Flows and processes may indeed span great distances, but this fact alone does not make their jurisdiction global. This false sense of scale only exacerbates the abstracted quality I mention above. Because we are rarely encouraged to examine the particular embeddedness of distanciated processes, globalisation remains an analytical category and not a daily experience.

For these reasons I do not feel that globalisation – at least in its sociological rendering – is the most productive discursive arena in which to discuss the cultural transformations which mark the present era. I want to suggest that transnational anthropology, with its greater emphasis on micro-processes, contextuality and lived experience – what Ulf Hannerz calls 'forms of life'[83] – can provide us with a richer conceptual language for thinking about peoples and identities located in and between nations, states and territories – in short, to help us recognise and appreciate salient new forms of world politics. A review of recent contributions from the field of anthropology will help to illustrate this point.

Transnational anthropology and political 'forms of life'

I mentioned earlier how critical approaches to anthropology have contributed to our understanding of the translocal by recognising the increasing unbounded-ness of community. I also want to say something, though, about how anthropology contributes to this endeavour through its own particular concep-tion of the political. Anthropologists have not been predisposed to look for politics in the form of the state. Traditionally, they have seen themselves as working in a social space well 'below' and far removed from the state. The peoples they have studied have not been represented as possessing the sorts of political cultures that produce and sustain state forms. The tendency of anthro-pologists to constitute the anthropological 'field' as a space devoid of politics and unconnected to wider political contexts has recently been criticised by those ethnographers working in the critical genre initiated by Clifford and Marcus' *Writing Culture*. However, one positive implication of this limited vision has been, I would argue, that anthropologists have learned to recognise 'the political' in other forms of life. Given its particular expertise, anthropology is capable of offering considerable insight into the politics of culture and cultural identity. Given that a great deal of the politics in translocal space relates, as we will see, to culture, it is not surprising that anthropology has been at the forefront of theo-rising the translocality of culture. Before I go on to look at some of these contributions, I need to say something about culture and, more specifically, how I see its relationship with politics.

While culture is certainly one of the most widely (ab)used concepts in social analysis, what it actually means is usually far from clear. For some analysts it is a safeguard behind which to retreat when some phenomenon escapes easy explana-tion. Culture is sometimes whatever is left over when all other explanations have been exhausted. However, to conceive of culture as some form of explanatory variable is to miss the point. Culture is not a thing. Despite its grammatical func-tion, I would not even want to see it is a noun. Like the political, culture is more a way of being, a *mode*. It refers first and foremost to the negotiation, articulation and inscription of *meaning* within and between social contexts. Several anthropologists have deployed culture in ways which hint at this connotation. Take for example Clifford Geertz's classic definition of culture as 'an historically transmitted pattern of meanings embodied in symbols, a system of inherited conceptions expressed in symbolic forms by means of which men communicate, perpetuate, and develop their knowledge about and attitudes toward life'.[84] While this is useful, it is still lacking in many respects. It gives the impression that one might go out into the world collecting specimens of 'meaning' and then be able to write something about the various cultures which produce these meanings. That is to say, the implication seems to be that there are meanings out there which belong to particular cultural systems conceived as bounded entities. Furthermore, Geertz's notion of a 'historically transmitted pattern' tells us very little about the temporal aspects of meaning. Without doubt, symbols endure. But to speak only of historical transmission does not help us to understand how meanings shift, implode and/or disappear over time. There are serious normative implications here as well. To focus on the historical transmission of meaning is to allow cultures to be dictated by those who write their 'official' histories, masking complex structures of power/knowledge in the public elaboration of meaning. In my study of Muslim communities in translocal spaces, for example, there is a great deal of emphasis on how cultural forms change over time and how they are (often drastically) modified through the act of moving from one social context to another.

Ulf Hannerz's rendering is somewhat more succinct. For him culture is 'the social organization of meaning'.[85] He makes no claims about systems or histories, and his idiom emphasises ongoing, active ('organising') processes. Again, though, we don't get any sense of how meanings change or of the uses to which they are put. This is why I prefer not simply to make the linkage culture = meaning, but rather to emphasise the ways in which culture emerges from the negotiation of meaning. It is here that the political begins to appear. Arjun Appadurai recognises this when he stresses the notion of 'situated difference' in relation to culture. For him culture is not a thing in itself, but rather a *dimension*:

> Culture is not usefully regarded as a substance but is better regarded as a dimension of phenomena, a dimension that attends to situated and embodied difference. Stressing the dimensionality of culture rather than its substantiality permits our thinking of culture less as a property of individuals and groups and more as a heuristic device that we can use to talk about difference.[86]

Appadurai recognises, however, that not all differences in the world are related to culture. In the context of his ideas about cultural globalisation (post-national politics, translocal identity) there is a need to focus on the production of political identity; hence, he suggests that 'we regard as cultural only those differences that either express, or set the groundwork for, the mobilisation of group identities'.[87] This is commensurate with what I have described above as the politicisation of identity. In other words, in what Appadurai sees as culture, I recognise the difference which engenders political antagonism and contestation.

What is not fully elaborated in Appadurai's thinking, however, is this notion of the 'group' – i.e. the 'culture'. Any analysis of 'identity', or 'community' can easily stray into an essentialist mode which involves constructing boundaries around some social phenomenon (person, nation, culture, religious community, etc.) and assigning it certain timeless characteristics or traits. It is, quite literally, to impute an *essence*. According to Pnina Werbner, this sort of analysis 'obscures the *relational* aspects of group culture or identity, and valorise[s] instead the subject in itself, as autonomous and separate, as if such a subject could be demarcated out of context, unrelated to an external other or discursive purpose...It is to imply an internal sameness'.[88] What must be stressed above all is the sense in which the construction of group identity is inherently a socio*political* process, involving as it does dialogue, negotiation and debate as to 'who we are' and, moreover, what it *means* to be 'who we are'.

Seeking to distinguish between essentialist and non-essentialist modes of thought, Gerd Baumann speaks of the difference between 'dominant' and 'demotic' discourses on culture and community. The dominant discourse, he points out, aims towards closure. It seeks to reduce cultural complexity to the simple equation: 'Culture = community = ethnic identity = nature = culture'.[89] The demotic discourse, on the other hand, problematises the boundaries of culture and community. It sees cultural identity as contingent and negotiable. It should be pointed out that these two modes are not deployed solely by ethnographers; that is, they are not simply descriptions of how analysts objectify and study culture. Communities and 'cultures' often vacillate in their own self-representations between dominant and demotic modes of identification, and this is usually indicative of the politics within those communities. Werbner summarises the point nicely:

> The argument about ethnic naming highlights the fact that it is not only Western representations of the Other which essentialise. In their performative rhetoric the people we study essentialise their imagined communities in order to mobilise for action. Within the spaces of civil society, the politics of ethnicity in Britain are not so much imposed as grounded in essentialist self-imaginings of community. Hence, ethnic leaders essentialise communal identities in their competition for state grants and formal leadership positions. But – equally importantly – such leaders narrate and argue over these identities in the social spaces which they themselves have created, far from the public eye.[90]

She is referring here to a politics which takes place not in the public spaces of formal institutions, but within spaces and forums that we do not usually see. Award ceremonies, weddings and mosques are all important instances of such spaces. These places do not relate to activities which we would normally consider to be political, but all are examples of practices which can and often do involve the narration and appropriation of political identity. This is why it has become all the more important to emphasise the dialogic nature of community. As Werbner continues: 'A moral community is not a unity. It is full of conflict, of internal debate about right and wrong...Such debates...involve competition for the right to name: Who are we? What do we stand for? What are we to be called? Are we Muslims? Democrats? Pakistanis? Socialists? Blacks? Asians?'[91]

The dominant discourse of identity which arises out of such situations is often quite literally the 'dominant' discourse in that it represents the strongest voices within any community: those who have managed in the demotic debate to impose a discursive hegemony which negates dissenting voices of internal difference. 'Instead of seeing the different forms of identity as allegiances to a place or as a property', argues Chantal Mouffe, 'we ought to realise that they are the stake of a power struggle'.[92] This will become apparent later when we go on to look at Islam in translocal spaces. I will be arguing that encounters between the Muslim and his Muslim 'other' give rise to competing discourses as to what Islam is and who may speak on its behalf.

According to Lila Abu-Lughod, one method of avoiding essentialist modes of analysing culture is to 'write *against* culture'. By this, she means that we need to move away from conceptions of culture as something that can be fixed, measured off and described – in short, we need to stop using culture as an ascriptive category. Looking at traditional anthropological discourse, Abu-Lughod has noted that culture has often functioned primarily to 'make other'. However, she warns of the dangers inherent in taking the particular situatedness of a few individuals as representative of an entire culture:

> When one generalises from experiences and conversations with a number of specific people in a community, one tends to flatten out differences among them and to homogenise them. The appearance of an absence of internal differentiation makes it easier to conceive of a group of people as a discrete, bounded entity who do this or that and believe such-and-such...The erasure of time and conflict make what is inside the boundary set up by homogenization something essential and fixed.[93]

Instead, Abu-Lughod suggests that we might more usefully write what she terms 'ethnographies of the particular'. By this she means that we need to pay close attention not only to peoples' situatedness in particular sociocultural contexts, but also to their situatedness *within* these contexts. What power relationships obtain in any given community, and where are individuals positioned *vis-à-vis* these structures? What individual meanings do subjectivities derive from the signifying practices of a culture?

> In writing 'against' culture (or ethnicity) we thus seek to discover more hidden forms of identification and to highlight the arguments of identity *within* ethnic collectivities about who 'they' are and thus who may legitimately represent 'them' and 'their' interests or loyalties in the public arena.[94]

Incoherence therefore needs to be stressed as much as, if not over, coherence. We need to understand the ways in which people 'are confronted with choices, struggle with others, make conflicting statements, argue about points of view on the same events...and fail to predict what will happen to them or those around them'.[95] A great strength of Abu-Lughod's argument is that she does not see her concentration on 'particularity' as simply a privileging of micro- over macro-processes. For her, the particular is by no means synonymous with the local:

> [A] concern with the particulars of individuals' lives [need not] imply disregard for forces and dynamics that are not locally based. On the contrary, the effects of extralocal and long-term processes are only manifested locally and specifically, produced in the actions of individuals living their particular lives, inscribed in their bodies and their words. What I am arguing for is a form of writing that might better convey that.96

In this she reflects the insight – already touched upon briefly above – that 'the field' and 'the village' no longer exist (if indeed they ever did) as closed, bounded spaces. An emphasis on translocality hence emerges as an effective route away from essentialist conceptions of culture. Let us move on to look at some of the ways in which recent anthropological thought has contributed to our understanding of translocal political identities and the unboundedness of community.

The traditional methodologies of anthropology have assumed that peoples and cultures inhabit more or less bounded spaces – and relatively small ones at that – and therefore that one needed only to visit the 'village' in question in order to gain knowledge of a given people or culture. This is the classic model of the participant-observer anthropologist at work in 'the field'. It is an approach which suffers from two major shortcomings. First of all, it does not by and large recognise that supposedly rooted peoples are usually being 'studied' by a very unrooted and displaced observer, that the act of moving between, say, a home university and the field is actually a constitutive act in the ethnographic process. In this regard greater self-reflexivity on the part of anthropologists is required. Second, and more importantly, 'the time-worn anthropological tradition of viewing culture in terms of separate, spatially incontiguous entities, each placed in their own territories, bears little resemblance to the mobile and culturally complex lives that people can be seen to lead today'.97 It is becoming increasingly apparent that one cannot so easily map peoples and cultures today by reference to static, fixed localities. As people move, the meaning of locality can itself shift such that it comes to refer to more than just a geographic notion of 'here'. Identity and place increasingly travel together. Uprooted and diasporic cultures reconstitute homes away from home, and hence the imagination of new distanciated communities means that 'the local' can spread itself across and between bounded spaces. As Olwig puts it, 'important frameworks of life and sources of identification should…be sought in the cultural sites which have emerged in the interstices between local and global conditions of life'.98 Her work on the people of the West Indian island of Nevis is a prime example of how anthropology becomes transnational. In order to gain a better picture of contemporary Nevisian life, Olwig found that she had to carry out her fieldwork in four separate 'fields': Nevis itself; New Haven, Connecticut, a key destination of early twentieth century Nevisian migration; Leeds, England, which received many Nevisians in the 1950s and 1960s; and the US Virgin Islands. She alludes to the sense in which her presence in any one of these fields could only tell part of the story:

> Even though the field work of necessity was grounded in specific locations, it took place within a non-local cultural space related to the network of ties which connected individual Nevisians residing in these separate locations. Thus a great deal of the Nevisians' daily life was oriented towards activities and concerns of relevance to people and places in other points in the global network, giving me the feeling that Nevisian culture kept escaping me – *it always seemed to be where I was not.*[99]

Transnational anthropology seems to better appreciate the fact that people are increasingly mobile and that their identities are now configured in relation to more than one locality – or towards localities which have been effectively 'stretched' across space. Peoples and cultures are therefore not to be understood solely by reference to what is taken to be their 'place', but rather by the ways in which they define themselves between and across such places. The general orientation to which I refer might then be summarised as follows:

> Anthropologists…[are] beginning to critique the idea that settled life in particular places necessarily is a 'normal' state of being. A great deal of attention is therefore now being directed at the cultural and social significance of moving in space and the transnational communities which may result from this.[100]

These people and place dynamics become even more interesting when we begin to consider how they mediate political identity. How do these processes affect and/or change nations and states? If we take these two categories to be representative of traditional notions of the political then an emphasis on transnational relations allows us to move beyond the boundaries of conventional politics. This task has a vital normative component insofar as the peoples and cultures involved are often 'invisible' because they do not conform to the modern political imaginary. Official radars do not see them as participants in transnational networks and members of distanciated communities, but rather as objects attempting to cross state borders. Consequently there are anthropologists who emphasise the ways in which transnational subjectivities are subjugated by the hegemony of state borders:

> It is in this border area that identities are assigned and taken, withheld and rejected. The state seeks a monopoly on the power to assign identities to those who enter this space. It stamps or refuses to stamp passports and papers which are extensions of the person of the traveler who is 'required' to pass through official ports of entry and exit.[101]

Other writers see the relationship between state and political identity as more ambiguous. Ulf Hannerz, for example, argues that '[c]ontemporary state forms, and contemporary ideas of nation and nationalism, are themselves in large part items of transnational diffusion'.[102] In this regard the state can often play an important role as a 'broker' between locality and the transnational; and here it is often the nation – an amorphous form of community (or at least less institutionalised than civil society) constructed as simultaneously 'of the state' *and* 'of the people' – which 'mediates between state and form of life'.[103]

The nature and role of the nation in the context of transnationalism is especially problematic. On the one hand there is a sense in which the nation is an integral aspect of trans*nation*alism. Many anthropologists stress the extent to which transnational processes are a vital constitutive aspect (rather than a negating force) of the national groups they have studied.[104] On the other hand, however, we can always point to many ways in which the rise of transnational processes challenges the hegemony of national identity – at least in its monist forms. Hannerz suggests that we can increasingly find people today with whom the nation finds little purchase as a 'source of cultural resonance'. He argues that there are those who partake in largely 'transactional' relationships with the nation, such that they become capable of activating the national aspect of their identities when and if it suits them, but then abandon the nation when it no longer serves any useful purpose.[105] Transnationalism, according to Hannerz, largely runs against the grain of the nation:

> These [transnational] relationships are sensed not to fit perfectly with established ideas of the nation, and in this way the latter become probably less pervasive, and even compromised. The feeling of deep historical rootedness may be replaced by an equally intense experience of discontinuity and rupture, as in the case of the transcontinental migrant...such [transnational] ties may entail a kind and a degree of tuning out, a weakened personal involvement with the nation and national culture, a shift from the disposition to take it for granted; possibly a critical distance to it. In such ways, the nation may have become more hollow than it was.[106]

Khachig Tololyan concurs, arguing that 'the nation's aspiration to normative homogeneity is challenged not just by immigration but also by various forms of cultural practice and knowledge production'.[107] It is however difficult, as Hannerz points out, to detect the emergence of any social form which could play the role of a successor to the nation. In this regard, he feels that the nation may be changing rather than simply withering. But what would it mean to speak of changes to the nation, or of an emerging post-national politics? In order to begin answering this question we need to first recognise that the transnational is itself a site of national politics. As Basch *et al.* argue:

> Both the transnational processes that challenge bounded thinking and the pressures on transmigrants to reconstitute their identities in terms of nation-states and race reflect ongoing hegemonic contention within which

constructions of identity are constantly being reformulated, transformed, and modified...Consequently the newly reconceptualised categories represent simultaneously both resistance to domination and new hegemonic categories that perpetuate domination.[108]

We can get a sense of this politics just by looking at the connotations which various writers associate with the term 'transnationalism'. Thomas Faist, for example, seems to yearn for a modicum of scientific rigidity in his definition of 'transnational social spaces'; these are sites which he sees as 'combinations of social and symbolic ties, positions in networks and organizations and networks of organizations that can be found in at least two geographically and internationally distinct places'.[109] Similarly, Basch *et al.* define transnationalism as: 'the processes by which immigrants forge and sustain multi-stranded social relations that link together their societies of origin and settlement...[they] take actions, make decisions, and develop subjectivities and identities embedded in networks of relationships that connect them simultaneously to two or more nation-states'.[110] Neither of these sources appears to recognise the epistemological problems associated with speaking about 'internationally distinct places' or clearly-defined 'societies of origin and settlement'. Part of the point is precisely that these processes render the existence of 'distinct places' almost impossible, and that the sharp distinction between societies of 'origin' and societies of 'settlement' no longer obtains. One is no longer simply 'from' one (bounded) place; rather, identities are oriented in relation to complex translocal flows. 'Although there may be a tendency in the new work merely to widen the object, shifting from [bounded] culture to nation as locus', writes Lila Abu-Lughod, 'ideally there would be attention to the shifting groupings, identities, and interactions within and across such borders as well'.[111]

Michael Kearney provides us with a more useful idiom when he notes the ways in which contemporary transnational processes 'blur' the social, cultural and epistemological categories of modernity. For him, transnationalism has two meanings: 'One is the conventional one having to do with forms of organization and identity which are not constrained by national boundaries, such as the transnational corporation. But I also wish to load onto the term the meaning of transnational as post-national in the sense that history and anthropology have entered a post-national age'.[112] He is alluding here to that quality of transnationalism which I find most promising, but which is also the most difficult to theorise: the possibility of new forms of post-national politics. It is in this context, I want to argue, that we should view transnationalism as a space of resistance in that it allows us to reimagine the boundaries of political community and to question hegemonic notions of the political. As Basch *et al.* argue:

[B]y conceptualizing transnationalism, not as flows of items and ideas, but as social relations constructed by subordinated populations, we may be contributing to social movements that think beyond what is deemed thinkable...Transnational spaces, overflowing with daily life experiences that are not congruent with hegemonic boundaries of identification, provide a terrain for new and different subjectivities and public descriptors.[113]

It is in this sense that we might begin to think of transnationalism as possessing certain emancipatory qualities which allow us to move towards a political imaginary beyond the categories and requirements of the territorial state. The quality of emancipation derives from being able to represent oneself and being recognised as speaking with a legitimate voice within public spheres that do not conform to the fixed boundaries of the state. This is necessary because transnationalism creates forms of political identity which do not fit the taxonomies of political modernity. Hybridity and cultural melange often feature heavily in these spaces, and such syncretisms often give rise not only to new post-national forms but also to reformulated understandings of what and where the nation can be. Thus I disagree with Faist when he asserts that in addition to novel supranational identities, transnational diffusion 'encompasses...[the] resurgence of ethnic and national identities'.[114] The notion of 'resurgence' would seem to suggest that there exist given forms of ethnicity and nationality which are somehow lying dormant, waiting to be reactivated by transnational activity. As I understand it, however, the transnational – or, in my terms, the *translocal* – is a space in which new forms of (post-)ethnic and (post-)national identity are constituted, and not simply one in which prior identities assert themselves. Forms of political identity are heavily contingent, and hence the boundaries of our imagined communities can be shifted through reimagination.

So what happens when these shifts occur? What might a post-national politics look like, and how can we theorise it? I want to point to the importance of what Arjun Appadurai calls *ethnoscapes* in the emergence of post-national political forms. By this term he refers to 'the landscape of persons who constitute the shifting world in which we live: tourists, immigrants, refugees, exiles, guest workers, and other moving groups and individuals [which] constitute an essential feature of the world and appear to affect the politics of (and between) nations to a hitherto unprecedented degree'.[115] I would go further and argue that these ethnoscapes do much more than simply 'affect' politics between nations; they actually constitute forms of politics unto themselves. These post-national politics question the boundaries of statist political community by giving rise to political identities disembedded from the context of the territorial nation-state. For Appadurai, a key dynamic in the emergence of post-national politics is to be found in the relationship between these ethnoscapes and the increasing prevalence of 'deterritorialising' processes. This is a notion which covers more than the obvious cases of transnational corporations and capital flows. It also refers to flows of people and forms of identity which are increasingly capable of transcending the boundaries of state and territory. Furthermore, the fragmenting qualities of transnational processes are such that disparities between place and purpose become features of daily life: 'For many national citizens, the practicalities of residence and the ideologies of home, soil and roots are often disjunct, so that the territorial referents of civic loyalty are increasingly divided for many persons among different spatial horizons: work loyalties, residential loyalties, and religious loyalties may create disjunct registers of affiliation'.[116] In other words, the state becomes relativised: increasingly these days, political life is elsewhere.

Asserting that the hyphen which links nation and state 'is now less an icon of conjuncture than an index of disjuncture', Appadurai goes on to examine the ways in which these disjunctures in the imagination of political community might be seen as a constitutive aspect of post-national politics. He does so by relating the uncoupling of nation and state to deterritorialisation. 'One major fact that accounts for the strain in the union of nation and state is that the nationalist genie, never perfectly contained in the territorial state, is now itself diasporic [and] is increasingly unrestrained by ideas of spatial boundary and territorial sovereignty'.[117] One might be tempted here to point out the extent to which so many contemporary political movements state their goals in nationalist terms. Appadurai's preference, however, is to read situations such as those found in Serbia, Sri Lanka, Punjab or Nogorno Karabakh as 'trojan nationalisms'. He means by this that avowedly 'nationalist' projects such as these are so heavily permeated with sub-, trans- and even non-national elements as to render it almost impossible to speak of a nationalism outside transnationalism.[118] 'Territorial nationalism', he claims, 'is the alibi of these movements and not necessarily their basic motive or final goal'.[119] This point is then further elaborated in connection with a critique of the limits of our current national imaginaries:

> Although many antistate movements revolve around images of homeland, soil, place, and return from exile, these images reflect the poverty of their (and our) political languages rather than the hegemony of territorial nationalism. Put another way, no idiom has yet emerged to capture the collective interests of many groups in translocal solidarities, cross-border mobilizations, and postnational identities. Such interests are many and vocal, but they are still entrapped in the linguistic imaginary of the territorial state.[120]

There are thus 'actually existing social forms and arrangements that might contain the seeds of more dispersed and diverse forms of transnational allegiance and affiliation'.[121] Appadurai argues that there exist formations of finance, recruitment, co-ordination, communication and reproduction that go beyond mere transnationalism to verge on the truly postnational.[122] In this regard he cites the importance of various Christian, Hindu and Muslim organisations (the last of which I will examine more closely in chapter four) as examples of 'full-service global movements that seek to alleviate suffering across national boundaries while mobilising first-order loyalties across state boundaries'.[123] Rather than conforming to stereotyped media images of fundamentalism, perhaps these are 'more humane motives for affiliation than statehood or party affiliation and more interesting bases for debate and cross-cutting alliances'.[124] In this regard, I would also argue that these sorts of affiliations need to be seen as important forms of politics in their own right. A central purpose of this book will be to demonstrate why this is the case.

In summary of his thinking on the post-national, Appadurai offers the following:

> It remains now to ask what transnations and transnationalism have to do with postnationality and its prospects...As populations become deterritorialized and incompletely nationalised, as nations splinter and recombine, as states face intractable difficulties in the task of producing 'the people', transnations are the most important social sites in which the crises of patriotism are played out...[I]t is possible to detect in many of these transnations (some ethnic, some religious, some philanthropic, some militaristic) the elements of a postnational imaginary...[T]ransnational social forms may generate not only postnational yearnings but also actually existing postnational movements, organizations, and spaces. In these postnational spaces, the incapacity of the nation-state to tolerate diversity (as it seeks the homogeneity of its citisens, the simultaneity of its presence, the consensuality of its narrative, and the stability of its citizens) may, perhaps, be overcome.[125]

A worthy cause certainly, but what shortcomings can we identify in Appadurai's approach? Several writers have pointed to limitations here. Basch *et al.*, for example, offer an indirect but valid criticism of theorists such as Appadurai who celebrate the unboundedness of community. An approach which stresses the contingency of cultural boundaries, they suggest, runs the risk of ignoring the importance which boundaries can play in many political contexts:

> To develop a perspective that emphasises the constructed nature of bounded units is not to deny the significance of boundaries once they are constructed...Boundaries, whether legally created borders, as in the case of nation-states, or socially forged boundaries, as in instances of group ethnicities, once conceptualized, are given meaning and sentiment by those who reside within them. They acquire a life of their own. Conceived as culturally distinct, these social constructions persist and therefore shape and influence people's behavior and daily practices.[126]

Karen Fog Olwig has also raised questions about certain aspects of Appadurai's work. She worries that a mere reorientation of anthropology from the village to transient sites may lead us to 'focus on the more short-lived and flimsy contexts of modern life and therefore risk exaggerating its transient and "uprooted" character'.[127] While she undoubtedly has a point here, there is a sense in which Olwig is also missing the point. As I read them, most transnational anthropologists – and certainly those sympathetic to Clifford and Marcus – are not arguing for a simple re-orientation of anthropology from 'local' village to transnational space. Rather, their argument is that increasingly today *all* localities, be they island villages or world cities, need to be viewed as spaces of movement and transnational diffusion. '[T]he importance of embedding large-scale realities in concrete life-worlds', writes Appadurai, '[is to] open up the possibility of divergent interpretations of what *locality* implies'.[128]

It is this emphasis on the changing nature and vital importance of locality which distinguishes Appadurai's approach to sociocultural globalisation — a term which, as will become increasingly clear, I see as interchangeable with socio*political* globalisation: '[i]n such a theory, it is unlikely that there will be anything mere about the local'.[129] In his recent work Appadurai has given even greater weight to locality, talking more of 'translocality' and less of 'transnationalism'. This seems to me an intuitive extension of post-nationalism's logic, for to speak incessantly of trans*nationa*lism is only — at least semantically — to perpetuate the nation rather than move beyond it. For this reason in the chapters that follow I prefer to designate *translocal spaces* as my primary object of inquiry. In so doing my intention is to emphasise the ways in which sociocultural globalisation is about the mediation of distanciated communities, which increasingly take non-national forms, across and between locality/translocality. As will be made clear later, I do see certain spaces (e.g. migratory or global cities) as more translocal than others. For the time being, however, I am simply concerned to point out that almost every locality today possesses some aspect of translocality.

Conclusion: IR as translocal politics

Let me conclude by recapping the key arguments I have made in this chapter. I began with a critique of state-centrism in IR and highlighted some of the key sociocultural transformations which question the hegemony of this structure. I suggested that we need to question today the extent to which the imagination of political identity remains nationalised — that is, whether political identity remains the exclusive reserve of a single national-territorial referent. The approach I would endorse involves re-orientating the trajectory and widening the arc of analysis in international relations such that its emphasis lies less on the examination of bordered, bounded and fixed entities and concentrates instead on the ways in which international sociopolitical life manages increasingly to escape the constraints of the territorial nation-state. This would be commensurate with Giddens' focus on time-space distanciation; that is, seeking to move beyond the undue reliance which has been placed on understanding society as a bounded system and positing instead a 'starting point that concentrates upon analysing how social life is ordered across time and space'.[130] This involves the reconceptualisation of international relations such that 'the political' is not understood as a practice or set of practices which pertains only to relations between given (that is, prior and self-evident) actors within specific territorial units, but rather as a space of interaction situated across and between many territories — interaction which is itself *constitutive of new political identities*. It is when the nexus of globalisation and political practice is viewed in this sense that the possibility of translocal politics begins to emerge.

Translocal spaces are hence constituted by those technologies and infrastructures which allow peoples and cultures to cross great distances and to transcend the boundaries of closed, territorial community. Translocality does not refer simply to a 'place', nor does it denote a collectivity of places. Rather it is an abstract (yet daily manifest) space occupied by the sum of linkages and connections *between* places (media, travel, import/export, etc.). The notion of locality is included within the term in order to suggest a situatedness, but a situatedness which is never static. Translocality can be theorised as a mode, one which pertains not to how peoples and cultures exist *in* places, but rather how they move *through* them. Translocality is hence a form of travel. Furthermore, I want to argue that translocality disrupts traditional constructions of political identity and gives rise to novel forms of political space. In this sense we can claim that certain spatial extensions (i.e. 'places') such as migratory or global cities are characterised by a high degree of translocality. In other words, translocality can be used to refer to places which peoples and cultures occupy, but in doing so it seeks to draw attention to the dynamics of distanciation at work within such locales rather than to the 'locatedness' of these places.

In summary, under globalising conditions we see that political identities are becoming increasingly disembedded from the context of the territorial nation-state. What I am seeking is a conceptualisation of this fact which does not address the political subject's alienation from the nation-state simply by attempting to produce a new, more inclusive model of the state. Rather, I am trying to refigure the scope of international political theory such that it becomes more capable of recognising and accounting for new political spaces and the identities they construct. As William Connolly puts it:

> Instead of defining the most basic problem as one of general alienation or fragmentation and the most fundamental response as one of achieving a more harmonious collective identity [i.e. a new version of the state], one may define the problem as an intensification and territorial extension of pressures for normalization that, ironically enough, then produce fracturing and fragmentation by defining an enlarged variety of types that do not or cannot conform to established standards of normality.[131]

Translocality is hence about recognising forms of politics situated not within the boundaries of a territorial space, but rather configured across and in-between such spaces. It is – as I have said – about studying what flows *through* localities rather than what is 'in' them.

My core thesis, then, might be stated as follows. In an increasingly globalised environment, the rigidity of bureaucratic and institutional structures such as the nation-state have allowed mounting pressures to produce a certain amount of cracking and fragmentation in their frameworks. The inherent fluidity of political identities, however, has allowed them to flow into, through, and out of these crevices – merging and syncretising as they go – thus creating new forms of politics whose dynamics hinge on spatial distanciation rather than on the persistence of a fixed territorial space. The multifaceted nature of identity has, under *translocality*, brought forth a diverse new set of political practices. These involve the possibility that any given individual may have ties and identity claims which pertain to more than one nation or state (or neither). Furthermore, the activities of such individuals are not limited to a single political space, either in terms of territory or discourse. One's presence in a particular territorial state does not restrict one from engaging in transnational relations which seek to politicise a component of self-identity which is not 'of' the territory from which these activities emanate. 'The empowering paradox of diaspora', writes James Clifford, 'is that dwelling *here* assumes a solidarity and connection *there*. But *there* is not necessarily a single place or an exclusivist nation'.[132] In other contexts the meaning of the 'translocal' becomes richer still. Instead of referring to dynamics and politics which operate across and between distinct, bounded nations, the idea of the translocal comes to refer to political practices which are simultaneously configured in relation to multiple spaces. A translocal identity does not belong to a single, distinct community or locale which, say, happens to be talking with, negotiating with or buying from a (single) other; rather, both localities can be seen as constitutive of the single individual. This is what we mean when we speak of hybridity – the presence of melange and syncretism in the construction of self-identity. For Homi Bhabha, this hybrid 'third space' 'displaces the histories that constitute it, and sets up new structures of authority, new political initiatives, which are inadequately understood through received wisdom'.[133] The political implications of these hybrid spaces will become evident when I go on to look at Muslim translocalities in later chapters.

In this chapter I have been concerned to map the conceptual ground upon which translocal identities are constructed under globalising conditions, and to frame some of the dynamics which underpin new forms of post-statist political space. In so doing I have also sought to critique some of the ways in which international relations has traditionally configured relations that are inter-, trans- or post-national. In this regard I would echo David Campbell when he asks whether international relations, in its present form:

> is adequate as a mode of understanding global life given the increasing irruptions of accelerated and non-territorial contingencies upon our political horizons, irruptions in which a disparate but powerful assemblage of flows – flows of people, goods, money, ecological factors, disease, ideas, etc. – contest borders, put states into question (without rendering them irrelevant), rearticulate spaces, and re-form identities.[134]

Can IR produce a post-national geography based not on horizontally arranged and contiguous, exclusive territories but rather on multiple, overlapping allegiances and post-territorial politics? The various processes of cultural displacement surveyed in the chapter are constitutive of new forms of political identity and translocal spaces which locate the political outside the normative boundaries of the territorial state. We need to write IR so that it speaks to this fact.

The same forces which have brought about translocal spaces have also given rise to phenomenal increases in the extent to which people communicate and encounter each other across the boundaries of cultures, ethnicities, nations and other communities – indeed, translocality has been responsible for bringing about significant changes in the nature and shape of these boundaries as well. In addition, the processes of decolonisation and a changing international labour environment have resulted in new dynamics of migration which have challenged (if not eradicated altogether) the very possibility of the homogenous nation-state. The era of translocality has hence radicalised our encounters with difference in such a way that we are increasingly forced to recognise the contingency of our own conceptions of society in the face of 'the others'. As Mike Featherstone puts it, '[t]hings formerly held apart are now brought into contact and juxtaposition. Cultures pile on top of each other in heaps without any obvious organizing principles. There is too much culture to handle and organize into coherent belief systems, means of orientation and practical knowledge'.[135] Over the last fifty years or so, globalising processes have also given birth to translocal actors on a scale which is historically unprecedented; ethnic minorities, diaspora groups, and migrant workers are all examples of this phenomenon. When bodies travel, so obviously do cultures. But what is the nature of a 'travelling culture' and what metamorphosis does it undergo in the process of transit?

2 Before, during and after the West
'Islam', Muslims and the umma

The sheikh [of the land of Halba] removed his turban and rubbed his hand across his head, then put it back and said, 'Freedom is the sacred value accepted by everyone.' I protested. 'This freedom has overstepped the boundaries of Islam.' 'But it is also sacred in the Islam of Halba.' Frustrated, I said, 'If our Prophet were to be resurrected today he would reject this side of your Islam.' 'And were he, may the blessings and peace of God be upon him, to be resurrected', he in turn inquired, 'would he not reject the whole of your Islam?'

(Naguib Mahfouz, *The Journey of Ibn Fattouma*)

Theory is no longer naturally 'at home' in the West – a powerful place of Knowledge, History, or Science, a place to collect, sift translate and generalise. Or, more cautiously, this privileged place is now increasingly contested, cut across, by other locations, claims, trajectories of knowledge articulating racial, gender, and cultural differences. But how is theory appropriated and resisted, located and displaced? How do theories travel among the unequal spaces of postcolonial confusion and contestation? What are their predicaments? How does theory travel and how do theorists travel? Complex, unresolved questions.

(James Clifford, 'Notes on Travel and Theory')

In the first chapter of this book I sought to explain why international relations needs to engage more closely with literatures that offer a sophisticated political sociology of globalisation. To this end I suggested that IR might be able to interact profitably with fields such as anthropology, postcolonial studies and transnational sociology. I also argued for an expansion of the theoretical parameters of 'the political' within international relations as a means to better understanding the political dynamics of what I termed translocal space. I concluded the chapter by submitting a query about the nature of the 'travelling' cultures and politics we find in translocality. In the rest of the book I will go about providing an answer to this through an exploration of the changing boundaries of Muslim political community. Obviously I could never hope to offer a comprehensive study of globalisation and political Islam within the space available to me here. Instead, in the context of this book I will focus on two important aspects of translocality identified in Chapter One, the *movement of peoples* and the rise of *communication and information technologies*, and examine how they are experienced by a selection of political communities within the contemporary Muslim world. I want to suggest that by studying the 'grass-roots' impact of globalisation in this way, we can perhaps discover important things about how transnational and globalising forces affect the configuration of Muslim political identity in relation to other identities, both Muslim and non-Muslim. Furthermore, I want to argue that these same processes are also helping to transform the boundaries of political community in Islam. In essence I am seeking to understand what happens to Islam when, as a theory, it travels. Islam is particularly interesting here in that as a religion it is already, at least in theory, a non-territorial force. As a normative code, Islam is equally valid wherever a Muslim might find himself. At the same time, however, throughout history different territories – or 'places' – have significantly mediated Islam and continue to do so today. We also find here a very strong, and, as I will later argue, overdetermining sense of what Edward Said would call Islam's 'point of origin'.

The specific questions I asked at the end of the previous chapter about what travelling cultures look like and what happens to them in translocality will be held in stasis for the duration of the present chapter. In this chapter I want to explain how I understand Islam's discursive function in the context of debates on religion and politics. I will first explain why I think an emphasis on Muslim subjectivity rather than on something called 'Islam' will be more helpful in our explorations of shifting identities in translocal space. In order to illuminate the wider context into which Muslim politics are articulated today I will review Bobby Sayyid's theory on Eurocentrism and the emergence of Islamism. I will suggest that he offers a powerful account of how the decentring of the West has allowed non-Western voices – and Islam in particular – to be heard, but then fails to give adequate attention to competing discourses *within* Islam as to what Islamism should be. It is my argument that such debates and negotiations over Muslim authenticity and authority are particularly rich when they take place in translocality – especially when compared to the Islam of various territorially and discursively bounded lifeworlds. I then go on to look at one important elaboration of Islamic political community, the notion of the umma, in two historical settings: the early years of Islam in Medina, and the colonial environment of the late nineteenth and early twentieth centuries. Both are contexts in which the umma had particular salience as a political category, and both play important roles in animating contemporary Muslim political imaginaries and discourses.

The metatheoretical parameters of Islam

I want to begin with some comments about a particular choice of terminology. In the context of this study, I will assign a connotation to the term 'Muslim' which is somewhat different from the seemingly synonymous designation 'Islamic'. On my understanding, to speak of a *muslim* (in Arabic, 'one who submits') is simply to speak of a subject-consciousness which considers itself to possess or practice a form of identity which derives from something called Islam, regardless of what form one's consciousness of the latter takes. I choose to emphasise the 'Muslim', then, in order to orient this study towards exploring the self-descriptions of those who consider themselves to be practising something called Islam. That is not to say, however, that I am advocating a form of methodological individualism. Indeed, I fully realise that individuals only exist as such through constitutive interaction with wider communities and normative systems. Rather, I am seeking to avoid the essentialism which can so easily be engendered by speaking about a single (absolute) system called Islam. In the same way, the term *Islamic* is problematic in that it would appear to suggest that there exists a body of thought or discursive practice which can be identified as 'authentic' or 'real' Islam. I wish the reader therefore to be aware that when I do use the term 'Islamic', I mean it to be seen within the context of a particular community's (or individual's) understanding of Islam. Occasionally, I will also use the term 'Islamism', which I take to refer to the attempt to articulate a political order based around Islam. My aim is to emphasise the multiple, cross-cutting interpretations which produce and reproduce various understandings of this religion across an equally diverse range of sociocultural contexts. So I enter this discourse with caution and fully cognisant of the fact that, as Edward Mortimer states, '[f]or me, in my condition of *jahiliyya* [pre- or non-Islamic ignorance], there is no Islam, in the sense of an abstract, unchangeable entity, existing independently of the men and women who profess it. There is only what I hear Muslims say, and see them do'.[1] It is therefore only possible to work within the confines of the various discursive fields which Muslim communities produce, and without recourse to any Archimedian perspective from which 'Islam' as a totality can be observed. At the same time, however, I do not want to suggest that those Muslims who claim that there is only one Islam are wrong in their conviction. Indeed, there is a very strong sense in which there is only one Islam. I see the signifier *Islam* in its singular, universal manifestation as playing a very particular (and vitally constitutive) role in Muslim political communities. Like Bobby Sayyid, I would suggest that Islam can be most usefully viewed as a form of *master signifier:*

> The master signifier functions as the most abstract principle by which any discursive space is totalized. In other words, it is not that a discursive horizon is established by a coalition of nodal points [e.g. 'Islamic' practices], but rather by the use of a signifier that represents the totality of that structure. The more extensive a discourse is, the less specific each element within it will be: it will become simply another instance of a more general identity. The dissolution of the specificity and concreteness of the constituent elements clears the path for a master signifier becoming more and more abstract, until it reaches a limit at which it does not have any specific manifestations: it simply refers to the community as a whole and it becomes the principle of reading that community.[2]

I take this to mean that Islam does not refer to a specific set of beliefs or practices, but rather that it functions as a totalising abstraction through which meaning and discourse can be organised.

Some writers have tried to come to terms with the diversity of the Islamic world by speaking of 'Islams' in the plural.[3] Their motivation is usually to escape the essentialising practices of Orientalism which on the one hand seek to impute some essence or immutable quality to Islam, and on the other to avoid confirming the discourses of those contemporary Islamist ideologues who wish to portray their interpretation of the religion as the one and only 'true' Islam. By positing the existence of a multitude of 'Islams', however, these writers risk reproducing the very essentialism they wish to combat and also severely relegating Islam's legitimacy as a religious doctrine. This is an approach which flies in the face of the fact that the vast majority of Muslims, despite a clear cognisance of their religion's diversity, see themselves as adhering very firmly to a single Islam.[4] To speak of 'Islams' is to be haunted by a sense of boundaries; it gives the impression that there is some point where one Islam leaves off and another picks up. I prefer to think of Islam as something far more fluid. This is why when speaking of Islam, I prefer to see different aspects of a single master signifier, with each aspect becoming 'another instance of a more general identity'. Islam can hence be seen as a single discursive field – a 'lifeworld' perhaps – yet one whose borders are constantly changing. In this sense there is only one Islam, but this does not necessarily have any direct correlation with the lived experience of being (or making oneself to be) a Muslim, nor does it have to impart any essence or teleology to the religion. Islam is narrated, yet the multiple forms of this narration do not destroy but rather build a greater whole. Talal Asad captures this well when he writes:

> While narrative history does not have to be teleological, it does presuppose an identity [e.g. 'Islam'] that is the subject of that narrative. Even when that identity is analyzed into its heterogeneous parts (class, gender, regional divisions, etc.), what is done, surely, is to reveal its constitution, not to dissolve its unity. The unity is maintained by those who speak in its name, and more generally by all who adjust their existence to its (sometimes shifting) requirements.[5]

The singularity of Islam does not, therefore, have to be seen as inimical to the social construction of Islam. It offers to its believers a set of meanings, but as Veena Das argues, these meanings are 'not to be interpreted once, and correctly, but continually reinterpreted, for meanings assigned to the word of God by human efforts can only be approximations'.[6]

Once we have recognised the plurality of meanings derived from Islam, we will want to go on to ask something about the nature of these meanings. What does Islam 'mean' to the Muslim? In what form does its significance manifest itself? As Aziz al-Azmeh notes, 'Islam appears as an eminently protean category'. According to him, Islam refers variously to a religion, a history, a community, a culture, an 'exotic' object and a complete political programme.[7] So while Islam is a product of discourse and social construction, it is also usually seen to fall within one of several conceptual categories – most commonly perhaps, that of *religion*. The point I wish to make here is that when we observe Islam from within an epistemology which assigns it to a distinct sphere of activity then we have already to some extent delineated the limits of what Islam can or cannot be. That is, insofar as we invest the concept of religion with a particular significance or set of meanings (which inevitably derive from our own experiences of it, e.g. seeing religion as primarily concerned with founding myths, the transcendental and questions of eschatology), we necessarily bring traces of that same template of meaning to any other phenomenon whose outward form leads us to give it the label 'religion'.

I am not seeking here to argue that we are somehow unjustified in treating Islam as a religion, nor am I advocating the point of view of those writers – usually Orientalists[8] or, ironically, some of the more extreme Islamists – who have a vested interest in arguing that Islam is far more than a religion and hence that one cannot make any meaningful distinctions between categories such as religion and politics in Islam. Rather, I simply wish to point out that when we calibrate our discursive horizons with reference to totalising categories, we inevitably view our chosen object of observation through a particular lens. For example, if we commence our analysis with a presumption that these things called 'religions' inhabit a realm called 'the private', this will necessarily mediate our perception of any religion which assumes a very prominent public role (i.e. it will be seen as somehow 'out of place'). Talal Asad argues that there can be no universal definition of the category religion because 'not only [are] its constituent elements and relationships historically specific, but that definition is itself the historical product of discursive processes'.[9] I wish, therefore, in the present context to treat Islam not merely as one example of the more general category religion, but rather as a discursive construct which operates as an important bearer of social meaning within particular communities. What we must be careful of, however, is the tendency in much writing to allow the appellation 'Islamic' to overdetermine the meanings we assign to objects, ideas and people as if something is suddenly wholly transformed when it becomes associated with Islam. Again it is usually those standing to gain the most from emphasising the exceptionalism of Islam (Orientalists and the more extreme Islamists) who engage in this sort of descriptive practice:

> [For them] there are 'Islamic cities' unlike all other cities, 'Islamic economies' to which economic reason is inapplicable, 'Islamic politics' impenetrable to social sciences and political sense, 'Islamic history' to which the normal equipment of historical research is not applied. Facts are disassociated from their historical, social, cultural and other contexts, and reduced to this substantive Islamism of the European [and extremist] imagination.[10]

Likewise the ease with which Islam becomes *the* explanatory variable of any given sociocultural condition. For example, when women are discriminated against in predominantly secular societies (e.g. the United States or the United

Kingdom) the culprit is usually seen to be something called 'patriarchy' (i.e. a historical-structural explanation is given); however, similar discrimination in predominantly Muslim societies is usually immediately ascribed to Islam. In this sense, Islam often offers the easy way out, both for analysts seeking a quick explanation and for the policy-makers of the societies in question who want to sidestep the structural causes of gender inequality and the mistreatment of women by referring to 'cultural' causes which are conveniently 'out of their hands'. I do not want to go too far with this, however. I do not want to suggest that an object is wholly untouched by its association with Islam, nor do I wish to claim that Islam has nothing to do with the ways in which Muslim women are treated. Any object is at least partially constituted through conjunction with a discursive field such as Islam. Islam cannot therefore be dismissed as nothing more than a 'secondary element'. Rather, what needs to be asked is *why* the language of Islam is used for the articulation of various socio-political projects:

> Enumerating the variety of functions of Islam does not answer the question of why it is that its name is evoked. For anti-orientalists its importance is due merely to its use as a source of symbolic authority and validation – in other words its instrumentality. They, for the most part, do not enquire why it is that Islam is being used in this way. Islam matters. Therefore, it needs to be theorized.[11]

Hence while 'Islamic economies' or 'Islamic histories' do not possess uniquely 'Islamic' ontologies, the coupling of history and Islam does have an important discursive function related to the production of authority and authenticity. This will be made more clear when I go on to discuss the nature of politics and religion in the context of Islam.

I have already mentioned the problems associated with taking Islam simply as an example of the category we call religion without attending to the political implications of doing so. When one sets out to write about political communities within an ostensibly 'religious' tradition, the question of the distinction between religion and politics – and whether such a thing even exists – becomes vital. This issue is particularly pertinent in the case of Islam because it is often claimed that in this context there is no distinction to be made between religion and politics. Many commentators subscribe to the formula *al-islām d''n wa dawla* ('Islam is both religion and state') which they claim has been a core assumption of Islamic thought since the medieval period,[12] although there are other writers who suggest that this particular creed began appearing in Islamist writings only very recently.[13] Either way, it is certainly not true to say that there have been no historical divisions between the 'clergy' and structures of the Islamic state – much the same way that it would be ridiculous to maintain that there has never been any overlap between Church and Emperor in the European Christian tradition. The terms din and dawla may not correspond exactly to what is usually understood by religion and state in conceptual terms, but the very fact that we have separate lexemes to distinguish din and dawla means that there is some notion of difference in operation here. While Islamic political history has indeed seen cases of symbiotic, mutually-legitimising alliance between *ulamā* (religious scholars, sing. *'alim*) and various temporal dynasties, it has also given us periods of bitter acrimony and open conflict between the two. But this is not the point. The question of a distinction between religion and politics is not one that can be answered simply by identifying the agents of each ('clergy' and 'state') and then looking for overlap or disjuncture between them. What we are faced with here is rather a question about whether 'the religious' and 'the political' are modes which occupy the same *discursive space*. My claim is that, in fact, they do occupy the same discursive space in the sense that they can both be seen as forms of *social authority*. I want to make this argument by referring back to how I defined 'the political' and 'political community' in the previous chapter. We recall that one important aspect of the political involves ethical claims or the assertion of a normative vision. In this regard there is a great deal of overlap between politics and religion in that they both posit a particular idea of 'the good'. I want to define social authority by linking it to these normative projects. On my reading, authority does not refer to one's power to control or coerce behaviour, but rather to one's capacity to command allegiance to a particular set of ethical claims (e.g. Islam or Marxism). In the same way that I have defined political community as the object of a particular mode of politics (i.e. a norma-tive project), we can also now define the same community as the constituency of a given social authority. By emphasising the ethical components of religion and politics we are able to read both as forms of social authority rather than as modes which occupy disparate spaces. When I speak of Muslim political community, however, I am not seeking to imply that the ethical claims of 'the political' take precedence over those of 'the religious' in Islam. Rather, my aim is to emphasise the political (i.e. negotiational or dialogic) aspect of this commu-nity. In this sense a *Muslim political community*

> relate[s] to widely shared, although not doctrinally defined, traditions of ideas and practice…[T]he forms of political contest and discourse as well as the meanings of traditions vary widely, but a constant across the Muslim world is the invocation of ideas and symbols [i.e. an ethical code], which Muslims in different contexts identify as 'Islamic', in support of their organ-ised claims and counterclaims.[14]

In summary, I believe that contemporary debates about the compatibility of reli-gion and politics in the modern world – the sort often waged today between Islamists and 'liberal secularists' – need to be viewed not as instances of moder-nity confronting premodernity (*à la* Orientalism) or as wholly incommensurable worldviews (according to the extreme Islamists), but rather as an encounter between two forms of social authority – both eminently modern – reified by the passing of Western modernity's totalising reign over the discursive field of the modern. This latter claim, borrowed from Bobby Sayyid, will have to be substan-tiated, and this I will do in the next section. My point in doing this is to recognise that we cannot say anything meaningful about Muslim political discourse in translocality without first understanding something of how Islam fits into the 'wider picture' of debates about Western hegemony, modernity and postmodernity. This is especially important insofar as many of the Muslim communities we will be examining in later chapters live in and are confronted by the West on a daily basis. Their conversations with the West, I will be arguing later, play an important role in defining who they are as Muslims and also what Islam is in the face of the West.

'Islam', modernity and the West

As I have said, it is impossible to comprehend contemporary Muslim political discourse without first situating it in a complex set of debates about Western hegemony, modernity and, to some extent, postmodernity. The literature here is vast and I could never hope to cover it comprehensively in the space available. I will therefore focus only on those aspects of the debate which are necessary for developing a reading of Islamism as a form of post-hegemonic discourse. Although the emphasis of this book is primarily on conversations taking place *within* Islam, it is vital that I also give some attention to the relationship between Islam, modernity and the West, especially since much of the 'internal' debate within translocal Islam is about how to respond to the West. We encounter an immediate difficulty, though, in that the labels 'West' and 'Islam' are themselves highly problematic. One of the first questions we might be tempted to ask concerns the commensurability of the two categories which these words describe; that is, we might want to assert that because 'Islam' and 'the West' are words that refer to totally different types of things, they simply cannot be compared – end of story. If, however, we look carefully at each of them as instances of political discourse, then dialogue is enabled.

Taken at face value, 'Islam' is the name of a religion while 'the West' is a geographic signifier conventionally used in reference to those cultural spheres in which power, social organisation and *logos* are legitimised and explained in terms of a master signifier derived from the history of European reason. In this sense, then, the West is purely a discursive creation and something that does not so easily correspond to one category or another (e.g. religion, ideology, etc.) of the standard taxonomy of analytical abstractions which the West has created for its own use. So how can we best characterise the relationship between these two discursive constructs, Islam and the West? The opinions on this issue in the literature are numerous and diverse. Some see inherent, irreconcilable tension and hostility between the two, while others claim them to be entirely compatible. We also find every possible position between these two poles. This vast spectrum of opinion can be explained in part by the fact that different writers work with very different conceptions of what constitutes Islam and the West, and also at varying levels of essentialism/abstraction. There is often a tendency in the literature, as I mentioned earlier in this chapter, to posit a monolithic Islam and then to compare it with an equally undifferentiated West. Aside from the production of severely stereotyped images on both sides, there is a much more serious problem with this kind of analysis. It would seem that the goal here is usually one of determining whether Islam and the West are harmonious – that is, the extent to which they can 'go together'. They are treated as two given (or predetermined), separate objects, and the task is to see if they are compatible.

This line of inquiry, I would argue, is wholly unproductive. On the one hand it is pointless insofar as the high level of abstraction involved – 'Islam' vs the 'West' – prevents us from determining the extent to which the socially embedded manifestations of these phenomena actually correspond to the master signifiers (which is not the point anyway), and hence whether or not the latter are 'compatible'. This method also tells us very little about the ontologies of Islam and the West, or about the extent to which they might actually have important influences on each other's very existence.

The anthropologist Talal Asad has remarked on a certain asymmetry in exchange between the West and the non-West, namely that 'people from non-Western countries feel obliged to read the history of the West…and Westerners in turn do not feel the same need to study non-Western histories'.[15] As a generalisation this is a fair point, but the nature of 'cross-reading' between the West and the non-West has, of course, been far more complex. There are various ways to view this relationship. An Orientalist reformulation of Asad's statement would most likely read something like this: 'People from non-Western countries have been obliged by the West to read and indoctrinate themselves with the history of the West, but Westerners do not feel the need to study non-Western histories except to confirm that non-Western histories are heading in the wrong direction'. This sort of discourse is usually constructed by using a set of binary oppositions – e.g. reason vs dogma, democracy vs despotism, civilisation vs medievalism, modernity vs tradition – with the first component of each pair corresponding to the West, and the second to the non-West.[16] I am most interested in this last pair, 'modernity vs tradition', because modernity seems to me the most general or abstract quality of all those on offer, the one which best subsumes the others (reason, democracy, civilisation) and is often seen to be most intimate, if not actually synonymous, with the West.

Modernity, though, is somewhat ambiguous in character. Part of the problem seems to be that no one is quite sure exactly what 'modernity' means. Is it simply a description of certain qualities, or is it a normative project? At various points throughout its discursive history modernity seems to have been associated with almost every intellectual trend since the European Renaissance: humanism, secularism, enlightenment, liberalism, capitalism, communism etc. What we should note here is the crucial qualifier 'European'. The implication is that modernity is something produced by and constitutive of the West. Despite the fact that references to this latter appellation are ubiquitous, 'the West' – as I have noted above – is itself a highly problematic concept. It is one of those terms which everyone seems to know and understand, yet which is most difficult to define with any kind of analytic precision. It is a space (both physically and discursively) which contains an enormous corpus of thought, history and culture. Although it ostensibly refers to a place, or put another way, a 'where', I believe we gain a better understanding of the discursive function of the West if we view it more as something that describes variously a 'who', a 'what', a 'when' and a 'why'. In other words, there tends to be an assumption that certain people are Westerners (the 'who'), that these people embody norms and ideals which derive from a particular Western history (the 'what'), that this history reaches its maturity during the phase we call modernity (the 'when') and that the entire Western project is underpinned by the logic of a particular *telos* (the 'why').

It is more difficult, however, to define the substance of each of these categories. Different writers choose to define and deploy the West in different ways within the various schemes and frameworks they construct. Very often readers consulting the indices of recent grand treatises on social or historical theory for an entry on 'the West' will find themselves referred elsewhere – advised perhaps to 'see Europe', or 'see capitalism'. These re-routings can offer us a few hints as to the discursive space occupied by the West. It could also be said that in attempting to trace the origins of the West as a discursive category what we really want to know is something about how the West is thought. Stuart Hall contends that our discourses on the West act in four main ways:

1   As instruments of classification which permit us to define various societies according to a binary opposition, West or non-West. In this sense they 'set a certain structure of thought and knowledge in motion'.[17]
2   As sets of images or systems of representation which serve to associate (both verbally and visually) particular cultures, peoples and traits with various normative categories – e.g. Western democrats = good, non-Western 'oriental despots' = bad. These are similar to the binary oppositions I referred to above.
3   As abstract standards of comparison which allow us to determine the extent to which societies and cultures are distinct from one another. 'Non-western societies can accordingly be said to be "close to" or "far away from" or "catching up with" the West. It helps to explain *difference*'.[18]
4   As determinants of the criteria according to which societies are ranked and judged – that is, they 'produce a certain kind of *knowledge* about a subject and certain attitudes towards it'.[19]

It should be pointed out that the typology of Western discourse outlined by Hall above is most prevalent within Western societies themselves. The process of 'Westernisation' can perhaps therefore be thought of as the attempt by the West to propagate these discourses about itself (i.e. as *the* criteria for the 'good life') beyond its own borders. Furthermore, at the discursive level the West has sought to acquire hegemony, to represent itself as a 'universal' and 'natural' mode. By doing so it has set itself up as the benchmark by which any and every theory (or community) is to be judged. For example, there is often this idea that Islam, in order to be seen as valid, must first experience the same sequence of epistemological progression found in Western self-descriptions: secularisation leading to enlightenment leading to democracy, capitalism and all the other 'good stuff' – in short, 'modernity'. In this sense Islam remains trapped within the West's hegemonic description of the history of knowledge. The West, in order to evaluate Islam, needs to place it somewhere along the timeline of European epistemology and more often than not this becomes a process of what Johannes Fabian has termed 'pushing the other back in time'.[20] This is where descriptions of Islam as 'medieval' or 'traditional' enter the picture. Islam becomes yet another object to be catalogued, categorised and named.[21]

The problem here is the way in which the West de-historicises itself. Europe wants to claim the particularity of its own historical experience as a universal, as a set of ideas and values that should be binding on all humankind. What it fails to acknowledge is that what it represents as universal is nothing more than another particularity, albeit one which has succeeded in acquiring hegemonic status. In this sense there is no sharp distinction to be drawn between modernity and tradition because modernity is revealed as a form of tradition. As Asad writes:

> When people talk about liberalism as a tradition, they recognise that it is a tradition in which there are possibilities of argument, reformulation, and encounter with other traditions, that there is a possibility of addressing contemporary problems through the liberal tradition. So one thinks of liberalism as a tradition central to modernity. How is it that one has something that is a tradition but that is also central to modernity? Clearly, liberalism is not a mixture of the traditional and the modern. It is a tradition that defines one central aspect of Western modernity. It is no less modern by virtue of being a tradition than anything else is modern...Once we set that grand narrative [of 'Western' modernity], that normative history aside, we can start asking not, 'What should such-and-such a people be doing?', but 'What do they aim at doing? And why?'. We can learn to elaborate that question in historically specific terms. This certainly applies to our attempts to understand politico-religious movements, especially Islamic movements. It is foolish, I think, to ask: 'Why are these movements not moving in the direction History requires them to?'. But that is precisely what is being asked when scholars say: 'What leads the people in these movements to behave so irrationally, in such a reactionary manner?'[22]

In other words, we have to stop asking the sorts of questions in which the 'correct' answers are already predetermined by the interrogatory act. What Asad is arguing for here is a form of inquiry which moves beyond a paradigm in which the particularity or 'tradition' of Western norms is allowed to masquerade as a form of objective 'science'. In terms of methodology, he gives us some indication as to what kinds of questions need to be asked. Where we run into problems, however, is at the level of conceptual discourse. If a concomitant of Western universality is that it becomes impossible to engage in any sort of theorising without resorting to Western conceptual categories then it would seem that we are trapped. Even the act of advancing 'non-Western' claims becomes yet another instance of Western discourse. Is there any escape from this paradox? Some think so. In the next section I want to look at one such argument developed by Bobby Sayyid. Through a series of adroit theoretical manoeuvres he seeks to free Islam from Western hegemony by refiguring the condition of *post*modernity as one in which the West is de-centred and Europe provincialised.

Islam beyond Eurocentrism

In his *A Fundamental Fear: Eurocentrism and the Emergence of Islamism*, Bobby Sayyid seeks to read political Islam as a discourse which emerges out of cracks in Western hegemony. His first move in this process is to establish the modern character of Islamist thought. Taking Imam Khomeini as his representative Islamist, Sayyid argues – with supporting evidence from a variety of political sociologists – that despite the conventional depiction of Khomeini as an archaic extremist, his political theory can in fact only be understood in the context of modernity. Because Khomeini's writing relies heavily on categories associated with Western political thought, e.g. 'the people' as political agents and the legislative properties of the state, we must understand him as a thoroughly modern theorist. Nowhere in his principal treatise, however, does Khomeini refer to Western political theory. He writes as if it does not exist. Most commentators, Sayyid notes, are unimpressed by this. They tend to see the modernity of Khomeini's thought as sufficient evidence of its Western character (i.e. modernity and the West are effectively conflated). What these writers are claiming, in effect, is that Khomeini's non-Western credentials are weak. What he proposes as 'authentic tradition' is actually Western theory dolled up in Islamic garb. Talal Asad, however, takes issue with this line of thought. For him it reproduces an essentialist dichotomy between tradition and modernity which, as we have seen above, simply does not exist:

> [M]any writers describe the movements in Iran and Egypt as only partly modern and suggest that it is their mixing of tradition and modernity that account for their 'pathological' character. This kind of description paints Islamic movements as being somehow inauthentically traditional on the assumption that 'real tradition' is unchanging, repetitive, and non-rational. In this way, these movements cannot be understood on their own terms as being at once modern and traditional, both authentic and creative at the same time.[23]

The largest problem with this conventional discourse on modernity, according to Sayyid, is that modernity and the West are used interchangeably, *as if they are the same thing*. He goes on to argue that within the West, modernity operates as a tautological structure which constructs *itself* as the West: 'Modernity positions itself as a ruptural moment which divides history in two. It is this rupture that gives birth to the West and marks it off as being unique'.[24] Sayyid is therefore faced with the following problem. He has established that Islamism is something modern and wants to maintain this characterisation. At the same time, however, he realises that the Eurocentrism of modernity dooms it to be a quality associated exclusively with the West. Consequently, by asserting that Islamism is modern he is also saying that it is Western (for if Islamism = modernity and modernity = the West then Islamism = the West). He is now faced with a range of options. He could affirm the Western nature of Islamism, but believes that this would severely dilute the efficacy of the West as an analytical concept. He could retract his claim that Islamism is modern but is loathe to do this because he is fully convinced by the argument that Islamist theory (at least in its Khomeinist form) contains elements that did not exist before the modern age. So he decides to go the ambitious route:

> A third option would be to see in Islamism an attempt to articulate a modernity that is not structured around Eurocentrism. That is, to take seriously the Islamists' claims to being a movement dedicated to a denial of the West, but not to read in this rejection of the West an attempt to re-establish 'traditional' agrarian societies. To do this means renegotiating the identity of modernity as well as that of the West.[25]

The project here is to construct an Islamic modernity, one which retains modern features but which elaborates them without reference to or conjunction with Western political theory, a modernity divorced from the West.[26] Sayyid's strategy here is complex. He does not reach his destination by describing a specifically 'Islamic' form of modernity, or by enumerating the various features which such an entity might possess. Rather, he concentrates his efforts on the crucial task of decoupling modernity from the West. It is here that the notion of Eurocentrism becomes important in his argument.

> I define eurocentrism as the discourse that emerges in the context of the decentring of the West; that is, a context in which the relationship between the western enterprise and universalism is open to disarticulation and re-articulation. The discourse of eurocentrism is an attempt to suture the interval between the West and the idea of a centre (that is, a universal template). Eurocentrism is a project to recentre the West, a project that is only possible when the West and the centre are no longer considered to be synonymous. It is an attempt to sustain the universality of the western project, in conditions in which its universality can no longer be taken for granted.[27]

Sayyid links this trend with the rise of a post-modern condition in the sense of a scepticism towards metanarratives à la Jean-François Lyotard. The West is seen to be gradually losing its discursive monopoly on all that is good, and Eurocentrism functions to preserve the linkage between the West and universality. It is in this light that Sayyid would want to read Francis Fukuyama's claims about the 'End of

History'. Other writers confirm that Sayyid is not alone in his assessment. Mehrzad Boroujerdi, for example, informs us that many intellectuals in Iran interpreted the downfall of Soviet-style communism not as a victory for the Western model, but rather as an indication of Western weakness. For them, Marxism and Liberalism are both 'Western' ideologies, and share a great deal of conceptual presumptions. 'These presumptions manifest themselves', he writes, 'in realms such as the stripping of nature's divine essence, the advocacy of science and secular knowledge, and the privileging of mind and body over the soul'.[28] On this reading the events of 1989 are seen as a precursor to further decline in the Rest of the West. Eurocentrism thus operates as a form of 'genetic engineering' in which the West seeks to maintain the integrity of its genealogies.

> What this means is that the denunciation of Islamists for using Western categories is actually the reconstruction and maintenance of particular genealogical traces. It is not that Khomeini uses concepts which are themselves western, but that the description of the concepts as western retroactively constructs them as such. It is not only that Islamists are engaged in an operation of fabrication – that is making up stories about their authentic selves, 'pretending' that the clothes they wear are 'Islamic' – but also that those who reject Islamist narratives of authenticity do so by making up stories about the West.[29]

In order to maintain its hegemony, the West needs to make a claim to cultural copyright on any form of non-Western thought by insisting that Islamist discourse, for example, is nothing more than a rehearsal of ideas whose 'authentic' origins are to be found in the history of the West.[30] In this sense Eurocentrism is an attempt by the West to assimilate all would-be competitors, to police and discipline them within its own 'universal' jurisdiction. It would seem that on Sayyid's reading, Islamic voices are not getting louder but rather Western voices are getting weaker. The West is experiencing a crisis of representation, no longer able to posit itself as the sole guardian of universality. This attenuation of Western discourse is allowing non-Western voices, such as those of the Islamists, to be heard; for when the West is relatively quiet, the rest of the world seems louder. The West responds to this in one of two ways. Either it seeks to portray these newly amplified Islamist voices as part of a dangerous global Islamic revival (and here begin discourses on Islam's irrationality, despotism, and 'medieval' social attitudes) or it claims that the Islamists are simply rearticulating Western ideas in Islamic language, and hence constitute nothing more than an isolated protest movement *within* the West. Sayyid, however, argues that as we move further away from modernity – totalised at its zenith as a purely Western narrative – and into some form of *post*modernity, the West is effectively decentred. A metaphor of lunar eclipse springs to mind, all the more appropriate because the crescent moon is a symbol of Islam. It is as if the moon (the 'non-West') has been eclipsed by the shadow of the earth ('the West') for the last several centuries. The decentring of the earth ('postmodernism') allows the moon to be seen again. Obviously there are complicating factors here – important questions, for example, about who revolves around whom – but the general image I think holds true.

There is much of merit in Sayyid's argument; it is well-developed and theoretically sophisticated. Yet I fear also that in some respects it suffers from its own forms of reductionism and essentialism. In the first chapter of *A Fundamental Fear*, Sayyid expresses his dissatisfaction with the ways in which most Western commentators have attempted to account for Islamism. Having reviewed the relevant literature, he identifies five explanatory paradigms that tend to dominate Western scholarship on Islam: in (1) Islamism is due to the failure of nationalist secular elite governments in predominantly Muslim countries; (2) sees a lack of meaningful political participation as the main catalyst for pro-Islamist sentiment; in (3) a disenfranchised petty bourgeoisie turns to political Islam in a quest for power; (4) offers an explanation based on the flow of petro-dollars and uneven economic development; and finally (5) sees Islamism as a nativist response to cultural erosion, the protest of weakened Muslim identities in the face of a Western global system.[31] 'These narratives on the causes of "Islamic Fundamentalism"', Sayyid writes, 'assume that it is possible to understand what emerges from a crisis by understanding the nature of the crisis itself'.[32] In other words, he does not believe that these explanations tell us anything about why it is that Islam becomes the specific language of political (re)articulation. Arguing a similar point, one writer notes that 'Islam is treated as an explanatory phenomenon rather than a phenomenon which has to be "explained" '.[33] So Sayyid wants to obtain an explanation for the emergence of Islamism not through Western objectifications of Muslim societies but rather by focusing on transformations in the status of the West itself. It is this which leads him to focus on Eurocentrism and a postmodernity in which the West has become decentred.

Now I see two problems with this argument. First of all I think it too Eurocentric – not in the sense of reflecting European concepts or values, but because Sayyid seems to want to understand the emergence of Islamism exclusively by reference to changes in the West. In doing so he neglects the role of theorising *within* Islam which, as I will argue later, has also been undergoing some profound transformations in recent years. Ironically, we might even say that his argument is too structural or 'infrastructural' in that it focuses on how something called 'the West' is shifting in relation to other 'non-Western' units; that is, it concentrates primarily on changing configurations of hegemony. I agree with Sayyid that the usual explanations offered by Western commentators do not help us to answer the question 'Why Islam?' At the same time, though, there is more to the story than Sayyid's account of a decentred West would have us believe. On my reading, there is another element that needs to be included. At first glance it probably bears a passing (although false) resemblance to explanation (5) – and perhaps also (1) – above, which sees Islamism as a response from 'weakened' Muslim identities to a Western-dominated global system. While I certainly do not see Islamism as a 'nativist' response to Muslim cultural erosion – indeed, I will be arguing later that in many ways Islam is flourishing today, or at least has the potential to do so – I do see in Islamism (and read in Islamist discourses) a response to Western hegemony. This is why I believe we also have to leave room for reading Islamism as a form of *post-colonial discourse*. As it became obvious that the various projects of decolonisation and national self-determination (premised on the almost sacrosanct model of the autonomous nation-state) which unfolded in the 1960s and 1970s were no panacea, and that, if anything, the new nation-states were simply once again trapped within a structurally determined system in which Western dictates – economic, political and cultural – reigned supreme, a new language was sought. One with no ties to the West, something 'of our own making', something beyond the Western matrix. Marxist experiments did not count for they were only local variations on yet another Western ideology. So Islam emerges as the most coherent, non-Western alternative. Although he does not explicitly link the term to Islamism, Sayyid's account is haunted by the notion of *authenticity*. What emerges from this discourse on authenticity, however, is not an anachronistic, medieval throwback but an Islam which speaks itself in terms of rejuvenation: *nahḍa* (renaissance), *iṣlāḥ* (reform), *tajdīd* (renewal). Muslim identities are not 'eroded' by the West, but rather it is the decentring of the latter – which Sayyid has so persuasively established – that allows Islam to be articulated in new ways. Political Islam is an attempt to articulate a *different* modernity – or what James Clifford has referred to as a 'discrepant modernity'.

The second problem with Sayyid's thesis is related to this last point about the articulation of Islam in new ways. By focusing on Khomeini, which he needs to do in order to establish the non-Western character of Islamism, Sayyid falls into the trap of essentialising political Islam. He neglects the enormous diversity of opinion within the Muslim world about what an Islamic political order should look like – and, more particularly, what its relationship with the West should be. There are those who believe that Islam desperately needs to reform itself – not because Muslims no longer consider its values to be superior to those of the West, but because the world is changing (see Chapter One), and hence Islam needs to change with it. Sayyid recognises that the world is changing, and that one of the consequences of this is the relativisation of the West. He sees this as a precondition which allows Islamism to emerge, but does not inquire into the nature of this Islamism except to assert its modern and non-Western character. Arguing strongly against this mode of depicting the non-West, Revathi Krishnaswamy writes:

> The complex 'local' histories and culture-specific knowledges inscribed in post-colonial narratives get neutralised into versions of postmodern diversity, allowing 'others' to be seen, but shorn of their dense specificity. Class, gender, and intellectual hierarchies within other cultures, which happen to be at least as elaborate as those in the West, frequently are ignored.[34]

Thus while I believe Sayyid makes an effective set of arguments for explaining the circumstances under which the discursive field of modernity (or postmodernity) becomes open to non-Western – and in this case, Islamist – voices, he does not go far enough in examining the implications of this vicissitude for Islamism itself. Although it is fair to say that Islamism refers to the attempt to articulate Islam to a political order, such attempts are made in a variety of shapes and colours. To take Khomeinist discourse as representative of Islamism is to mask a variety of alternative Islamist imaginaries – many of which have been enabled by the very same transformations Sayyid identifies, but which would nevertheless advocate a path to Islamist reform significantly different from Khomeini's. So while he is correct to argue that the de-centring of the West opens up universality to disarticulation, he also needs to recognise that by the very same token, Islam is now open to rearticulation.

In order to gain an understanding of some of the other ways in which Islam is being articulated as a political project today we first need to trace the history of the concepts and ideas deployed by contemporary Muslim political theorists. What sources of social authority (i.e. ethical claims) do they turn to in order to legitimate their politics? What has it meant to speak of political community in Islam and how do Muslims conceive this community? I propose to answer these questions by undertaking a brief historical investigation of sorts. It will constitute an attempt to reconstruct the course of an intellectual journey which began in Medina, 622 AD, and whose most recent detours and re-routings (call them decolonisation and translocality) have landed it firmly in twenty-first century Europe and North America. The two periods with which I will concern myself here are of paramount importance in the global history of Islam. I have chosen them because they both represent instances in which a particular notion of community, the umma, was mobilised as a politicised identity (i.e. an identity constructed in the face of antagonism) and as an alternative political order. The two periods studied here are doubly important in that they also provide the intellectual resources upon which a great many contemporary Muslim theorists draw. The first account, that of the early Muslim community in Medina explores the 'point of origin' for a very well-travelled set of ethical claims and demonstrates how Islam constituted a new form of politics and social authority in the context of seventh century Arabia. The second account reveals how Muslim thinkers in a wide variety of sociocultural and regional settings collectively turned to Islam and the umma as a form of anti-colonial discourse during the nineteenth and early twentieth centuries. It is the 'global' nature of this response which particularly interests me, seeing in it as I do the first modern expression of Muslim translocality.

Migration into community: the *umma* of Medina

The first meaningful expression of Islamic polity occured in the Hijazi (Western Arabian) oasis of Medina – then called Yathrib – in the third decade of the seventh century.[35] The year 622 marks both the origin of the Muslim community and year one of its calendar. In that September, Muhammad – as God's Messenger and Prophet of a 'new' religion[36] – followed several dozen of his followers from their native city of Mecca on the *hijra* (migration) to Medina. Notables from among the feuding clans of the latter settlement had agreed to recognise Muhammad's prophethood and to accept his arbitration in settling their disputes. This invitation allowed the Prophet and his followers to escape a Mecca which was becoming increasingly hostile towards his monotheistic message. With the large Jewish population in Medina perhaps more predisposed to Muhammad's form of monotheism, the early Muslims were provided with the opportunity to regroup while establishing an entirely new political base.[37] The dispute with Mecca was, however, to continue for almost a decade until victory over the city was finally consolidated in 630 AD.

The following account will seek primarily to understand how the first Muslim community came to be constituted at Medina. In essence, the normative model which developed in these early years eventually came to form the very basis of the *sharī'a* (Islamic law). The authoritative deeds and dictums of the Prophet (his *sunna*) have, along with the *Qur'ān*, come to constitute the two primary sources of social authority in Islam. The traditions of the first emigrants and their supporters in Medina have been recorded, interpreted, and coded as sources of jurisprudence which carry a mythical warrant even today. The themes, events, and personages of these years are constantly referred to – and aspired to – in contemporary Muslim discourse. In the context of Medina I will not be dealing with a particular set of texts or a single author; rather, I will be presenting this oasis society in its totality as a model, a source of emulation for later generations of Muslims. We start the clock, then, with the decisive break, the founding of the community: we begin with the hijra.

The first migration has become an enduring symbol and its resonance can be heard today in the names of several Islamic movements such as *Takfīr w'al-Hijra* in Egypt or *al-Muhajirun* ('The Emigrants') in London. The hijra has taken on a significance much wider than the specific historical event itself. It has come to symbolise deliverance from oppression and *jāhilīya* (pre-Islamic ignorance), and the institution of a new social paradigm in which 'the good life' would accrue from submission to the will of a single divine source. As Ira Lapidus puts it: 'For Muslims the word has come to mean not only a change of place, but the adoption of Islam and entry into the community of Muslims. The hijra is the transition from the pagan to the Muslim world – from kinship to a society based on common belief'.[38] In theory, then, the hijra represented an idiomatic shift with regard to the manner in which community was to be imagined. Social cohesion based purely on clan and kin was seen as a source of constant strife and feuding, whereas a 'community of believers' could strive to transcend this base tribalism in the name of a greater unity. In Islam, the core doctrine of *tawhīd* (unity of and in God) reflects this concern. For those who participated in the first migration, then, it was not the geographic move from Mecca to Medina which mattered, but rather the much more dramatic (and initially, one would imagine, disorienting) split from their tribal kin-groups. These affiliations had been the crux and core of social solidarity in Arabia at the time, and to leave them behind in the name of Islam signified a major break with traditional practice. The umma, or world community of Muslims, therefore had its initial incarnation in the original group that accompanied Muhammad on the hijra in 622.

It is difficult for the modern commentator to discern exactly what was implied by the term umma in the context of Muhammad's new Medinan society. As it occurs in both the Qur'an and other primary source material from the period, we may attribute several possible meanings ranging anywhere from Muhammad's closest followers to all living creatures (Sura vi. 38). The etymology of the word is also ambiguous. The instinctive tendency has been to connect it with the Arabic *umm*, meaning 'mother', but it seems more likely that the term is derived from analogues in Hebrew and Aramaic, both of which refer to 'community'. It has even been speculated that the word is ultimately Sumerian in origin.[39] In modern discourse, umma often appears as a central normative concept which appeals for unity across the global Muslim community. Its evolution in early Islamic society, however, was somewhat more particular.

The umma of Medina was originally a sort of 'defence pact' which united the city's clans in a pledge to protect Muhammad and his followers. This alliance system was codified in a document usually referred to as the Constitution of Medina. In essence, this 'treaty' provided an overarching sense of authority for the anarchic settlement. Because it demanded complete loyalty from all factions it also effectively prevented the formation of unstable alliances between clans. Just who was included in its initial jurisdiction is however not easy to determine a situation made all the more ambiguous by the fact that the documents we have from this period appear to contain several disparate usages of the term, reflecting various modifications and amendments during the Medinan years. Does it refer to relations of kinship, religion or territory? It would seem that the umma as it was conceived at the time of Muhammad's arrival included elements of all three. Certainly it was initially confined to the major clans of Medina and several local Jewish and Christian groups, in addition to the Muslim emigrants themselves. In this sense its connotation is not significantly different from that of 'the large tribe'. As the Prophet managed to consolidate his authority in Medina, however, the character of the umma began to evolve. It is likely that Muhammad became increasingly capable of demanding a commitment to his religion (or at least a renunciation of idolatry) on the part of those who would seek to enter into confederacy with his community. Impressed by the success of his raids against Meccan caravans, it soon became obvious to neighbouring nomadic tribes that the political winds were blowing Muhammad's way and many were anxious to pledge their loyalty to him in return for the shelter of his expanding *dhimma*, or 'security system'.[40]

If we want to speculate as to the character of the umma of Medina we can perhaps best view it as a conglomerate of various communities – tribal, confessional, and confederal. Certainly a good deal of traditional practice with regard to the formation of alliances and kinship ties was preserved in Muhammad's new mini-state, with the overtly 'religious' aspects of the community being confined largely to Muhammad's close followers. As far as Allah's Messenger was concerned, the main imperative at this point was to bolster his numbers and to widen the basis of his popular support. If this involved the occasional pact with a pagan clan, so be it. The realisation of the religious universal would come gradually. The basis of social solidarity was, to some extent, still based on the traditional tribal idiom, albeit with a new focus of collectivity that could (and did) prevent a return to civic conflict and factionalism. Although references to the umma seem to disappear from the Qur'an after the first years following the hijra, we can still see from early Medinan verses that Allah envisaged a unique role for his community.[41] As the propagation of Islam by conquest began in earnest following the death of the Prophet, so did the notion of a wider umma naturally regain its currency. Indeed, so venerated is this early period in Muslim thought that its precedents have been recorded in copious detail so that they may be passed on to future generations as an authoritative example of how Islam is meant to be practised. The political community of Medina has no equal in its influence. For forty years, from AD 622 to 661, Islam, in the eyes of its adherents, attained near purity. Although schisms began to form from the day the Prophet died (and probably even before), the reign of the first four caliphs – Muhammad's successors as leaders of the Muslim community – is considered to have been a period of enlightenment, justice and prosperity. It was under these leaders, collectively known as the *rashīdūn* or 'rightly-guided' caliphs, that Islam began its incredibly rapid expansion. It was also under them that the first authoritative edition of the Qur'an was produced and the various sources of social authority were systematised into religious law, the shari'a.

> Since the death of the Prophet, Islam has never recovered the special circumstances permitting its double expression as symbol and politics: Muhammad put a political order in place by designing immediately and quite adequately a process of symbolization by which every judicial-political decision took its justification and finality from a living relationship with God.[42]

Did Muhammad and his close followers know that in an attempt to preserve this 'living relationship' their every act would be scrutinised, interpreted, reinterpreted and later codified in *fiqhi* (jurisprudential) literature? Did they know that the stories told about them, as passed down through a secure chain of transmitters, would become the basis for an entire legal system? Medina is a memory, distant yet tangible, pulling at the modern Muslim mind like a magnet. We might invoke here Lawrence Durrell's description of Alexandria in the 1930s as 'a city half-imagined, yet wholly real'. It is a vivid model, something to be desired. Muslims today, and especially those who constitute the diasporic communities examined in later chapters, are increasingly returning to the sources of this early period for guidance as to where 'real' Islam can be found. Returning to our history, though, there are questions that need to be answered about the politics which emerged from the Medina period. What of the debates which ensued after Muhammad's death over who was to succeed him as leader of the Muslims? Did these contestations signify the birth or the death of a political community? We could perhaps suggest the following: that with the passing of the Prophet, Islamic political community ceased to exist and *Muslim* political community – as a space of negotiation – came to take its place. The very fact that today we find competing accounts of the Medinan period – in both Western and Muslim histories – bears testimony to its importance in the Islamic imagination. In this sense, the social construction of Medina in contemporary Islamist discourse can be seen to constitute a vital form of Muslim politics.

We rapidly lose track of tiny Medina in the years following the Prophet's death. A system of political succession, embodied in the institution of the caliphate, was established. However, through a series of assassinations, conspiratorial machinations and eventually, open civil war, the locus of political power in the Muslim community began to shift quite significantly. Factions and breakaway groups (such as the Shi'a and the Khawarij) began to multiply, and the first of Islam's many territorial dynasties was established. Over the coming centuries, 'Islamic' capitals were declared in locales as diverse as Baghdad, Damascus, Córdoba, Cairo, Nishapur, Samarqand and Constantinople, among others. This geographic plurality was accompanied by a new diversity in religious thought. Islam's initial schism, that between Sunni and Shi'a, became more complex as subdivisions within these approaches began to develop. In the Sunni tradition, for example, there eventually emerged four distinct systems of jurisprudence, each with its own founding father and chain of disciples. A complex religio-political system emerged during the medieval period, composed of a class of religious scholars (the ulama), a shari'a-based judiciary and its courts, and the political dynasty, where the caliph ruled in theory as the leader of both a religious and a political community. The centuries following the death of Muhammad, then, saw a phenomenal expansion of Islam as it came to claim territories from the edge of Western Europe right across to the archipelagos of Southeast Asia. In the process of this diffusion the Prophet's umma was split into a myriad range of dynasties, sects and ethno-national regimes, with the caliphate moving continuously between the various power centres identified above.

In my historical account I will be omitting the thousand years between Medina and the nineteenth century for a number of reasons. Although it is a fascinating period, I do not consider it particularly germane to the arguments I wish to make in this study. First of all the expansion and accompanying fragmentation of the Muslim community makes it difficult to speak of the umma in any sense other than its most minimal description of the world community of believers. Second, I do not see the umma's relevance during this period as a form of *politicised* community in the sense of collective mobilisation against an external antagonism. One may wish to interject that Islam's struggles during the Crusades or against various invasions from Central Asia can be viewed as such a collective mobilisation. While it is undoubtedly true that these conflicts clearly had their non-Muslim 'others', I am choosing not to include them in my account because there is a strong sense in which they were confined to particular regions of the Muslim world and did not serve to constitute the umma (in the sense of the wider multicultural, multi-regional Muslim world) as a single political community. As Ira Lapidus points out:

> The first Muslim reaction [to the Crusader states] was, by and large, indifference. Syria was so fragmented as to preclude any unified opposition to the intruders; several more little states among many did not much disturb existing interests. *The fact that these new states were Christian was not exceptional* – the Byzantines had also ruled northern Syria, and there was a substantial, if not a majority, local Christian population.[43]

Relatively large populations of Christians had already been living peacefully in Muslim lands for several centuries as protected peoples of the book (*ahl al-kitāb*). There is therefore a very strong sense in which during the Crusades, the Christians had a much stronger notion of the Muslim as 'other' than the Muslims did of the Christians. My thousand-year leap into the colonial era of the nineteenth century is therefore justified, I believe, in that this latter period marks the re-emergence of the umma as a key concept in Muslim political discourse in the face of the challenge posed to Islam by the West. Furthermore, the case of the colonial period is one in which a common threat (European imperialism) affected more or less the entire Muslim world from Morocco to India and even Indonesia and Malaysia. During this period, Muslim anti-colonial activists travelled widely throughout the Muslim world seeking to inspire their fellow believers to throw off the yoke of European colonialism in the name of a greater umma. In this regard, the early modern struggles of the colonial era serve as a key point of reference for Muslims today, many of whom view the continued dominance of the West as the perpetuation of European imperalism. There is thus an intrinsic link between the Muslim voices of the early colonial period and the contemporary Muslim post-colonial discourse referred to above.

Pan-Islam and the colonial umma

Let us begin this second set of historical discourses by noting that by and large their 'points of origin' lie not in the nominal centre of the Muslim world, the Sultanate and Caliphate of Istanbul, but in Persia and the Indian subcontinent – hence offering what Richard Bulliet has termed 'the view from the edge'.[44] The rise of European imperialism had a profound effect on many Muslim minds, and proved to be the catalyst for several generations of thinkers whose primary occupation was the removal of the unbelievers from Muslim lands. This could only be accomplished, they believed, through a concerted effort towards Pan-Islamic unity and a 'reawakening' of the Muslim conscience. Hence an intellectual agenda was to be combined with a programme of organised political activism. It is not surprising that some of the loudest voices in this cause came from those regions in which the European presence was strongest. Another important factor which distinguished these activities from previous attempts to reform the Muslim body politic – and one which will be explored more fully in Chapters Four and Five – relates to the nature of the personalities involved. Where before the religious establishment, that is the ulama and legal scholars, had held a virtual monopoly over the ability to interpret, formulate, and propound legitimate political causes in the name of Islam, this was quickly changing. The lay Muslim was increasingly invested with a new religio-political efficacy. Rapid increases in literacy rates and the proliferation into these regions of what Benedict Anderson has termed 'print-capitalism'[45] were undoubtedly contributing factors. As we will see, the ideologues of the Islamic revival in the nineteenth and twentieth centuries often came from outside the exclusive circles of religious scholars, having their origins instead in the educated, professional, middle classes.

'Pan-Islam' as a form of anti-colonial discourse had already been proposed in India in the eighteenth century by writers such as Shah Waliullah (1703–62), but did not become a political ideology in that region until later.[46] The first exponent of a full-blown Pan-Islamic political project was Jamal al-Din al-Afghani (1838–97), an Iranian-born intellectual, journalist, activist and travelling-theorist *par excellence* who spent time in Calcutta, Cairo, Istanbul and Paris during his active career. Al-Afghani's major life concern was the presence of foreign powers – and most specifically, Britain – in Muslim countries. He believed that the Muslim peoples would never manage to remove the Europeans unless they were united, and it is this conviction which led him to develop his Pan-Islamic programme. The Islamic world, he asserted, had fallen into decline through lack of unity and a loss of religious consciousness. Al-Afghani's charisma and oratory powers ensured him an influential position wherever he went. He often managed to gain access to the highest echelons of power in the various destinations of his travels, finding favour with Emirs, Shahs, Khedives, and Sultans alike. So controversial were his views, however, that he almost always found himself out of favour (and usually expelled from or detained in the country in question) within months of his arrival. Al-Afghani spent time in Europe as well, editing influential Muslim newspapers and journals in Paris, where he also engaged in debate with leading French intellectuals such as Ernest Renan. The intrigues which governed imperial politics in the late nineteenth century ensured that the Pan-Islamic union of Muslim countries which al-Afghani had envisaged (centred most likely in Istanbul) never came to fruition. His message of unity, the rejuvenation of the umma in its widest sense, did however resound throughout much of the Muslim world, earning him a devoted following and producing several influential disciples along the way.[47]

One such adherent was the Egyptian Muhammad Abduh (1849–1905), a pioneer of Islamic reform in the Arab world who early in his career had been closely associated with al-Afghani. Abduh had received a religious education at home and was later a student at the eminent al-Azhar university, the oldest institution of religious learning in the Muslim world. The pedantic rote system of empty memorisation which he found at al-Azhar severely disillusioned Abduh, and led him to take on educational reform as a dominant theme throughout his life.[48] When al-Afghani arrived in Egypt, Abduh quickly fell in with his circle and the two of them later ended up together in Paris, editing an influential Arabic newspaper. After several years of teaching in Beirut, Abduh returned to Cairo. He then proceeded to hold a number of senior positions both in the state legal system and on the administrative council of al-Azhar. Several years before his death he was promoted to the position of Grand Mufti of Egypt, using the authority of this position to institute both educational and social reforms – in the latter case, expounding comparatively liberal attitudes towards the role and rights of women and stressing the need for education, science and modernisation.

Abduh mourned the passing of Muslim supremacy from the world, and in his writings often invoked the golden age of Islamic military power and Muslim achievements in the fields of science and philosophy. Indeed, part of his message was a claim that the Europeans had managed to gain the upper hand by appropriating and developing Muslim knowledge. He also vociferously sought to refute popular European arguments which asserted that the decline of the Arab world had something to do with Islam.[49] The revival of the umma ideal was also an important element in Abduh's thought. Like many before him and many who came after, Muhammad Abduh looked back to the early community at Medina as a source of inspiration, a model of civic unity. His emphasis on the notion of *shūra* (consultation) is quite telling. Abduh sought to emphasise the need for Muslims to take their political fate into their own hands. Resistance to European domination, according to Abduh, was a duty of all Muslims. A community of believers could never be properly constituted, he wrote, so long as foreign powers prevented the implementation of the shari'a, and so long as Muslims were willing to blindly imitate foreign ways.[50] With its emphasis on grass-roots activism, Abduh's message later became an important inspiration for many Islamic movements in the Arab world – not least of which was the enormously influential Muslim Brotherhood, founded by Hassan al-Banna in 1928. For our own purposes, the salience of the Pan-Islamic reformers of the late nineteenth century, such as al-Afghani and Abduh, lies in their call for Islam to wake to its plight, and for Muslims to engage with and to shape their futures themselves, free from foreign domination. This, then, represented a politicisation of the umma – and a new challenge to colonial authority. According to Reinhard Schulze:

> After 1870, the colonial situation created completely new conditions in most Islamic countries: many Islamic citizens felt culturally separated from 'their' state. First, in certain areas of control such as law or education, there were attempts to reclaim sovereignty or to defend the existing sovereignty. After 1900, an Islamic macrocosm was created in which people tried to uphold their civil identity in the face of the colonial states. Here in the virtual space of Islam, they found it possible to articulate their civil identity even though their influence on real state power was minimal. A characteristic of this macrocosm was the reference to the wholeness of the Islamic community (umma), which Islamic intellectuals wanted to represent politically. In this

they were able to practise the sovereignty which had been denied them in the colonial states.[51]

The notion of Pan-Islam was by its very nature implicitly anti-national. It asked Muslims to place their loyalties beyond the nation-state, and to look to a greater collective, the umma. The political realities of many countries with large Muslim populations was such, however, that tensions inevitably arose between both desires, the national and the religious. Colonial resistance in India, for example, had its strongest base in nationalist sentiments. Those with religious aspirations, however, identified the nation-state with Europe and foreign influence and sought an indigenous source of solidarity instead; this, at least for the Muslims, took the form of the umma. The difficulty for many Islamic sympathisers lay in reconciling religious and national aspirations. Freedom was of course the paramount goal, and these two tendencies represented rival methodologies. Certainly the nationalists could claim that their approach was more likely to succeed, and more likely to be perceived as legitimate on the international stage. Those who advocated the umma, however, sought to emphasise the authenticity of their option and to portray it as an autonomous alternative with no European ideological baggage (i.e. a non-Western form of modernity). Indeed, they claimed, nationalism had been the root of endless suffering and conflict throughout history. The spiritual nature of solidarity in the umma would ensure that it remained free from the concomitant malignancies of nationalism. Underlying these approaches, then, were two very different normative models for the constitution of community, one based on territorial history and the other on religious heritage. One approach asked that the country be imagined as autonomous and Indian. The other, transcending borders, sought autonomy by imagining the Muslims of India into a union with their co-religionists. In this regard it was a schizophrenic time for India's peoples, and for its Muslims in particular.

One prominent figure, who in his long and productive career ranged from nationalist sympathiser to Pan-Islamic activist (and everywhere in between), was Abul A'la Mawdudi (1903–79). Mawdudi's family background had prejudiced him against British rule from a very young age. The family were Muslim notables who had served the court of the Moghul dynasty in its dying years and, following the Great Mutiny, had found their social standing significantly reduced.[52] Deeply steeped in his classical Indian heritage, Mawdudi's father made sure that his children received a traditional primary education, which excluded modern subjects such as English and the sciences. Mawdudi did eventually take up these subjects for several years before his formal education was brought to a halt at the age of sixteen upon the death of his father. He moved to Delhi and took up journalism, writing enthusiastically for a number of pro-nationalist causes. Much of his effort at this time was focused on trying to rally Muslims behind the pro-national Congress Party. After some time he attracted the attention of prominent figures within the Jami'at-i 'Ulama-i Hind (Society of Indian Ulama) who invited the young Mawdudi to edit their official newspaper. It was under their influence that he first became active in Muslim politics, although his interests in this regard were initially oriented towards the Muslim community in India rather than towards Pan-Islamic doctrine. Mawdudi also underwent the prescribed course of religious training which would licence him as an 'alim (religious scholar) – a fact which did not emerge until after his death since he never sought to publicise this status or to make use of it politically.[53]

How would we characterise Mawdudi's approach to political community? During the 1920s his increasingly cordial relations with the Muslim movement brought him closer to the doctrine of Pan-Islam. Twice during his career, in the 1930s and again in the late 1960s, Mawdudi was a vocal advocate of this ideal. He repeatedly appealed for religion to be made the primary source of social solidarity in the Muslim world. In the context of the Cold War, this call was tantamount to an alternative form of non-alignment. Mawdudi sought the establishment of an international union of Muslim states in order to rejuvenate Islam's efficacy in world politics. He pointed to similar organisations such as the British Commonwealth and the Organisation of African Unity. In particular, Mawdudi cited the case of the European Communities. If a region as disparate as Europe could move towards greater union, he argued, then there was no reason why the Muslims should not be able to do so as well.[54] Mawdudi bemoaned the ambivalence and lack of religio-political consciousness in the Muslim world:

> What is regrettable is that all these Muslim countries are following the same doctrine of nationalism that they had imbibed from their Western masters...They are not even fully conscious of the revolutionary rule of Islam, because of which they are linked to each other, which can unite their Muslim populations into one umma, [and] promote goodwill and co-operation among them.[55]

For Mawdudi, the existence of an Islamic state was absolutely necessary for the achievement of social justice. He believed, therefore, that Islamic reform had to come from the top down. He did not see violent revolution as a viable option, seeking instead to bring about Islamisation from within existing state structures.[56] That is not to say, however, that Mawdudi advocated Islamic authoritarianism. Rather, he had his own particular take on *khilāfa* (the caliphate), one which sought to invest this concept with an essentially democratic character. Mawdudi took as his starting point the Qur'anic stipulation that sovereignty belonged to God alone (*al-hukm l'il-allah*), and hence no temporal institution or ruler could ever be anything more than a viceregent of God.[57] Further, Mawdudi argued, because God promises authority to the entire community of believers in the Qur'an, every member of the umma is therefore implicated in the caliphate: 'Every believer is a Caliph of God in his individual capacity. By virtue of this position he is individually responsible to God. The Holy Prophet has said: "Everyone of you is a ruler and everyone is answerable for his subjects." Thus one Caliph is in no way inferior to another'.[58] In Mawdudi's scheme the virtue of shura (consultation) is paramount. This method is to be used first and foremost in the selection of a head of state in order to prevent the establishment of a dictatorship or other autocratic regime.[59] In theory, this principle is also to be extended such that it covers every aspect of governance, rendering state authorities answerable to the people and in effect functioning as a form of 'check' on authoritarianism:

> The position of a man who is selected to conduct the affairs of the state is no more than this: [someone to whom] all Muslims (or, technically speaking, all caliphs of God) delegate their caliphate for administrative purposes. *He is answerable to God on the one hand and on the other to his fellow 'caliphs' who have dele-gated their authority to him.*[60]

Mawdudi's theory amounts to a popularisation of the caliphate, an attempt to remove its elitist connotations and to place it firmly in the hands of the people. Rather than emphasising the political community's subordination to the caliph (or head of state), he instead emphasised the caliph's subordination: first to God, and then to those co-caliphs (i.e. 'the people') who have placed their trust in him. Mawdudi coined the term 'theodemocracy' to describe this model.[61]

Mawdudi's 'party', the Jama'at-i Islami, can to some extent be seen as a successful expression of these principles. With its intervention in Pakistani politics, a new socio-political force was added to the equation. In the years following the parti-tion of India, the nature of the Jama'at was somewhat ambiguous. It was neither a conventional political party *per se*, nor an affiliate of the ulama. It could perhaps best be described as a powerful lobbying group which depended heavily on its grass-roots legitimacy for much of its influence. In this sense it acted as a mediating force between the state, the ulama and the people – an attempt to articulate Islam according to public opinion and to reinvest the umma with social authority. These tendencies in Mawdudi's thought can be seen as a continuation of the aforemen-tioned disenfranchisement of the ulama, the disintegration of their monopoly on religious authority. For although Mawdudi, as an alim, was technically one of them, he made a point of never using this fact to grant himself greater religious authority on the political platform. And though he undoubtedly did grant the ulama a privileged place with regard to the determination of constitutional ques-tions,[62] he also clearly denied them any exclusive jurisdiction over religious matters:

> Nobody can…claim in Islam to enjoy spiritual monopoly, and the '*Mulla*' or '*Alim*' is not a titular head claiming any inherent and exclusive rights of interpreting religious laws and doctrines. On the contrary, just as anybody may become a judge or a lawyer or a doctor by properly qualifying for these professions, similarly whosoever devotes his time and energy to the study of the Qur'an and the *Sunnah* and becomes well-versed in Islamic learning is entitled to speak as an expert in matters pertaining to Islam.[63]

Abul A'la Mawdudi's thought has had an enormous impact on successive genera-tions of Islamist intellectuals, perhaps most notably on the Muslim Brotherhood's Sayyid Qutb (1906–66). Qutb had read much of Mawdudi's work and often referred to him in his own writings. Qutb's *Ma'alim fi al-Tariq* ('Signposts on the Road') was banned by the Egyptian authorities as a subversive work, and based on its contents he was convicted of attempting to overthrow the Egyptian state and hanged in 1966. Qutb's reputation as a 'radical' was further reinforced when his ideas turned up in a rehashed format in the writings of the ideologue whose group, *al-Jihad al-Islami*, assassinated Egyptian President Anwar Sadat in 1981.

It is via figures such as Mawdudi and Qutb, then, that we reach the personalities and discourses of twenty-first century political Islam. It is these thinkers who have taken on the responsibility of theorising Muslim political community into an era of rapid globalisation. Unprecedented media coverage, rumours about a 'clash of civilisations', and repeated calls for them to justify their beliefs in the face of a supposedly universal trend towards liberal democracy are some of the challenges they face. During the colonial era Muslims developed a greater sense of 'globality' (and they continue to do so today), an awareness of the world as a single political space and of their position within its configurations of hegemony. Until this time Islam had been largely introverted in its attitude towards intellectual developments in the non-Muslim world. The rise of the West hence served as an important wake-up call by forcing Muslims to relativise their senses of identity in the context of a wider, global picture in which the West held the upper hand. Although this book will seek to analyse contemporary Muslim political community from a different viewpoint – stressing Islam's *internal* conversations within translocal space – an examination of the Islam/West nexus in modern history and the early years of the umma is vital for gaining some insight into how Muslims are imagining their political communities today, especially as these early periods serve as key reference points for contemporary Muslim political discourse.

We can also see from these brief historical interludes that religion and politics are not irreducible concepts by any means, and therefore characterising their relationship in such dichotomous generalisations (separation or union) really tells us very little about how they are actually experienced as sources of social authority. Religion, by its very nature, often *is* a form of politics. It constructs antagonisms and friend/enemy images structured through discourses about believers and unbelievers, orthodoxy and heterodoxy. At this point I should reiterate that the realm of the political is by no means coterminous with the state; politics can often have nothing whatsoever to do with structures of territorial power. Rather, 'the key to understanding the intricate and intersecting relationships between religion and politics lies…in the *nature of authority*'.[64] Sources of social authority are received and understood in a variety of ways by a given political community, and often this reception will be dependent on where they (community *and* authority) are located within the social discourse of a particular time and place. Social authority is hence never immutable. In fact, it is necessarily always contingent in that it depends on the continued existence of the social environment which produced it in the first place. As social environments are changed, so are structures of authority transformed. In the case of Islam this has manifested itself in the present era in a decline in the efficacy of the religious scholars, and an increased confidence on the part of individual Muslims with regard to (re)interpreting the ethical claims of Islam for themselves. The consistent efficacy of authority, then, has been the exception rather than the rule throughout our histories. Religion and politics, I would thus argue, must be analysed within a scheme which views them as complex, mutually constitutive sources of social authority, rather than simply as either 'unified' or 'separate' from one another. Translocal spaces, as we will see in the following chapters, are particularly interesting in the case of Islam because they often form the sites in which competing Muslim claims to authority are played out.

Conclusion: reading the Muslim translocale

I began this chapter by saying something about what I understand Islam to be at the level of metatheory. I focused on its role as the master signifier for a variety of discourses and suggested that we can most usefully understand political Islam today by focusing on 'Muslims', that is, those subjectivities which understand themselves to believe in and practice something called Islam. I then went on to examine how we might go about understanding the relationship between religion and politics in the context of Islam. I suggested that rather than seeing religion and politics as two separate categories, each with its own area of jurisdiction, we view them instead as forms of social authority. In order to explain the wider political context in which Muslims imagine the umma today I reviewed Bobby Sayyid's theory on Eurocentrism and the emergence of Islamism. I found his account of how non-Western voices are amplified in the wake of a declining Western hegemony convincing, but was less satisfied with his treatment of Islamism as an example of this phenomenon. By failing to differentiate between competing models of Muslim political order, Sayyid misses one of the most important aspects of this new discursive latitude: the fact that Islam can itself now be renegotiated within a translocal 'public sphere'. In order to gain a better understanding of contemporary discourses on political community in Islam I then undertook a survey of how the notion of the umma has been elaborated in two historical contexts which often serve as key points of reference for contemporary Muslim political discourse: the early years of Islam in Medina, a source of emulation and enlightenment for Muslims both today and throughout Islamic history; and the Pan-Islamic responses of Muslim thinkers during the colonial era of the late nineteenth and early twentieth centuries, a period marked by Western hegemony in which the umma was reconstituted as an important form of political community in the wider Muslim world.

Crucially, though, I want to make the point that the politics of 'Islam and the West' is but one side of the story. Another politics, that of Islam and its own 'internal others', is becoming increasingly important in the present translocal climate. Hegemony in its Western guise is not the only obstacle contemporary Islam needs to negotiate; there is also hegemony within. Across the plurality of

Islamist thought *Islam* is still undoubtedly the master signifier, but there is an enormous conceptual diversity as to the proper relationship between this signifier and its signified(s). It is for this reason that I have argued for an emphasis on the 'Muslim' rather than on 'Islam'. Furthermore I want to argue that it is within what I have termed translocal spaces that a great deal of internal Islamist debate takes place. Many of these contestations are found in various sections of the Muslim diaspora, a set of communities constantly overshadowed by the presence of the West. In these contexts the parameters of the umma are in flux: a community longing for the purity and stability of Medina's golden age, but one that also realises – like the Pan-Islamists of the colonial era – that contemporary circumstances are very different.

In the first chapter I provided some examples of the ways in which translocality challenges traditional statist notions of politics and political identity. The present discussion has provided us with a framework for thinking about Islam and I want to go on now to provide a similar set of tools for conceptualising translocality. In the next chapter I will focus on the discursive forms and spaces of politics that emerge in translocality and explain why they are relevant for our exploration of diasporic Muslim communities.

3 Modes of translocality

Travelling theory, hybridity, diaspora

It may well be that writers in my position, exiles or emigrants or expatriates, are haunted by some sense of loss, some urge to reclaim, to look back, even at the risk of being mutated into pillars of salt. But if we do look back, we must also do so in the knowledge-which gives rise to profound uncertainties-that our physical alienation from India almost inevitably means that we will not be capable of reclaiming precisely the thing that was lost; that we will, in short, create fictions, not actual cities or villages, but invisible ones, imaginary homelands, Indias of the mind.

(Salman Rushdie, *Imaginary Homelands*)

I'm not saying there are no locales or homes, that everyone is-or should be-traveling, or cosmopolitan, or deterritorialized. This is not nomadology. Rather, what is at stake is a comparative cultural studies approach to specific histories, tactics, everyday practices of dwelling *and* traveling: traveling-in-dwelling, dwelling-in-traveling.

(James Clifford, 'Traveling Cultures')

On three occasions between 1649 and 1661 the Moroccan traveller, scholar and (undoubtedly) theorist Abu Salim 'Abdullah al-'Ayyashi plied the deserts between North Africa and the Hijaz region of western Arabia. His routes led him through Islam's holiest cities and several of its most renowned places of learning. All his itineraries – citing extended stays in both Cairo and Jerusalem – and a full gamut of impressions from joy to disillusion were faithfully recorded in his two volume *Ma' al-Mawa'id*.[1] In it, Abu Salim never hesitates to mention (and critique) local variations of Islamic practice at the many junctures of his journey, or to detail accounts of his debates with scholars of diverse Islamic religio-juridical traditions. From the somatics of prayer to contesting genealogies of religious authority, each new idiosyncrasy is digested and reflected upon. All the while, of course, Abu Salim's own 'strange' idiom of Islam was carefully entered into the catalogues of his various hosts. The observer becomes the observed, the curator is himself curated.

Or consider the young Ali Shariati, future ideologue of Iran's Islamic Revolution, as a student in the Paris of the early 1960s.[2] Repulsed by the urban hedonism of the French capital yet at the same time captured by the vigour of its intellectual life, Shariati's transformation during these years was considerable. In Paris his Islam becomes eclectic. The Shi'ism of his homeland loses its monopoly over his religious imagination; soon non-Shi'ite and even Western interpretations of Islam begin to find their way into his thought and writing. Religion is now a sociopolitical imperative rather than a source of dogmatism: Shariati's journey becomes Islam's journey.

And so theory travels. That which 'is' in one place elsewhere becomes undone, translated, reinscribed; this is the nature of translocality: a cultural politics of *becoming*. But what does it mean for theory and culture to travel? Now that I have clarified my understanding of how Islam and its various corollary terms function at the level of metatheory, and also given some representative historical examples of how Muslims have imagined political community, I want to move on to look at some of the broad issues raised today by the encounter between Islam and the set of processes we have called translocality. In so far as I will be aiming to identify the key, overarching features of this encounter, the discussion which follows might best be viewed as a backdrop against which the more empirical explorations of the next two chapters will take place. In the first chapter I looked briefly at some of the ways in which an alternative reading of globalisation allows us to recognise the complexity of transnational cultural flows. I argued that far from representing the universalisation of Western culture, translocality actually serves to open up new spaces of discourse in which travelling theory, hybridity and shifting idioms of identity are the most salient characteristics. In the present chapter I want to engage in a more in-depth exploration of several aspects of translocality, explaining briefly how each is relevant in the context of translocal Islam. I will first look generally at the notion of 'travelling theory', a set of ideas which helps us to understand how cultures and ideas are transformed through movement from one social context to another. Notions of travelling theory, I want to suggest, are particularly relevant in regard to those political identities – discussed in Chapter One – which move through and across translocal space. This in turn leads to a discussion and critique of hybridity theory. Various tropes referring to the fusion and intermingling of cultures and tradition are examined here, and I argue that in the context of Muslim translocality hybridity theory is particularly useful for understanding the nature of encounters and dialogue between different interpretations of Islam. The chapter then concludes with some general comments on the nature of translocal/diasporic identity claims. I suggest that the celebration of diaspora and migrancy found in much of the post-colonial literature tends to assume a very particular (and Eurocentric) form of ironic subjectivity, and therefore has difficulty dealing with those identities which predicate themselves on what is perceived as an 'authentic rootedness'. Returning to the notion of culture, I claim that we need to pay careful attention to structures of power/knowledge and differentiation *within* various cultural contexts. The translocal politics of travelling cultures such as Islam are, I suggest, a particularly rich object of inquiry in this regard.

Travelling theories

Translocal spaces, I have argued, represent sites through which a great many cultures travel. Not only do peoples and their 'theories' pass through translocalities, they also travel within these spaces. By this I mean that the cultural complexity of translocal space is such that it often becomes easy for meaning to move, shift or slip. I want to begin by exploring how we can conceptualise such a thing as travelling theory. In other words, what happens to ideas when they become portable? In the first section of this chapter I will discuss travelling cultures and will be seeking to demonstrate the ways in which the movement of theories can often lead to movement *within* those theories.

'Traveling Theory' is the title of an essay by Edward Said that first appeared in his 1984 collection *The World, the Text and the Critic*. Said takes as his point of departure the fact that like peoples and institutions, ideas and theories also *travel*: 'from person to person, from situation to situation, from one period to another'.[3] For him, cultural and intellectual life are dependent on this circulation of ideas. In this sense the movement of theory is often a precondition for intellectual creativity. Said's main concern is with the ways in which theories change when they become translocal. He is keenly aware that ideas have to negotiate borders in much the same way that people do: 'Such movement into a new environment is never unimpeded. It necessarily involves processes of representation and inst-itutionalization different from those at the point of origin. This complicates any account of the transplantation, transference, circulation, and commerce of theo-ries and ideas'.[4]

Said identifies four stages which he believes are common to how most theories travel. The first of these he calls a point of origin ('or what seems like one') where a set of ideas are first elaborated or enter discourse. In the case of travel-ling Islam, the point of origin can be understood in two ways. In one sense it refers to the sociocultural contexts of the countries from which diasporic Muslims originate, but at the same time I also think we need to view the mythical period of early Medina as a form of 'point of origin' in Islam. The seventh century umma draws the Muslim imagination so strongly that nearly all forms of travelling Islam, even after they have been significantly transformed, still refer back to this point of origin. The second component of Said's scheme is the 'distance traversed' – the act of travelling itself – in which a theory or set of ideas moves from the point of origin into a different time and space. The medium through which this occurs can be almost anything, but we might usefully think here of 'vessels' such as migrant communities, exiled intellectuals, transnational publishing houses or electronic media. In the case of translocal Islam, all of these have played a significant role in bearing tradition across great distances. Third, our itinerant theory will necessarily encounter a set of condi-tions which mediates its acceptance, rejection or modification in a new time and place. For travelling Muslims these are usually the European and North American societies in which they settle; but, as we will see, there is also the factor of the 'Muslim other' to take into consideration. In other words, the conditions which Islam as a travelling theory encounters are not only determined by non-Muslim cultures, but also by competing interpretations of Islam. What finally emerges in the fourth stage of Said's process is an idea which has been transformed by its new uses; in short, a new (albeit well-travelled) theory. In our case what emerges is a 'new Islam', often invested with a greater critical capacity and a sense of its own contingency. It is this final stage of theory travelling which seems to most interest Said:

> What happens to it when, in different circumstances and for new reasons, it is used again and, in still more different circumstances, again? What can this tell us about theory itself – its limits, its possibilities, its inherent problems – and what can it suggest to us about the relationship between theory and criticism, on the one hand, and society and culture on the other?[5]

These are all questions which will be examined in the next chapter when we look at the ways in which translocal spaces bring about shifts in the meaning and significance of various Muslim practices.

Some writers have, however, questioned the universal relevance of Said's depiction of travelling theory. James Clifford, for example, wonders whether this four-stage scheme is appropriate for those theories which travel in post-colonial contexts:

> [Said's four] stages read like an all-too-familiar story of immigration and acculturation. Such a linear path cannot do justice to the feedback loops, the ambivalent appropriations and resistances that characterize the travels of theories, and theorists, between places in the 'First' and 'Third' worlds. (I'm thinking about the journey of Gramscian Marxism to India through the work of the Subaltern Studies group, and its return as an altered, newly valuable commodity to places like Durham, North Carolina or Santa Cruz, California in the writings of Ranajit Guha, Partha Chatterjee, Dipesh Chakravorty, etc.)[6]

Despite his apparent concern to redress the Eurocentrism of Said's formulation, Clifford seems to fall into a version of the same trap himself with this. The dialogue is still too one-way, from the West to the Rest and vice versa. It ignores theories and ideas that travel between and within regions of the so-called 'Third World'. The implicit 'us' (First World) and 'them' (Third World) logic here seems to exclude the possibility that 'we' are not necessarily involved in some of the conversations that 'they' have amongst themselves. What is interesting in the case of Islam is the ways in which reformulated interpretations of religion are sometimes enabled through translocality to *travel back* to their points of origin, in other words re-enacting the travelling process in order to bring 'home' revised theories which then go on to travel within the 'Third World'.

In his essay Said traces the development of Lukacsian Marxism from Lukacs himself in the Hungary of 1919, through the elaborations of his disciple Lucien

Goldmann in post-World War II Paris, and on up to Raymond Williams' uses of Goldmann in Cambridge during the 1970s. What emerges from this is a sense of ideas shifting, twisting and *learning* to fit new contexts. Said puts emphasis on the need for a critical capacity on the part of those who 'receive' travelling theories. For him there is no point in simply reiterating time and time again those aspects of a theory which were radical at the point of origin. To do so would be to risk turning a methodological breakthrough into a methodological trap. 'Once an idea gains currency because it is clearly effective and powerful', he notes, 'there is every likelihood that during its peregrinations it will be reduced, codified, and institutionalized'.[7] The environment in which an idea was conceived becomes almost mythological and those who commit themselves to this 'originary' source become intransigent:

> [The] original provenance...dulls the critical consciousness, convincing it that a once insurgent theory is still insurgent, lively, responsive to history. Left to its own specialists and acolytes, so to speak, theory tends to have walls erected around itself, but this does not mean that critics should either ignore theory or look despairingly around for newer varieties.[8]

In other words, there is every likelihood that through extensive travel a theory will lose its radical (i.e. transformative) edge. This does not mean, however, that all is lost. When a theory travels it can also sometimes take on a new critical consciousness – towards both itself and other theories. The intransigence of acolytes can be countered by theorist-reformers willing to take their theories on the road again. These last points are particularly complex in the case of travelling Islam. In this case, the original theory has become fragmented. There are those Muslims who 'soften' their Islam in order to more successfully blend in with the values and norms of their new society, while others adopt extremely hardline political positions in an attempt to differentiate themselves and their religion from its new surroundings. These various political responses to translocality will be explained further in Chapter Four.

According to Said, what matters above all in travelling theory is the continual presence of a critical discourse: 'the...recognition that there is no theory capable of covering, closing off, predicting all the situations in which it might be useful'.[9] Furthermore, he wants to disallow the possibility of privileged, free-floating or 'objective' readers. 'No reading is neutral or innocent', Said argues, 'and every reader is to some extent the product of a theoretical standpoint, however implicit or unconscious such a standpoint may be'.[10] When a theory travels it splits, multiplies and reproduces such that what we eventually end up with is many theories. Within any set of ideas, then, there will be multiple and often competing discourses on the nature of the 'true' (or originary) idea. Part of travelling theory's task is to capture this sense of fragmentation. Muslims in translocal spaces often come into contact with other Muslims who interpret and practise Islam in disparate fashions. There often ensue debates about the nature of 'real' Islam and about who is licensed to speak on Islam's behalf.

Communications and media technologies, as we will see in Chapter Five, also serve to intensify these translocal politics.

Towards the end of 'Traveling Theory' Said also deals with another way in which theory can travel. This is the sense in which the meaning(s) of a given concept can often be seen to cover great distances when charted through the oeuvre of its author(s). As an example of this, Said traces the development of Michel Foucault's ideas on power and resistance. He finds that the early Foucault has very little engagement with the concept of power. By the middle of his career, however, the power/knowledge nexus has become very much the foundation of his thinking. In his later career the possibility of engaging with power disappears once again since Foucault – at least on Said's reading – has become convinced that 'power is everywhere' and any attempt to resist hegemony would only be founded on a false consciousness serving to reproduce pre-existing power structures.

> The disturbing circularity of Foucault's theory of power is a form of theo-retical overtotalization superficially more difficult to resist because, unlike many others, it is formulated, reformulated, and borrowed for use in what seem to be historically documented situations. But note that Foucault's history is ultimately textual, or rather textualised; its mode is one for which Borges would have an affinity. Gramsci, on the other hand, would find it uncongenial. He would certainly appreciate the fineness of Foucault's arche-ologies, but would find it odd that they make not even a nominal allowance for emergent movements, and none for revolutions, counterhegemony, or historical blocks. In human history there is always something beyond the reach of dominating systems, no matter how deeply they saturate society, and this is obviously what makes change possible, limits power in Foucault's sense, and hobbles the theory of that power.[11]

We find similar discourses in travelling Islam surrounding concepts such as *ijtihād* (independent reasoning). Traditional sources of religious authority such as the ulama often attempt to maintain a monopoly on the capacity to engage in this practice or, in some cases, to claim that this kind of thinking is no longer permitted. Many of the new Islamist intellectuals, as we will see, dispute the ulama's totalisation of the discursive field and assert instead that any and all Muslims are vested with the capacity to practise ijtihad. The very fact that they are able to find a discursive space in which to subvert genealogies of power – powerful forms of active critique in their own right – shows that hegemony is never complete. The presence of the theoretical other, which discursive identity always necessarily implies, means however that the discursive conditions for the erasure of theoretical identity are also present. Antagonism, if not immanent, is therefore at least possible. Furthermore, and to reiterate a point that has been made above, the antagonists of any discursive field are not necessarily always to be found outside that field. The imagined boundaries of any such space are teeming with a politics from within; hence debate and negotiation must be seen as vital constitutive elements in the discourse.

One obvious weakness in Said's explication of travelling theory is his hesitation to more fully elaborate the mechanisms through which meanings shift as theory travels. The readers of Said's essay, argues Abdul JanMohamed:

> wait to see what specific modifications in the situation are responsible for this [shift in meaning], what kind of border has in fact been crossed, [and] what are the socio-political differences between the two locations that can bring about such changes. Perhaps because he senses the reader's expectations, Said insists several times that relocation *in itself* precipitates the transformation.[12]

To be fair, it is doubtful whether Said ever intended to provide anything like a comprehensive study of the various technologies – discursive and otherwise – which enable theories to change through travel. Surely his intention was simply to offer a metaphor for reading certain aspects of intellectual life. JanMohamed does however draw our attention to questions which must be asked (and answered!) if anything like a thorough understanding of those theories which travel is ever to be achieved. In this respect, Chapters Four and Five (the one dealing with discursive technologies, the other with electronic technologies) of the present book might be read as an attempt to do just that. In them, we will examine the specific mechanisms – such as intergenerational conflict, minority status, and the intellectual challenges of the West – which prompt meanings to shift in translocal Islam.

While most of what I have written above stresses the senses in which travel transforms theory, it should also be mentioned that there exists another politics of travelling theory, one which concerns itself primarily with the establishment and maintenance of hegemony. This relates to the fact that theories need to be made mobile by their authors if they are to have any pretence to universality. Propagation is imperative. If a theory aspires to the hearts and minds of all (wo)men then it must make itself appear to belong to all (wo)men. Its applicability must be seen to be universal and it must lodge itself in our imaginations as something like a 'natural state of affairs'. In this sense a theory must do its utmost to avoid being associated too closely with what Said would term the 'point of origin', for the wearing of local colours can easily taint cosmopolitan credentials. As James Clifford puts it:

> Conventionally, theory has been associated with big pictures – trans-cultural and trans-historical. Localization undermines a discourse's claim to 'theoretical' status. For example, psychoanalysis loses something of its theoretical aura when it is found to be rooted in bourgeois Vienna of the turn of the century and in a certain male subjectivity for which woman is object and enigma.[13]

This aspect of travelling theory has for obvious reasons been most prevalent in the post-colonial literature. It seeks to prohibit any theoretical hegemony, be it a discourse on colonialism, capitalism or democracy, from articulating and representing itself as somehow 'natural' and/or rootless. It demands that any theory – and especially those wandering out of the West – declare its origins. Any set of ideas must be located in the particular sociocultural context in which it was elaborated, with all structures of power/knowledge clearly displayed. This is as true for liberal democracy and 'Muslim hegemony' (see below) today as it was for the colonialisms and ideologies of yesteryear. The younger generation of diasporic South Asian Muslims, for example, often questions the Islam of its parents, regarding the latter as tainted with the 'local culture' of the subcontinent and therefore not 'true' Islam. This has in many cases prompted a return by the younger generation to another point of origin, Muhammad's Medina, which it regards as a source of 'pure' Islam. In this we see that theories travel not only in space, but also in time.

Travelling theory hence provides us with useful ways of thinking about the politics of translocal space. It does so mainly in two ways. First, travelling theory allows us to conceptualise distanciating processes as a source of cultural politics in which meanings are transplanted and rearticulated from one context to another. Second, insofar as this transition implies a *pluralisation* of theory, we can see that the notion of travelling theory also helps to explain how competing interpretations of a given culture come to exist – and how they seek hegemony by gaining a monopoly of the discursive field. In the next section, I will elaborate a more specific quality of translocal/travelling cultures, namely their tendency towards *hybridity*, the intermingling of disparate discourses and cultures.

Dialogic politics: hybridity and internal difference

The literature is currently replete with references to the fusion and melange of cultures. Multiculturalism, it seems, reigns supreme – if not as an ethos then at the very least as an ontological condition. Creolisation, syncretism, hybridity: all variations on the polyglot self. While it might ostensibly seem that these tropes refer to the same general phenomenon, closer scrutiny reveals that they have somewhat different connotations associated with them. When we examine their situatedness in the literatures we find strong normative components in each. In the case of one rendering, hybridity, we find a veritable political manifesto. This latter rubric is hence particularly interesting. In what follows I want to look at some of the claims that have been made on the behalf of hybridity. I will accept several and reject others. I then want to develop my own idiom of hybridity, one which captures some of the very particular features of cultural melange in travelling Islam.

The term hybridity has its origins, of course, in biology, but the connotations associated with the term have changed quite significantly over the last hundred years. It was originally seen to represent a loss of purity, an authenticity compromised by the insertion of an alien element which tainted the whole. However, the rise of Mendelian genetics in the mid-nineteenth century signalled a shift in this conventional wisdom. Hybridity increasingly came to be seen as a desirable condition, one in which the cross-fertilisation of different gene pools produced stronger, richer offspring.[14] Social attitudes and the social sciences were both slow to pick up on this new rendition of the cross-breeding trope, and it has only been in the present decade that writers have begun to use the term with any regularity.

One notable exception here is Mikhail Bakhtin. His linguistic rendition of hybridity was elaborated as early as the 1930s and became a major influence on later hybridity theorists – particularly, as we will see, those working in a post-colonial mode. Bakhtin's thinking is worth briefly examining, constituting as it does the first important attempt to understand hybridity in relation to language and society. Bakhtin begins with a direct answer to the obvious question: 'What is a hybridization? It is a mixture of two social languages within the limits of a single utterance, an encounter, within the arena of a single utterance, between two different linguistic consciousnesses, separated from one another by an epoch, by social differentiation or by some other factor'.[15] He then goes on to draw a distinction between what he calls the conscious, 'intentional' hybrid and the unconscious or 'organic' hybrid. The former he sees as an artistic device in which an author *deliberately* juxtaposes two languages so that they might both unmask each other, coming together, as he puts it, '[to] consciously fight it out in the territory of the utterance'.[16] The point here is to use the one language to illuminate the other by bringing them (unexpectedly) face to face within a *single space* (e.g. Islam): 'Therefore an intentional…hybrid is a *semantic* hybrid; not semantic and logical in the abstract (as in rhetoric), but rather a *semantics that is concrete and social*'.[17] The 'organic' hybrid, on the other hand, is a far more passive creature. There is no deliberate or strategic placement of language here, no use of 'conscious contrasts and oppositions'. This organic hybrid seems to be more about the accidental collusion of different languages and worldviews within the same utterance. That is not to say, however, that the unintentional hybrid possesses no creative or revelatory properties. On the contrary. '[U]nconscious hybrids', Bakhtin writes, 'have been…profoundly productive historically: they are pregnant with potential for new world views, with new "internal forms" for perceiving the world in words'.[18] For him, this kind of hybridisation is one of the primary motors of historical and linguistic change. Travelling cultures naturally bump into one another. For our own purposes it will be most useful to read the intentional hybrid as a 'political' hybrid in the sense that intentional hybridity involves the manufacture of antagonism by deliberately placing two disparate conceptual languages together within a single discursive space. There are implications here, I will argue later, for the nature of the encounter between the Muslim and his 'internal other' (i.e. also Muslim) in translocality.

For me the most problematic aspect of Bakhtin's theory is the question of the boundary between the two languages (or cultures, theories, worldviews) which encounter each other within the hybrid. It seems tempting, at least initially, to accuse Bakhtin of essentialising the components of his hybrid utterances in the sense that he seems to be suggesting we can identify two languages which are somehow 'separate'. I will be returning to this problem later when I develop an idiom of hybridity linked to my earlier discussion of culture and politics. I want to go on now though to look at some of the ways in which other contemporary theorists have used hybridity theory.

Various notions of hybridity can be found in contemporary literature, each with its own strategic logic. In post-colonial theory, for example, the term has a metaphorical function within a wider political discourse. All accounts, however, speak of hybridity as a form of encounter, a coming together of disparate cultural forms into a new fusion or melange. Some view this process as highly desirable while others are mixed in their assessments; often this depends on the larger normative scheme in which a writer is situated:

> Hybridity evokes narratives of origin and encounter. Whenever the process of identity formation is premised on an exclusive boundary between 'us' and 'them', the hybrid, born out of the transgression of this boundary, figures as a form of danger, loss and degeneration. If, however, the boundary is marked positively – to solicit exchange and inclusion – then the hybrid may yield strength and vitality. Hence the conventional value of the hybrid is always positioned in relation to the value of purity, along axes of inclusion and exclusion. In some circumstances, the 'curse' of hybridity is seen as a mixed blessing.[19]

The idiom of hybridity found in post-colonial and cultural studies tends to view the subject-self as a juncture for multiple cross-currents of identity. In this sense hybridity is a description of *simultaneous difference*. It becomes a metaphor for the post-colonial condition itself, and is celebrated as a means by which to resist the totalising assignations of identity and value which emanate from hegemonic centres. This line of thought is often heavily informed by terminology borrowed from literary criticism such as W.E.B. Dubois' notion of 'double consciousness' or Bakhtin's 'dialogic imagination'.[20] One of the most prominent exponents of post-colonial hybridity is Homi Bhabha. His explication functions well as a summary of the post-colonial approach:

> In my own work I have developed the concept of hybridity to describe the construction of cultural authority within conditions of political antagonism or inequity. Strategies of hybridization reveal an estranging movement in the authoritative, even authoritarian inscriptions of the cultural sign. At the point at which the precept attempts to objectify itself as a generalised knowledge or a normalizing, hegemonic practice, the hybrid strategy or discourse opens up a space of negotiation where power is unequal but its articulation may be equivocal...Hybrid agencies find their voice in a dialectic that does not seek cultural supremacy or sovereignty. They deploy the partial culture from which they emerge to construct visions of community, and versions of historic memory, that give narrative form to the minority positions they occupy; the outside of the inside: the part in the whole.[21]

Bhabha thus seeks to actualise the latent *political* potential of Bakhtin's intentional hybrid, translating it into a manifesto of active post-colonial agency.

Colonial authority depends on the imagined integrity of a single voice in order to subjugate and in this sense hybridity is its greatest threat. If colonial discourse is brought into a hybrid articulation, that is a situation in which the language of colonial authority can be unmasked by the language of an other, then the monologism on which its power is based will be undermined. Hybridity demonstrates to colonial authority that it cannot be what it claims. '[It] intervenes in the exercise of authority not merely to indicate the impossibility of its identity but to represent the unpredictability of its presence'.[22] Authority is hence revealed as a contingent rather than natural force through an encroachment into the homogenous space of authority which requires this contingency to articulate itself.

> Hybridity is the sign of the productivity of colonial power, its shifting forces and fixities; it is the name for the strategic reversal of the process of domination through disavowal (that is, the production of discriminatory identities that secure the 'pure' and original identity of authority)...[C]olonial hybridity is not a *problem* of genealogy or identity between two *different* cultures which can then be resolved as an issue of cultural relativism. Hybridity is a problematic of colonial representation and individuation that reverses the effects of the colonialist disavowal, so that other 'denied' knowledges enter upon the dominant discourse and estrange the basis of its authority its rules of recognition.[23]

In Bhabha's work, hybrid identities are seen to inhabit what he calls a 'third space', an area of discourse which is neither here nor there but rather *interstitial*. Within these spaces hybridity is seen to be an anti-hegemonic force which seeks to force any would-be totalising narrative to come face to face with a challenge to its own supposed purity: the absolute rendered contingent by the positing of a dialogic difference. 'Such assignations of social differences', writes Bhabha, 'where difference is neither One nor the Other but *something else besides, in-between*, find their agency in a form of the "future" where the past is not originary, where the present is not simply transitory'.[24] The third space is hence one in which real 'newness enters the world' and not simply a space in which prior cultures are conjoined:

> For me the importance of hybridity is not to be able to trace two original moments from which the third emerges, rather hybridity to me is the 'third space' which enables other positions to emerge. This third space displaces the histories that constitute it, and sets up new structures of authority, new political initiatives, which are inadequately understood through received wisdom...The process of cultural hybridity gives rise to something different, something new and unrecognisable, a new area of negotiation of meaning and representation.[25]

I would want to suggest that such 'third spaces' are often coterminous (in a queer sort of terminosity which never quite ends) with what I earlier defined as translocal space. Furthermore, on entering such spaces we would quite likely find them to be inhabited primarily by travelling theories. We can see in this the important link between post-colonial hybridity and translocality. My reading of hybridity's post-colonial aspect is, however, somewhat different from Bhabha's. Like him, I recognise the power of the hybrid to disrupt the hegemony of colonial authority by revealing to it its own contingency. In post-colonial theory, the colonial subject is conventionally taken to be equivalent with European or Western hegemony. In my deployment of Bhabha's hybridity, however, I wish to insert Muslim hegemony in place of Western hegemony or colonialism. In other words, I am using hybridity as a way to read difference and disjuncture *within* Islam. By 'Muslim hegemony' I am referring to those sources of social authority in Islam which seek to represent themselves as the privileged readers of tradition or the bearers of 'true' Islam. Their identity can vary from context to context but they will often be either traditional ulama or 'new' Islamist intellectuals of a more extreme tendency – two groups which, ironically, often find themselves at odds with each other. Hybridity emerges as a tool that can be used against them by 'other' Muslims seeking to speak for Islam, or, in other words, seeking to enter the same discursive space. The methodology is again similar to that of post-colonial hybridity, namely to demonstrate to the ulama and the hardline intellectuals that their supposedly 'correct' readings of Islam are nothing more than the product of particular historical contingencies. We will see examples of this process at work in the next chapter.

Another understanding of hybridity which emphasises its ability to give voice to the marginalised but which is not explicitly tied to post-colonial discourse is to be found in the work of Ulf Hannerz, an anthropologist whose work we briefly examined in Chapter One. In place of hybridity, however, he speaks of 'creolisation'. Language is the chief metaphor evoked by Hannerz in explaining this idiom of mongrelisation which is seen to involve the pushing and pulling of hegemonic forces between traditions and the exercise of meaning within specific structures of social organisation under varying spatio-temporal conditions. The defining feature of creolisation for Hannerz is the confluence of widely *disparate* cultures which interact in the context of a centre-periphery relationship. However, he also argues that:

> [t]he cultural processes of creolization are not simply a matter of constant pressure from the center toward the periphery, but a much more creative interplay. As languages have different dimensions such as grammar, phonology, and lexicon, and as creole languages are formed as unique combinations and creations out of the interaction between languages in these various dimensions, so creole cultures come out of multidimensional cultural encounters and can put things together in new ways.[26]

Thus the periphery in creolisation is invested with a new ability to 'talk back' to the core as it increasingly adopts the organisational forms and commodity models of the latter. Hannerz's idiom of hybridity is useful for conceptualising at least one aspect of Muslim translocality, that of language. In the chapters to come I will refer on several occasions to the emergence of something like an 'Islamic English'. This dialect represents a fusion of, for example, American street slang and Islamic terminology. Muslims in translocal spaces will often use the noun *dhikr* (the praising of Allah through ritual recitation) as a verb. One American Muslim, for instance, complains that 'we cannot sit and *dhikr* for like three hours and expect to help the community'.[27] Other American Muslims speak of 'giving *shahadas*', the testimony or creed affirming one's belief in the uniqueness of God and Muhammad's Prophethood. Here is the periphery seeping into the core. While Hannerz's model of hybridisation effectively counters the unidirectional globalisation-as-homogenisation paradigm, it does possess its limitations. His concentration on creolisation processes which occur between 'highly differentiated' cultures and traditions limits the applicability of his approach because as translocality evolves it becomes more and more difficult to determine exactly where the boundaries between 'significantly disparate cultures' lie. Hence Hannerz's creolisation theory does not provide a framework for understanding the processes by which hybridisation occurs *within* a particular tradition when various interpretations of that culture come face to face with each other in the context of translocal space.

Another idiom of hybridity can be found in William Rowe and Vivian Schelling's work on popular culture in Latin America. Here hybridisation is seen as 'the ways in which forms become separated from existing practices and recombine with new forms in new practices'.[28] The distinctive feature of this model is its emphasis on the encounter between 'existing' and 'new' practices: the old meets the innovative, memory meets modernity. A second theme in their approach, and one which is particularly pertinent in the present context, is that of deterritorialisation. This focuses on the changing set of meanings which are mapped on to objects as they move between cultural spaces. 'With the transition', they write, 'symbols become detached from their previous contexts…handicraft objects [become] ornaments in cities instead of being used for eating, cooking and so on'.[29] We see a similar phenomenon in the changing meanings attached to Muslim rituals such as the daily prayer in diaspora. In the context of the 'point of origin' or homeland for example, prayer might have been performed almost mechanically with little soul-searching or introspection. In diaspora, however, the Muslim encounters discourses which stress the importance of Islam as a spiritual and moral force in the context of a wider society (i.e. the West) which is perceived to be lacking in these respects. When the 'theory' of devoutness meets the 'practice' of prayer in diaspora, the meanings assigned to the latter are transformed such that it comes to be seen as a new form of self-awareness and identity.

The final set of ideas regarding hybridity that I want to look at before moving on to my critique of the theory brings us quite firmly into the realm of translocal space. These ideas represent a macro-worldview which seeks to problematise the 'globalisation as homogenisation' thesis and which quite explicitly figures itself as a rewording of globalisation *as* hybridisation. Jan Nederveen Pieterse rejects those versions of the globalisation thesis which claim an increasing synchronisation of world cultures, especially those which reduce the trajectory of cultural flow to the universalisation of Western modes. As he argues:

> [The globalisation-as-homogenisation] approach overlooks the counter-currents – the impact the non-Western have been making on the West. It plays down the ambivalence of the globalising momentum and ignores the role of the local reception of Western culture; for example, the indigenisation of Western elements. *It fails to see the influence non-Western cultures have been exercising on one another*...It overrates the homogeneity of Western culture and overlooks the fact that many of the standards exported by the West and its cultural industries themselves turn out to be of culturally mixed character if we examine their cultural lineages.[30]

In examining the nexus of globalisation and hybridity, Nederveen Pieterse identifies two key forms of this phenomenon: (1) *structural hybridity*, which is seen to involve the emergence of new forms of social organisation in the wake of weakening nation-states (e.g. transmigrant communities); and (2) *cultural hybridity*, characterised by increasingly intensified encounters between cultural forces and systems of meanings in which the boundaries of these practices are readjusted so as to include material from the others: 'the doors of erstwhile imagined communities opening up'.[31]

The first emphasises a new plurality in the available modes of social organisation, all of which are seen to exist and to operate simultaneously depending on which model of community is most relevant to a given sphere of interaction. 'What matters', argues Nederveen Pieterse, 'is that no single mode has a necessary overall priority or monopoly'.[32] Examples of the modes of organisation mentioned in this regard include the transnational, international, macro-regional, national, micro-regional, municipal and local. The institutional frameworks at work here are seen to bridge and criss-cross various functional levels, with footholds in more than just one of these areas – often in several. The cultural aspect of globalised hybridity is seen to involve the blurring of boundaries, cultural cross-over, and – perhaps most importantly – *interculturalism* as opposed to multiculturalism.[33] Nederveen Pieterse makes mention of a feature common to many migrant groups, the appearance of mixed-culture patterns in the second-generation which combine both elements of 'home culture' (often only within the domain of the private, but increasingly in the case of Islam also within a new 'Muslim public sphere' – see below) and 'outdoor culture', that is, the practices of the culture of residence.[34]

These two areas of globalised hybridity are seen by Nederveen Pieterse to be intrinsically inter-related: 'Structural hybridisation, or the emergence of new practices of social cooperation and competition, and cultural hybridisation, or new translocal cultural expressions, are interdependent: new forms of cooperation require and evoke new cultural imaginaries'.[35] This thinking leads him to draw a distinction between two different types of culture which he terms 'territorial' and 'translocal', respectively. The former understands the content and substance of culture to be primarily the product of a distinct territorialised locality while the latter category stresses the roles of diffusion and boundary crossing as determinants of cultural form. What makes discussions of transcultural relations difficult, argues Nederveen Pieterse, is that these two very different notions of culture tend to be used interchangeably without any recognition of the importance not only of distinguishing between them, but also of viewing transcultural relations itself as an encounter between these two understandings of meanings – one static, the other 'travelling'. Like Nederveen Pieterse, my interests lie more with understanding hybridity in relation to those cultures that travel. His understanding of globalisation is also similar to my own, although I have elected to use the term translocality because it focuses on the spatial framing of moving culture.

One way to imagine this spatial framing in the context of translocality is to picture the emergence of 'gaps' in the global architecture, a 'liminal space that cuts across inside/outside, a space that is neither within the state nor an aspect of the international state system but animates both'.[36] Many writers from a variety of disciplinary projects are writing about 'gaps' (my own colloquialism) using an equally diverse range of terminologies and theoretical rubrics. James Rosenau has his 'Frontier';[37] Michael Kearney and Renato Rosaldo write about ethnographies in the 'borderzones';[38] Homi Bhabha finds hybrid identities in the interstices of a 'third space'[39] – and this is then echoed in Smadar Lavie and Ted Swedenburg's proposition of a 'third time-space'.[40] Susanne Hoeber Rudolph analyses non-state identities as a form of 'transnational civil society'[41] and Arjun Appadurai looks to 'translocalities' to find the contours of a post-national geography.[42] Each of these tropes is of course a world unto itself, and it would do them (and their authors) great discursive violence to simply conflate them. There is however a sense in which all of these theorists are writing about very similar phenomena, but with the obvious caveat that each does so within his or her own normative and (usually) disciplinary context.

These new identity spaces are not by any means replacements for the state system as we know it. They do not provide structures for global governance, nor systems for the application of transnational justice. Gaps are not regimes. Rather, they contribute to plurality and hybridity in the world polity.[43] We can also see them as trenches, the bunkers from which marginal identities combat the rigidities of institutionalised hegemony. Fluid creatures leak openly from their dilapidated habitats, mixing and matching as they encounter each other in travel. Bhabha is worth quoting at length here, recognising as he does:

> the dilemma of projecting an international space on the trace of a decentred, fragmented subject. Cultural globality is figured in the *in-between* spaces of double-frames: its historical originality marked by a cognitive obscurity; its decentred 'subject' signified in the nervous temporality of the transitional, or the emergent provisionality of the 'present'...What must be mapped as a new international space of discontinuous historical realities is,

in fact, the problem of signifying the interstitial passages and processes of cultural difference that are inscribed in the 'in-between', in the temporal break-up that weaves the 'global' text...[A] willingness to descend into that alien territory...may reveal that the theoretical recognition of the split-space of enunciation may open the way to conceptualizing an *inter*national culture, based not on the exoticism of multiculturalism or the *diversity* of cultures, but on the inscription and articulation of culture's *hybridity*. To that end we should remember that it is the 'inter' – the cutting edge of translation and negotiation, the *in-between* space – that carries the burden of the meaning of culture. It makes it possible to begin envisaging national, anti-nationalist histories of the 'people'. And by exploring this Third Space, we may elude the politics of polarity and emerge as the others of our selves.[44]

Bhabha's concern with the 'anti-national' allows us to bring in Arjun Appadurai's conception of *translocality* as a space in which the hegemony of nationalist politics is challenged by forms of life which refuse to recognise the limits of the state as the limits of its politics. The *trans*local is the space that bridges *place*, a 'dwelling-in-travelling'. In one sense we are speaking of an empowering distanciation, the ability to defy by not staying put, by not allowing the state to render one 'static'. At the same time, however, translocality is also dislocation and displacement. It is about being neither here nor there, neither one nor the other. 'Living in the border', write Lavie and Swedenburg, 'is frequently to experience the feeling of being trapped in an impossible in-between'.[45] To inhabit the borderzone is thus to threaten the hegemony of an international relations with a very limited capacity to 'see' other forms of politics outside its statist framework.

The various approaches summarised above form a representative selection of hybridity theories. Each, of course, is specially formulated to serve the particular purposes of its author. My aim has been to give some indication of the many diverse notions of cultural hybridity to be found in the literature and to show how they can be related to the core themes of this book. Inevitably, of course, hybridity theory also has its shortcomings. I propose now to offer some possible critiques of the hybridity approach and then to use these as a tool for producing my own idiom of hybridity.

Nederveen Pieterse raises the important question of whether there is anywhere any such thing as an *un*hybridised culture. That is, since any and every cultural tradition can be said to have been formed from divergent origins, does the analytical category 'hybrid culture' actually possess any analytical utility? '[I]f we accept that cultures have been hybrid *all along*, hybridisation is in effect a tautology: contemporary accelerated globalisation means the hybridisation of hybrid cultures'.[46] As the anthropologist Talal Asad puts it:

Let us be clear: to speak of cultural syncretism or cultural hybrids presupposes a conceptual distinction between preexisting ('pure') cultures. Of course, all apparent cultural unities are the outcomes of diverse origins, and it is misleading to think of an identifiable cultural unity as having neutrally traceable boundaries. But the term *hybridity* (like *amalgam* or *composite*) does not seem to me very useful in thinking about this problem.[47]

Lavie and Swedenburg allude to the same issue when they write that 'hybridities which result from the interminglings of disparate cultures necessarily implicate cultures that themselves are already syncretised, always in the process of transformation. All cultures turn out to be, in various ways, hybrid'.[48] According to Jonathan Friedman, any analysis which tries to understand hybridity as a coming together of 'distinct' cultures is therefore engaging in a form of 'confused essentialism'.[49] This problem seems to occur even in post-colonial accounts of hybridity. There seems to be little explicit recognition amongst many post-colonial writers of the vast heterogeneity within their own cultures – or indeed, that their societies are themselves the products of creolised histories and hybrid encounters. The need to hold up a culturally authentic alternative to the 'hegemonic imagination' (be it a form of political community or moral system) leads them to gloss over their own diversity and to invest their culture with misplaced purity. They also seem to ignore the fact that any such alternative must itself have been produced and maintained by an indigenous system of hegemony. In short, the post-colonial position tends to forget the myriad of power relations which obtain within its own society, be they caste systems or religio-juridical hierarchies. It would seem, then, that an obsession with the nature of hegemony between coloniser and colonised blinds many of these writers to the multiple histories, forms, and hence the tensions of actual cultural performance within themselves and the very societies they seek to critique.

It is here that we return to Bakhtin's original formulation of linguistic hybridity. We will recall his assertion that within a hybrid utterance one is able to identify two different, that is, one and an *other*, cultures. If he is able to say that there are two languages in any given hybridity then there must be some (essentialist) criteria by which he differentiates between or draws boundaries around these cultures. Bakhtin, however, is most adamant to deny this:

> [T]here is no formal – compositional and syntactic – boundary between these utterances, styles, languages, belief systems; the division of voices and languages takes place within the limits of a single syntactic whole, often within the limits of a simple sentence. It frequently happens that even one and the same word will belong simultaneously to two languages, two belief systems that intersect in a hybrid construction – and, consequently, the word has two contradictory meanings, two accents.[50]

This statement would seem to be somewhat contradictory. Bakhtin denies the existence of any boundary between the two languages, but in speaking about two 'different' languages, that is, the one and its other, he is necessarily implying the existence of a boundary between them. Although he does not explicitly address this apparent inconsistency at any length, I do believe that there is a reading of Bakhtin which allows us to work around the problem and it hinges on the nature of the dividing boundary. Bakhtin claims that there is no *formal* border between the two languages of a hybrid, that is to say no announcements or signs in the road, nothing to tell us that we are passing from one language to another. This does not mean however that there is not some other kind of boundary here. Somehow we still know how to recognise the internal differentiation within an utterance that signals the presence of hybridity. This is possible, I want to argue, only by virtue of our own hybridity. I mean by this that we must already be familiar with the two languages of the hybrid utterance – and hence somehow hybrid ourselves – in order to even recognise them as two languages. This does not necessarily imply a given, formal boundary between the languages, but rather a cultural situatedness which permits us to assign double-meanings. Our cultural vocabularies must therefore be broad enough to identify the interplay between 'different' signifying codes within a single discursive space. The boundary between the two languages is therefore culturally contingent, for without prior cultural competence the hybrid cannot emerge. I hence want to relate hybridity to what I said earlier about culture and politics. In the 'third space' of hybridity, where multifarious cultural forms come into contact with one another, politics is bound to occur; a set of hegemonic relations thus emerges *within* each specific instance of hybridity. The intermingling of symbols and practices is not the end of the story by any means, but rather should pose another set of questions with regard to the nature, structure and hierarchy of power relations within a given hybridity. Nederveen Pieterse seems to be one of the few hybridity theorists to explicitly recognise this:

> Relations of power and hegemony are inscribed and reproduced *within* hybridity, for wherever we look closely enough we find the traces of asymmetry in culture, place, descent. Hence hybridity raises the question of the *terms* of mixture, the conditions of mixing and mélange. At the same time it is important to note the ways in which hegemony is not merely reproduced but *refigured* in the process of hybridisation.[51]

Again, for all its concern with relations of power, the post-colonial idiom seems to lose all interest in hegemony at the very moment of hybridity. Do the cultures which meet in this space stand on an equal footing? Are power relations reproduced as they obtain 'outside' the hybrid space? Is hegemony inverted? What are the determinants of power asymmetry within creolisation? These are the questions which any theory of hybridised politics must seek to answer.

The criticisms rehearsed above, I believe, seriously discredit the utility of the concept of hybridity when deployed in the context of what is often called 'cross-cultural' analysis. Because all cultures are already hybridised to one extent or another it becomes meaningless to refer to this ongoing process as anything new or distinctive. And while translocality may indeed serve to intensify the encounters which lead to hybridisation, is there anything further to say once this point has been made? If we want to think of hybridity as something that involves the intermingling of discrete, bounded, originally 'pure' cultural entities then the answer is a most resounding no. I believe, however, that the limitations we have uncovered actually serve to show us a route to somewhere that hybridity may be of some use, namely the study of encounters and exchanges *within* a particular cultural space as they are experienced in translocality. I have already alluded to this in my explanation above of how I want to read Bhabha's post-colonial hybridity as a means of conceptualising difference and disjuncture within Islam. This approach allows us to bypass the trap in which all (essentialised) cultural systems are hybrid. This is achieved by concentrating not on syncretisms between supposedly distinct (and somehow 'pure') traditions, but rather on the convergence of differing interpretations within a single discursive space (e.g. Islam). The concomitant of such an approach would be a shift in the focus of our analysis such that we look more at the nature and distribution of authority and hegemony within the hybridised scheme itself. In the case of Muslim transnationalism, as we will see, a politics of authenticity and authority becomes a key motif when the canon of Islam is increasingly forced to account for and reconcile itself with any number of competing self-interpretations within translocal spaces.

So what does the politics of hybridity within travelling cultures look like? Having posited a politics of cultural anti-essentialism, outlined the qualities of travelling theory and then advanced a particular interpretation of hybridity, I want in the final section of this chapter to say something about how these concepts can be best contextualised in the translocal communities that are the objects of this inquiry. I will be arguing that in their conventional critical guise, the metaphors of migrancy, diaspora, rootlessness and hybridity are easily over-celebrated. The freedom they imply in one particular reading can and often is perceived as a loss elsewhere. I also want to suggest that in certain cultural contexts the notion of hybridity is itself politically charged. In translocalities marked by a prominent dialogue and politics between 'host' and 'diasporic' cultures, hybridity is often a complicating factor because subjectivities are forced to converse not only with Others outside their culture but also with the Others within.

Diasporic conversations

A limbo of national or cultural identity – a defining characteristic of the translocality mapped in Chapter One – is becoming increasingly common in a global society which possesses the infrastructure to import, export, shift, modify and exchange peoples and their bodies of knowledge on an unprecedented scale. Edward Said makes an eloquent allusion to this condition:

I think culture has to be seen as not only excluding but also *exported*; there is this tradition which you are required to understand and learn and so on, but you cannot really be *of* it…and then of course the whole problematic of *exile and immigration* enters into it, the people who simply don't belong in any culture; that is the great modern or, if you like, postmodern fact, the standing outside of cultures.[52]

Faced with this situation, can the only answer be an appeal for the imagination of new forms of political space which will appreciate community's discontents? Or, in so far as this condition can only be represented as a community of *non-community*, would any new form of polity (even at its most tolerant) not necessarily somehow deprive society's 'in-betweens' of a condition that is simultaneously treasured and maligned? Historically it would seem that the answer has been to syncretise, that is, to develop from fresh (or to borrow from outside) models of community which can be grafted onto a *prior* body of cultural material so as to preserve its 'authenticity'. At face value this might seem like just another rendition of hybridity, yet there is a crucial distinction:

Syncretism and hybridity are similar in some respects but not the same by any means. Syncretism involves impregnating one culture with the contents of another in order to create a third, stable culture while hybridity involves an ambivalence about both of the original cultures, thereby leading to the creation of a slipzone of indeterminacy and shifting positionalities. This is a state of unbelonging, in effect a form of freedom, nomadism, homelessness, or vagrancy – even opportunism – because it settles on nothing but difference itself.[53]

Much is often made of the postmodern qualities of displacement and alienation: the subject is split, de-centred, in flux. Identities are fractured, reality is elsewhere. '*One [does] not have to belong*, one [can] simply float, effortlessly, through a supermarket of packaged and commodified cultures, ready to be consumed'.[54] It is as if, in the wake of global capitalism and the technologies of travel and communication, the whole notion of belonging has become *passé*, an antiquated relic of a modernity which sought to classify, name and place peoples whenever and wherever possible. Aijaz Ahmad renders this condition instead as an *excess of belonging*: 'not only does the writer have all cultures available to him or her as resource, for consumption, but he or she actually belongs in all of them, by virtue of *belonging properly in none*'.[55]

There are, I believe, two key problems with the ways in which some post-colonial and metropolitan discourses celebrate the empowering qualities of migrancy. The first relates to the fact that post-colonial discourses tend to be marked by an abstracted literariness which often refuses to engage with the concrete, material contexts in which subjects – and even neo-hegemonic subjects – find themselves today. Pheng Cheah, for example, refers to the post-colonial idiom of hybridity as 'a theory of resistance that reduces the complex giveness

of material reality to its symbolic dimensions and underplays the material institution of neocolonial oppression at a global-systemic level'.[56] The second
problem, which is related to the metropolitan celebration of the liberating
qualities of migrancy, travel and hybridity, might be seen as more epistemological in nature. It relates to the disparity between those travelling subjectivities
which posit what they 'know' as the core of their identities and those which
question even the possibility of 'knowing'. Many 'postmodern' theorists of travel
tend to write in sympathy with the latter; that is, with a certain cosmopolitan
irony, an ambivalence towards identity, belief and belonging. Are all travelling
theories required to take up this same ironic stance, though? In order to travel a
theory certainly needs to give up on its rootedness to some degree; but must it
also give up on *itself*? As Homi Bhabha notes, there are those for whom hybridity
is tantamount to heresy:

> The fundamentalist charge [against Salman Rushdie's *The Satanic Verses*] has
> not focused on the misinterpretation of the Koran, as much as on the
> offence of the 'misnaming' of Islam: Mohamed referred to as Mahound, the
> prostitutes named after the wives of the Prophet. It is the *formal* complaint of
> the fundamentalists that the transposition of these sacred names into
> profane spaces   brothels of magical realist novels – is not simply sacrile-
> gious, but destructive of the very cement of community. To *violate the system of
> naming* is to make contingent and indeterminate…the shared standpoint of
> the community, its traditions of belief and enquiry.[57]

There exist vast numbers of migrant subjectivities that find it difficult to simply
relativise their identities. In many cases the politics is just too strong. Ironically,
Salman Rushdie alludes to this himself when he writes that:

> The effect of mass migrations has been the creation of radically new types
> of human being: people who route themselves in ideas rather than places, in
> memories as much as in material things; *people who define themselves – because
> they are so defined by others – by their otherness*; people in whose deepest selves
> strange fusions occur, unprecedented unions between what they were and
> where they find themselves.[58]

Giving up on belonging is not so easy when constantly confronted with an
antagonism which labels one as 'other', thus continually forcing the politicisation of identity. In the absence of this antagonism hybridity is more easily
celebrated. Once the political enters the picture, however, forcing one to
define oneself (or defining one on one's behalf), it becomes much more difficult to retreat behind a negative, ironic sense of identity, or 'violate the system
of naming'. What is engendered is the need to speak oneself in terms which
transcend the (trans)locality of migrant dwelling, to posit something that is
not *of* (and hence cannot be domesticated by) the nation-state. As James
Clifford puts it:

Positive articulations of diaspora identity reach outside the normative territory and temporality (myth/history) of the nation-state…Resistance to
assimilation can take the form of reclaiming another nation that has been
lost, elsewhere in space and time, but that is powerful as a political formation here and now.[59]

I will be arguing in the next chapter that in many respects the umma concept in
Islam functions as a similar form of nostalgia. There is a need to find a centre
beyond the metropolis – one which is closed to the 'other', a space he is unable
to enter. It must not, however, be a 'place' because:

If this centre becomes associated with an actual 'national' territory –
rather than with a reinvented 'tradition', a 'book', a portable eschatology –
it may devalue what I called the lateral axes of diaspora…The empowering paradox of diaspora is that dwelling *here* assumes a solidarity and
connection *there*. But *there* is not necessarily a single place or an exclusivist
nation.[60]

For many Muslims the Qur'an functions as that portable eschatology, an identity
bearer in the form of a book which passes easily across boundaries. Diasporic
hybridity thus possesses a language which can transcend the nation-state – but in
a sense this is the easy part. There are always multiple hybrid polities within
territorial spaces, ones which cannot always slip so easily through institutional
gaps. This brings us back to the point just made above about hybridity and
otherness. Politics, as a mode of antagonism based on ethical claims and one
which seeks to separate insiders from outsiders, does not take too kindly to the
ambiguities of hybridity. The political requires hybrid subjects to enunciate
themselves from a position of identity, that is, to *align* their hybridity.
Radhakrishnan alludes to this when he speaks about the semantic insufficiency
of hybridity in the Rushdie case:

In other words, Rushdie was being asked: In what identitarian mode or 'as
who' are you a hybrid? Obviously, the self-styling of hybridity from its own
point of view left too much unexplained. Was Rushdie hybrid as a Muslim,
or as an Indian, or as a Westerner, or as a Londoner, or as a metropolitan
intellectual-artiste? And even if one were to hyphenate all of these identities,
one still has to face the question of unequal mediation. Among the many
selves that constitute one's identity, there exists a relationship of unevenness
and asymmetry, since each of these selves stems from a history that is tran-
scendent of individual intentionality.[61]

It is thus only when a hybrid is called upon to represent itself that we gain
some insight into the negotiations of unevenness and asymmetry that constitute
politics *within* hybridity. This is why when we witness the articulation of any
political identity we need to ask questions about the politics through which this

identity has been able to emerge. Political identity must be seen as a product of the constitutive relationships with both internal *and* external 'others'. It is therefore an assertion of belonging to one group and not to an*other*, but one which can be made only after an internal negotiation about what it *means* to belong. Our task, then, is not one of dissolving all positive identities in a grand celebration of postmodern unboundedness. But neither is it one of naming, *identifying* or 'fitting-into-little-boxes'. Belonging and identity are both clearly still with us and will continue to be so for the foreseeable future. We should therefore be devoting ourselves to the task of understanding the contexts in which particular political identities come into being and the circumstances which mediate boundaries of inclusion/exclusion. We should not be asking an identity *what* it is, but rather *why* and *how* it is. I have argued that certain readings of tropes such as travelling theory and hybridity can help us to do this – especially where we are dealing with instances of translocal space. As I have argued in Chapter Two, and will emphasise again in later chapters, a Muslim's sense of 'belonging' to Islam often functions as a crucial form of anti-hegemonic discourse and therefore cannot always simply be relativised through irony. This is particularly true of those seeking to politicise their Muslim identities in diaspora. Ziauddin Sardar, writing from a Muslim standpoint, alludes to Islam's scepticism towards ironic postmodernism in a recent book.[62]

There is also a third problem from which most discourses on hybridity and diaspora suffer: a tendency towards Eurocentrism. There is often disproportionate attention given to translocal traffic from the 'periphery' to the 'centre', the Rest to the West. It is as if there are not significant flows of people moving around within the Rest. Unsurprisingly, it is often these people whose experiences of migrancy are the most traumatic. The pitiful condition of migrant workers from South Asia working in the Arab Gulf states – regarded as little more than cheap labour and possessing no meaningful political representation – is a case in point. 'Their dehumanised condition', argues Revathi Krishnaswamy, 'casts an inescapable shadow upon the exuberance that characterises metropolitan perceptions of migrancy. Clearly the grim realities of migrant labour inflect the notion of migrancy in ways that make it difficult to link consistently freedom and liberation with movement and displacement'.[63] Living as a Muslim in diaspora is therefore not always about celebrating a new vitality in religion. For the first generation of migrants, especially, constitutive recognition of Islam from the non-Muslim majority societies in which they settled was not easy to obtain. For them being a Muslim was a struggle rather than a form of liberation. While the younger generation has generally displayed a greater willingness to reassess and renew its Islam, this process has often brought about conflict both with the older generation (whose Islam is viewed as 'conservative' and/or 'culturally tainted') and with wider societies in which Islam is still seen as very much 'the other'. Translocal Islam is hence a form of 'third space' or interstitial political identity in which the political community of the host society is not accepted or embraced (in terms of configuring one's political identity) but, crucially, neither is that of the cultural 'point of origin', nor its Islam. We might do well here to recall Lavie and Swedenburg's characterisation of diasporic identity as a borderzone or 'impossible in-between'.

Conclusion: the cultural politics of translocal identity

Theory has done its fair share of travelling in this chapter. I first addressed the question of how meanings change through movement from one social context to another. Here I examined a set of ideas surrounding the notion of 'travelling theory'. This trope showed itself to be useful in understanding the transformation of ideas and cultures in translocal spaces, and also in helping to explain the existence of competing interpretations and idioms *within* a culture. The potentialities and limitations of hybridity theory were then assessed. It emerged that a focus on hybridity is perhaps most meaningful when discussing encounters between variations of an ostensibly homogenous cultural system under translocal conditions. Within the margins of pure locality – which, as we have seen, is becoming a virtually non-existent state of affairs – hybridity can endure unproblematised. Indeed, in such circumstances hybridity is usually not even recognised as such by its practitioners because, in the absence of any competing claims to the tradition, it appears to be a wholly natural condition. Cultural hybridity only really becomes an issue when translocality enters the picture. An encounter with the translocal can often throw up alternative interpretations of cultural authority and authenticity which suddenly bring the hybridity of 'local traditions' into sharp relief as they are brought face to face with their own contingency. Travel, migrancy and hybridity, I went on to argue, should not be celebrated as part of a postmodern carnival, or as an ontological fad. Diaspora is not our new 'natural state'. Mike Featherstone puts it well:

> To be aware of the construction of local communities, societies and nation-states as sedentary homelands does not mean that we should switch to the opposite assumption that the normal condition of beings is, or should be, one in which everyone is a 'nomad' or a 'traveller'...The challenge to theorizing today is how to construct theories of communal living in localities which do not merely represent sedentariness as the norm, but seek to consider its various modalities, including displacements into images of imaginary homes/homelands. Such theories also need to take into account the ways in which those inhabitants who engage in various modes of travel manage to construct and live out their various affiliations and identities.[64]

The key point which arises from this – and one which will figure heavily in my later treatment of Muslim political community – is the fact that within any given culture or community we find various and often competing conceptions of what that identity is and what it means. The politics of identity is therefore not based only on the presence of an external other against which communities and cultures may define themselves, but also on the process of negotiation and debate taking place *within* a given community. In this regard we might want to speak about the presence of an 'internal other'. We should also note that it becomes all the more difficult here to speak of any such thing as a 'given' culture or community since culture is actually the product of a dialogue involving both internal and external others. Within what I have termed *translocal space* this dialogue is all the more complex. The sheer multiplicity of subject positions and their concomitant cultural politics ensures that the production and representation of identity in these spaces will be intricate. This is especially the case when we are dealing with a cultural form such as Islam, whose global sociocultural jurisdiction is extremely wide. For example, in the migratory or global city, Islam is forced to contend not only with a vast array of non-Islamic others but also with an enormous diversity of Muslim opinion as to the nature and meaning of Islam. In such spaces Muslims will encounter and be forced to converse with interpretations of their religion which they have either been taught to regard as heretical, or which they perhaps did not even know existed.

In this connection it should be noted that what primarily interests me in the case of Islam, and what consequently will constitute my focus in the following chapters, are the ways in which translocal encounters modify how 'authoritative' and 'authentic' *meanings* are found in transnational religion – that is, the ways in which a system of symbols and laws is made relevant or acculturated to groups of people in particular places and times. Translocal spaces and the travelling theories and hybridities which inhabit them, I have argued, are the forums in which complex negotiations of Muslim identity take place today. In these spaces difficult questions about the viability of various Islamic political discourses become increasingly prominent, traditional sources of authority and authenticity are fragmented and Islam, as a travelling theory, comes face to face with its own otherness. Questions are being asked about who speaks for Islam today, and the classical sources of 'Islamic' knowledge, along with their traditional agents, are facing new challenges from Muslims increasingly confident about taking religion into their own hands. In subsequent chapters I will delve into the 'real world' of contemporary Muslim life in order to witness some of these changes. I outline the key features of Muslim diasporic politics and seek to understand the interplay between notions of authenticity and authority as they move between translocalities. In other words, I ask questions about *how Islam travels*. In what senses can we speak today of the changing boundaries of Muslim political community, and how are Muslims in translocal spaces reimagining their umma? By focusing on these questions I hope to provide a set of representative images which might give some indication as to how globalisation is lived in specific albeit sometimes heavily distanciated sociopolitical settings. In the chapters to follow we will see that the idioms of political community developed in Medina and during the colonial era both still possess significant discursive purchase in the translocal Muslim political imaginary today. What does 'Islam' mean to Muslims in the face of continuing Western hegemony? How do the politics of authority and authenticity figure in Islam's translocal spaces? What kind of umma do Muslims imagine today, fourteen centuries after Medina?

4   Living Islam: politics and community in the Muslim diaspora

Can one be a foreigner and be happy? The foreigner calls forth a new idea of happiness...Posited, present, sometimes certain, that happiness knows nevertheless that it is passing by, like fire that shines only because it consumes. The strange happiness of the foreigner consists in maintaining that fleeting eternity or that perpetual transience.

(Julia Kristeva, *Strangers to Ourselves*)

This stronger difference, this sense of being a 'people' with historical roots and destinies outside the time/space of the host nation, is not separatist. (Rather, separatist desires are just one of its moments.) Whatever their eschatological longings, diaspora communities are 'not-here to stay.' Diaspora cultures thus mediate, in a lived tension, the experiences of separation and entanglement, of living here and remembering/desiring another place.

(James Clifford, *Routes*)

Now that we have an understanding of what is meant both by translocality and by Islam, we can go on to explore *translocal Islam*. The notion of *diaspora* and more specifically of a 'Muslim diaspora' will be a recurrent trope throughout the discussions to follow. This term has been making increasingly frequent appearances in various literatures of late, but there is little consensus as to its exact connotations.[1] Despite this definitional plurality, diaspora does seem to possess something like a core dynamic, one that is perhaps best summarised by looking at the idea embodied by its Greek root: 'a dispersal or scattering of seeds'. The notion of travel is hence intrinsic to diaspora. It is about people moving from one place to another – but remembering where they came from, perhaps even desiring to return. Diaspora is also about how that place travels with them, and how it changes in travel. As Eickelman and Piscatori write: 'What seems clear is that travel and home – motion and place – constitute one process, and that in travelling beyond one's local time and space, one enters a mythical realm where home, the "fixed point" of departure and return, is re-imagined and further travel inspired'.[2] 'Travelling theory', as examined in the previous chapter, is hence central to any understanding of diasporic identity.

In the various cases which we will encounter throughout this chapter, the notion of 'travel' fulfils several functions. Often it will refer quite directly to a particular Muslim people leaving a specific national context, entering a new one and coming to terms with that experience – watching (and making) their Islam change with them. Sometimes it will refer to something more akin to a state of mind, a space in which old ways of knowing are relativised, questions asked and new forms of knowledge generated. In this sense travel is about how Islam flows through translocalities and what happens when it meets challenging 'non-Islamic' ideas as well as unfamiliar versions of itself. There is also a third form of travel at work here, one which runs through many contemporary Muslim discourses. For the most part this third sense is just another rendering of the standard diasporic idiom, a story of absence and desire, of home and away. This 'home', however, is not a place in the spatial sense of the nation-state, but rather an imagined nexus of past and future, something that once was and which could be again. We are speaking here of how ideas also travel through *time*. In this regard, James Clifford speaks of 'articulations of diaspora identity [which] reach outside the normative territory and temporality (myth/history) of the nation-state...[taking] the form of reclaiming another nation that has been lost, elsewhere in space and time, but that is powerful as a political formation here and now'.[3] For many Muslims there is a diasporic yearning beyond national geography: the umma of Medina in the first half of the seventh century. They remember Islam's very first journey, the hijra (see Chapter Two), the migration from ignorance (jahiliya) to unity in God (tawhid). Fatima Mernissi suggests that Muslims today suffer from a form of *mal du présent* experienced 'as a desire for death, a desire to be elsewhere, to be absent, and to flee to the past as a way of being absent. A suicidal absence'.[4] It is more than just a desire to return to the past, however, for there is also an aspiration here to remake Medina, a hope that this past might be achieved in the future. It is in this sense that Muslims see the umma as an object of diasporic desire. Although their Islam may have stopped to rest at many places along the way – such as the Indian town of Deoband where in 1867 a religious school (*madrasa*) to which many of today's Asian migrants in the UK adhere was founded, or Cairo, 1928 where Hassan al-Banna was forming the now transnational Muslim Brotherhood (*al-Ikhwan Muslimin*) – there is still a sense in which all Muslims today are part of a diaspora whose 'home' is the umma of the Prophet's Medina. It is here that we find a potent reminder of the fact that theories travel not only across space but also across time.

In this chapter I want to explore some of the more tangible aspects of the contemporary Muslim diaspora. What happens to Islam, I will be asking, when it travels, migrates or becomes otherwise 'transplanted'?[5] How does this travelling affect ideas about politics in Islam and how does it cause Muslims to rethink their theories of political community as I defined it in Chapter One. In this sense I am viewing the condition of diaspora as one in which profound changes can occur, and where new ideas are formed. Vertovec and Peach note that '[o]ne mode of modifying meanings occurs through a particular kind of self-consciousness which the condition of "borderlands"...or minority status stimulates'.[6] I am particularly interested in how the latter condition – that of minority status – affects Muslim thinking in diaspora. In some cases, as we will see, this predicament has led Muslims to re-read, re-interpret and re-assert many of the core textual sources of Islam (such as the Qur'an, *ḥadīth* and *uṣūl al-fiqh*) in new contexts and in light of unfamiliar situations, often to quite dramatic effect. One example of this which I will explore below is the way in which new interpretations of the classic texts are used to encourage and legitimise a more prominent position for women in the public sphere. My point, then, is to demonstrate that when Islam travels there are engendered not only conversations with the societies into which it enters, but also important dialogues within Islam itself – in other words, engagement with the Muslim 'other'. This constitutes a politics of cultural negotiation in which different conceptions of Islam are mediated and new critical capacities emerge. Although the majority of the case study material on which I draw pertains to Muslims living in the West, I do not wish to imply that it is only through contact with the West that Muslims come to practice self-critique. As we will see below (and more comprehensively in Chapter Six) Islam already possesses a rich conceptual language for engaging in critical modes of theorising in the sense of asking questions about the hegemony of particular Muslim narratives and the political implications of particular interpretations of Islam. And although the West – as we shall see – does at times play an important role in encouraging such critical thinking in Islam, I wish to concentrate primarily on the ways in which *translocality*, as a space in which encounters with myriad peoples, ideas and theories takes place, modifies Muslim political thought.

A number of writers have undertaken studies of specific Muslim communities in diaspora, or of Islam in particular cultural contexts.[7] There has not yet, however, been any attempt to produce a general study of travelling Islam or to fit these Muslim communities into a wider translocal or global framework.[8] This might be seen as the task of the present book. Rather than offering a comprehensive study of a single Muslim diaspora, I wish to draw on examples from many such communities in order to produce a more general picture of how Islamic thought changes in translocal spaces. My methodology involves re-reading the secondary literature into the translocal context and then supplementing it with a series of my own interviews with diasporic Muslims. It might do well at this point to briefly clarify what it is I mean when I speak of a 'diasporic Muslim'. This can best be accomplished by breaking the designation down into its constituent elements. By 'diasporic' I am referring simply to those Muslims whose families have moved between sociocultural contexts separated by considerable distance during the past two or three generations *or* those Muslims who have spent significant periods of time outside their countries of origin, be it for reasons of education, labour or political exile. Both of these rubrics can be related to the global transformations which I identified as the defining features of translocality in Chapter One. The notion of 'Muslim' is, however, somewhat more difficult. For example, although there are approximately fifteen million Muslims currently living in Western Europe, many of them are only 'nominally' Muslim, belonging to a category which some writers call the 'culturalist' Muslim.

This term refers to those people whose ethno-historical roots qualify them as Muslims, but who do not regularly practice their religion. These are people, then, whose sense of identity is not usually strongly informed by Islam. Felice Dassetto has recently estimated that up to 60 per cent of Europe's Muslims fall into this category.[9] Following our discussion in the previous chapters, though, I am well aware of the dangers involved in trying to label or fix these identities. Because it often changes from context to context, political identity is never an immutable category; identity always needs to be situated and therefore also understood as a product of particular sociopolitical circumstances. Viewing identity in this way helps us to understand how in Bradford, at the height of the Rushdie Affair in 1989, thousands of people who might otherwise have been regarded merely as 'culturalist' Muslims could take to the streets in protest against what they perceived as a grave insult to Islam. It is hence only by placing forms of behaviour within specific *political* contexts – i.e. in relation to the negotiation of normative boundaries (see Chapter One) – that we can understand the politicisation of Islam. In order to simplify matters somewhat I will be concentrating here not on people of Muslim 'background', but rather primarily on individuals whose self-descriptions and identities *do* involve Islam (however defined) as a key (and often primary) component. These then are people who conscientiously try to live their lives as Muslims, seeking whenever possible to make their religion relevant to daily experience.

The chapter will proceed as follows. After some brief comments on religion and travel in the Muslim context (with a few historical examples) I will make some general observations on the condition of contemporary Muslim diasporas, paying particular attention to issues related to minority status. I will also look at how their identification with 'Islam' can prompt ambivalent or even openly hostile receptions in certain societal contexts while at the same time rendering Muslims and their needs almost invisible to wider society. I then turn to a number of broad themes and debates in order to illustrate how Islam and Muslims change through travel. The various aspects of translocality outlined in the previous chapter – travelling theory, hybridity and diasporic 'third space' – should all be kept in mind as we progress through these various themes. The areas I will be looking at are encounters and debates with the Muslim 'other' (a rich source of hybrid discourse – see Chapter Three), the critical renewal of Muslim thinking on politics, community and gender, and, finally, the translocal aspects of diasporic Islam. The chapter concludes by briefly explicating some of the broader themes related to travelling Islam and Muslim diasporas in the wider context of translocality and globalisation.

Islam, religion and travel

The notion of travel is central to many religions. It may take the form of pilgrimage (to shrines, saints, temples and cities), or perhaps a spiritual journey, but the general idea here is the same: movement from one place to another becomes vested with meaning. Quite often the significance of travel relates to some form of transformation such as a shift from ignorance to enlightenment, or from profane to sacred space. The underlying theme is again similar, that movement induces change or produces some form of difference. But there is more than only travel *in* religion, for religions travel themselves. They move and settle, then become displaced and migrate again, a process repeated across space and through time. Inevitably, religions change. As Stuart Hall puts it, 'I view this as a constant process of breaks, interruptions and reorganizations, in which the religious formation is reordered, rearranged, dislocated and repositioned, so as to provide new religious languages and practices within which to articulate new historical realities'.[10] As people migrate and disperse, their religions travel with them. 'These obviously constitute physical movement[s] from one place to another', write Eickelman and Piscatori, 'but owing to the power of the religious imagination they involve spiritual or temporal movement as well'.[11] Religions often enter new and unfamiliar contexts where they undergo subtle changes – or even, depending on their reception, quite dramatic ones. Much, however, stays the same. Religious symbols and languages may become invested with new meanings, but they still function to provide a framework of familiarity and a sense of identity. Indeed, some of the more difficult experiences – as we shall see below – come about precisely when a religion does not appear to be making the changes required of it by a new sociocultural setting.

Islam possesses its own rich vocabulary of travel. In many ways the hijra, the emigration of the Prophet and his Companions from Mecca to Medina in 622 is Islam's most enduring symbol. There is also the pilgrimage to Mecca, the *ḥajj*, which every Muslim is obliged to perform at least once during his or her lifetime. Other relevant tropes include *riḥla* (travel for education), *isrā'* (the Prophet's nocturnal journey to Jerusalem), and *ziyāra* (the visitation of saintly shrines and graves). Many of these terms have enormous metaphoric purchase beyond the actual physical act of movement.[12] We have already remarked on the importance of the hijra. Its significance lies in the notion of moving from paganism, tribalism and, above all, unbelief, into a community of monotheistic faith. It is a symbol whose resonance can still be heard in the name of Islamist groups today such as *al-Takfir w'al-Hijra* ('Excommunication and Migration') in Egypt or the diasporic *al-Muhajirun* ('The Emigrants') in London. The call for Muslims to quit 'un-Islamic' lands still finds adherents today and often figures heavily in the rhetoric of those religious leaders who seek to discourage Muslims from living in the West. But connotations of the hijra have themselves been subject to diasporic mediation. The late Ismail Faruqi, an archetype of the modern Muslim migrant, sought to reverse the rhetoric by calling on Muslims in the West (of which he was one) to regard themselves as having made a hijra *to* the West. Faruqi, a scholar-activist trained at the famed al-Azhar in Cairo as well as at a number of secular institutions, encouraged his fellow Muslims in diaspora to live their lives as companions of Muhammad, *as if they had just arrived in the city of the Prophet*: 'Now that you are in Madinah, what is your task?…Your task…is the saving, the salvation of life, the realization of the values of dignity, of purity, of chastity, all the nobility of which humans are capable'.[13] We can also look to the recent response of a religious scholar ('alim) in Mecca who when approached by several Algerian students enquiring what Islam had to say about Muslims staying in Europe or America, produced a treatise which argued that in some senses travel to these countries is actually obligatory for Muslims. He cites the importance of education and the acquisition of advanced science and technology, without which the Muslim world would be dependent on the West. Also noted is the fact that circumstances in the West are such that the proper practice of Islam is in some senses easier there.[14] 'Islam explicitly encourages and even enjoins certain forms of travel', write Ahmed and Donnan. '[T]he movement of Muslims from one part of the world to another, whatever the purpose, resonated with the historical foundations of their religion'.[15]

Islam has of course been travelling for centuries. The Muslim world, stretching from the West coast of Africa to the Indonesian archipelago – and more recently into Europe and North America – has known countless examples of movement and migration both within and across its borders. 'The expansion of Islam', argues Ross Dunn, 'was a cultural process, but it was also a *social movement*, a complex migration of people who were driven to seek new experiences from all sorts of personal and public motives'.[16] Conquering caliphs, itinerant scholars and mobile merchants are hence very much the stuff of Islamic history.[17]

> At some level, Islamic civilisation worked as an eminently international system of social links and cultural communication. We might ask, for example, to what extent Muslim commercial diasporas, *sufi* brotherhoods, and perhaps even 'old boy networks' of urban scholars and craftsmen linked Islamic frontier lands not only with the metropolitan centres but with each other…[This fact] requires us to break out of scholarly specialities rigidly defined in space and take the trans-hemispheric view.[18]

Far from being simply a medieval phenomenon, Muslim travel must also be seen as a key component of the history of modernity. 'Cosmopolitan Islam', as Nederveen Pieterse notes, 'extending through caravan and maritime trade, through diasporas and settlements, through knowledge networks and through military expansion, has given shape to the historical dynamics of globalization, of which world capitalism is one manifestation'.[19] This is another reason why, as Bobby Sayyid observed in Chapter Two, it is impossible to simply separate Islam from modernity.

Islam has produced its fair share of famous 'wanderers', of whom the most celebrated is probably the fourteenth-century traveller Ibn Battuta. He and those like him have bequeathed to us a rich literature of travelogue, a genre known as rihla.[20] We find here a veritable tapestry of Muslim life across the continents, with the great diversity of religious practice recorded in high detail. Such travel had an interesting effect on those who undertook it, one which I will be drawing our attention to below. Abderrahmane El-Moudden argues that '*rihla* [travel] is ambivalent: through it the traveller becomes more closely linked to the idea of the

Muslim community as a whole, but at the same time learns what is specific to his own people and culture'.[21] Travel is hence a condition in which 'local' knowledge becomes relativised and subject to transformation through entering translocality. In the previous chapter we touched upon a contemporary example of this 'epistemological reordering', that of 'Ali Shariati in Paris. I pointed out that Shariati's Islam became eclectic in Paris, having been disembedded from the Iranian context in which it was originally elaborated. The intellectual idioms which Shariati encountered in Paris also had a profound effect on his religious consciousness:

> Shariati's western education...opened his eyes to the scholarly works and interpretations of non-Shi'ites on Shi'ism. Subsequently, his Shi'ism became very different from that of its official custodians in Iran. He was more concerned with the socio-political content, message and implications of what was being written on Islamic issues than the Shi'ite credentials of those who were writing them...Shariati's unabashed preference for the works of non-Shi'ite, and especially non-Muslim, scholars on Islamic issues infuriated the Iranian clergy. To them Shariati was suggesting that they ought to learn their Islam not only from non-Shi'ites, but from non-Muslims.[22]

Shariati came to be influenced by a number of Western thinkers in Paris, among them the celebrated Orientalist Louis Massignon, the sociologists George Gurvitch and Jacques Berque, and the philosophers Jean-Paul Sartre and Jean Cocteau – not to mention Frantz Fanon, with whom he exchanged several letters discussing issues related to colonialism and the developing world.[23] This is a useful first glimpse of contemporary Islam in diaspora. Much of what Shariati and his religion experienced is typical of travelling Islam and many more similar examples will be provided below. Before moving on to look at these cases let me say something about the more general aspects of the contemporary Muslim diaspora.

Living (and revising) Islam in diaspora

The contemporary movements and migrations of Muslim peoples can be seen as part and parcel of the global sociocultural transformations outlined in Chapter One. Global labour divisions, decolonisation and 'disorganised capitalism'[24] have all been contributing factors. Some of the countries most affected by these forces – most notably the Indian subcontinent, which has recently seen large waves of migration departing for Europe, North America, the Arab Gulf and Africa – have significant Muslim populations. Some of these are sojourners, labour migrants who move fairly regularly between their 'home' and countries of employment. Others have settled permanently in new societies, often in Europe and North America. Many millions of Muslims have been on the move in recent generations as a result of these transnational processes. They have provided passage for much of the travelling Islam examined below.

Islam, by its very nature, travels well. It can be, and often is, elaborated in many different ways in an equally diverse range of settings.[25] What happens, though, when Islam moves beyond contexts in which Muslims are a majority? What tools does Islam possess to communicate and negotiate across cultures? Nederveen Pieterse argues that there is a tension within Islam, 'a global project organised in local structures', that becomes particularly pronounced in diaspora.[26] Surveying the textual sources of Islam, Omar Khalidi remarks that 'what is baffling is the serious deficiency in the Islamic ideology of a theoretical framework that would be the guiding principle for Muslims in minority situations'.[27] This theoretical gap becomes a chasm once we realise that up to 40 per cent of today's Muslims live in minority situations.[28] This status, as we will see, involves a number of advantages and disadvantages. It means coming to terms with an unfamiliar set of circumstances, a requirement to engage with new cultures and an ability to adjust to inevitable changes in one's own tradition. 'We cannot assume', argues Barbara Metcalf, however, 'that the old and new cultures are fixed, and that change results from pieces being added and subtracted. Instead, new cultural and institutional expressions are being created using the symbols and institutions of the received tradition'.[29] We are therefore not talking about cases of loss and gain, or of aspects of Islam simply 'disappearing' in diaspora. What we see is a far more complex *hybrid* condition, one in which Islamic meanings shift, change and transmutate, where things *become something else*. Likewise Islam becomes represented in new forms and via new media – a phenomenon which will be explored in depth in the next chapter. Television, the Internet and 'secular' literature now suddenly all become sources of Islamic knowledge. The Muslim subjectivity also often becomes more aware of its religion in minority situations. In the 'homeland' Islam was an intrinsic aspect of that context's lifeworld, one which was taken for granted. In diaspora, however, Islam becomes yet another stigma of foreignness, a sign of the other. This causes the Muslim to objectify his or her religion and to engage in a self-examination or critique of Islam and its meanings.[30] Migration is hence a rupture, an important break which can lead to changes in the significance of Islam and of being Muslim.[31] My argument is thus that we need to focus on the dynamic qualities of travelling Islam, to draw greater attention to the ways in which things change when they migrate. It must be understood that Islam's passage into diaspora constitutes but a single stage of its journey; this transition in turn enacts a form of internal peregrination: travelling Islam becomes travel *within* Islam. In order to appreciate this dynamic we need to re-orient our analysis of Islam to focus on flux and disjunction rather than on stability and continuity. As will become clear, the translocal spaces of diasporic Islam seem to provide fertile venues for the rethinking and reformulation of tradition and the construction of an Islam for generations to come.

Let us move on now to examine some examples of how Islam has travelled in diaspora, acquired new meanings and re-interpreted old ones. Our discussion will be divided into three theme areas: encounters and *debates within Muslim communities*; rethinking and *reformulating Islamic thought (politics, community, gender)*; and the influence of *transnational* forces. A few qualifiers and caveats before we begin, however. It will soon become apparent that the vast majority of the examples I use relate to Muslims living in 'the West' (Europe and North America). As I have already mentioned above, I do not wish to imply that Islam changes only in the West. I have chosen to focus on Muslims living in these regions for three reasons. First, there is a growing literature on Islam in the West, providing a good range of case study material; second, the sociopolitical environment of the West is particularly conducive to engaging in public debate; and third, we find very high concentrations of translocal space in the West – especially in migratory and global cities such as London, Paris, Bradford and Berlin. Obviously Islam also travels in other parts of the world, often encountering significantly different cultural dynamics and new sets of problems. I hope to investigate these extra-Western translocal processes in a subsequent study.

As will also soon become clear, this case study draws on examples and illustrations from a diverse range of Muslim diasporic contexts. There are however several specific Muslim movements whose discourses crop up throughout the text. All of them are most prevalent in the British context (where the bulk of my research was focused), and constitute a useful snapshot of the Muslim political spectrum. They are:

1   Hizb ut-Tahrir/al-Muhajirun, a movement which originally emerged in the Middle East in the early 1950s. Strict advocates of the re-establishment of khilafa (the political system of the Caliphate), Hizb ut-Tahrir found little support in the Arab countries. The group then became notorious around British university campuses in the 1990s for allegedly promulgating anti-Semitic sentiment. Al-Muharijun emerged out of a split which occurred in 1996 over the question of co-operation with other Muslim movements. The fundamentals of its political agenda, however, are essentially the same as Hizb ut-Tahrir's.

2   Young Muslims UK, a group established in the UK in 1984 as a successor organisation to the Islamic Youth Movement which had originally been set up by a group of diasporic intellectuals sympathetic to Pakistan's Jama'at-i Islami party. Young Muslims UK, however, has expended considerable effort to distance itself from Abul A'la Mawdudi, the Jama'at-i Islami's ideologue, and to concentrate instead on creating an Islam whose teachings resonate with the needs and circumstances of the new generation of diasporic Muslims in the West. The pursuit of an Islamic political order in the UK, for example, is not part of the Young Muslim UK's agenda, as it is in the case of Hizb ut-Tahrir.

3   the Tablighi Jama'at, a quiescent movement founded in 1927 in India, which claims not to be interested in (statist) politics. The group's activities focus almost exclusively on travelling 'missionary' work among Muslim communities worldwide, emphasising the importance of personal spiritual purity and collective harmony.

Because people and meanings migrate together, a new sociocultural environment often means a new Islam. In diaspora many Muslims find that their religion has assumed new significance, or that its symbolic connotations have somehow shifted. Much of this is related to the transition from majority to minority status, the act of moving from an environment in which Islam is an integral component of the cultural landscape to one in which the wider resonance of its language finds no echo. For many there is a heightened awareness of Islam as what was once taken for granted is discovered anew. Islam becomes a memory-aid, something with which to remember who one is. Fellow Muslims also take on greater significance. In Muslim-majority homelands, one rarely thought to make the distinction between Muslim and non-Muslim; 'Muslimness' was natural and self-reproducing – a part of everyone.[32] The diasporic Muslim, ever aware of his 'otherness', comes to see other Muslims in a special light, as participants in a similar predicament. 'Back home I could relate Islamic thinking in a religious manner', one Muslim told me, 'but in diaspora I gained a greater sense of Islam's *social* relevance'.[33] Even in travel, however, many things stay the same, or refuse to travel beyond a certain point. I want to focus, however, on that which changes, and particularly on its relationship with that which stays the same, because it is often on the border between these two forces – inertia and dynamism – that *politics* emerges.

A number of writers have commented on the ways in which the passage into diaspora transforms Muslims' symbols and spaces. These changes usually take one of three forms: an alteration in the significance assigned to particular ideas and practices; the 'translation' of Muslim symbolic language and thought into a translocal dialect; or the construction of new forms of religious expression. I will briefly deal with each of these in turn.

The spatiality of the mosque in The Netherlands provides an interesting example of how the role and significance of 'religious' institutions changes in diaspora. Several writers have emphasised the extended sociopolitical functions which the mosque fulfils for Muslim migrants. More than simply places for prayer, mosques become spaces which mediate between diasporic communities and the wider society. They often offer Dutch language instruction, financial aid, shops and a whole host of other social services geared towards serving the needs of diasporic Muslims. In this sense they operate as a point of interface between Islam and Dutch society, a window through which the former views (and constitutes) the latter. 'As such', writes Sunier, 'they are organizations which initially provided private goods (i.e. religious services) only, but which developed into organizations which seek to obtain public goods (related to the position of group members in society)'.[34] The diasporic mosque hence operates as an effective example of the blurring between public and private which occurs in translocality. Hamid Naficy makes a similar point with regard to the Iranian-exile media in Los Angeles. Although many of the Iranians currently living in exile left their homeland in order to escape Khomeini's Iranian Revolution, Naficy finds that after time religious symbols lose their negative connotations and become instead associated with a nostalgia for Iran. 'The twin ambivalence of exile and nationalism', he writes, 'served to gradually attenuate and destabilise the anti-Islamist idea of an exilic nation'.[35] This creates a new hybrid discourse in which the

Islamist politics of Khomeini can be viciously attacked in one television programme, followed by a focus on the beauty of the *azan* (the call to prayer) in the next.

A second type of shifting meaning relates to the translation of Muslim symbols and language into relevant or analogous diasporic dialects. This involves finding expressions of Islam which resonate in the new sociocultural environments which they enter, making 'Muslim' life applicable to diasporic life. In previous sections we have looked at the important roles which language and popular culture can play here – the expression of Islam in sport, for example, or in Western dress; also, the availability of Islam in English via the modern media. Other changes relate to the symbolic languages used by Muslims to express their religion's significance. Fischer and Abedi relate how Iranian students studying in the United States just prior to Khomeini's revolution encountered various discourses of Islamic liberation. The symbology of Islam was translated into the contemporary political context with the Shah depicted as Pharaoh, and Khomeini as the Shi'a martyr Husain. The challenge of communism was countered with claims that Islam was more egalitarian, more concerned with the plight of the people. The heroes of Shi'a mythology became religious leftists fighting on behalf of the downtrodden – a hybridised image borrowed from the writings of Ali Shariati.[36] The same two authors also offer us an account of the meanings ascribed to Islam by a young African-American Muslim woman. Her position as a woman and as part of a racial minority heavily informs the significance she finds in Islam – and also the significance she does *not* find, the areas where she believes Islam fails. In her view, Islam needs to deepen its analysis of class differences and pay more attention to how the abuse of women is often legitimised in its name.[37]

Systems of thought and political agendas also undergo significant changes when they travel, inevitably translated into new idioms by those who carry and receive them in unfamiliar contexts. Much of this has to do with translocal disembedding processes which remove ideas from the sociopolitical environment in which they were initially established, and rearticulate them in new settings – the classic 'travelling theory' (see Chapter Three). This effect can be illustrated by looking at what happens to some of the more radical breeds of Sunni Islam when they enter translocality. Many groups espousing these ideologies have been banned from countries in the Middle East or, in the ironic case of the Committee for the Defence of Legitimate Rights in Saudi Arabia, persecuted for setting up an Islamic opposition in a state that was already supposedly Islamic! Hizb ut-Tahrir is one such organisation. Although originally founded in Jerusalem in the 1950s, Hizb ut-Tahrir has enjoyed little political success in the Middle East. Many Arabs find their Islamist programme far too simplistic. They thrive in diaspora precisely because of the generally low level of Islamic knowledge that exists among many migrants. 'They are able to impress people in the UK by throwing around a few Arabic words', one interviewee told me, 'but that doesn't get them very far in the Middle East where people know better'.[38] Clearly some political ideologies have no choice but to travel. Other Muslim groups have also benefited from the journey into diaspora. Many of them are sectarian minorities – such as the Alevis of Turkey or the Ahmadiyya of Pakistan – who face intense persecution in their own countries. Certain Sufi brotherhoods, banned or circumscribed in their places of origin, have also found 'a new lease of life' in countries such as The Netherlands.[39] These groups' flourishing can be seen as the result of three factors. First, they enter into a society in which they have no 'history' and where the negative connotations associated with them in the wider societies of their original homelands are largely absent. Second, the fact that Islam is usually in a minority situation in diaspora often means that differences between Muslims are de-emphasised. Similarities between these sects and other forms of Islam are hence accentuated. Third, some of these groups adhere to beliefs and practices perceived by many as being closer to Western norms. Several writers mention this fact in relation to the Alevis. Their practices regarding women's dress and public behaviour, often read as 'libertine' in Turkey, are seen as 'liberal' in Europe.[40]

A third form of shifting meaning pertains to the creation of 'new' expressions of Islam, or substitutes for those which have been lost in travel. Some writers have pointed to the 'portability of Islamic ritual',[41] the fact that Islam is not spatially confined: 'When Islam leaves its original landscape, what travels are not the marabout shrines not the rural folk practices and brotherhoods, but the Qur'an and Qur'anic teachings: the Qur'an is portable Islam'.[42] This is fine and well for those orthodox Muslims who require little more than books and a place to pray (which, in theory, can be almost anywhere), but what about those forms of Islam which depend on very specific places (e.g. the graves and shrines of various saints) or on particular configurations of social relations in order to sustain their religion? Think of the Alevis mentioned above and the difficulties they have in sustaining their notions of religious community in diaspora. Clearly not *all* forms of Islam travel well. '[If] the religious symbols and rituals are no longer affirmed by the social environment…they [will] lose the character of certainty which underpinned their existence'.[43] In many cases the religious rituals and personnel of the homeland provide particular services and fulfil certain needs specific to time and place; in diaspora these become redundant. The women who visited marabout saints in Morocco appear to have little need for them in diaspora.[44] The social services provided by Sufi orders in the countries of origin are superfluous in The Netherlands.[45] Contrast this with the way the mosque has managed to re-invent itself as a form of diasporic community centre.

Muslim political theories also sometimes have trouble travelling, or retaining their cutting edge in diaspora. The role of many thinkers thus changes in diaspora. Dr Ataullah Siddiqui of the Islamic foundation mentioned that Abul A'la Mawdudi's thought is now often little more than a 'starting point' for young, educated, highly literate Muslims. 'Mawdudi gives important confidence to young Muslims', he says, 'and they can then go on to find something else.'[46] We have already seen the ways in which Mawdudi's thought is often combined with that of other (sometimes antithetical) tendencies in diaspora. Imam Khomeini and the Islamic Revolution often find themselves in a similar predicament. One African-American Muslim, for example, finds Khomeini's message empowering in the face of anti-hegemonic struggle, but berates him for a lack of thorough class analysis and also takes issue with some of his ideas about non-Muslims.[47] Some analysts suggest that the apparent limited export potential of the Iranian revolution is connected to its particular national and sectarian context:

> While in the early days of the revolution the adjective 'Islamic' was taken literally, in practice the revolution took the form of an Iranian/Shii populist movement. For example, when Hujjatiyeh Seminary began to train jurisconsults in the *Jafari* (Shii) school of jurisprudence, the school lost a great number of Sunni students. One student from an African country told me, 'Had I been trained well in my own Sunni school of jurisprudence in Qum, I would have been the best agent for the export of the revolution for you. But instead, I simply have to leave because I did not come here to train as a Shii'.[48]

Ideas often carry the marks of their own specificity within them. These, once activated, can sometimes render a theory inert. Hence the difficulties some reform-minded theologians encounter when trying to introduce innovative forms of thinking into Islam. Too often they are accused of being 'Western' or 'secular' – two terms often viewed as synonymous.[49] The West, or at least the idea of something called 'the West', lurks in the background of diasporic Muslim discourses. For many Muslims living in Europe or North America 'the West' is simply part of life, the infrastructure of daily existence. For others, however, it is a haunting force, something to be reckoned with, a spectral 'other'. Thus questions arise as to whether new forms of diasporic religious practice constitute 'authentic' Islam.[50] This is where the boundary drawing (and the politics) begins. Islam begins to be seen as something that needs to be protected and steps are taken to guard against the encroachment of Western influences.

So, as we see, sometimes Islam can only travel so far. Fortunately, the younger generation of diasporic Muslims seems more willing to engage in active exchange with the West. This does not mean, however, that they simply 'accept' the West or conform to its requirements; young Muslims are far from uncritical in this regard. Rather, there seems to have occurred a shift in the way they view the West. One interviewee told me that the West is now regarded less as an intrusion and more as a challenge. 'Muslims want to make sense of their own tradition in light of this challenge', he explained.[51] Today's diasporic Muslims understand the foundations of modern political theory and practice. Recent arrivals in diaspora, many of whom are political exiles, find that being in the West affords them a better perspective from which to view the predicament of the modern Muslim movement. 'When you're in Kashmir or wherever, out of touch with the wider movement and other Muslim tendencies', one recent arrival told me, 'you realise only the need for change, but not the *dire* need that exists. By looking at Islamic movements from the West one is able to identify those areas and imperatives which have not been discussed'.[52]

Encounters and debates with the Muslim other

The numbers bode well for Europe's next generation of young Muslims. Britons of Pakistani and Bangladeshi descent, for example, almost doubled in number between 1981 and 1991, with nearly half of them now born in the UK. The age dispersion compared with that of white Britain is also striking. There are almost twice as many under-16s among the South Asian population, and only 2 per cent of this community is over the age of 65 compared to 17 per cent among Britain's white population.[53] Within a decade this generation will be ready for participation in Muslim public life, but *whether* they will be able to do so is another question. As Jørgen Nielsen points out, many mosque organisations are 'firmly in the control of the immigrant generation, their parents, and only the most perceptive of these [are] beginning to co-opt their children into the power structures'.[54] It is not just a matter of parents keeping children out of mosques, however. Young Muslims, as we will see, are largely dissatisfied with the Islam of their parents. The generational divide is hence one of the defining features of the Muslim diaspora today. But what are the terms of this debate?

Notions of identity are undergoing some major changes for the current generation of young Muslims in Europe. They are aware that the Islam of their parents was learned in a different sociocultural setting and in a different era. This older generation received both direct and indirect socialisation into their religion at home, school and in the wider Muslim majority societies which constitute their homelands.[55] The parents of many young Turkish migrants, for example, will have studied Islam in primary school in Turkey for at least two years. Furthermore, Islam here was part of a wider lifeworld which provided a continuing infrastructure for the reproduction of religion and belief. This system, however, does not travel well into diaspora.[56] Some writers note that when Islam is transplanted, 'the religious symbols and rituals of Islam are no longer affirmed by the social environment, and they thus lose [the] character of certainty which underpinned their existence [in the homeland]'.[57] There arises therefore a question as to the continued relevance of Islam as it was traditionally practised at various 'points of origin'. The responses of the new generation to this ambivalence generally take one of two forms. Some young 'Muslims' turn away from their religion, regarding it as an unwanted vestige which serves no purpose in diaspora other than to mark them out as different. These people often go the secular route, voiding Islam from their lives and doing their very best to integrate into their new cultural environments; in other words, becoming as British or German or American as possible. For this group, issues concerning race and ethnicity sometimes become the new obstacles; Islam is usually only an issue here when it is projected on to them by virtue of their 'Muslim background'.[58]

Other young Muslims, however, choose to reaffirm their Islam. By doing so they remain in diaspora, but the object of their migrant desire – the place to which they seek to return – changes. Pakistan or Morocco ceases to be an imaginary homeland and instead that role falls to Islam. As Elizabeth Scantlebury notes, '[a] significant number of young Muslims are rejecting a religio-ethnic identity in favour of a search for "True Islam" '.[59] This also often involves questioning their parents' lifestyles and Islamic credentials. Much of what the older generation sees as Islam is dismissed by the younger generation as tainted, or as mere 'cultural' practice. This questioning 'takes the form of trying to strip away the varying cultural traditions that first generation migrants have, rightly or wrongly, assumed to be Islamic, from the "essential core" of the religion'.[60] Hanif Kureishi's short story and subsequent film *My Son the Fanatic* depict exactly this kind of situation from the point of view of a father whose son has apparently 'returned' to Islam. This is often explained as a search for identity, a response by diaspora's discontents to their disenfranchisement and loss of self in a minority context. Some young Muslims have been led to join radical organisations such as the aforementioned Hizb ut-Tahrir which states as its goal the establishment of an Islamic state in Britain. Many of these activists attempt to 'hijack' mosques, using them as pulpits for noisy propaganda. For the most part mosque administrators are tolerant of such behaviour. '[They] have nowhere else to go to let off steam. We tolerate them because they are lonely in London and angry at the wrongs in their own countries...[But] there is no discipline. Every boy is a leader'.[61] The older generation is often quite ambivalent about these self-appointed imams. 'They do not like the young firebrands shouting at the mosques', one informant told me, 'but at the same time they are also happy that their children still see Islam as an important part of their lives'.[62]

Many young Muslims, however, are not so tolerant of their parents. They complain that the older generation still tries to live as it did in its societies of origin, that is, as if Muslims were still in the majority: 'They would talk Pakistani politics constantly, but never neighbourhood politics...they didn't want to engage with non-Muslims'.[63] The sectarian conflicts and divisions between religious schools of thought are also seen by the younger generation as a negative aspect of their parents' Islam. Many young Muslims view these ethno-theological debates as pointless time-wasting that only generates dissent. As Dilwar Hussain, a former member of Young Muslims UK's executive board, told me, '[W]e dealt with this by deciding that it would not be a public issue for us. We saw the *madhhab* debate as something that was important for our parents' generation and we didn't want to fall into or continue their debates since we realised that this would be a source of disunity'.[64] Some Muslim community leaders have taken this into consideration when formulating their platforms. For example, when the Manchester Council of Mosques was set up in 1989, one of its stated aims was 'to provide the younger generation with pure Islam – quite untainted with sectarianism'.[65] But the real source of dissatisfaction for young Muslims relates to a much broader issue, the question of whether the older generation is able to engage with Western society and to produce an Islam for this particular habitat. The religious leaders – imams, ulama and sheikhs – are viewed as particularly problematic in this regard:

These ulama often seem to be living in a different world; they have very little sense of the important issues of the day. They have fixed minds and are very fixed in their views. In terms of politics they have created their own internal politics concerning different institutions and traditions, but they aren't dealing with the larger political issues. No questions are being asked and there is no reasoning.[66]

Most of all, these religious leaders do not enter into dialogue with the West. It is therefore difficult for them to advise younger Muslims on how best to make Islam relevant to European or North American settings, and how to relate to the issues faced by young people today. Phillip Lewis refers to the interesting case of two father-and-son imams in Bradford. While both teachers use the same basic materials, the bilingual son is able to ensure that a lesson has been understood in both English and Urdu and also to pepper his lectures with references to the objects and imagery of contemporary British popular culture. Also, with regard to particularly sensitive issues such as contraception, it is usually the son who is approached for advice and not the father.[67] The question of religious leadership is hence a vexed one, and is closely related to ideas of 'dispersed authority' discussed in Chapter Two. That is, clear sources of leadership and guidance are not always forthcoming; rather, 'Islamic knowledge' is to be found spread amongst a variety of disparate sources. Many young Muslims also find the intellectual quality of their elders to be inferior. As one prominent imam remarked, 'most of the imams in this country lack the basic training required to lead the prayer in a village mosque, not to mention in a place of worship in a more sophisticated and intellectually superior society'.[68] Much of this dissent stems from the fact that what we are dealing with here, as Tariq Modood reminds us, is 'a semi-industrialised, newly urbanised working class community only one generation away from rural peasantry'.[69] It is therefore not surprising that the older generation feels more comfortable having Islam taught and read to them by an imam from their own village and in a language that they understand.[70] The phenomenon of 'transnational ulama' – religious scholars (or 'travelling theorists') who move frequently between diasporic communities and their countries of origin is largely a consequence of this preference for religious leaders from more familiar environs. Such 'imported Islam' does not, however, meet with either the approval or the needs of the younger genera-tion. It has been noted that because this Islam is taught by individuals with little knowledge of daily life in the West, it often only serves to alienate young Muslims.[71]

The employing of *imams* from the countries of origin of the migrants is seen as ignoring the needs of the British-born members of the community. This may be in the area of language since very few of these *imams* speak English fluently. *Qur'an* schools held in the mosques are then perceived as being very unattractive to children who are used to the variety of teaching methods in

state schools. Very few mosques are seen as providing a programme specifically aimed at the younger generation.[72]

Many of these imported teachers, however extensively trained in religion they
may be, possess little first-hand experience of life in the diasporic environment.[73]
They therefore find it difficult to accommodate the needs of young Muslims.
Many writers point to the necessity of developing new, effective leadership structures for the next generations. Parents and imported imams are finding that their
Islam has less and less resonance for their children. Dassetto and Nonneman
argue that one of the major questions facing diasporic Muslim communities
today is how the transition 'from the Islam of the fathers to the Islam of the
sons' (and increasingly, as we shall see, the daughters) will take place.[74] As the
reliance on transnational ulama decreases,[75] yet another question arises as to
where the next generation of imams will be educated.[76] Young Muslims who
write on Islam in English without a knowledge of Arabic are often not taken
seriously by the more traditional ulama – who then find themselves counter-
accused of being narrow-minded and out of touch with their surroundings.[77] As
Phillip Lewis argues, 'the task confronting Muslims in developing the Islamic
tradition in English is thus considerable. It is by no means clear which institutions are equipped for such a task. It is difficult to envisage the *'ulama* and their
centres of learning as equal to such an undertaking'.[78] Such developments are,
however, imperative.

Recently we have seen some encouraging signs in this regard. The establishment of organisations such as Young Muslims UK is a step in the right direction,
offering as they do resources for Muslims seeking to make Islam relevant to their
own hybrid condition. Dilwar Hussain is a good example of someone who has
been affected positively by this trend. Islam was not a particularly large part of
his life as he grew up. In fact, he was quite suspicious of any form of organised
religion. In his late teens he attended several meetings of Young Muslims UK on
the advice of his friends and liked what he saw.

> I began to feel more comfortable with Islam because it was being articulated
> in a language I could understand by my own peer group; in English rather
> than Urdu or Arabic. Everyone was in Western dress. I began to think that
> maybe I'd misunderstood Islam…So I began to read widely about the reli-
> gion, entering into a period of inquiry. I didn't just accept Islam. I had a lot
> of questions that I wanted answered first, about the treatment of women for
> example. After I had received satisfactory answers I then felt ready to make
> a commitment to Islam. I got my answers from the leadership of the Young
> Muslims rather than from the mosque; the imams there are quite fixed in
> their views and don't like it when people ask too many questions.[79]

What is crucial here is the rendering of Islam in an idiom comprehensible to
those Muslims who have grown up in Western society and who possess certain
Western norms in addition to Islam. Indeed, this process is in many ways about

emphasising the areas in which these value systems are co-extensive or highly similar. It is also, as I will argue later, about setting both vocabularies, Islam and the West, in motion – helping them to travel towards each other.

Much of this will involve bringing Islam into the forums of popular culture and making it available via a wide variety of media (see Chapter Five). Religion has to be seen to offer something to those young Muslims who find themselves unemployed, alienated or lost in the majority society. Some argue that this can be accomplished by attempting to relate aspects of wider popular culture in, say, the United Kingdom to a Muslim identity. Aurangzeb Iqbal, a Bradford solicitor, has suggested that sport might be one route by which this could be done.[80] To this end he has organised a number of football matches for young Muslims in the UK. Iqbal emphasises the need for Muslim role models and the importance of prominent Muslims showing the younger generation that Islam can be compatible with success in the West. In this regard he outlines his own version of 'upwardly-mobile Islam':

> Islam tells you to dress smartly, to spend upon yourself, you are not supposed to hoard money. It's wrong to have a big bank balance or build a massive house in Pakistan that no one lives in. That's wrong. Spend that money on your kids, on private education, don't hoard it. Have a nice house, invite your neighbours in regularly. Set yourself high standards, so that other people think, 'I like that, I would like to be like that'.[81]

Others emphasise the importance of language which, as we have seen, is one of the issues which most divides the generations. There is hence a need to make Islam widely available to those young Muslims whose first (and sometimes only) language is English. The importance of publications such as *Q-News* and *The Muslim News* (see Chapter Five) is therefore difficult to underestimate. *Q-News* 'appeals to young, educated Muslims, impatient of sectarianism, and is able through an international language, English, to access innovative and relevant Islamic scholarship'.[82] This publication has also contributed enormously towards the availability of sound religious advice through a column by the late Dr Syed Mutawalli ad-Darsh, a prominent religious scholar in the UK. Every fortnight in *Q-News* he would dispense *fatāwā* (juridical opinions; singular *fatwā*) on a vast range of issues relevant to Islam in modern society. Many of these were answers to questions sent in by readers on marriage, sexuality and contraception – topics which young Muslims often find it difficult to raise with traditional ulama in local mosques. Several Islamic publishing houses in the UK have also dedicated themselves to producing useful materials for English-speaking Muslims. Among them are Ta-Ha in London and the publishing wing of the Islamic Foundation in Leicester. This latter organisation generates a wide range of literature ranging from children's books to treatises on Islamic economics and the translated works of Abul A'la Mawdudi (the prominent Pakistani Islamist whose political thought we briefly examined in Chapter Two). 'We try to make our coverage general', they say, 'so that any tendency or movement – and especially their children – can use our books'.[83] The Foundation also produces literature targeted at non-Muslims in public life in order to help them understand the beliefs and circumstances of their Muslim employees, colleagues, constituents and pupils.[84] Another writer mentions the emergence of what she terms 'Islamic English' among some certain Muslim communities. She mentions, for example, the Islamically-inflected phraseologies specific to African-American Muslims in the United States.[85]

The imperatives, then, are clear. Today's young diasporic Muslims are trying to build their lives in a highly urbanised and often cosmopolitan environment. They require an Islam to match this setting. The traditional frameworks of their parents and the associated institutions of religious scholarship are perceived as being in desperate need of transformation. In this regard, publications such as *Q-News* have provided important forums for debating intra-Islamic politics and the future of Muslims in diaspora.[86] Yet doubts still remain as to the viability of 'reformed' ulama within the stagnant religious structures of the older generation. As Lewis notes, 'Even where an able student…becomes an 'alim, it is an open question whether mosque committees will be able or willing to offer him the salary and job security he deserves. There is a real danger that there will be a haemorrhaging of the most able into the state educational system'.[87] Islam's diasporic scholars need to transcend the ghettos into which they are perceived to have confined themselves. They need to re-invent themselves as the role models for a diasporic Islam that knows where it is: 'The future of Islamic living will depend on ulama with vision, ulama who are in touch with the problems of today and who can show how Islam is relevant to contemporary life'.[88]

Intergenerational issues have not been the only source of conflict in the Muslim diaspora. There are other debates going on within these communities, many of which pertain to questions about the boundaries of who and what Islam is. These conversations are intensified in translocal spaces due to the sheer volume of human traffic that flows through them. Muslims in diaspora come face to face with the myriad shapes and colours of global Islam, forcing their religion to hold a mirror up to its own diversity. These encounters often play an important role in processes of identity formation, prompting Muslims to relativise and compare their self-understandings of Islam. Eickelman and Piscatori point out that in translocal spaces:

> [Muslims have] direct contact with the real differences of language, sect, race, and customs that unavoidably make up the *umma*. Contrary to the conventional wisdom of western social scientists, therefore, the encounter with the Muslim 'other' has been at least as important for self-definition as the confrontations with the European 'other'.[89]

Other writers point out that before this century's migrational waves, interaction between different kinds of Muslims was often minimal. These groups tended to live in fairly closed communities, often with only limited knowledge and contact with other understandings of Islam. Their arrival in migratory and global cities, however, has required them to interact with each other to a far greater degree, and hence also to become more aware of their religion's internal variety and vicissitudes.[90] 'With globalisation', one diasporic Islamist told me, 'we are forced to confront different interpretations of Islam, you can't hide away from them'.[91] One also finds groups or movements whose Islam has been deemed heterodox or even outlawed in their homelands – minority 'sects' such as the Ahmadis or Alevis – with whom contact may have previously been proscribed.

What, then, has been the effect of this new intra-Islamic melange? Many community leaders had hoped that the circumstances of diaspora would lead Muslims from different parts of the world and cultural backgrounds to focus on that which is common to them all, as prescribed by scriptural norms.[92] In other words, they have been anticipating the emergence of a new form of cosmopolitan Islam devoid of 'ethnic' or 'local' distortions. In this sense it was hoped that diaspora might provide the opportunity for greater Muslim unity. Too often, though, it seems as if the call for greater unity has been viewed by many Muslims as a call for more *uniformity* – a political manoeuvre by one school or tendency trying to force its own particular brand of Islam on the entire Muslim community. The consequences of diasporic diversity have therefore been a mixed blessing. In the early period of settlement sectarian differences were rife, and many of these still endure. In addition, as we will see, there are a number of ongoing debates about orthodoxy/orthopraxy, 'modernism' and the political agenda. The situation is not, however, only one of strife. I will also be arguing that there are a number of important ways in which these encounters with the Muslim other are contributing towards the development of a more tolerant and progressive climate. By holding a mirror up to its 'hybrid self' (see Chapter Three), Islam is better able to gauge what needs to be changed.

Sectarian conflict has been a constant feature of the Muslim diaspora in its modern history. Sometimes this has manifested itself in the form of ethnic factionalism. Coventry, for example, saw Deobandi and Barelwi (the two most common sectarian schools in British Islam) dissent take the form of a confrontation between Pakistanis and Gujeratis, with each side in turn accusing the other of being 'Wahhabis'.[93] At other times theological orthopraxy has been a key source of disagreement. In Manchester the same two schools had another falling out when the Deobandi imam of the Central Mosque refused to attend festivals associated with saints, a practice of which his tradition does not approve.[94] This incident hints at another common divide within diasporic Islam, that between 'puritanical' movements such as the Wahhabis and Muslim Brotherhood and those Muslims more inclined towards a 'popular' Islam centred on saints and festivals, such as the various Sufi orders.[95]

In other settings we find a similar (but perhaps inverse) form of politics involving those Muslim sects whose interpretations of Islam are considered taboo in various home societies. Among the migrant Turkish community in Berlin, for example, 'orthodox' Sunnis often condemn fellow Turkish Alevi Muslims as heretics.[96] And in The Netherlands the debate over government licensing for the ritual slaughtering of meat heated up when it was discovered that the authorities had initially sought religious advice from an imam of the Ahmadiyya – a group outlawed by the Pakistani state – who, it was claimed by a consultant specialist on Islam, are 'considered to be heterodox by probably more than 95 percent of the Muslims in Holland'![97] The issue of which sects receive 'official' state approval is thus the source of some particularly interesting politics within diasporic Muslim organisations, many of which are sponsored by prominent Muslim states such as Saudi Arabia, Pakistan and Iran. The combination of sectarian divisions and this transnational patronage has meant that Muslim organisations have often been of a very fragmentary nature.[98] In the early days of Muslim settlement in Europe this severely hampered campaigns for the provision of *ḥalāl* ('permissible'; in this case, slaughtered in accordance with religious regulations) meat and Islamic education. The politics surrounding associations in the UK such as the Union of Muslim Organisations, the Council of Mosques of the UK and Eire and the Muslim Parliament have often wasted time that could have been spent on more pressing issues faced by Muslims in diaspora. Other Islamic organisations in Europe have had similar problems. For example, the *Diyanet* movement – which constitutes the voice of 'official' Turkish state Islam abroad – has refused to participate in the Higher Council of Belgian Muslims because adherents of the *Milli Görüs* group, an anti-Kemalist movement associated with the *Refah* party in Turkey, were also involved.[99]

Another form of debate, one which is often co-extensive with the intergenerational conflicts examined in the previous section, relates to the divisions between so-called 'modernising' and 'traditional' tendencies in diasporic Islam. This antagonism can take many forms in daily life, and often comes into play when questions related to issues such as gender relations and the permissibility of certain 'Western' practices arise. One writer gives the example of a 'modernising' religious leader in London who was consulted by two young women over the question of whether, according to Islam, women are allowed to initiate divorce. These women had already asked the same question of other 'culture-centred' – and therefore 'traditional' – scholars and had been told that in Islam women do not have the choice to separate from their husbands. From the modernising scholar, however, the women heard a different opinion.

> [He] told them that, according to his interpretation of Islam, women had the choice of initiating divorce too. This calmed the situation, through providing them with empowerment. They were able to inform their husbands and families of the 'correct' authoritative Islamic position within this particular belief framework…[The 'moderniser'] was able to prove, through his interpretation, that he was 'correct'. It demonstrated to [him] that in his view, many Muslims lack understanding of basic principles regarding Islam. He reflected, however, that the erroneous 'traditional' perspective often prevailed in similar cases – and that he was in a 'minority'.[100]

Many young Muslims today are part of this broadly modern disposition. However, even within this tendency there is conflict, some of which has received considerable media attention even in the wider majority society. Much of the debate here is over the question of what the younger generation of diasporic Muslims should regard as its political imperatives, and, more specifically, how it should deal with the West.[101] The modernist tendency subspeciates into two broad camps, usually identified as 'moderates' and 'radicals'. Most prominent among the latter in the UK has been the Islamist organisation Hizb ut-Tahrir, a movement we have examined briefly in other contexts above. This group's stated goal is the establishment of an Islamic state and khilafa, governance according to principles outlined by the Qur'an and the example of the Prophet.[102] Although many may see this as an eminently 'traditional' agenda, Hizb ut-Tahrir's methods are distinctly modern.

> Hizb ut-Tahrir's radical Islamic theology is the very antithesis of Marxist atheism, but it operates on classical Leninist lines. Core activists…travel the country, setting up closed cells in towns and universities, whose members are indoctrinated in the party's beliefs and worldview. The activists move on, but the new cadre-members are left behind to infiltrate the Muslim establishment, such as established student Islamic Societies and try to take them over. For many young British Muslims Hizb ut-Tahrir provides a set of ready-made answers to both political issues and the questions of personal identity that often draw alienated individuals to extremist organisations.[103]

Hizb ut-Tahrir has undoubtedly forced young Muslims to deal with questions and issues which they might have otherwise avoided, its noisy tactics effectively allowing it to define the political agenda for the younger generation. 'I would be dishonest if I said I hadn't been influenced by them', reported one interviewee. 'The rise of Hizb ut-Tahrir had a strong impact on the other movements. Until then many other groups had been politically apathetic. They were forced to react and relate to the issues – such as khilafa – that Hizb ut-Tahrir had put on the agenda'.[104] Many began to switch camps, abandoning groups such as the Tablighi Jama'at which some view as limited in transformative potential. Even such traditionally 'quietist' movements were forced to politicise to some degree in order to answer Hizb ut-Tahrir's challenge. Some see the latter's disruptive strategies as marking them out as a form of modern day *khawarij*, an early puritanical sect which broke away from mainstream Islam in the years following the death of Prophet. Other Muslims believe that groups such as Hizb ut-Tahrir and its offshoot al-Muhajirun fulfil a useful polemical function by provoking the more quiescent movements, and are willing to mute their own objections so long as the more radical groups stay within the boundaries of what is halal.[105] The very definition of these boundaries is, however, a large part of the ongoing debate.

Strangely enough, the rise of Hizb ut-Tahrir has also had a unifying effect among young Muslims. Opposition to the 'radicals' has, for example, brought together previously antagonistic groups such as the Deobandi-influenced Tablighi Jama'at and the Barelwis. Even other Islamists seeking to implement an

Islamic political order have expressed dissatisfaction with Hizb ut-Tahrir's methods. They are well aware that global spaces are firmly under the gaze of the world's media, and that one therefore has to be careful of what one says. 'If you have a slogan that makes you look funny – for example, the claim that you're going to implement *khilafa*, a programme that needs many more elements and perhaps several hundred years – then you'll never be taken seriously.'[106] By unifying these various tendencies in opposition, Hizb ut-Tahrir has, in the words of one observer, 'played a positive role in a negative way'.[107] A similar phenomenon was observed during the height of the controversy surrounding Salman Rushdie's novel *The Satanic Verses*. This episode 'revealed the need for broader organizational frameworks, as well as setting new agendas for common action'.[108] Other writers have also highlighted the role of crisis situations and perceived threats (such as the Gulf War of 1991) in uniting the Muslim diaspora.[109]

There is now a more general trend towards communication and interaction across sectarian divisions. Much of this is linked to the younger generation's distaste for such differences, as discussed in the previous section. Until the 1990s, many mosques and their leaderships remained introverted, rarely seeking contact with other schools and tendencies. In contrast, the present decade has seen significantly increased interaction between different Muslim movements, particularly in the translocal spaces of more urban and cosmopolitan areas such as London.[110] Mosques have emerged as a particularly salient form of Muslim public sphere in this regard, forming the sites of a growing number of intra-Muslim conversations. This is also reflected in the way some mosque associations now organise their leaderships. The Bradford Council of Mosques, for example, has consciously avoided having religious scholars associated with its administration in order to minimise sectarian issues.[111]

There are ways in which diaspora provides an environment highly conducive to dialogue and exchange between the multitude of different schools of thought in travelling Islam. It seems to be the case that many ideologies lose their specificity when they travel. The processes of becoming disembedded from the sociocultural contexts in which they were originally elaborated also loosens their fixedness. It becomes easier to adapt them to new contexts, or to combine them with ideas previously viewed as incompatible. One of my informants, for example, remembers being particularly struck by a speech he heard in London about the need to remove the Islamic Revolution in Iran from its national and Shi'a context, and to make it relevant to the entire umma.[112] These transplantations can also give rise to new hybrid formulations which cater for the specific needs of migrant Muslims. Thus in diaspora we often find curious syntheses of thinkers and systems of thought. Fischer and Abedi, for instance, refer to an African-American Muslim woman who described herself as simultaneously having been a follower of Abul A'la Mawdudi *and* the Tablighi Jama'at movement.[113] This is interesting because the Tablighis usually do their best to avoid politics, while Mawdudi's thought emphasises the need for Muslims to be politically *active*. In diaspora, however, these ideas combine with little difficulty, each fulfilling a different aspect of an individual's sociopolitical and identity needs. Some Muslims also find it easier in diaspora to engage with other schools of thought without losing sight of their own Islam. 'You learn to adjust to other tendencies', says Dr Ataullah Siddiqui, 'and to be at ease with other interpretations of Islam without feeling that you are diluting your own beliefs'.[114] He recalls meeting significant numbers of Shi'a Muslims for the first time in the UK, and also being struck by how easy it seemed to be for many Arab Muslims to talk across and combine different schools of thought. Others note that in diaspora, religious thought often takes on a new dimension. 'I have become more tolerant', says one Deobandi mufti, 'and my knowledge has become "live". You see, knowing something about a school of thought and actually coming into contact with someone from that school are two very different things'.[115] This comment usefully reflects the fact that it is often very difficult to tell anything about an individual's personal religious belief or behaviour by looking at what movement or tendency he or she supposedly belongs to. '[The] individual opinions of members of a specific organization do not always concur with the ideological contents of the organization', notes one analyst.[116] Obviously such groups *can* play an important role in political situations, but we need to bear in mind the dangers of conflating unity and uniformity. In any case, there are a great number of issues whose salience cuts right across the wide range of Muslim discourse, generating, at times, a 'convergence in public rhetoric'.[117] This is often the case, as we have seen, when Muslims perceive themselves to be facing a common threat, for example, during the Rushdie Affair or the Gulf War of 1991.[118] There are also occasions when different tendencies will borrow from each other's ideologies in order to compensate for aspects missing from their own programmes. Thus, Sufi and Deobandis in Britain have at times adopted the political agenda of the Jama'at-i Islami. Werbner notes that as such 'discourses "travel" across the sectarian divide…they come to be imbued with new meanings'.[119] Groups who share broadly similar principles also co-operate in various ways. Muhammad al-Mass'ari of the Committee for the Defence of Legitimate Rights explained that his 'radical' movement did its best to avoid being publicly associated with other, more 'moderate' Gulf Islamists such as the Bahrain Freedom Movement. During his group's first year in exile they also did not attend mosques which received Saudi money so as not to jeopardise those institutions' sources of funding.[120] Intra-Muslim political discourse is also enriched by this interaction. 'In London I have contact with the whole spectrum of the Islamist movement', says Dr Sa'ad al-Faqih, 'and I am forced to communicate politically. Dialogue is very important, especially with those with whom you disagree'.[121] The dialogue to which he refers is wide-ranging, covering issues from Islamic conceptions of democracy and the participation of Islamists in 'non-Muslim' elections to questions of gender roles and intra-Muslim co-operation within diaspora.

It would be dangerous, however, to get carried away by these apparent trans-sectarian trends, for there are still significant forces militating against intra-Muslim discourse. Many Muslims still know that the pressures for greater 'unity' are – as we have already mentioned – often nothing more than demands for greater 'uniformity'. Ever wary of this predicament, independent-thinking Muslims often have difficulty finding like-minded peers, preferring instead to go it alone.[122] For them, safety in individuality is more important than safety in numbers. And there are always those schools of thought and mosques which simply refuse to come out of their shells. But many Muslims *are* reconciling themselves to Islam's heterogeneity and seeking dialogue with other traditions. They realise that this internal diversity can only be a good thing, and that it in no way threatens the integrity of Islam; rather, they see it as an intrinsic part of their religion. A conversation recently overheard in a mosque demonstrates this: 'Look, Islam is the hand, and every finger is a part of that hand. But every finger is different. It wouldn't be a hand if it didn't have five fingers, all different'. There is a hadith in which the Prophet reassures his followers that *ikhtilāf al-umma raḥma*: 'differences of opinion in the community are a blessing'. An appreciation of this ikhtilaf (diversity) is crucial for the development of diasporic Islam. The signs are that many Muslims are realising its importance. As the leadership of the diaspora passes to the next generation, all signs are that a greater sense of unity will emerge among young Muslims;[123] but this will be a unity based on difference, an awareness that it is only through recognising plurality within that Islam can adapt to life in diaspora. Encounters and debates with the Muslim other have hence played a central role in defining Islam's political agenda. In this sense the condition of diaspora can actually contribute towards the development of critical thinking in Islam. Critiques not only of the West, but also – and more importantly – of Islam itself. In diaspora Muslims face new questions, and these require new answers. There is hence an intrinsic link between the shifting meanings of travelling Islam, the rise of a new generation, intra-Islamic debate and the renewal of Muslim theories on religion, politics and community.

Rethinking Islam: politics, community, gender

In this section I want to review a series of Muslim discourses related to the nature of politics, the boundaries of community and constructions of gender. I will argue that the renewal and reformulation of such notions is contributing to the emergence of something like a 'Muslim public sphere'. I also want to demonstrate that the condition of diaspora has provided the primary impetus for this innovative thinking. Increasingly today, translocal spaces are enabling and encouraging the articulation of a new critical Islam.

Towards a critical Islam

A new breed of Islamic intellectual, often schooled and living in the West, is staking strong claims to the Muslim's right to reflect upon tradition, and to make moral choices based on responsible and rational readings of Islam's textual sources. Shabbir Akhtar, for example, quotes Qur'anic verses forbidding compulsion in religion and enjoining confessional tolerance. For him these suggest 'a specifically Islamic manifesto on freedom of conscience and convic tion'.[124] For such thinkers, one's life in the West is therefore not to be lamented but rather embraced, offering as it does the opportunity to re-read, reassess and re-assert the validity of Qur'anic teaching in new contexts.[125] In this regard we might recall al-Faruqi's celebration of hijra 'to the West', or the Meccan 'alim who pointed to the obligation a Muslim has to seek knowledge and religion wherever it might take him. Indeed there are those, such as Zaki Badawi, who firmly believe that it is from Muslim contexts in the West that the most radical and innovative Islamic thought will emerge.[126] He sees France as potentially very fertile in this regard because it is there that Muslims face the greatest diffi- culties. These challenges, he hypothesises, will produce the most creative solutions.[127]

Another phenomenon closely related to life in diaspora is the way in which the traditional ulama are increasingly finding themselves bypassed in favour of, for instance, Muslim youth workers, in the search for religious knowledge. We saw this in the case of Dilwar Hussain, who explained that by asking questions in the mosque he seemed only to inflame the tempers of impatient, doctrinally rigid imams. In the Young Muslims UK, however, he found a leadership willing to devote the time and effort necessary to answer questions and show young Muslims how their religion is relevant to contemporary life in the West.[128] Some writers have depicted the traditional religious scholars as purveyors of an internal hegemony, an ahistorical reading of the sources which seeks to posit an essential, immutable Islam. 'They all profess to be upholding the essence of Islam', argues James Piscatori, 'yet in fact all are reinterpreting doctrine. They establish new, supposedly fixed points while denying that shifts of emphasis, nuance or meaning also occur'.[129] Thus we find Shabbir Akhtar arguing for an explicit 'critical Qur'anic scholarship' and also for 'a new theology, responsive to the intellectual pressures and assumptions of a sceptical age'.[130]

Many contemporary thinkers urge Muslims to go back to the sources and read for themselves, exercising good judgement and trusting in their own personal opinions as to what the texts mean for Islam today. Fazlur Rahman, for example, argues that Muslims should read the Qur'an and the *hadith* without relying on bulky, medieval commentaries. His claim is that these sources 'were misconstrued by Muslim scholars in medieval times, made into rigid and inflex- ible guides – for all time, as it were – and not recognised as the products of their own times and circumstances'.[131] Another prominent religious scholar urges young Muslims in the West to undertake 'a fresh study of the Qur'an...not with the aid of commentaries but with the depths of your hearts and minds...You should read it as if it were not an old scripture but one sent down for the present age, or, rather, *one that is being revealed to you directly*'.[132] Young Muslims are hence told to imagine themselves as Muhammad (a controversial proposition in itself), and to recognise that just as the Qur'an was revealed to the Prophet in a partic- ular setting in space and time, so must its message be made to speak to the particular circumstances of diasporic life.

There are indications that this call is being heeded. Young Muslims in the West often meet informally to discuss the Qur'an and other textual sources, attempting to read them anew and 'without the intervention of centuries of Islamic scholarship'. Schooled in a tradition that teaches them not just to blindly accept but to ask questions, young Muslims are deploying this inquisitiveness on the early texts in order to find in them the contours of an Islam for the here and now.[133] There is hence no reluctance to delve into the usul al-fiqh, but there has been a shift in what Muslims are hoping to find there. Gone is the obsession with the somatics of prayer and correct bodily practice. The emphasis now is on wider questions concerning Muslim identity and relations between Muslims and non-Muslims.[134] Also less frequent now are intersectarian debates on points of fiqh. Some organisations, such as Young Muslims UK, have decided that one's choice of *madhhab* or school of thought should be a personal choice. Where the organisation needs to take a public position on some issue, however, this is decided by a process of shura (consultation) in which the views of various *madhāhib* (plural of madhhab) are considered. Again, this ethos reflects the style of education which many young diasporic Muslims have received. Reflection and comparison allows them to develop their own responses to the situations and challenges of life in the West; through this activity they are able to develop an emancipatory theology that 'allow[s] them to be European without breaking with Islam'.[135] This amounts to a strong reassertion of the principle and practice of ijtihad ('free thinking')[136] as a competence possessed by all Muslims and not simply an elite (albeit socially detached) group of ulama. For many young Muslims today, a legitimate promulgator of ijtihad is anyone who speaks to a particular question or cause with morality, perspicacity and insight. The status of *'alim* is hence no longer a prerequisite for being recognised as a valid source of Islamic authority. One interviewee, for example, told me that he regarded someone like the Tunisian Islamist Rashid Ghannoushi – who has recently written extensively on the compatibility of Islam with Western doctrines of democracy and civil society – as far more qualified to practice ijtihad on the topic of politics than, say, an Azhar-trained 'alim.[137] Pnina Werbner notes how:

> For a younger generation of [Muslims] growing up in Britain the definition of what Islam is and means may well come to be increasingly constituted not by the Qur'an and Hadith, but by dissenting political ideologies…[Their] texts increasingly fuse a multicultural rhetoric of antiracism and equal opportunity with the ethical edicts of the Qur'an and Hadith.[138]

Fischer and Abedi's conversation with an American Muslim confirms this point in a more lucid vernacular:

> I don't go out and say, 'Everybody come to the mosque.' I don't do that anymore, because the mosque is not what people need. People need to know how to feed themselves. People need to know how to survive. People need to

know their class interests. And the application of Islam as something that comes out of the mouths of the imams is not doing that.[139]

Young Muslims today are hence seeking to create an Islam that addresses the social predicaments and daily experience of life in the modern West. They have neither the time nor the patience for South Asian idioms of Islam from the last century. These traditions, as Phillip Lewis notes, were 'honed in conflict with British hegemony, ranging from accommodation to isolation and defiance. The need now is for a critical and constructive exchange both within these traditions and with the majority society'.[140]

It is in the cosmopolitan, translocal spaces of cities such as London and Bradford that this kind of exchange is taking place. The myriad range of cultures, ideas and people that flow through these spaces produces rich sites of hybridised intellectual activity. The syncretisms and interminglings which inhabit these cities also constitute the cutting edge of critical Islam – and also, occasionally, the edge that cuts too deep. It is no coincidence that Salman Rushdie's now infamous novel of translocal hybridity, *The Satanic Verses*, is set in the British capital. London's status today as a global city – in many ways even a gateway to the world or nodal point for cross-cultural transit – ensures constant cultural intercourse on an unprecedented scale. It is also an environment in which such conversations can be openly expressed, assessed and reformulated. In this sense, Western translocal space stands in stark contrast to the situation in many Muslim majority states where the capacity to stray publicly from officially-prescribed doctrine is heavily circumscribed. Western translocalities, on the other hand, offer the aspiring Muslim intellectual the opportunity both to *express* and *encounter* alternative readings of Islam. It is not surprising, therefore, that so many exiled and diasporic Muslim activist-intellectuals choose to make their homes in the global city.[141] This fact stands in stark opposition to a statement by Dominique Schnapper to the effect that 'Muslim intellectuals in Europe are faced with the task of setting the terms of necessary compromise between faith and participation in communal life'.[142] On the contrary, it is often more likely that a Muslim would have to live with such a compromise in Saudi Arabia than in London. Schnapper also invokes the concept of *ḍarūra* ('imperative need') to explain how medieval scholars used to find it possible 'by learned and subtle argument' to legitimise transgressing the boundaries of doctrinal prescription under circumstances of absolute need, and these were often associated with a Muslim's presence in a non-Muslim state.[143] Her implication seems to be that Muslims in Western Europe may need to resurrect that principle today. (Perhaps she is even suggesting that such drastic measures constitute the *only* means by which the Qur'an can 'travel'?) I would want to argue, however, that the evocation of darura by many of today's diasporic Muslims took place well before their 'hijra to the West'. Indeed, I would suggest that for them, the departure from their societies of origin was itself seen as an act of darura because in many cases the West provides them with the best possibility of fulfilling the

Qur'anic injunction against compulsion in religion. Not only are they able to speak their religion more freely in diaspora, but it is also here that they come to know the Muslim 'other'. Dialogue, self-reflection and, gradually, *critique* all flow from this process. As a collective exercise, we are witnessing the deconstruction of Islam by Muslims themselves:

> The old way has to be analysed into discrete parts so that Islam can be identified...one [then] proceeds to 'reassemble' these Islamic components together with the components arising out of the migration and settlement experience into a new complex whole which functions more successfully in European, urban, industrial life.[144]

A new perspective emerges in which a Muslim is able to see his religion both in relation to the norms and structures of the majority society *and* in relation to other idioms and interpretations of Islam. It is as a result of this wider breadth of vision that a critical renewal of Islam is now beginning to emerge. It is therefore not simply a case of bringing one's Islam into translocality, for the very act of doing so necessarily involves a relativisation of Islam – an act which, by questioning the parameters of normativity in Islam, becomes inherently *political*.

Reformulating politics and community

Not only is this new Muslim discourse political in nature, but one of its chief concerns is explicitly to rethink Islamic conceptions of politics and political community. A major impetus for much of this thinking has been the minority status of Muslims in diaspora. This condition has led Muslims to enquire as to the nature of the Islamic self – especially as regards its position *vis-à-vis* non-Muslims. In the early years of migratory settlement, Islam was very much about drawing an 'othering' line, about marking oneself off as different and also somehow 'apart' or disengaged – almost as if the Muslim was blind to the non-Muslim other. The new generation of Muslims also wants to represent difference, but most certainly does not want to advocate any form of *exclusion*. In this sense, diasporic Islam is very much about the reformulation of Muslim political identity. The social reality of large numbers of Muslims living within non-Muslim majority societies has prompted some theorists to rethink the categories through which identity and community are represented in Islam. 'The whole notion of "the other" in Islamic theology is changing', says Dilwar Hussain. 'We live side by side now, in each other's domains. Islam is in the West and the West is in Islam'.[145]

Classical Islamic thought created an essential dichotomy between two ontological spheres: *dār al-islām* (the domain of Islam) and *dār al-ḥarb* (the domain of strife or war). Traditionally, the former refers to those regions in which the principles of Islam are upheld under the rule of a Muslim sovereign. The latter, on the other hand, 'is that which is not [under Muslim rule], but which, actually or potentially, is a seat of war for Muslims until by conquest it is turned into [dar al-islam]'.[146] Hence there is an essential element of antagonism between these two abodes, for dar al-harb represents a space in which Muslims, at least in theory, are in conflict with non-Muslims. Dar al-harb therefore does not represent a country or people to which Muslims are simply indifferent, but rather one which Islam is actively seeking to steer towards the Straight Path. There are also some madhahib which recognise a third such classification, that of *dār al-'ahd* (the domain of treaty). This represents a region in which Muslims and non-Muslims have entered into some form of agreement as regards the conduct of relations between them, usually to the greater benefit of the Muslims by way of a tributary tax exacted from non-Muslim communities. This latter category, however, has not appeared in Muslim writing with anything like the frequency of the first two.

It is not surprising that these terms have been deployed most frequently during times of perceived conflict between Muslims and non-Muslims. The colonial era marked one such period. The notion that the West was somehow a land of unbelief which might one day be brought under Islamic rule found particular resonance in the colonised imaginations of the Middle East, India and Southeast Asia. At that time it was perhaps one of the clearest Manichean expressions of the global situation. There was clearly an 'us' (those Muslims ruled by colonial Europe) and also a 'them' (the colonising powers who would themselves one day be subject to Muslim rule), dar al-islam, dar al-harb. Such notions also exercised the minds of Muslim political theorists in the early years of decolonisation, forming the basis of programmes such as Sayyid Qutb's (see Chapter Two) – seeking to depict the depravity and corruption of the West.

Although many of the more radical Islamist tendencies today (such as Hizb ut-Tahrir and al-Muhajiroun) still use this vocabulary in its traditional idiom, there is also a sense in which we can argue that concepts such as dar al-harb and dar al-islam are currently undergoing certain transformations. Broadly, this rethinking of political community is taking two forms. First, there are those Muslim thinkers seeking to apply the label dar al-harb to their own Muslim majority states. The argument here is that none of these governments is 'truly Islamic' and hence cannot be seen as dar al-islam. Classical Islamic law requires Muslims to depart from any Islamic state which lapses into dar al-harb; hence the connection with diaspora. Many of the political activists who criticise their governments in this manner end up as exiles in London or Paris. The Islamic opposition in the Arabian Peninsula is a prime example of this trend. The second way in which these categories are changing relates to the reformulation of dar al-islam. There are those theorists who wish to claim that the only requirement for a country to qualify as dar al-islam is that Muslims must be allowed to practise their religion with complete freedom. Some writers also emphasise the extent to which Muslims are actually more often able to fulfil the scriptural obligations of their religion in the West than they are in their own countries.[147] There have even been those who have suggested that because there is no such thing as a true dar al-islam then there is also no such thing as dar al-harb because they are necessarily always defined in opposition to each other; without one, the other does not exist.[148] Admittedly, those thinkers willing to view the West as dar al-islam are still a very small (but growing) minority; often they are accused by both the more extremist tendencies and the mainstream of having become too 'Westernised'. There is evidence, however, that even the adherents of mainstream orthodoxy are starting to rethink political community in Islam.

At a recent seminar in France a group of ulama came together to discuss the problems faced by Muslims living in Europe. Many of them had had first hand experience of life in the West, and were also well regarded in the Muslim world.

> The seminar discussed several issues, one being the issue of nationality and citizenship. They found that Muslims living in a non-Muslim majority country could no longer be classified as living in the House of War or *Dar al-Harb*. These terms, they decided, do not convey the contemporary realities…The *Ulama* made it clear that in the contemporary situation, 'we cannot classify non-Muslim nations as the abode of war'. They are, in their view, *Dar al-Ahad* or the 'Abode of Treaties'.[149]

So although the West has not been deemed a domain of Islam, it has at least been 'officially' upgraded to dar al-'ahd. If we elaborate this shift in thinking, however, we can see that it has some very serious implications for the ways in which diasporic Muslims go about their politics. Jacques Waardenburg refers to a 'New Islamic Discourse' emphasising active participation in community life rather than the political introversion which characterised the early phase of Muslim immigration and settlement. Muslims will no longer hold themselves apart from the majority society but *will* continue to distinguish themselves from it by offering an alternative order, Islam. These claims are to be seen as addressed both to state authorities and to society at large.[150] 'The Muslim community in Europe is searching for a new idiom through which to express itself', says Ataullah Siddiqui.[151] This takes the form of seeking a recognised and legitimate place in the public sphere. We can best understand this shift in Muslim political thought by viewing it as a response to the condition of diaspora, and as an inversion of yet another category of classical Islamic political thought, that of the dhimma. This term refers to non-Muslims (and usually ahl al-kitab: 'people of the book', meaning Christians and Jews) living under the protection of a Muslim ruler in a Muslim majority state. In the European Muslim diaspora, however, the situation is reversed. Muslims are now in some sense the dhimma. I want to argue that the emphasis on 'community building' and 'political conscience' that marks the new Islamic discourse must be seen in the context of this new minority position.

Muslims are hence constructing new frameworks for the practice of Islamic politics in response to the condition of diaspora. These constitute new strategies and are not simply replicas of community in the societies of origin.[152] But what do these new strategies imply? What do they mean in the context of the transition from Europe as dar al-harb to Europe as dar al-'ahd? My claim is that this shift represents a new Muslim disposition towards political engagement and the emergence of an 'active' approach to the theory and practice of Muslim politics in the public sphere. The difference also affects, as Ataullah Siddiqui points out, one's 'whole perception of living. *Dar al-Harb* suggests temporality, otherness, and a sense of compulsion. *Dar al-Ahad* suggests participation, belonging and responsibility'.[153] This is also therefore a new discourse on Muslim political community (see Chapter One). Some, such as Jocelyn Cesari, argue that through the new associations formed by young Muslims in France, 'a new form of citizenship is emerging, [one that refers] to concrete and local action rather than voting or involvement with political parties. In other words, the *civil* dimension seems to be more relevant than the *civic* one'.[154]

We also find here a blurring of the distinction between public and private, as discussed in Chapter One. These forms of Muslim political activism can, in some senses, be seen to constitute a movement of religion from the private into the public sphere. 'Islam', as Cesari argues, 'cannot be confined to the mosque and to the realm of the private as Catholicism has been'.[155] There is hence a confusion, she claims, on the frontier between public and private. Mosques can be seen as an institution on the border between these two realms, as attempts to 'set up small sections of Islamic civil society which overflow into urban [public] space'.[156] As Pnina Werbner notes:

> [U]rban mosques in Britain are centres of communal affairs, drawing labour migrants-turned-immigrants and sojourners into communal activities. The mosque is the base for teaching collective discipline, organization, and internal fund raising, the springboard for regional and national political alliances, and a training ground in polemics and adversary politics. Mosques link town and country and constitute public arenas for political debate. Many of the lay speakers are self-employed businessmen who, as recent immigrants, are excluded from other public spheres.[157]

Werbner also points out that the various discourses heard in these mosques – including those of the Sufi orders – do not confine themselves to 'religious' (i.e. private) issues. Contemporary political issues of the day, such as racism and the distortion of Islam by the media, are hotly debated, responses planned and action co-ordinated.[158] In many ways this has been the case with the mosque down through the ages, even in the time of the Prophet when the mosque delineated a space in which Muhammad's nascent umma – the first Muslim diaspora – could assess and respond to the predicaments of minority life in Medina.

Many young Muslims would hence like to see Islam as something political (i.e. as a mode of contesting authority – see Chapter One), but not necessarily as 'Political Islam', in the sense of extremism or fundamentalism. For them, an Islam confined to the realm of private ritual is irrelevant in the modern West. 'This is not reality', says one young Muslim, 'we cannot sit and *dhikr* [the praising of Allah through ritual recitation] for like three hours and expect to help the community'.[159] Well aware of this fact, Dilwar Hussain is trying to reassert aspects of Islamic thought in a contemporary light. His research focuses on the notion of *maṣlaḥa* ('public interest'), seeking to reframe this concept as an important feature of contemporary Muslim life. The great medieval theologian al-Ghazali once claimed that maslaha was the end goal of the entire body of shari'a (holy law); Hussain believes this to be particularly true today. For him an emphasis on public interest means that the question of whether a particular practice should or should not be permitted needs to be viewed in the context of its effect on the entire community rather than simply deemed halal or *ḥaram* ('forbidden') by an 'alim with his nose buried in a collection of *fatawa* (religious edicts) from the tenth century. 'This is particularly relevant in cases where Muslims are living in circumstances where the situations of daily life are not covered clearly by the texts', he argues. 'When things are changing so quickly, one cannot rely exclusively on analogical deduction (*qiyās*) from the sources...[so] we need to find a new flexibility when dealing with juridical issues'.[160] Hussain wants to invert the classical conception of *maslaḥa*, which sees it primarily as a means of 'closing the gates to evil', and to concentrate instead on maslaha refigured as 'opening the gates to good'. 'For example', he says, 'there's the idea of opening the gates for women to play a role in public, and seeing this as a "good", as something in the public interest: *maslaḥa*'. The question arises, however, as to who holds the keys to these gates – a question to which Hussain, as yet, has no answer. 'That's what I'm working on now', he says optimistically.

We see, then, the importance that Muslims today are laying on re-reading and reassessing the textual sources of Islam in new contexts. There is a particular imperative here in the realm of political theory and community. Plurality is of the essence, according to many thinkers today. They highlight the need for Muslims to increase their '*umma* consciousness', and are developing 'a more open understanding of the notion of the global community of Muslims than many commentators – Muslim and non-Muslim alike – have heretofore proposed'.[161] In the Qur'an, Allah reminds Muslims that had he wanted to he could have made them one, but instead created many nations and peoples so that they might get to know each other.[162] This injunction to 'know the other' is at the root of much contemporary thought on cultural pluralism in the umma. As Anwar Ibrahim, one of the most progressive thinkers in this area, argues:

> Recapturing the meaning of [the *umma*] would necessitate that Muslims engage with other people, nations, worldviews, religions and ideologies to work for a set of moral objectives that we can and must define together. But it takes us much further. It requires that we respect the *Umma* of other people...the history of the *Umma* has shown exemplary, almost unique models of multiracial, multicultural, multireligious, pluralist societies. If ever we had the need of recovering such an imperative, it is now.[163]

In this regard there would appear to be some degree of discursive overlap between a new umma consciousness and recent thinking in Western critical theory. The notion of dialogue and some form of 'communicative action' (informed by tradition) within a 'public sphere' seem to be intrinsic to both.[164] Several Muslim writers have already embarked on this kind of dialogue, offering theoretically sophisticated treatments of postmodernity and its relationship to Islam.[165]

Gender, Islam and diaspora

Another common concern for modern Muslim and Western social theory is gender. In Islam, gender represents yet another area where the influence and efficacy of traditional authority and practice appear to be waning. Today more Muslim women than ever before are to be found in the public spheres of diaspora – in places of work and in higher education. 'Most Muslim women are educated in a Western tradition which makes few concessions to Islam, and increasing numbers are working outside the home, exposed to non-related males and thereby transgressing gender norms'.[166] To some extent this is a reflection of a socioeconomic environment in which families have found it increasingly necessary to have wives and daughters enter employment in order to supplement their incomes. Some local authorities in the UK and other countries have responded to this changing climate by offering single-sex job-training schemes. Even some distinctly 'Muslim' forums, such as the innovative magazine *Q-News*, now have a mainly female staff. In other cases, modifications to immigration policies have worked to the benefit of young women. Phillip Lewis explains, for example, how a woman with a regular income and house in her name finds it more easy to 'import' a fiancé into the UK from South Asia   and this provides a rationale for 'unwomanly' behaviour that her parents' generation will find satisfactory.[167]

More and more Muslim women, another analyst suggests, seem to be taking Islam into their own hands. They are not hesitating to question, criticise and even reject the Islam of their parents. Often this takes the form of drawing distinctions between *culture*, understood as the oppressive tendencies which derive from the parents' ethnosocial background, and *religion*, a 'true' Islam untainted by either culture or gender discrimination.[168] Young Muslim women are hence often more religiously self-conscious than their mothers or grandmothers, seeing in Islam a 'progressive' force which allows them to move away from their increasingly unfamiliar South Asian roots, but at the same time also to avoid submission to Western cultural norms. 'Dress codes, methods of arranging marriages, gender-roles are, in these circumstances, losing their importance as symbols of Islam', argues Jørgen Nielsen. 'The emphasis appears to be changing towards the underlying values of ethical and spiritual principles'.[169] In this sense Muslim women in diaspora are starting to formulate their own Islam.

Members of the Al-Nisa women's group in London and grassroots organisations in Bradford, Birmingham and other places, spend hours every week analysing the kind of Islam that would help to empower them instead of limiting their capacities. They talk openly and passionately about contraception, abortion, adoption, rape, the education of their children, how men can be better fathers and husbands, geopolitical changes and ecological problems.[170]

In some cases diasporic Muslim women are engaging in such discussions in spaces with an even higher public profile. Nico Landman notes how the presence of an Islamic broadcasting organisation in The Netherlands has been a major influence in raising the visibility of 'headscarved and very self-confident and emancipated Muslim women in the Dutch media' in recent years.[171]

Women are also being taught Islam in school. Here they are equipped with the intellectual tools necessary for critiquing Islam and all those who speak in its name. 'This poses uncomfortable questions for the custodians of the Islamic tradition' writes Phillip Lewis. The ulama, an all-male institution, are now facing large numbers of young Muslim women no longer prepared to have Islam dictated to them. Many feel that for too long women have followed Islam blindly, never daring to ask questions; reading and theorising, certainly, but never articulating. This, however, is changing.

> You're allowed to ask questions. [Allah] made us with the ability to be curious about things, so we should. But that fear [of asking] – and I had that fear, too – will keep your mouth closed. You'll just do it. And I grew out of that. I started asking questions, because, logically, you know, Allah knows what's in your heart. He knows what's in your mind, so why be a hypocrite?[172]

More than simply questioning, many Muslim women in the West – or at least those that have passed through its places of learning – are seeking to re-interpret Islam for themselves. Beyond just doubting, they are actively going to the sources, especially the Qur'an and the hadith, in order to discover the 'Muslim woman' for themselves. It has been suggested by a number of writers – Muslim and non-Muslim, male and female – that the Medina of the Prophet Muhammad was actually an environment in which the women of Arabia could flourish as never before, enjoying unprecedented freedoms and rights. It was the codification of Islamic law, after the death of the Prophet, that most likely put an end to this liberal climate.[173] Today's Muslim feminists therefore return to the earliest sources in order to read back into Islamic history a veritable women's revolution that has so conveniently been forgotten. Such effort has produced one of the most fascinating pieces of Islamic historiography to be published in recent years, Fatima Mernissi's *Women and Islam*. In this book Mernissi, a Moroccan sociologist, undertakes a rereading of several volumes of hadith, Qur'anic commentary (*tafsīr*) and the biographies of Muhammad (*sīra*) in order to piece together an image of early Medina, 'when women had their place as unquestioned partners in a revolution that made the mosque an open place and the household a temple of debate'.[174] In another disruption of established Islamic order, the Pakistani academic Riffat Hassan has sought to question the very methodologies which underpin the collection, classification and confirmation of the Prophet's hadith.

> She concludes that traditional Hadith criticism, which focused on a study of the reliability of the transmitters and the chain of transmission to establish their authenticity and reliability – *isnad* criticism – needs to be supplemented with criticism of their content, *matn*, to ascertain whether such are in conformity with Qur'anic teachings.[175]

Furthermore, it is not only the medieval scholastic tradition which has come in for criticism by Muslim feminists. Self-avowedly 'modern' movements such as the Jama'at-i Islam have recently been reproached for their 'un-Islamic chauvinism'.[176] The Jama'at often promulgates a very stereotypical ideal of feminine virtue in which the woman is assigned a particular space, the domestic realm, and her role therein glorified. The politics so central to their Islamist programme is still very much only within the purview of men.

A modern movement which does not seem to make so strong a distinction between the roles and competence of men and women is the Tablighi Jama'at – a group we touched upon very briefly in the first chapter. The Tablighi movement is a transnational, 'apolitical' network for religious propagation whose core mode of operation involves despatching 'missionary tours' to travel to wherever Muslims are to be found in order to encourage greater religious devotion and observance. Associated with the Deobandi school of thought, it is a group that works almost exclusively *within* the Muslim community. The conversion of non-Muslims is hence not its aim. Although its origins lie in the Indian subcontinent, the Tablighi Jama'at is globally active with a large European headquarters complex in Dewsbury, Yorkshire.

The Tablighi Jama'at attitude towards women, suggests Barbara Metcalf, may be somehow tied to the way in which it conceives or, rather does *not* conceive its ideas about politics:

> I would argue that the reason political Islamic movements (such as the Jama'at-i Islami in Pakistan) emphasise women's domestic roles, in contrast to the Tablighis Jama'at, is due to the distinctive status accorded to women's roles and feminine nature in the discourse of modern nationalist politics and its accompanying notions of the private and public realms. Jama'at-i Islami is a movement forged in the context of the institutions of the nation-state, which examines and reconfigures Islam to adapt to the principles of a social order mandated by modern national politics.[177]

The Tablighi Jama'at, on the other hand, stands largely outside the order imposed by the nation-state system. Through its focus on missionary travel, the movement primarily inhabits translocal space. 'The Tablighis, in terms of rhetoric and cosmopolitan membership', write Eickelman and Piscatori, 'direct followers toward the pan-Islamic *umma*'.[178] It has no interest in participating in or even heeding national politics. For Tablighis, one does not reform society through political activity, but rather through concentrating on producing moral individuals. For the Tablighi Jama'at, 'political inclinations are not entombed in the Qur'an but are rather daily reshaped by judgements about who is most likely to provide justice and development'.[179] Although the group shuns political activity of any kind, its fervent apoliticism becomes, in a sense, a form of (anti)politics. As Dassetto observes:

> [T]he very radicalism of their faith and their methods of reference are powerful elements in a critique of political systems, particularly those defining themselves as Islamic. Everything suggests that the Tablighs, far removed from power by virtue of their position in society, instead of attaching themselves to it engage in challenging its legitimacy. They go to the heart of the problem of power in 'Muslim' countries without touching it.[180]

In this regard other modern Muslim movements, particularly those who are politically active, have difficulty making sense of the Tablighi Jama'at. Their quietism is often dismissed as devotional obsession – an other-worldly disengagement with the world. Indeed, many young Muslims in the West question the group's staying power given its seeming reluctance to engage with the political imperatives facing young diasporic Muslims today. However, I want to argue that there are senses in which the Tablighis Jama'at can be read as a movement or tendency whose practices challenge received notions of space and power in Islam – particularly as regards gender. These innovations, however, relate not so much to new things that women do, but rather to what Tablighis men do that most other Muslim men do *not* do.

Although Tablighis women do occasionally travel, the vast majority of the group's *da'wā* ('missionary') activities are undertaken by men. There are a number of interesting points to be made about the nature and style of this travelling. First of all, Tablighis men 'devalue the public realm' by pointedly avoiding politics. They hence do not claim any particular position or space of masculine power or virtue. At times Tablighis men have come in for criticism from other Muslims because their frequent sojourning is seen as a neglect of the masculine duty to protect and care for the family. The Tablighis style of discourse and inter-personal communication is also very simple and humble. While travelling the men are all expected to acquire a strong set of domestic skills. They wash clothes, cook, clean and maintain the integrity of the group – roles usually associated with women. Other aspects of Tablighis Jama'at discourse also seem to contribute to a reconfiguration of gender roles:

> A talk given at an annual Tabligh meeting, for example, reminded men that women also had a responsibility to Tablighi, and that men should not only refrain from objecting but should actively facilitate women's participation by providing child care. The speaker reminded his audience that since the Prophet had said that women have the right to refuse to nurse should they

want to, women certainly could decline to provide child care for a task so important as Tablighi.[181]

Thus there do appear to be certain ways in which Tablighiis practices contribute to a reconfiguration of gender roles in Islam. At the same time, however, the group's reluctance to bring its views into the public sphere mitigates against their wider propagation. Similarly, Tablighis Jama'at's translocal character does much to widen the boundaries of political community in Islam, yet their refusal to speak this translocality in political terms raises questions as to the group's continued efficacy. Its numbers, however, continue to grow. Perhaps there is in this model of the 'mobile madrasa'[182] a new idiom of (anti-)politics or a discrepant translocality – one in which the gendered notions of public and private are gradually being eroded.

'Long distance' Islam

In this final section I want to briefly examine some of the translocal aspects of diasporic Islam. Travelling Islam, as I understand it, does not simply depart from a 'point of origin', arrive in diaspora and then settle permanently, but rather continues to flow across a range of transnational networks. It is also mediated by various 'distanciated' political actors seeking to establish translocal constituencies for the furthering of their own aims and interests. Finally, we will also need to say something about the 'trip home' – that is, about what happens when expatriot Muslims bring reformulated idioms of Islam back to their societies of origin.

We can meaningfully speak today about the existence of something like a global infrastructure for the maintenance, reproduction and dissemination of Islam. This 'regime' possesses no central authority and there is very little co-ordination between its various constitutive elements. Nevertheless, through a diverse range of organisations, technologies and transnational structures the contours of a translocal Islam are beginning to emerge. We have already mentioned several of the institutions which collectively form this infrastructure such as the 'imported imams' who travel back and forth between homeland and diaspora, and the myriad regional and transregional Muslim organisations which mediate daily life for believers in a variety of national settings. In addition, we can also point to the role played by various communication and information technologies, from the circulation of a wide range of English-language books on Islam via international publishing networks linking Washington, DC with Durban, London and Karachi,[183] to cyberspace debates between Muslims and madhahib in Internet chat rooms. Diaspora television programmes also play a role in the sustenance of long distance communal and religious ties,[184] as does the live broadcast of the hajj in many Muslim countries and its subsequent availability on video.[185] A more in-depth analysis of some of these media forms will be undertaken in Chapter Five.

Migratory spaces and global cities also figure heavily in translocal Islam. With their culturally diverse and highly mobile populations, cities such as

London are important nodal points for travelling theories and often serve as factories for the production and import/export of (reformulated) ideology. As Adam Lebor puts it, 'Positioned halfway between the Middle East and the United States, with easy access to Europe, the hub of a global communications network, and with decade-old ties to Islam's lands, London has now become the *de facto* intellectual capital of the Middle East'.[186] It is therefore not surprising that a number of transnational movements have chosen to set up shop in diaspora. We can think here of the Tablighis Jama'at, an eminently translocal organisation, whose European 'headquarters' in Dewsbury co-ordinates and despatches missionary tours to destinations all around the world. Travelling Tablighis of many ethno-national backgrounds – although mainly from the Indian subcontinent – pass through the centre on their way to Canada, Malaysia, South Africa and Mecca. As Barbara Metcalf observes, 'Dewsbury...looks more like Pakistan than does Pakistan itself. In Tabligh participants are part of this contemporary world of movement even as they transcend cultural pluralism by the re-lived Medina their actions create'.[187] It is in groups such as the Tablighis Jama'at – a movement both translocal and post-national – that the umma, in the sense of a community of believers unhindered by geographical or national boundaries, finds its truest expression in Islam today. In terms of politics, the Tablighis dwell in a translocality that challenges the spatial confines of political community. More crucially, however, they advocate an understanding of the political which in many ways seems to resonate with Warren Magnusson's vision of 'global popular politics' (see Chapter One). Theirs is, in essence, an inverse normative model in which the good does not emanate from an ethical institution (i.e. the state) but rather from an emphasis on the collective power of the ethical 'self'.

There are also many Muslim organisations with more familiar institutional frameworks, such as the transnational Muslim World League (MWL); many of them have their own state sponsors such as Saudi Arabia, and often maintain offices in a number of regions with large Muslim populations, including Europe. We also find innumerable 'local' or country-specific associations devoted to providing services for Muslims in particular national settings. These various types of Muslim organisation engage in a range of activities from securing the provision of halal meat at the neighbourhood level to the encouragement of high national standards in the teaching and practice of Islam. The 'normative' character of many of these groups often gives rise to a politics of authenticity centred around debates about who and what constitutes 'real' Islam. Van Bommel reports an incident that took place in Belgium in 1974, when a delega-tion of Muslims from The Netherlands arrived in Brussels at the Benelux offices of the Muslim World League in order to invite a speaker from the League to address Muslims in Holland. The imam-director of the centre, however, had been under the impression that all Muslims in The Netherlands were somehow connected to the Ahmadiyya sect, a group viewed as heretical by many Sunni Muslims. 'Even though the delegation explained all about the true composition of the Muslim population in The Netherlands', writes van Bommel, 'both the centre in Brussels and the head office in Mecca remained blind to the needs of Muslims in Holland for several years more'.[188]

Certain state and state-run organisations have also played a 'watchdog' role over diasporic Islam. During the first attempt to establish a supra-national mosque in The Netherlands, for example, several Middle Eastern governments balked at providing financial support because they were unsure 'if the migrant communities were able to give a true representation of Islam'.[189] In a more 'proactive' approach, the Turkish state seeks to export its strict regulation of religious practice through an institution in Europe called the Turkish-Islamic Union for Religion (*Diyanat Islerli Türk Islam Birligi*). The Diyanat attempts to standardise and control Islamic education and also to administer various mosques. Although its stated aim is simply 'to care for the Turkish commu- nity…in all affairs related to the Islamic religion', the Diyanat can also be seen as an extension of the state's security apparatus in that it seeks to provide a buffer against Islamism in Turkey by mitigating some of the more radical tendencies abroad.[190] It is therefore not surprising that on a number of occa- sions and over a range of issues the Diyanat has locked horns with another Muslim organisation, *Milli Görüs*, the diasporic representatives of Turkey's Islamist *Refah* party (now defunct). This case provides a useful example of some of the ways in which states are being forced to respond to the non-territorial nature of translocal politics.

Governments are also wary of other transnational Islamist movements, many of whom have offices or operations in London. Indeed, there has been so much emphasis on radical Islam in the British capital of late that some '[have] even been prompted to talk of London being the base for a new "Fundamentalist International", a sort of Muslim Comintern'.[191] The Al- Mass'ari affair, during which the British government sought to deport a dissident Saudi Islamist in order to protect its trade interests in the Kingdom, was a particularly high-profile manifestation of this trend. Other attention has focused on 'charity groups' in the UK, such as Interpal, which have been accused of raising funds for Hamas and other militant groups abroad.[192] Muslim opposition leaders from Bahrain, Syria, Pakistan and Tunisia are all based in London. The most famous of these, Rashid Ghannoushi, the exiled leader of Tunisia's banned *Nahdha* (Renaissance) movement, is a key theoretical reference for many contemporary Muslim political thinkers. Positioned within translocality, Ghannoushi has made a number of key interventions in the debate on Islam and democracy, and, through the relatively intense media interest in his situation, managed to set the tenor of Islam's political agenda in diaspora and beyond.

On some occasions, Muslim states have actually sought to use translocal Islam to further their own political goals. The Rushdie Affair was a prime example of this. There is a sense in which this incident can be read as an instance of Saudi- Iranian rivalry, with each state engaging in a rhetoric of 'holier-than-thou'. Riyadh and Tehran have been competing for the religious high ground ever since Iran's Islamic Revolution in 1979. In this light, Khomeini's fatwa might be viewed as Iran's trump card, allowing Tehran to claim the strongest 'Islamic' response to Rushdie's novel. Saudi Arabia's reaction to *The Satanic Verses*, tempered by its close ties to the West, had mostly consisted of support for demonstrations and other protest activities in the UK channelled through the Jama'at-i Islami. Indeed, the initial impetus which eventually led to the Bradford protests and burning of the book did not come from Britain. Rather, the Leicester-based Islamic Foundation had contacted all of the UK's leading Muslim organisations only after the novel was brought to their attention by contacts in South Asia. 'The fervour of the British Muslim response', notes one analyst, 'can thus be explained in part, though certainly not wholly, by this competition between groups – Saudi, Iranian, and South Asian in inspiration – for the high ground.'[193] There is therefore a geopolitical dimension to the Rushdie Affair, a sense in which it has to be understood – at least to some degree – as the appropriation of translocal Islam (and its various networks) by political actors pursuing wider agendas. Yet this is not the geopolitics of neo-realist international relations. There is no clear 'level of analysis' here. The backstreets of Bradford, Khomeini's Tehran and various sub-, inter- and transregional Muslim organisations were all mutually constitutive of this episode. 'If the Rushdie affair has demonstrated anything', writes James Piscatori, 'it is that "international", while obviously not incorrect, is inadequate to explain the interconnected networks that are at work'.[194]

Finally, we come to the question of what happens when travelling Islam returns home. The 'repatriation' of Muslims, either temporarily during holidays or family visits, or more permanently after the expiration of short-term labour contracts or reverse immigration, constitutes a key dynamic of Islam's translocal infrastructure. Once again, perceptions of religion shift. There are those who bring back with them a new conviction, the belief that the experience of diaspora has allowed them to discover 'real Islam'. For some this new certainty is the product of an extensive examination of both Islam and self in diaspora, an Islam reformulated through encounters with new ideas and conversations with the Muslim other. For others, the conviction is the result of a negative diasporic experience, one that has allowed the migrant to relativise his or her opinion of both Western culture and the society of origin. As one Turkish migrant in Turkey put it: 'I think that we, as Muslims in Europe, will in the end bring real Islam to Turkey. Only we as migrants have experienced into what kind of society the present leaders of Turkey are trying to change our homeland'.[195] But there are also those returning Muslims reassured at finding once again the familiar religious idioms of their home. This is particularly true for those forms of Islam which rely on symbols and sites that do not travel well. Landman has noticed this phenomenon in Holland's Moroccan migrants.

> During their holidays in Morocco they will attend the annual memorial days (*mawsim*) of deceased saints and visit their graves in order to obtain a blessing. Also they will visit living holy men in their country of origin, e.g.

when they suffer from illness and have more faith in the *baraka* [holy force] of a saint than in the skill of Dutch doctors.[196]

Thus migrants still look to their homelands and often, in some ways, understand their Islam best in relation to these societies. And what of these societies into which they re-enter? What do those who have remained at home think of their culture 'being defined and practised in novel and sometimes disturbing ways'?[197] They are undoubtedly told many stories; of strange places and strange Muslims, of new festivals and different *madhahib*, of other ways of reading and knowing Islam. Debates about authenticity inevitably ensue, and perhaps also arguments about the 'Westernisation' of Islam. For their own part, the returning migrants may see their home societies as backward – although they would be wrong in this, for all cultures travel even when they stay in the same place. Whether there is agreement or disagreement does not matter. Whatever the outcome, new ideas are digested and gradually incorporated into the discursive fields of the home society. 'The very elasticity of the diasporic tie', write Ahmed and Donnan, 'ensures the reciprocal redefinition of identity at both ends of the migratory chain as elements of culture rebound first this way and then that'.[198]

Other translocal Muslims see themselves as playing a role within the context of a much wider picture. For those who have developed something like Ibrahim's '*Umma* consciousness', travelling in Islam also means helping Islam to travel. 'Muslims in diaspora have a more global sense of Islam', says one 'alim, 'and hence have a role to play in the globalisation of the religion'.[199] This means articulating Islam in terms that non-Muslims can understand, but it also means rearticulating Islam to *Muslims* in new ways. In Indonesia, for example, the father of one of the most prominent female preachers (*muballigha*) Ibu Alfiyah Muhadie, spent twelve years in Mecca where he undoubtedly came into contact with modernist interpretations of Islam. Upon his return he began to disseminate these ideas in the local Islamic school, and was an important influence on his daughter who now works on projects which 'strive to empower women by preaching Islam in such a way that it can be turned into a motivational force toward economic development'.[200] Diaspora offers a unique context for the reassessment of theories, beliefs and traditions, while translocality enables these new reformulations to travel the world. For some Muslims this offers the greatest hope for rethinking Islam:

> In order to have *ijtihad* [independent judgement] you need freedom of thought. This does not exist in most Muslim countries. We Muslims in the West should debate, discuss and disseminate our ideas because this will encourage Muslims living where there is not freedom to do the same, or at least to make use of the materials and ideas we produce.[201]

In the time of translocality the Muslims of the diaspora thus have a vital role to play. It is they who are in the best position to engage in a sustained critical renewal of their religion, and it is also they who can most effectively speak this new Islam to the world.

Conclusion: fission and fusion in Muslim translocality

This chapter has covered considerable ground. In it, I have sought to provide something like a 'case study' of what happens to Islam when it travels – and particularly when it enters into and settles amongst non-Muslim societies in the West. My portrait of diasporic Islam has been created by combining three component themes, each of which illustrates a different aspect of the greater translocal whole: *debates within the Muslim community* reveal the nature of the Muslim other; politics, community and gender provide useful indications of some of the ways in which Muslims are *rethinking Islam*; and the section on *Muslim transnationalism* reminds us that these translocal diasporic reformulations can never be viewed in isolation from the rest of the world.

I realise that many of the apparent generalisations I have made throughout this chapter are quite specific to the particular Muslim contexts they inhabit. Nevertheless, I still believe them to be usefully illustrative of some wider trends. One consequence of translocality is that we become increasingly aware – if we were not already – that it is meaningless to speak of Islam in the sense of a single, monolithic, entity. By understanding how Islam travels we are also able to comprehend how those Muslim discourses labelled as 'fundamentalist' are, at least in part, a product of politics *within* Islam itself. Translocal and hybridising forces only serve to intensify these politics. 'But rather than being the manifestation of inherent tendencies within Islam', writes one pair of authors, 'such dispositions may instead be seen as the intersection of hegemonic Islamic discourses with common global processes, in relation to which processes many Islamic communities are similarly situated'.[202] This politics is the result of a tension within Islam. Muslims are having difficulty deciding whether globalising processes are culturally neutral – that is, something to which they can subscribe (and perhaps even something they can produce themselves) without seeing their norms and traditions diminished; or do they need to be wary of another agenda, of a set of global processes seeking ultimately to suppress and subvert their claims to difference?

> The Muslims are very confused; they don't know which way to go on this one. On the one hand globalisation seems to be opening up the possibility of the *umma* – previously a utopic category of political thought – becoming a *social reality*. Globalisation seems to resonate with the Qur'anic injunction to 'get to know one another'. Muslims like the technologies as well. But on the other hand, some aspects of it seem to be just another form of Western imperialism.[203]

Thus within the umma we see translocality producing two seemingly contrary effects. On the one hand a heavily dispersed community of believers is brought closer together, communication between them is enabled, and dwelling within what might be imagined as a single space – the notion of 'globality' discussed in Chapter One – becomes realisable. Yet at the same time the same forces which bring Muslims together are also working to separate them: fission within fusion. Translocality makes Islam more aware of its own internal difference; it highlights the Muslim other by making him/her visible and thus forcing confrontation. This in turn is giving rise to a new breed of diasporic Muslim, '[a] people in whose deepest selves strange fusions occur, unprecedented unions between what they were and where they find themselves'.[204] The umma is affirmed and realised in diaspora while simultaneously fragmented, broken down into subunits which generate novel combinations.[205]

Within the spaces of diasporic Islam there is also emerging a new form of interstitial identity – a 'third space' to use Homi Bhabha's terminology – in which the politics of the majority society is not embraced, but neither is that of the 'homeland', especially among the younger generation. This creates forms of hybridised political identity which, as we pointed out in Chapter Three, have to be conceptualised as somehow 'in-between'. When viewed in the context of translocality, or when these identities travel, there is also enacted a new mode of 'relating internationally' – one in which the boundaries of political community are constantly open to negotiation and renegotiation. Thus we must agree with Eickelman and Piscatori when they argue that traditional dichotomisations of 'inside/outside' and 'internal/external' are unhelpful in understanding the dynamics of these Muslim politics.[206] Many see in this Islam the seeds of a new idiom of political community as authentic as it is modern, one that perhaps moves even beyond modernity. 'Viewed in this perspective', suggests James Clifford, 'the diaspora discourse and history currently in the air would be about recovering non-Western, or *not-only-Western*, models for cosmopolitan life, non-aligned transnationalities struggling within and against nation-states, global technologies, and market – resources for a fraught co-existence'.[207] In the next chapter, I will go on to explore some of the ways in which these debates over authenticity, authority and (post)modernity play themselves out in the context of the increasingly widespread use of communications and information technology in Muslim translocal politics.

5   Transnational Public Spheres

Information and communication technologies in the Muslim world

First, there is the polysemy of the word 'communication', torn as it is between the domains of leisure and work, between the spectacular and the ordinary, between culturalist and technicist versions, or tossed about between a meaning confined to the area of media activity and a totalizing meaning that elevates it into one of the basic organizing principles of modern society.

(Armand Mattelart, *Mapping World Communication: War, Progress, Culture*)

The impulse to write is clearly related to the changes engendered by British domination and western technology, including the printing press, which permitted easy dissemination of writings, and new modes of transport, which permitted easy travel. [Muslims] were discovering new worlds as they were discovering, or creating, new ways of thinking about themselves.

(Barbara Metcalf, *The Pilgrimage Remembered*)

As has become clear from our discussion thus far, Islam means different things to different people at different times. Whether one chooses to speak of a multiplicity of 'Islams'[1] or of being 'Muslims through discourse'[2] the underlying point is the same: within the religious tradition we call Islam there exist any number of interpretations as to what Islam is, what it means, and who possesses the authority to speak on its behalf.[3] This internal diversity is the result of the myriad cultural, ethnic and national influences which have mediated Islam as it spread across much of the Middle East, Africa, Asia and – more recently – into Western Europe and North America. The resulting syncretisms and interminglings have bequeathed to Islam a rich body of cultural material replete with difference, hybridity and, at times, contradiction. As is the case with any other major religion, the history of Islam has been a history of heterogeneity. As Dale Eickelman notes:

Even eternal truths are necessarily revealed in a specific language and setting. Revelation 'in Arabic, that ye may be understood' (Qur'an 12: 2) has significantly different implications for a seventh-century Arabian merchant, a nineteenth-century Bengali peasant, a Turkish *Gastarbeiter* in Bonn, and a twentieth-century Malaysian university student.[4]

What happens, then, when this complex world discourse comes into contact with a force that can claim an equally broad geographic reach, the socially transformative effects of communications, media and information technology (IT)?[5] Islam, and political Islam in particular, has exhibited a wide variety of responses to this aspect of translocality. Certain features have been eagerly appropriated while others have been vociferously rejected. Indeed, as we will see, there have been occasions where IT has been mobilised by Muslims explicitly in response to aspects of the 'globalised' media (e.g. the spread of American culture) which they seek to repudiate. The themes which I have developed in previous chapters will be further elaborated here through a survey of Muslim political discourse in the context of translocal information technology. How, I ask, have the technological trappings of translocality affected both normative practice in Islam and the lived experience of 'being Muslim'? My purpose in this chapter, then, is to examine the ways in which the impact of globalised communications and information technology on various forms of one particular tradition, Islam, has led both to the imagination of new political communities and to the reimagination of traditional categories of social authority.

The chapter will begin with some general comments on Islam, the media and IT followed by a brief examination of how early forms of print technology led to a decline in the efficacy of traditional sources of Muslim authority and an opening up of the discursive space of 'authentic' Islam to competition from a multitude of newly literate, educated voices. The digitisation and mediatisation of Islam via more recent technologies is then surveyed, and some speculation is offered as to how these processes will lead to further changes in the structures and hierarchies of religious knowledge in Islam. I go on to look at how such transformations have become particularly pronounced at the 'peripheries' of the Muslim world (e.g. Southeast Asia and Africa) and also within the Muslim diasporas of Europe and North America. Diasporic uses of the Internet are then examined as an example of new forms of translocal, distanciated community. I go on to analyse the politics surrounding the Internet in the Arab Gulf countries as a contrasting form of 're-localising the translocal'. In conclusion, I argue that media and information technologies have played a large role in the emergence of a new breed of translocal Islamist intellectual whose activities – often explicitly anti-statist in nature – represent a form of hybridised, counter-hegemonic 'globalisation from below'.

Communications, the media and Islam

In a recent book, David Morley and Kevin Robins provide a useful summary of the transformative capacity of modern media and communications technology:

We are seeing the restructuring of information and image spaces and the production of a new communications geography, characterised by global networks and an international space of information flows; by an increasing crisis of the national sphere; and by new forms of regional and local activity. Our senses of space and place are all being significantly reconfigured. Patterns of movement and flows of people, culture, goods and information mean that it is now not so much physical boundaries – the geographical distances, the seas or mountain ranges – that define a community or nation's 'natural limits'. Increasingly we must think in terms of communications and transport networks and of the symbolic boundaries of language and culture – the 'spaces of transmission' defined by satellite footprints or radio signals – as providing the crucial, and permeable boundaries of our age.[6]

The presence, or rather the *ubiquity*, of media is a dominant theme of our age. Everything and everyone is to some extent the subject or object of mediatising processes; communications and information technology have hence become dominant forces both in terms of how we represent ourselves and of how the 'other' is represented *to* us. Given that Islam is often seen today as a 'significant other' of the west, we would expect to find a great deal written on Islam and the media. Unfortunately, the theme of 'othering' tends to dominate most treatments of Islam and the media. This is largely because images of Islam as the 'other' tend to feature quite heavily in treatments of Islam *by* the media. The uses and abuses of Islam by the mass media in the West have hence been the subject of a number of studies.[7] A number of writers, however, have examined the ways in which media and communications technologies have affected the particular Muslim societies into which they have entered, such as Davis and Davis' work on Moroccan youth culture and its exposure to Western media;[8] Lila Abu-Lughod's studies of Bedouin culture on audio cassettes and the Muslim politics of television in Egypt;[9] and Steven Barraclough's survey of Islamist responses to satellite television in Pakistan, Iran and Egypt.[10] Until recently, though, very little work had been done on the ways in which Muslims and Islamists were themselves making use of the new communication and information technologies.[11] Much of what did appear along these lines tended to be scaremongering about how Islamic 'fundamentalists' were using communication and information technology to plot the destruction of the Western world.[12] What has been missing until recently is any serious, sustained attempt to understand the role of information technology in the context of the sociology of knowledge in Islam. How have these technologies transformed Muslim concepts of what Islam is and who possesses the authority to speak on its behalf? How are they changing the ways in which Muslims imagine the boundaries of the umma? In order to begin answering these questions we need to briefly examine the first modern 'information technology' revolutions in Islam, the arrival of the printing press and mass education.

'Print Islam': subverting genealogies of religious knowledge

The salience of technology in bringing about religious change in Islam has been well documented.[13] In early Islam, oral transmission was the preferred mode of disseminating religious knowledge with each 'alim granting his student an *ijāza* ('license') which permitted him to pass on the texts of his teacher. Literacy among wider populations, even in urban centres, was very low. This state of affairs allowed the ulama and their associates (scribes, calligraphers, etc.) to maintain a virtual monopoly over the production of authoritative religious knowledge. We should note here that in a sense it is almost mistaken to speak of Islam's holy book as a form of 'scripture'. The Qur'an is, quite literally, a recitation[14] – the literal word of God as revealed to Muhammad. It is a collection of words whose message resonates most strongly when read aloud or given voice. Even to this day, the process of learning the Qur'an is first and foremost an exercise in memorisation and oral repetition. This goes some way to explaining why the Muslim world hesitated to embrace the technologies of 'print-capitalism' for almost three centuries. It was the experience of European colonialism and the concomitant perceived decline in Muslim civilisation which paved the way for the rise of print technology in the nineteenth century. The book, pamphlet and newsletter were taken up with urgency in order to counter the threat which Europe was posing to the Muslim umma. This process heralded the final stage in the transition from an oral to a print-based culture in the context of religious knowledge.[15] The ulama were initially at the forefront of this revolution, using a newly expanded and more widely distributed literature base to create a much broader constituency. An inevitable side-effect of this phenomenon, however, was that the religious scholars' stranglehold over religious knowledge was broken. Gradually Muslims found it easier and easier to bypass the ulama in the search for authentic Islam and for new ways of thinking about their religion. As Eickelman notes, '[e]ven when persons in authority [e.g. the ulama] thought they were using new technologies to preserve the old, new elements and patterns of thought were introduced with the telegraph, newspapers, magazines and an expanded (even if not mass) educational system'.[16] The texts were, in principle, now available to anyone who could read them; and to read is, of course, to *interpret*.

> Books...could now be consulted by any Ahmad, Mahmud or Muhammad, who could make what he [would] of them. Increasingly from now on any Ahmad, Mahmud or Muhammad could claim to speak for Islam. No longer was a sheaf of impeccable *ijazas* the buttress of authority; strong Islamic commitment would be enough.[17]

The new media opened up new spaces of religious contestation where traditional sources of authority could be challenged by the wider public. As literacy rates began to climb almost exponentially in the twentieth century, this effect was amplified even further. The move to print technology meant not only a new method for transmitting texts, but also a new idiom of selecting, writing and presenting works to cater for a new kind of reader.[18]

> Those who can interpret what Islam 'really' is [could] now be of more vari-
> able social status than was the case when mnemonics were an essential
> element in the legitimacy of knowledge. The carriers of religious knowledge
> [would] increasingly be anyone who can claim a strong Islamic commit-
> ment, as [was] the case among many of the educated urban youth. Freed
> from mnemonic domination, religious knowledge [could] be delineated and
> interpreted in a more abstract and flexible fashion. A long apprenticeship
> under an established man of learning [was] no longer a necessary prerequi-
> site to legitimizing one's own religious knowledge.[19]

Through this revolution, religious knowledge was 'objectified'. That is to say, it became a subject open to debate within the public sphere. Islam was something which could be represented; its identity was now open to negotiation by a constituency previously prohibited from speaking on its behalf.[20] The fragmenta-tion of traditional sources of authority is hence a key theme with regard to the nexus of Islam and translocality. These transformations in the status and prove-nance of religious knowledge have, in the contemporary era, helped to give rise to what Olivier Roy has termed the 'Islamist new intellectuals'.[21]

> The new intellectual has an autodidactic relationship to knowledge.
> Knowledge is acquired in a fragmented (manuals, excerpts, popular
> brochures), encyclopedic, and immediate manner: everything is discussed
> without the mediation of an apprenticeship, a method, or a professor…The
> new media, such as radio, television, cassettes, and inexpensive offset
> brochures, make snatches of this content available. The new intellectual is a
> tinkerer; he creates a montage, as his personal itinerary guides him, of
> segments of knowledge, using methods that come from a different concep-
> tual universe than the segments he recombines, creating a totality that is
> more imaginary then theoretical.[22]

The rise of what we might call 'media Islam' or 'soundbite Islam' has thus been a major by-product of translocal information technology. A new class of 'hybrid' Muslim intellectual ('using methods that come from a different conceptual universe than the segments he recombines') has been the chief agent of dissemi-nation for mediatised Islam. With the current world communications infrastructure, ideas and messages now possess the capability to bridge time and space almost effortlessly, and the political implications of this new capacity are not easily overestimated. 'Modern Muslim revitalization movements have been linked with an early stage of global modernisation', writes Serif Mardin, 'and one can follow this link through the effect on the revitalization of modern communications'.[23]

These transformations have been particularly wide-reaching on the 'peripheries' of the Muslim world. In these areas, such as Southeast Asia and certain parts of Africa, the lack of communication with the 'centre' of the Muslim world – the Middle East – had meant that local cultures had developed idioms of Islamic practice largely in isolation from mainstream, scripturalist Islam.[24] As Victoria Bernal notes:

> Throughout much of their history, Muslims in different communities were cut off from each other to a considerable extent. Communication between the centers of religious learning and believers in the hinterlands was much more difficult than it is today, and the holy texts have been inaccessible to the many illiterate and semi-literate Muslims. Local history and culture thus contribute to the religious practices and beliefs of Muslims around the world. The line between custom and Islam often is ambiguous.[25]

However, as large numbers of students from the peripheries started to travel abroad for further education, things began to change. In Barbara Metcalf's words, Muslims '[discovered] new worlds as they were discovering, or creating, new ways of thinking about themselves'.[26] Horvatich has observed a 'politics of authenticity' emerging between itinerant students critical of the oral traditions in their villages and those local religious leaders who insist on the correctness of their 'Islam'.[27] The students, often labelled 'Ahmadi'[28] complain that through the oral tradition, religious leaders in their village keep Islam almost as a 'secret', arguing that religious knowledge should be widely available to everyone in textual form. For their own part, the orthodox village leaders maintain that they do not need to engage with other interpretations of Islam available through books and pamphlets because 'we know better than they'.[29] This dynamic leads Horvatich to argue:

> There is, thus, a dialectical relationship between public education and international movements of Islamic reform. Because many modernist discourses share 'ways of knowing Islam', and communication can take place in a common language in published texts distributed throughout the Muslim world, the [Muslims of the periphery] are receptive to and can engage in dialogue with other Muslim discourses. Knowledge of English and access to a somewhat reliable international postal system enable [these remote communities] to communicate with perceived Muslim centers of knowledge.[30]

More recently, increased access to various media networks from the Muslim centre have had an important effect on religious discourse in the periphery. The enormous media arm of the Saudi regime, for example, has managed to reach into Southeast Asia very effectively. Muslims in this region are hence often encouraged to emulate Saudi practices and to view the Muslim world from a Saudi perspective.[31] Some writers, however, have bemoaned the stifling effect of Saudi control over the Muslim media.[32] They argue that this monopoly has been a major obstacle to the development of more open and progressive forms of political debate in the Muslim world. Disillusionment with the authoritative powers-that-be (both on the periphery and in the centre) has increasingly led many Muslims towards the Islamist new intellectuals in their search for religious knowledge. That most of these new ideologues do not have a formal religious education does not seem to deter eager young Muslims; nor does the fact that the 'Islamic' information they dispense is often derived from Western academic methodologies.[33] If anything, the latter fact has helped to make the Islam of the new intellectuals even more appealing to the younger generation of contemporary Muslims since most of them are themselves the product of Western-style educational systems. For these students – many of whom are trained in the natural sciences and engineering – modern IT is a familiar idiom. For them it is only natural, therefore, that the future of Islam should lie with communications and information technology. What, though, is the nature of the nexus between Islam and IT? How have Muslims been making use of these technologies?

Digitising Islam

Muslims have been speculating about the utility of information technology in the organisation of religious knowledge for some time now. A first spate of books appeared in the late 1980s, speculating about, for example, the development of 'a science of Tawhid Cybernetics' involving the creation of a giant computerised library for the storage of all aspects of religious knowledge with the aim to use such a system as the database for an artificial intelligence platform capable of generating a prolific number of fatwas.[34] 'Upon completion of such a databank', writes Larry Poston, 'one would in effect have a computerised majlis al-shura ('consultative council') or a supranational, supercultural ulama capable of providing solutions to problems faced by modern Muslims.'[35] It was primarily through its potential as an organisational and storage tool that other Muslims were also introduced to IT. Abdul Kadir Barkatulla, Director of London's Islamic Computing Centre, explains that he first became attracted to computer-mediated data storage in his capacity as a scholar of hadith, a field which involves the archiving and retrieval of thousands upon thousands of sayings attributed to the Prophet and his Companions.[36]

However, the Anglo-centric nature of electronic media was for a long time a serious barrier to working with anything but the most well-known and oft-translated religious texts such as the Qur'an and those hadith collections available in English or other European languages. The rise of the Graphical User Interface (GUI) in the mid-1980s – typified by the Apple Macintosh operating system and Microsoft's Windows – served to rectify this problem to some extent. The graphical nature of the interface allowed computer operators to readily make use of non-Latin scripts which had previously been difficult to render in the old command-line format. Operating systems and word processors began to become available in various non-English languages – most notably for our purposes, in Arabic. Another important development here was the exponential increase in the storage capacity of the various magnetic media used by computers. This situation was again transformed with the advent of optical media such as the compact disc in the mid- to late 1980s. Computers graduated from storing programs and data on regular audio cassettes (very low capacity) to floppy discs (between just over 100kB and 1.4MB), to hard drives (20MB to several gigabytes), to the phenomenal array-based servers which chain together several high-capacity hard drives and provide enough capacity to store the complete contents of a small library. It is the read-only compact disc (CD-ROM), however, which has most transformed the consumer market in recent years with its ability to easily transport chunks of data as large as 650 MB between many computers. This provides enough capacity to comfortably store several multi-volume encyclopedias, hours of high-quality sound, or even a full-length video film.

What does this mean for Islam? Given the size of most Islamic texts, the CD-ROM has provided a medium which can contain the full text of several works. This means that the entire Qur'an, several collections of hadith, tafsir, and various fiqhi works can easily fit on a single disc. Barkatulla sees this development as having the greatest relevance for those Muslims who live in circumstances where access to religious scholars is limited, such as in the West. For him, such CD ROM selections offer a useful alternative. 'IT doesn't change the individual's relationship with his religion', he says, 'but rather it provides knowledge supplements and clarifies the sources of information such that Muslims can verify the things they hear for themselves'.[37] Barkatulla sees IT as a useful tool for systematising religious knowledge, but only those juridical opinions which have already been reached. In his terms, IT is only for working with knowledge that has already been 'cooked', not for making new judgements. To engage in the latter, he believes, one requires certain formal training and knowledge of specific methodologies.

> These resources are not intended to replace the religious scholars or commentators, but they mean that the scholars will not be able to get away with saying just anything. They will be held to account. They will have to check their sources twice because people will be able to go to the sources themselves and check to see if what was said in the pulpit corresponds with what is in the books... but IT is not for generating one's own fatwas.[38]

There are, however, those who disagree with Barkatulla. Sa'ad al-Faqih, for example, the leader of the Movement for Islamic Reform in Arabia and another keen advocate of information technology, believes that the average Muslim *can* now revolutionalise Islam with just a basic understanding of Islamic methodology and a CD-ROM. In his view, the technology goes a long way to bridging the 'knowledge gap' between an 'alim and a lay Muslim by placing all of the relevant texts at the fingertips of the latter. 'I am not an 'alim', he says, 'but with these tools I can put together something very close to what they would produce when asked for a fatwa'.[39]

The availability of such CD-ROM collections, all hyper-linked and cross-referenced, has created a new constituency for religious texts. Where Muslims would have previously had to rely on the expertise of the ulama when dealing with these books, they are now all available in a single medium which can easily be searched by any computer user. According to Ziauddin Sardar:

> Instead of ploughing through bulky texts, that require a certain expertise to read, a plethora of databases on the *Qur'an* and *hadith* now open up these texts and make them accessible to average, non-expert, users. Increasingly, the *ulama* are being confronted by non-professional theologians who can cite chapter and verse from the fundamental sources, undermining not just their arguments but also the very basis of their authority.[40]

Sardar then goes on to speculate about how all of the usul al-fiqh might be placed on a single compact disc, along with an expert-system[41] that would guide the user through the literature and, in effect, allow him to generate his own fatwas.[42] This sort of ijtihad toolkit would amount to a 'virtual 'alim', and hence pose a further challenge to the authority of the traditional religious scholars. 'With this technology I think we are beginning to see a breaking of the monopoly over religious knowledge', says Sa'ad al-Faqih.[43] It is unlikely, however, that such a system will replace the ulama any time soon. They still command enormous respect in many communities and would, in any case, surely challenge the claim that their methodologies – the product of centuries of study and exhaustive research – can be reduced to a set of coded computer instructions. According to Barkatulla, an 'alim himself, many ulama see the utility of information technology for the organisation of religious knowledge but believe that by becoming over-dependent on such 'gadgets', the capacity to internalise and think for oneself decreases.[44] At the same time, however, there is still an important sense in which the availability of religious texts on CD-ROM actually *increases* one's capacity to think for oneself – perhaps even hailing a new form of individual ijtihad.

The existence of such collections on CD-ROM has quickly become a reality in the past few years. The Islamic Computing Centre in London has been at the forefront of producing and distributing Arabic and Islamic materials in electronic format, and one only needs to glance at their product catalogue to confirm the enthusiasm with which Muslims have taken up this technology. In addition to several electronic Qur'ans (with full Arabic text, several English translations and complete oral recitation on a single disc) the Centre also sells titles such as WinHadith, WinBukhari, and WinSeera. Also available are several products which begin to approach the system which Sardar has envisaged. The Islamic Law Base, Islamic Scholar, and 'Alim Multimedia are all vast collections of religious texts such as the Qur'an, hadith, several volumes of fiqh covering all four schools of Sunni jurisprudence, biographies of the Prophet and his Companions, and more recent writing by figures such as Abul A'la Mawdudi. All of these databases can be kept open simultaneously and material between them is cross-referenced and fully searchable. In the United

States, the Aramedia Group offers a library of Islamic CD-ROM resources with a choice of Arabic, English or Malay interface. Also available are software packages such as SalatBase, a multimedia guide to prayer which covers proper bodily practices, ritual somatics and the particular problems associated with, for example, prayer during travel. Barkatulla also mentions an expert system under development in Kuwait called al-Mawarith. This package enables a user to determine how the assets of a deceased relative should be allocated to his or her heirs according to Islamic law. It can be adjusted to reflect the opinions of the various Sunni legal schools, and will also provide textual evidence from the Qur'an and hadith in order to 'authorise' its output.[45] Also widely available on the Internet are utilities for calculating prayer times and the beginning and ending of the fasting day during Ramadhan at any geographic point in the world, and for converting dates between the Hijri and other calendar systems.

That is certainly not to say that the ulama have been marginalised: the moon must still be visible to the human eye for Ramadhan to begin, regardless of whether or not the 'science' of an astronomical program on the computer insists that it is there. In fact, some religious scholars have become quite enthusiastic about computer technology themselves. 'Traditional centres of Islamic learning [such as al-Azhar in Cairo and Qum in Iran] did not respond to the opportunities offered by IT for about ten years', Barkatulla observes, 'but now they have to'.[46] Because the modern religious universities have developed comprehensive information systems, the more conservative, traditional institutions are now forced to respond in kind in order to keep up with the times. Barkatulla alludes to something like a 'race to digitise Islam' among leading centres of religious learning around the world. At the Center for Islamic jurisprudence in Qom, for example, several thousand texts, both Sunni and Shi'ite, have been converted to electronic form.[47] This would confirm Barkatulla's observation that while Sunni institutions tend to ignore Shi'ite texts, the Shi'a centres are digitising large numbers of Sunni texts in order to produce databases which appeal to the Muslim mainstream, and hence capture a larger share of the market for digital Islam.

Related technologies have also allowed for the emergence of what one author has called 'print Islam'.[48] Just as 'print-capitalism' facilitated the early nationalist projects of Benedict Anderson's imagined communities,[49] so have new technologies of mass printing and circulation provided Islamist movements with a new grass-roots base and important sources of popular mobilisation. As early as the late nineteenth century, Muslim reformers such as Jamal al-Din al-Afghani were printing and distributing leaflets in political protest.[50] Serif Mardin's study of the early twentieth-century Turkish religious leader Said Nursi emphasises the role of print technology and the communications revolution in propagating his ideas.[51] In the contemporary context, writers have pointed to phenomena such as the rise of 'Islamic books' (*les livres islamiques*), a populist genre which employs simple, vernacular language and colourful, eye-catching covers to tap into the newly-literate working classes of Egypt and Lebanon.[52] In another example, David Edwards indicates the importance of newspapers, pamphlets and magazines for the development and mobilisation of competing Islamic political ideologies in Afghanistan.[53] An important point to note in relation to the electronic publication of Islamic texts is that this medium allows for a new flexibility in the handling, transmission and, most importantly, the *renewal* of textual sources. This is not to say that the early sources can and should now be modified (i.e. tampered with), but rather that it is now possible to 'cut and paste' between them, creating novel combinations of references and textual evidence which can be made to appeal to a wider range of audiences. As Mahdi notes:

> In some respects, the book in electronic, machine-readable form will mean a return to one of the main features of the manuscript age: copies can be made and subjected to continuous change and improvement, free of the fixed form introduced by printing and movable type. With the use of various means of communication, it will be possible to make what is initially a single copy available immediately across the globe...with the possibility that, from one copy, an infinite number of copies can be made, used, and disposed of.[54]

Neither has the rise of electronic 'print Islam' eradicated the salience of the oral tradition. Electronic media are as adept with sound as they are with the written word. Audio cassettes, widely available and portable as they are, may well serve to give the oral tradition a 'new lease on life'.[55] Certainly we have heard much about the role of audio cassettes in Iran's Islamic revolution, where recordings of Khomeini's sermons were smuggled over from his Neauphle-le-Chateau head-quarters near Paris and, much to the Shah's dismay, widely distributed in Iran. The newspapers, pamphlets and magazines of Afghanistan's religious upheaval are increasingly giving way to the audio cassette.[56] The Friday sermon, or *khuṭba*, is today recorded at many mosques throughout the Muslim world and the distribution of these recordings, along with addresses by imams consciously emulating the rhetoric of prominent ideologues such as Sayyid Qutb, Ali Shariati and Mawdudi, serves to politicise Islam before a vast audience. Recordings of sermons by dissident Saudi ulama such as Safar al-Hawali and Salman al-'Awda also circulate widely both inside and outside the Kingdom, and this marks the first time that material openly critical of the Saudi regime has been heard by relatively large sections of that country's population. The website of a London-based Saudi opposition group has also made Salman al-'Awda's sermons available over the Internet using the latest audio streaming technology.[57] 'Now that media technology is increasingly able to deal with other symbolic modes', notes Ulf Hannerz, 'we may wonder whether imagined communities are increasingly moving beyond words'.[58]

Communicating Islam

'It is in their use as *distributive* and *decentralised* networks', writes one author, 'that [information technology's] greatest potential lies for Muslim societies and cultures'.[59] He is undoubtedly correct insofar as their political impact is obviously strongest when these media are distributed, broadcast or otherwise made available to a wider audience. By 1890, al-Afghani was making use of the telegraph to maintain rapid communications with opposition movements across the Middle East.[60] Today, '[t]elevision, radios, cassettes, videos, personal computers, photocopiers, facsimile machines and electronic mail are frequently, if not routinely, found in the homes and offices of Muslim activists, ulama, and Sufi *shaykhs* as well as those of government officials', note Eickelman and Piscatori.[61] Technologies such as telecommunications, television (both terrestrial and satellite) and, finally, the Internet – all of which serve to politicise Islam through their global reach – have led some authors to argue that '[w]e are witnessing the "deterritorialisation" of audiovisual production and the elaboration of transnational systems of delivery'.[62]

Telecommunications is undergoing something of a mini-boom in the Middle East, and sophisticated systems are already in place or planned for the urban areas of many Asian countries such as Malaysia, Indonesia and Pakistan. The latest GSM mobile technology is also available in many countries of the Gulf, Jordan, Lebanon and Pakistan, and is planned for Syria.[63] It is in the West, however, that Muslims have made the most widespread use of telecommunications technology for religious purposes. The Islamic Assembly of North America (IANA), for example, operates a Fatwa Centre which can be reached via a toll-free telephone number. The ulama of the centre will dispense edicts on virtually any subject to members of the Muslim community in North America.[64] In the Middle East, activists in groups such as Hamas have made use of Israeli cellular networks to stay in touch while moving around the West Bank and Gaza. Ironically, in one case this technology proved to be their downfall. The Hamas master-bomber Yahya Ayash ('The Engineer') was assassinated by Israeli security agents using a booby-trapped cellphone packed with explosives.

An offshoot of telecommunications, the fax, has also been widely used by Muslims in the Middle East – and especially by Islamist groups seeking to question the legitimacy of various regimes. Organisations in Algeria and Egypt have made use of the fax machine in voicing protest to their respective governments, and the 'fax cascade' tactics of Saudi dissidents in London have become notorious. At the height of its activity, for example, the Committee for the Defence of Legitimate Rights (CDLR) was sending several thousand faxes per week to the Kingdom where offices were forced to turn off fax machines at night in an effort to stem the flow. These faxes were reportedly photocopied and then distributed widely within the Kingdom.[65] The organisation's efforts have certainly caught the attention of the ruling regime and its 'official' clergy. The government was even forced to take the unprecedented step of urging Saudis (via a state-owned newspaper) to ignore the CDLR's faxes.[66]

Television, which in the Middle East is often state-owned and censored, is not a forum which has been extensively co-opted by Muslims for political purposes. We do find references, however, to instances of interface between politicised Islam and television. Abu-Lughod speculates about the impact of militant Islamist groups in Egypt on the standards of dress and appearance of television presenters, and

Eickelman discusses officially-sanctioned religious presentation on television as a form of national discourse.[67] Television, and satellite television in particular, certainly have been the objects of protests by both official religious voices and various Islamist movements, however.[68] In Algeria, for example, soldiers of the Armed Islamic Group (GIA) have in the past threatened the owners of satellite dishes.[69] Several Arab Gulf states and Iran have official bans in effect on the private ownership of the dishes. In practice, however, these bans are very difficult to enforce and the countries in question have in some cases been forced to provide rival satellite programming in an attempt to lure viewers away from 'sinful' and 'poisoning' Western programmes.[70] Saudi Arabia owns a vast media empire and controls much of the premier Arabic-language satellite programming via its Middle East Broadcasting (MBC) network. In 1996, an Italian-based satellite relay company with significant Saudi investment interests was forced to terminate its contract with the BBC after its Arabic-language television service gave air time to the Saudi dissident Muhammad al-Mass'ari and also showed a programme critical of Saudi Arabia's human rights record.[71] In at least one case Islamists have also turned to satellite television as a potential political tool. The Movement for Islamic Reform (MIRA), an offshoot of the CDLR in London, has rented a broadcasting slot on a satellite and is planning to begin transmitting propaganda programmes which question the legitimacy of the Saudi regime according to religious criteria. The group is hoping to take advantage of the several hundred-thousand satellite dishes currently in use in the Kingdom (see below).[72] One of the most interesting developments in this field is the phenomenal success of the Qatari-based satellite station Al-Jazeera. Through popular chat programmes such as 'al-itija al-muwakis' ('the opposite direction') – where religious and political issues are discussed in relative freedom – Al-Jazeera has been hailed by many in the Gulf region as the harbinger of a breakthrough in public discourse.

Diasporic Muslims and IT: new translocal communities?

'Academically, media studies and migration studies tend to function as separate fields', Ulf Hannerz writes, '[y]et in real life migration and mediatisation run parallel, not to say that they are continuously intertwined'.[73] His observation holds particularly true for diasporic Muslims, as they are currently both the subject and the object of considerable mediatisation. In what follows, I will be mainly concerned with the ways in which Islam makes use of or is rendered in various media for the consumption of other Muslims; in other words, I am interested in how Muslims use IT to talk to other Muslims.

We have already mentioned the development of something like an 'Islamic English', and this often constitutes the vernacular in which Islam is published and distributed in diaspora. Many young Muslims, as has been noted in the previous chapter, are bypassing the ulama and the imams in order to learn their Islam from pamphlets and books published in English. Diasporic magazines such as *The Muslim News* and *Q-News* are also important in this regard.[74] Beyond the various printed literatures, we also find a variety of audiovisual and multimedia material which caters for the specific needs of diasporic Muslims. Much of this is aimed at children, seeking to teach them Islam using imagery and language similar to the Western entertainment genres with which they are already familiar. Thus we find a Disney-style animated adventure video, *Fatih – Sultan Muhammad*, which claims to be the world's first Islamic feature animation production. 'In this inspirational adventure', the advertisement reads, 'your family will see how the Muslims used not only their faith – but also strategic and technological superiority – to be successful'. Another company offers a children's educational series with a format and style similar to the muppets of *Sesame Street*. *Adam's World* 'introduces children to Islamic morals, values, and culture in a manner that's both entertaining and educational…By adopting such a universal approach to video-based education, *Adam's World* has found its niche among children of over forty different ethnic backgrounds'. The various episodes have titles such as 'Happy to be a Muslim', 'Take me to the Kaba', 'Kindness in Islam' and 'Ramadan Mubarak'. A wide variety of Arabic-language learning aids and Islamic quiz games for children on both video-tape and CD-ROM are also available. We have already mentioned the SalatBase prayer guide. The same company also offers a series of video-tapes featuring interviews with prominent Muslims in the West such as the NBA basketball star Hakeem Olajuwon and Yusuf Islam, formerly the pop singer Cat Stevens. One title, 'Holiday Myths' offers advice on how Muslims should approach and deal with Western holidays such as Christmas, Halloween, Valentine's Day and Easter.

What about the Internet? It is perhaps here that some of the most interesting things are happening. We should begin by noting, however, that while many countries in the Middle East and Asia are starting to provide Internet access to their populations, the vast majority of Muslim users of the Internet are in Europe and North America.[75] If translocal information technologies are having a discernible effect on the imagination of political community in Islam, then it is to the various Muslim diaspora groups in the West – Arab, Iranian, South Asian – that we must turn to find it. In this sense the use of the Internet by Muslim diaspora groups provides us with one of the best examples of how localities become translocalities. As Arjun Appadurai observes:

> New forms of electronically mediated communication are beginning to create *virtual neighborhoods*, no longer bounded by territory, passports, taxes, elections, and other conventional political diacritics, but by access to both the software and hardware that are required to connect to these large international computer networks…Unlike the largely negative pressures that the nation-state places on the production of context by local subjects, the electronic mediation of community in the diasporic world creates a more complicated, disjunct, hybrid sense of local subjectivity.[76]

What then are the implications of this media revolution for those Muslim communities which inhabit global spaces? Can we meaningfully speak today about the emergence of new forms of Islamic virtual community? Where one much-cited author pointed to the pioneering efforts of New World 'creoles' in the formation of imagined communities,[77] Jon Anderson now speaks of the 'new creoles' of the information superhighway – political actors whose strength lies in their adoption of the enabling technologies of electronic print and information transfer.[78] We should not be too quick, however, to declare that the Internet is suddenly going to radically transform Muslim understandings of political community. We need to look realistically at the number of Muslims who actually have access to this forum, and we need to take careful note of each socio-political setting which receives information via this network:

> Transnational theories, fixated on media and forms of alienated conscious-
> ness distinctive of late modernity, tend to overlook the social organization
> into which new media are brought in a rush to the new in expression.
> Impressed by what Simmel much earlier called 'cosmopolitanism', we over-
> look measures of social organization in pursuit of media effects.[79]

In addition, we need to make sure that we have a more nuanced understanding of those Muslim identities which use the Internet. We cannot start talking about new forms of diasporic Muslim community simply because many users of the Internet happen to be Muslims. Noting that in many instances Muslim uses of the Internet seem to represent little more than the migration of existing messages and ideas into a new context, Anderson warns that '[n]ew talk has to be distinguished from new people talking about old topics in new settings'.[80] Yet we also have to acknowl-edge the possibility that the hybrid discursive spaces of the Muslim Internet can give rise, even inadvertently, to new formulations and critical perspectives on Islam, religious knowledge and community. But in order to comprehend the processes by which community is created, we also need to understand the circumstances under which these Muslim identities became diasporic. That is, how do other aspects of identity influence the terms of religious discourse on the Internet? Issues such as culture and religion, for example, are often discussed using methods of reasoning and debate which derive from the natural and technical sciences, rather than using the 'traditional' terms of discourse which one might find 'back home'. This reflects the nature of the professional/student life of many diaspora Muslims who are often technicians, engineers or research scientists.[81]

As regards notions of community in Islam, there is also the Internet's impact on 'centre-periphery' relations in the Muslim world to be examined. A country such as Malaysia, usually considered to be on the margins of Islam both in terms of geography and religious influence, has invested heavily in information and networking technologies. As a result, when searching on the Internet for descrip-tions of programmes which offer formal religious training one is far more likely to encounter the comprehensive course outlines provided by the International Islamic University of Malaysia than to find any information on the venerable institutions of Cairo, Medina or Mashhad. Government officials in Indonesia have recently begun to explore the potential of the Internet for raising the profile of Indonesian Islam.[82] The Ayatollahs of Iran have also jumped on the information bandwagon. Eager to propagate Shi'ite teachings, the scholars of Qom have digitised thousands of religious texts which they plan to make available over the Internet. An e-mail fatwa service is also planned.[83]

Recalling Appadurai's point that the key obstacle to participation in new forms of electronic community is a lack of the necessary software and hardware resources, we have to remind ourselves that the vast majority of Muslims cannot afford to pay for Internet access. When available in the Middle East and Asia, Internet accounts are usually prohibitively expensive and hence subscriptions tend to be limited to elite groups who are often more sympathetic to Western bourgeois values in any case. As noted above, it is usually amongst the diaspora Muslims of the Western world that we find the Internet being appropriated for political purposes. The American media, for example, has recently been full of scaremongering about 'radical fundamentalists' who use the United States as a fundraising base for their overseas operations. Reports often cite the Internet as a primary tool for the dissemination of propaganda by Islamic militants.[84] We are told, for example, that Islamist websites distribute the communiqués of Algerian militant groups and provide a forum for the teachings of Sheikh Omar Abdel-Rahman, the Egyptian cleric accused of masterminding the World Trade Center bombing.[85] In a recent piece, even Benedict Anderson seemed to sensationalise the advent of diaspora activists:

> [They] create a serious politics that is at the same time radically unaccountable. The participant rarely pays taxes in the country in which he does his politics; he is not answerable to its judicial system; he probably does not cast even an absentee ballot in its elections because he is a citizen in a different place; he need not fear prison, torture, or death, nor need his immediate family. But, well and safely positioned in the First World, he can send money and guns, circulate propaganda, and build intercontinental computer information circuits [*sic*], all of which can have incalculable consequences in the zones of their ultimate destinations.[86]

A more sober examination of the situation, however, would most likely reveal that very few of the Muslim groups who have a presence on the Internet are involved in this sort of activity. To be sure, there do exist several prominent sites which advertise information on 'digital jihad' and 'on-line activism', or which claim to provide resources for Islamist politicians,[87] but it is unlikely that any of these – which are often run by students or part-time volunteers – actually have the capacity to engage in the sort of international intrigues alluded to above. Recent events, such as the Oklahoma bombing, indicate that a country such as the United States probably has more to fear from disillusioned sections of its own population or various cult and millenarian movements than it does from the Muslim diaspora. There are also those who argue that the Internet has had a moderating effect on Islamist discourse. Sa'ad al-Faqih, for example, believes that Internet chat-rooms and discussion forums devoted to the debate of Islam and politics serve to encourage greater tolerance. He believes that in these new arenas one sees a greater convergence in the centre of the Islamist political spectrum and a weakening of the extremes:

> In these forums it is very important now for the leaders of various tendencies to make strong, reasoned arguments that stand up in debate because their followers are also there and they are listening. Not only that, but the followers are now able to go to the sources themselves in order to verify what their leaders have been saying. Sometimes you get extremists who argue only out of emotion or sensationalism, but do not present arguments with any reasonable methodology or evidence from the sources. Leaders are becoming sensitive to this need. They know that they have to conduct debate according to certain reasonable rules in order to maintain their credibility with the followers...Not just on the Internet, but also on satellite TV and in other media forums. The ulama come on and they take questions from people who corner them and force them to defend themselves. 'The people' force them to come up with stronger arguments...It's like one huge public debate that thousands of people are listening to.[88]

Thus for the overwhelming majority of Muslims in the West the Internet is mainly a forum for the conduct of politics *within* Islam. 'Internet forums permit bypassing traditional gatekeepers and adjudicators of interpretive rights, procedures and adequacy', writes Jon Anderson.[89] Because very few 'official' Muslim organs, such as the Organisation of the Islamic Conference, the Muslim World League or the various eminent religious schools, actually have any presence on the Internet, we can characterise many of the Muslim sites which do exist as 'alternatives'.[90] That is, in the absence of sanctioned information from recognised institutions, Muslims are increasingly taking religion into their own hands. The Internet provides them with an extremely useful medium for distributing information about Islam and about the behaviour required of a 'good Muslim'. Through various newsgroups and e-mail discussion lists, Muslims – many of whom are new converts – can solicit information about what 'Islam' says about any particular problem. Responses will be received from, recalling Francis Robinson's phrase, 'any Ahmad, Mahmud or Muhammad' on the Internet and this represents a further decline in the authority of the ulama. Not only that, notes Sa'ad al-Faqih, 'but someone will be given information about what "Islam" says about such and such and then others will write in to correct or comment on this opinion/interpretation'.[91] In this sense, the Internet resembles a publishing forum far more than it does a broadcasting forum because here 'users are producers, or may be producers'.[92] Given that most of this discourse involves diaspora Muslims, much of the conversation on these information networks tends to be about how Muslims should deal with various 'cultural' phenomena which they encounter in, say, Los Angeles, Manchester or The Hague. Dozens of 'meta-sites' have sprung up in recent years, offering hundreds of links to other areas of the Internet containing information and resources on Islam.[93] The Muslim Students Association network, for example, posts daily collections of news stories on Muslims and Islamic issues from around the world.

There has also been a great effort to make the classic works of religious learning as widely available as possible. Numerous websites offer various translations of the Qur'an and the hadith, and also articles by prominent contemporary Muslim thinkers. Various Internet forums co-ordinated by the Muslim Student Associations of North America allow Muslims to discuss and debate the merits of different tendencies within the modern Muslim movement.[94] A recent example of this has been a wide-ranging debate on the merits of the Jama'at al-Tabligh movement.[95] Just as the more marginalised sects of Islam have often found life to be easier in diaspora (see Chapter Four), so too have they found a new lease on life on the Internet. Power asymmetries are often evened out on-line, and the World Wide Web allows the Ahmaddiya movement to appear as 'mainstream' as any Sunni site. More traditional Islamic spaces such as the mosque have also not gone untouched by IT. In 1996, for example, the Muslim Parliament of Great Britain recommended that all mosques in the UK be wired up to the network in order to provide 'porn-free access to the Internet and [to] establish places where Muslims can socialise in a *halal* (permissible) environment'.[96]

The Internet has also served to reinforce and reify the impact of print-capitalism on traditional structures and forms of authority. Instead of having to go down to the mosque in order to elicit the advice of the local mullah, Muslims can now receive 'authoritative' religious pronouncements via the various e-mail fatwa services which have sprung up in recent months. The Sheikhs of al-Azhar are totally absent, but the enterprising young 'alim who sets himself up with a colourful website in Alabama suddenly becomes a high-profile representative of Islam for a particular, disseminated and distanciated constituency. Due to the largely anonymous nature of the Internet, one can also never be sure whether the 'authoritative' advice received via these services is coming from a classically-trained religious scholar or a hydraulic engineer moonlighting as an amateur 'alim. As we noted above, however, the authority of the traditional scholars is not easily undermined. Many of them, especially in the Middle East, command a loyal following based on personal charisma which cannot easily be poached away by an anonymous computer personality. Barkatulla points out that judgements and rulings associated with IT such as e-mail fatwas are not yet considered permissible evidence in shari'a courts because no reliable system for the generation of 'digital signatures' that can verify the identity and credentials of religious scholars as yet exists. And again, the impact of these services must be measured realistically based on the number of Muslims who actually make use of them. However, we can perhaps say that they are having a fairly significant effect with regard to those questions which concern the details of daily life for a Muslim in the West. Diaspora Muslims are likely to find it convenient to be able to turn to one of their own, someone who has also lived Western culture, so as to receive a hearing that is more sympathetic and more in tune with local affairs.

More than anything else the Internet and other information technologies provide spaces where Muslims, who often find themselves to be a marginalised or extreme minority group in many Western communities, can go in order to find others 'like them'. It is in this sense that we can speak of the Internet as allowing Muslims to create a new form of imagined community, or a reimagined umma: 'It is imagined because the members...will never know most of their fellow-members, meet them, or even hear of them, yet in the minds [and on the screens] of each lies the image of their communion.'[97] The various Islams of the Internet hence offer a reassuring set of symbols and terminology which attempt to reproduce familiar settings and terms of discourse in locations far remote from those in which they were originally embedded. We might recall the hybridised media discourses of diasporic Iranian television as described by Hamid Naficy.[98] Here, Islam functions simultaneously as a hated symbol of Khomeini's regime *and* as the object of a nostalgic longing, the desire for a lost culture and homeland. It is inevitable when such traditions travel that various processes of cultural translation are set in motion. The resulting syncretisms then give rise to new forms of Islam, each of which is redrawn to suit the unique set of sociocultural contingencies into which it enters. This is what is meant by the notion of 'globalising the local'; or to be more precise, the globalisation of cultural material which is then *re-localised* in new and distant translocalities.

The Internet in the Gulf: re-localising the translocal?

> This Internet issue has made everything else pale into insignificance. These networks are accessible to everyone; people can find political, security and porno-graphic materials, songs, films, and scenery there. Unfortunately, some of our officials do not pay attention to these things. I do not understand why they are so confused; why there is no logic to what they do; they are expanding these things. They should explain themselves.
>
> (Ayatollah Ahmad Jannati, Sermon at Tehran University)

What happens, though, when the Internet begins to spread into a region of the world populated by societies whose normative orientation takes strong issue with some of its content? What happens when IT-based discourses 'travel back' from diaspora to 'homeland'? The question of how translocality affects cultural dynamics in the Arab Gulf countries is extremely salient here. We need first to note that the Gulf does not by any means represent a parochial, primitive back-water. Rather it provides a fascinating case for understanding how rapid influxes of technology and industry impact upon traditional sociocultural patterns and prac-tices. Gulf society is itself already something of a hybrid, a merger between 'traditional' norms and forms of social organisation and the very latest in modern technology. The region's affluence is the result of its crucial role in world energy provision, and both of these factors have allowed (if not forced) the Gulf to undergo rapid processes of industrialisation and modernisation – processes that in other regions of the world usually occur over the space of many generations rather than in just over half a century. Given these circumstances it is inevitable that tensions emerge between the traditional and the modern. For the most part Gulf societies have demonstrated extreme flexibility and a willingness to exploit both the latest trends in technology and the global division of labour. The presence of an enormous Asian migrant labour force is well-known, and this phenomenon is prevalent at every level of social structure in the Gulf. Among Bedouin tribes in Saudi Arabia, for example, it is not uncommon to find camels being herded by Pakistanis rather than by Arabs. Likewise the trappings of modern technology. Bedouin in the UAE make extensive use of that country's GSM mobile telephone network; globalisation, it would seem, has even found its way into the desert.

The arrival of the Internet in the Gulf has been a complex affair. There is a distinction to be drawn here between the availability of Internet access for a limited number of specialised research institutes, and the availability of accounts to the wider public. Various universities and hospitals in the Gulf have had Internet gateways (often via Europe) since the early 1990s, but it is only since about 1995 that private accounts have started to appear in a few locations. The reasons for this are obvious. These countries are all ruled by conservative dynastic regimes which – to varying degrees – wield overwhelming editorial control over their respective media forums (all of which are nationalised). This has meant that local political issues receive virtually no coverage except via the occasional heavily veiled wording in a newspaper. All magazines, television programmes, films and videos from abroad are censored, with any references to the Gulf and its various regimes removed unless unequivocally laudatory. Bare skin and alcohol advertising are also banned, as are sexually explicit or other religiously questionable materials. Several Gulf states, such as Kuwait and Qatar, have been experimenting with a certain modicum of free press and participatory politics. Even there, however, there are tacit parameters which are not to be transgressed. For the most part, Gulf Arab society remains closed.

What then happens with the advent of the Internet, a medium which by its very nature is heavily resistant to any attempt at control, censorship or regulation? Governments in the Gulf find themselves in something of a quandary. On the one hand they are as anxious to take advantage of the Internet as they have been to make use of every other new technology. Its scientific, educational and economic potential have certainly not gone unnoticed in the Gulf. On the other hand they are worried about the perceived threat to their relatively closed societies. Pornography, sex, religious and political debate – all these things would suddenly be available to Gulf citizens. In addition, countries such as Saudi Arabia and Bahrain feel themselves under threat from exiled religious opposition groups who make use of the latest information technology to question the legitimacy of the regimes. The Internet services offered by groups such as the Movement for Islamic Reform in Arabia (MIRA) and the Bahrain Freedom Movement (BFM) in London have in the past been aimed primarily at fellow countrymen abroad, such as students and travelling businessmen. Internet access in the Gulf would provide these groups with a much-desired constituency which had previously been reachable only via the fax.[99] The challenge, then, has been to reconcile these two concerns – that is, to use the Internet as everyone else seems to be doing while at the same time finding some sort of means to prevent citizens from accessing 'undesirable' information and images.

This latter problem has been circumvented by two methods. The first, as noted above, has been to severely limit the amount of Internet access available in the country. Initially only specialised scientific and medical universities and research institutes were allowed onto the Internet, and all material accessed was noted. This parallels the situation in Iran where until early 1996 only higher education establishments could tap into the Internet, and then only over a clogged, high-traffic route via Vienna. The second approach to Internet control, known as the 'proxy-server system', involves the installation of hardware and software safeguards which prevent users from accessing specific sites known to be 'bad'. The system operators keep a list of all banned locations on the central server and any request for one of these sites by a user is refused. The websites of the various Gulf dissident organisations would, one might assume, be among the first on the list. The size of the Internet is a primary foil of this method, however. Sites divide, multiply and mirror themselves on a daily basis and it becomes impossible to keep track of where data is migrating to on the Internet – and hence also impossible to restrict access to all possible sites. 'The proxy-server system would be useless against us', says the exiled owner of an anti-Saudi web site, 'we would mirror [duplicate] the site so often that the authorities would never be able to keep up with us'.[100] Another method of censorship involves the computer searching all downloaded data, looking for references to banned keywords and scanning for graphic patterns that, for example, match those of naked bodies. This method, however, severely slows down one's connection to the Internet and is just as liable to fail in its efforts as it is to succeed.

A combination of these methods has been used in those Gulf countries which do allow public access to the Internet. The UAE's sole service provider, Etisalat, for example, has installed a proxy-server system which allows it to select the sites available to its users at any one time. They are also negotiating with a British security company for the installation of an elaborate system which would allow police to monitor all requests for data sent by UAE Internet accounts and would alert them whenever banned materials were requested by users.[101] Indeed it is the availability of such systems which has convinced many Gulf countries to gradually phase in the availability of private Internet access. Kuwait was first, followed by the UAE, Bahrain and Qatar. Oman went on-line in early 1997, but Saudi Arabia, the largest and most conservative of the Gulf states, hesitated until 1999, with its advertised dates for providing private Internet service being put back time and again. The authorities in Saudi Arabia announced that private Internet accounts would only be widely issued once a suitable 'moral gateway' has been installed. Effectively, this means routing all of the country's Internet traffic through a single system – most likely the King Abdul Aziz City for Science and Technology (KACST) – for 'ethical filtering' before sending it on to a variety of local servers operated by service providers.[102]

At this point it is too early to tell what the long-term impact of the Internet will be on Gulf society. Its presence has, however, already provoked a number of telling incidents. Dubai's chief of police, Major General Dhahi Khalfan Tamim has been vocal in emphasising the need to control access to the Internet and has even found himself embroiled in a public feud with the service provider Etisalat, a rare occurrence in the Emirates. The conflict centred around the question of who possesses jurisdiction to issue licenses for Internet access. Major General Dhahi claimed that the police and security forces were ultimately responsible for monitoring the flow of information in and out of the emirate, while the 60 per cent state-owned Etisalat insisted that its own expertise should have the deciding hand.[103] In other comments the Major General has expressed fears about Israel trying to disrupt Arab countries using the Internet and has also recommended that the UAE follow the lead of Singapore in placing tight restrictions on Internet access.[104] So it is difficult to read the politics behind an event such as the opening of the region's first Internet café in Dubai. This enterprise, which brings the Internet out into the open, can be understood in a number of ways. We might choose to see it as the popularisation of the Internet, as an indication that the Internet well and truly has arrived in the Gulf. In this case its installation in a very public space – a shopping centre – represents a victory of consumer demand over state authority. Alternatively, however, we might just as easily read the situation as one of government intervention. This rendition would hold that state authorities sanctioned the establishment of an Internet café precisely so that the network would be brought into the open. Instead of accessing the Internet from the privacy of their own homes where government monitoring is nearly impossible, the café encourages potential users to go on-line in a very public setting. According to this logic, people would be less likely to attempt to access questionable material under circumstances where they could be easily scrutinised.

The religious sector has also reacted to the arrival of the Internet. Islamist deputies in Kuwait, for example, submitted a bill to that country's parliament which called on the government to be wary of 'sin-inducing' material on the Internet which '[does] not suit our social values'.[105] The proposal also recommended that the government act swiftly to put control mechanisms in place. Two months later the Kuwaiti Ministry of Communications announced that it would regulate the country's main Internet connection point. 'This operation', they announced, 'will give us full control of the Internet in Kuwait, as well as full control of the necessary equipment. Anyone who wants to be an [Internet service] provider will have to do so under certain conditions which we are currently drafting.'[106] It is difficult to determine whether or not this new policy was prompted by the protests of the Islamist parliamentarians. Their publicisation of the issue, however, must certainly have been a factor.

In Iran users have been told that their e-mail has to comply with Islamic laws and traditions,[107] and in the Arab Gulf countries the various regimes have worked to ensure that Internet feeds entering their societies are devoid of controversial and sinful materials. By effectively reducing the content of the

Internet in this way and by heavily promoting their own Arabic-language sites, these countries can indeed manage to 'localise the translocal' to some degree. Recent plans to expand the region-specific GulfNet project are another pointer in this direction, an indication of how technologies from the 'outside' can be appropriated for purely local use. But this is only one side of the story. The arrival in the Gulf of networked forums such as the Internet offers the possibility of something for which Arab Gulf society is becoming increasingly impatient: a minimal public sphere. 'We have agreed to ban sex, religion and politics on the Internet to respect local laws', notes one user, 'but when someone downloads from North America and they discuss God, for example, the chatting continues and you learn something. The authorities can't do anything about this'.[108]

Another potential source of annoyance for the various regimes is satellite television. The Movement for Islamic Reform in Arabia (MIRA) is planning to tap into the estimated one million 'illegal' satellite dishes in Saudi Arabia in order to beam its message of Islamic reform straight to the Saudi masses. Sa'ad al-Faqih, the co-ordinator of the project, doubts that such activities will prompt a new crackdown on satellite dishes in the country. He notes that there are simply too many of them, and also that the increasingly small size of the dishes means they are often difficult to find. Ironically, it can also be argued that the regime actually wants Saudis to have access to satellite television, so that it can offer counter-propaganda via its own vast media arm that includes the European-based Middle East Broadcasting Corporation (MBC), ART and Orbit, the premier providers of Arabic-language satellite television. The sale of satellite dishes in the Kingdom also provides a lucrative income for those members of the royal family who traffic in them. MIRA is planning to rent time on a commercial satellite well outside Saudi jurisdiction. 'After all', says al-Faqih, 'the Saudis can't buy the whole sky.' He believes that satellite television will start to have a major impact in Saudi Arabia once he begins a series of phone-in programmes during which Saudis will be able to place anonymous, untraceable calls to the studio and will be able to express their criticisms of the government live on air, beyond the reach of the regime. Al-Faqih believes that once other Saudis see their fellow citizens stand up publicly to criticise the al-Sa'ud, they will gain the confidence to do so themselves. In his mind, the greatest imperative is to make Saudis aware that public criticism and debate about the politics and problems of their country are possible. Everything else, he believes, will follow from that. 'Once we have this up and running', al-Faqih insists, 'it will do much more damage to the regime than any bomb ever could'.[109]

Spaces of public debate are few and far between in the Gulf, with a few of the countries only just cautiously easing back on their tight control of the media. The socio-economic situation in the region – and especially in Saudi Arabia – is such that the citizens of these countries are increasingly coming to demand that they be treated *as* citizens; that is, that they be granted a certain number of political rights. High levels of unemployment among recent university graduates – who previously were guaranteed a government job upon completion of their degrees – have spawned a generation which is largely disillusioned with the al-Sa'ud regime. Substantial numbers of young Saudis suddenly find themselves needing to criticise the government, but without any effective forum in which to do so. Inspired by exiled groups such as CDLR and MIRA and also by charismatic local ulama, Islamist discourse is increasingly becoming their chosen language of protest. The regime is well aware of this potential instability and is hence very hesitant to allow the Saudi population access to computer-mediated communication. Preventing users from downloading pornography and sinful texts from 'Out There' is one thing. How, though, can governments prevent their citizens from talking to each other? There exist large sections of these populations which have no interest in Western nasties: problems closer to home are much more pressing. For them, computer networks in the Gulf provide a means by which local political issues can be discussed and debated, responses planned and actions co-ordinated. For them the Internet offers a semblance of political civility, albeit somewhat different in form from the model of 'civil society' which we derive from Western liberal theory. If we contextualise the sociopolitical implications of Gulf Internet use in this way, then the sense in which it represents a localisation of the translocal starts to become clear.

In the case of the Arab Gulf countries, therefore, a translocal force such as the Internet is 'made local' in two key fashions: (1) official censorship tries to reduce its content such that it fits within the normative constraints of Gulf Muslim society; while at the same time, (2) various religio-political communities in the Gulf may attempt to appropriate it as a form of civil society – perhaps explicitly in opposition to the various ruling regimes. Although the example of the Gulf was initially framed to serve as a contrast to the experience of the Internet in the Muslim diaspora ('re-localising' the translocal vs. a shift from locality to translocality), we have to recognise in the end that any dichotomy between these two identities, the translocal diaspora Muslim and the local Gulf Muslim, is false. Translocality means that individuals can move fluidly between these roles – picking and choosing as convenient, emphasising and de-emphasising as the situation demands. Translocal information technology has undoubtedly had a strong impact on Muslim politics wherever they have emerged; it has provided Islamists with effective new tools with which to network, disseminate information and raise their profiles. Increased interaction between various 'local' conceptions of Islam (as mediated by cultural, regional and national traditions) also serves to emphasise the heterogeneity within the religion. Finally, globalised information technology has provided new forums for the politicisation of Muslim discourses and the basis of a new framework within which Muslims might reimagine the umma. However, as Appadurai reminds us, the virtual umma feeds back into highly localised political discourses and nascent public spheres, such as the Islamist struggle against the Saudi regime.[110] In this sense, information technologies reveal the dialectical nature of locality and translocality.

Conclusions: new Islamist intellectuals and 'globalisation from below'

It has become apparent that the encounter between Islam and the translocal technologies of communication is as multifaceted as the religion itself. The rise of IT has led to considerable intermingling and dialogue between disparate interpretations of what it means to be 'Islamic'. The politics of authenticity which inevitably ensues from this also serves to further fragment traditional sources of authority such that the locus of 'real' Islam and the identity of those who are permitted to speak on its behalf become ambiguous. It is in this context that we have witnessed the emergence of a new breed of Islamist intellectual. 'For the new intellectuals', writes Olivier Roy, 'neither the transmission of knowledge nor the place of this transmission is institutionalised. Everyone is "authorised" '.[111] We can hear this latter point echoed in the writings of two Islamists who fit the 'new intellectual' profile well. Hassan al-Turabi, the ideologue of Sudan's self-styled 'Islamic experiment' suggests a broad answer to the question of who can be regarded as part of the ulama. 'Because all knowledge is divine and religious', he argues, 'a chemist, an engineer, an economist, or a jurist are all ulama'.[112] Likewise, Muhammad al-Mass'ari claims that '[e]very single Muslim, man or woman, is empowered to ijtihad. You do not need an ordination from any ruler or scholar'.[113] This language can be read as part of a discourse urging Muslims to turn away from jaded sources of traditional scripturalism and established authorities, and encouraging them instead to use their own faculties to assess the merits of various religious arguments.[114] This, in many ways, is an Islam with a distinctly modern, or perhaps even *post*modern, ring to it. The vocabulary here is eclectic, combining 'soundbites' of religious knowledge into novel combinations suited for complex, translocal contexts. 'What we see in the spaces that focus on the identities of the participants are mixed discourses, crossover talk between domains (notably science, religious, social and cultural issues), borrowing and trafficking in alternative forms and bases of authority and legitimacy', notes Jon Anderson.[115]

Furthermore, the discourse of the new Islamist intellectual is usually explicitly anti-establishment in nature. It seeks to question the legitimacy of the state, the institution and even society.[116] Neither the mosque nor the state is to be trusted as a source of authentic Islam, and this allows us to understand the popularity of cassette-based sermons and pamphlets on Islam which originate from outside these institutions.[117] The new Islam hence exists in spaces which institutionalised forms of politics cannot reach.

> The state has no means by which it can control the new Islamist intellectual in his social function. His thought does not correspond to his social position, he does not live from his profession, the networks of activities are on the fringe of institutions, when they are not entirely clandestine. He operates in *remote places* (meeting houses,

sites of worship, educational centers, [transnational diasporas]) and in spaces outside of the traditional society that the state has not resocialised.[118]

The new Islamist intellectual thus represents an interstitial political identity, one which inhabits the gaps between institutional forms. His rhetoric challenges the legitimacy of the state, and – insofar as translocal information technologies question the integrity of state boundaries – his practices challenge its spatiality.[119] As James Clifford writes, '[s]uch visions and counterhistories can support strategies for nontotalizing "globalisation from below". [This] phrase...is proposed to name transregional social movements that both resist and use hegemonizing technologies and communications'.[120] It is through information technology that we are able to read the hybridity of the new Islamist project. The communications medium serves as a form of *authority* (modern, post-traditional) through which an *authentic* message (Islam, ethicality) is transmitted. In this chapter we have seen some of the ways in which information technologies have mediated (and mediatised) Muslim notions of authority. We have also investigated the role played by IT in helping Muslims to create and sustain translocal communities reminiscent of the umma concept. To what extent, though, are the changing connotations of Islamic authority and authenticity in translocal spaces leading to a critical reimagination of the boundaries of Muslim politics? This is the question to be taken up in the final chapter.

6 Reimagining the umma?

Knowledge is to foresee, in order to obtain power. However, to be powerful, one should start by knowledge, and one cannot know without the condition of liberating oneself from the obsession of power.

(Mohammed Arkoun, *Pour une critique de la raison Islamique*)

[T]he networks and circuits in which transnational migrants and refugees are implicated constitute fluidly bounded transnational or globalised spaces in which new transnational forms of political organization, mobilization, and practice are coming into being.

(Michael Peter Smith, 'Can You Imagine?')

In this final chapter I want to work towards a closer weave of the two narrative strands running through this book. On the one hand we have an account of translocality, non-statist forms of community and the emergence of new 'distanciated' political spaces. On the other, a story about transformation within 'travelling Islam' and the diasporic Muslims whose lives it shapes. Although my text is peppered with numerous references (some more explicit than others) to the linkages I see between the politics of translocality and the reimagination of the umma, I want in this conclusion to make their relationship more clear.

In a recent essay, Dale Eickelman alludes to a nascent 'Islamic Reformation'.[1] Eickelman himself would be the first to admit the difficulties involved in trying to draw any hard and fast comparisons with the Christian Reformation. As he points out, Islam does not possess a clerical hierarchy or 'centre' against which one can rebel. This essay also is not in any way an attempt to 'push the other back in time' by suggesting that Islam is only now experiencing the upheavals which Christianity went through four hundred years ago. Rather, by referring to contemporary changes in Islam as a 'Reformation', Eickelman is indicating a trend in much of the Muslim world towards a greater critical awareness of religion. Muslims are increasingly willing to take Islam into their own hands, relying on their own readings and interpretations of the classical sources or following 'reformist' intellectuals who question traditional dogmas and challenge the claims of the ulama to be privileged sources of religious knowledge. Much of this is related, as we have seen in the previous chapter, to massive rises in literacy rates and the increased presence of religious issues in the public sphere as a result of globalised communications and media technologies. The authority of the written word is no longer the sole reserve of a select few, and the religious elite cannot compete with the myriad range of Muslim voices reading, debating and, effectively, *reformulating* Islam on the Internet, on satellite television and in a plethora of widely-distributed books and pamphlets. Thus, 'media Islam', the new intellectuals and popular religious discourse, I want to argue, are all contributing towards the emergence of what we might call a new 'Muslim public sphere'. Furthermore, I also want to suggest that translocality should be seen as that which both enables this reformist discourse and provides the spaces in which much of it is elaborated. In this conclusion, therefore, we will first examine several aspects of the latter influence, that of translocality, on Islam, before going on to assess the ways in which the Muslim reimagination of political community can be seen to constitute a new form of translocal politics.

Critical Islam and changing boundaries

Translocality has contributed significantly to the development of a critical Islamic discourse. In addition to the 'structural' factors mentioned above (e.g. increased literacy and the role of information technology), the objectification of religion which occurs as Muslims move through and dwell in translocal space (i.e. their capability to externalise and critique Islam) has opened up new avenues for rethinking and reformulating Islamic thought. Many authors have emphasised that diasporic Muslims live in the constant shadow of the West, and that their discourse is consequently over determined by the struggle against Western hegemony. I want to suggest, however, that translocality actually enables Muslims to focus on a different type of hegemony – namely, power asymmetries *within* Islam. By this I mean that in the process of displacing Islam from a particular national context and reconstituting it as a 'travelled' object in diaspora, Muslims develop an increased capacity to recognise, account for, and debate the difference within their religion. The relativisation of Islam which naturally occurs through travel allows Muslims to see internal hegemony, and translocality provides them with the intellectual environment in which to develop counter-hegemonic discourses. Talal Asad has argued that '[t]o secure its unity – to make its own history – dominant power has worked best through differentiating and classifying practices'.[2] The 'dominant power' to which he refers is usually taken to be a colonial or neo-imperial form – or at least something emanating from the West. I want to argue, however, that in translocality we often find hybridising manoeuvres which also seek to disclose the dominant powers within Islam. How, though, can we conceptualise such a thing as 'dominant power' in relation to Islam? We do so by looking for totalising discourses which claim the authority to represent the 'real' Islam and which also seek to label and classify 'deviant' Muslims. In the same way that the West reproduces its exceptionalism by repudiating any ethical claims which do not derive from its own tradition of modernity, so Islamic hegemonies (e.g. the Sunni majority) label and differentiate those readings of Islam which diverge from its orthodoxy (e.g. Shi'ism). This internal 'othering' is not, however, limited to theological debates. We see it also in the diasporic political arena, where groups such as Hizb ut-Tahrir portray themselves as the only movement pursuing a 'truly Islamic' political agenda, and in doing so are able to set the terms of the political debate (see Chapter Four). Competing tendencies are hence constantly forced to respond to Hizb ut-Tahrir's ethical claims, rather than advancing their own vision of political community.

One of the chief obstacles to critical thinking in Islam during recent years has been the fact that Islamist discourse is usually constructed around a set of claims represented as non- or even anti-Western in nature. To critique this discourse, therefore, would be to betray and weaken its anti-Western potential. Another component of the same discourse has been a drive to depict criticism itself as a Western, and hence anti-Islamic, practice. Unsurprisingly, therefore, one of the main strategies deployed by hegemonic Muslim political discourse (such as that of Hizb ut-Tahrir) is to portray any Muslim advocating a critical approach towards Islam as a 'closet Westerner'. A zero-sum game is constructed in which Muslims are either 'truly' Islamic (i.e. sympathetic to Hizb ut-Tahrir) or Western collaborators (i.e. critical of Hizb ut-Tahrir's political discourse). Muslim modernists who seek to combine Islamic political concepts with Western analytic methodologies are similarly condemned by fundamentalists and conservatives alike as 'Westernised'.[3] It seems the slightest hint of Western thought in a Muslim discourse immediately corrupts and invalidates any ideas which might emerge from it. The hybridity is not tolerated. In other words, the hegemonic discourse is basing itself on a claim to 'purity' and 'authenticity', what in Islam is sometimes referred to by the term *aṣāla*. Dismantling this hegemony requires two theoretical moves. The first, as Shaw and Stewart note, is to point out that authenticity and originality do not necessarily depend on purity and that both 'pure' and 'mixed' (i.e. hybrid) traditions can be unique.[4] 'Authenticity', rather, must be seen as a construct rendered by rhetorics of power and persuasion. '[C]laims of authenticity', argue Shaw and Stewart, 'depend on the political acumen and persuasiveness of cultural "spin doctors" who convert given historical particularities and contingencies to valued cultural resources'.[5] It is therefore necessary to open up a discursive space in which Muslim subjectivities can enunciate asala in the plural; that is, combat totalising discourses by articulating discrepant conceptions of Islam, and without being accused of having 'violated the system of naming'. Radhakrishnan alludes to this when he speaks of an authenticity based on 'multiple rootedness'. He envisages this as an interstitial site at which discourses of tradition and innovation can be creatively negotiated:

> What I mean by 'authenticity' here is that critical search for a third space that is complicitous neither with the deracinating imperatives of Westernization nor with theories of a static, natural, and single-minded autochthony...[T]here need be no theoretical or epistemological opposition

between authenticity and historical contingency, between authenticity and hybridity, between authenticity and invention.[6]

I want to argue that translocal spaces provide discursive environments conducive to such alternative articulations. As we have seen in Chapter Four, Muslims encounter a diverse range of interpretations and schools of thought in diaspora. As dialogue is enabled between these different tendencies, the differences between them are often attenuated. This diminution of difference, I believe, results from particular conceptions of Islam becoming disembedded from the 'lifeworlds' that sustain them in countries of origin, and, via translocality, resettled into circumstances in which they are in a minority. This process of relativisation allows Muslims to partake in a discourse of particularity, one in which their conception of religion is no longer universal. Crucially, however, and unlike hegemonic discourse, this is also a space in which no particular conception of Islam is *negated*. Difference is negotiated, rather than eradicated. As one observer puts it, 'You learn to adjust to other tendencies and be at ease with other interpretations of Islam without feeling that you are diluting your own beliefs'.[7]

That is not to say, however, that translocal Islam is a model of sectarian harmony. There are always forces working to narrow the boundaries of political community and seeking to monopolise the discourse of political legitimacy. What does one do, for example, about those extremists, such as Hizb ut-Tahrir, who refuse to engage with pluralistic conceptions of asala? This problem requires another set of theoretical manoeuvres. So far we have only dealt with the problem of opening up space for multiple articulations of Islam, a problem which, as I have argued, is largely solved by the condition of translocality. What we have not dealt with is the question of how one can engage in a critique of Islam without, according to the accusations of those such as Hizb ut-Tahrir, falling prey to Westernisation. One possible strategy is to turn the tables on the extremists and to construct a discourse in which *they* become the unwitting victims of Western hegemony. This is accomplished by observing that a large proportion of their own discourse is devoted to anti-Western rhetoric; so much so, in fact, that they end up neglecting to address the problems which most Muslims face on a day-to-day basis. That is to say, they are so obsessed with denouncing Western hegemony – and, in fact, have managed by and large to define the political field in relation to this very issue – that they do not engage with the substantive issues facing their constituencies. Some Muslim thinkers, notably in the West, have started to problematise the methodology of the extremists by pointing out that in many ways it simply serves to reproduce Western hegemony. 'As long as Islamic political thinkers are locked in a (one-sided) conversation with western political thought', writes Bobby Sayyid, 'they remain locked in a logic in which there is no space for anything other than the West'.[8] This sentiment is echoed by Akeel Bilgrami, who argues that '[a] failure to come out of the neurotic obsession with the Western and colonial determination of their present condition will only prove [to Muslims] that that determination was utterly comprehensive in the destruction it wrought'.[9]

This obsession with the West, it can be argued, has created an impasse whose logic runs something like this: 'If a critique of Islam is enacted then we Muslims are falling right into the hands of the West because this kind of (ironic) critique is a Western mode and hence will inevitably weaken Islam. If, on the other hand, we do *not* engage in a critical renewal of our religion then Muslims will never make any progress in the modern world'. To escape from this dilemma, two further moves are required. The first is to dismantle the assumption that critique is an exclusively 'Western' concept. This is accomplished by pointing out that because there is no historical necessity to Western hegemony then therefore there is also no legitimate Western totalisation of discursive modes.[10] This first move enables hybridity by permitting the intermingling of Islamic and Western modes within a single discursive space. Many Muslim thinkers in diaspora are happy to engage in this sort of hybridity today, seeing in it the power of Bhabha's post-colonial political hybrid – or, in other words, a method for undermining the coherence of Western hegemony.[11] I want to argue, however, that a far more radical methodology can emerge from this disjuncture, one that is particularly suited to the 'multiple rootedness' of translocal space: an Islamic critique of Islam. 'Critiquing Islam from within' is a notion that has gained particular currency in recent years among diasporic Muslim intellectuals in the West. The late Fazlur Rahman, for example, was a keen advocate of such a methodology.[12] For him, a Muslim critique of Islam does not mean questioning the authenticity of the Qur'an or hadith. Rather, what need to be unmasked are the dogmas developed over the centuries (e.g. the various madhahib and their subsequent corruptions) which were not specifically authorised by the Prophet. For Rahman, Islam has been bloated by intransigent theologies which have little or nothing to do with the ethical core of Muhammad's message. These dogmas, he believes, are often treated as if they, like the Qur'an, are somehow the untouchable word of God. There is thus a need to distinguish between what Rahman terms 'normative Islam' (Muhammad's 'true' message) and 'historical Islam' (the codification of these norms by various political hegemonies).[13] Too often, he argues, modern Muslims display a tendency to conflate these two. The juridical opinions (fatwas) of Islamic scholars, regardless of their renown, are nothing more than historically-situated opinion and therefore open to debate and, more crucially, abrogation.

Furthermore, Islam already possesses a rich critical vocabulary. In the twin concepts of *istiḥsān* and *istiṣlāḥ*, for example, we find the foundations of a form of critical reasoning. Istihsan is a method for deriving legal principles which contradict the conventional methods of analogical deduction. It has also been used by some classical scholars to describe the process of arriving at legal decisions for which no authority can be found in the traditions. Istislah is even more interesting because it possesses an inherent normative component. It refers to a methodology which seeks specifically to produce juridical decisions which are in the 'public interest' (maslaha – see Chapter Four). It is therefore intrinsically tied to notions of human welfare and finding 'the good'. Its ethical strength has even allowed some scholars to use istislah to question the validity of legal principles derived directly from the Qur'an and sunna.[14] There is also the concept of ijtihad, which refers to the exercise of independent judgement in determining one's opinion. This is, effectively, Muslim 'free thinking', and often figures heavily in situations, such as those faced by diasporic Muslims, where the classical sources provide little guidance in determining a correct course of action. Finally, there is also a sense in which a multiplicity of asala has already been institutionalised in Islam. We find this in the notion of ikhtilaf, which refers to differences of opinion among religious scholars. In order to deal with this plurality, Islamic orthodoxy has traditionally held that each opinion is of equal value, and therefore equally 'authentic'.[15] There is also a saying attributed to several of the early caliphs and sometimes even to Muhammad himself to the effect that differences of opinion within the umma should be seen as a sign of divine favour.

So what form is this critical thinking in Islam taking today? Not surprisingly, some of the most innovative ideas are coming from those thinkers who have either travelled abroad to study or who have had sustained contact with translocal critical theories. Rashid Ghannoushi, for example, the exiled leader of the Tunisian Islamist movement, has recently argued that ikhtilaf should be politically institutionalised. He means by this that a political community should possess the right to vote for or against the political implications of any given textual interpretation, and also to change its mind later if it so desires.[16] The implication here is that an opinion is not somehow inherently 'true' simply by virtue of having emanated from the ulama; rather, these opinions simply enter the 'public sphere' – that is to say, they become contestable and open to re-interpretation. Other Muslim scholars, from Egypt's Hassan Hanafi[17] to Harun Nasution in Indonesia, have attempted to re-read the traditional theological texts (*kalam*) so that they speak to the political imperatives of contemporary Islam.[18] There are also those, such as Fazlur Rahman, who have sought to critique some of Islam's orthodox political formulations. This is part of his broader project, outlined above, to remove interpretative agency from the hands of traditional scholars – and, more importantly for our context, from the state – and place it in the hands of Muslims. He argues, for example, that the slogan 'al-islam din wa dawla' (Islam is both religion and state – see Chapter Two) is often 'employed to dupe the common man into accepting that, instead of politics or the state serving the long-range objectives of Islam, Islam should come to serve the immediate and myopic objectives of party politics'.[19] The Iranian philosopher Abdolkarim Soroush has recently made similar arguments with regard to the situation in contemporary Iran. His message is particularly radical in that context because governance in Iran is, in theory, based on Imam Khomeini's principle of *wilayat al-faqih* ('governorship of the legal scholars').[20] This doctrine states that leadership of the Islamic community should be vested in the religious scholars because of their superior knowledge of the Sharia. Soroush, on the other hand, argues that no single interpretation of Islam is ever final and that therefore a religious state can never be ruled according to an 'official' political ideology.[21] It is not surprising that such a position has made him a controversial figure in Iran. He has been forced by the pressures of conservative Islam to take up a more translocal existence, and currently spends considerable time lecturing abroad.

One of the most radical projects of Islamic critique can be found in the work of Mohammed Arkoun, an Algerian-Berber whose academic career has been spent almost entirely in Paris. Arkoun has sought to deploy post-structural methodology as a critical tool in his investigations of the history of ideas in Islam. His genealogies of Islamic reason and authority, for example, are highly original contributions to the growing discourse on critical Islam.[22] Arkoun reads the hegemony of the early Muslim dynasties, for example, as a delinking of political action and symbolic creativity:

> Instead, there triumphed an inverse process whereby the symbolic capital carried by the Qur'an was utilised for the construction and imposition of an official, orthodox Islam: *official* because it resulted from political choices of the state, which physically eliminated opponents who stood for any other interpretations (the Shi'ite and Kharijite protesters, most notably); *orthodox* because the experts accredited by the political authorities gave credence to the idea that it is possible to read the Word of God correctly.[23]

By revealing the historical situatedness of these supposedly 'correct' readings, Arkoun is able to deconstruct layer upon layer of supposedly immutable theology. His is a theoretically sophisticated methodology which provides crucial support for the more general task of re-stating the nature and sources of Islamic authority – a task which, as we have seen, is most actively enjoined in the Muslim translocality. Many of the writers I have mentioned, such as Rahman, Hanafi and Arkoun, have at one time or another been 'travelling Muslims' and these translocal experiences have significantly influenced the development of their thinking by bringing them into contact with new peoples and bodies of theory, Muslim and non-Muslim alike.

How though has the combination of these critical ideas and translocality been transforming popular Muslim political discourse? As we have seen in Chapter One, a number of writers have been emphasising the ways in which globalising processes increasingly disembed peoples and their political identities from the context of the nation-state. I want to argue that one of the most tangible manifestations of this phenomenon can be found in what I have termed translocal Islam. To some degree, as we have already seen, this is a product of the transformations occurring within Islam related to the sociology of knowledge and the question of who is 'authorised' to speak (and 'act') on behalf of Islam. Muslims are turning away from the traditional religious scholars of their 'local' communities and creating 'translocal' political spaces in which the authority of disparate Muslim voices is recognised. Often, as we have seen, the intellectuals to whom young Muslims turn for inspiration live in (and between) distant lands. We have noted, for example, the transnational relevance of thinkers such as Mawdudi and Khomeini. We can also recall travelling Indonesian students challenging village tradition by using ideas from Pakistan and Saudi Arabia. The national identity (or state affiliation) of these thinkers is not important. What matters is that they are able to articulate a Muslim (and thus 'authentic') normativity well-suited to the circumstances and problems of contemporary life. 'One of the most basic consequences of the new relationship between the religious community and society', argues Schiffauer, 'is that one no longer automatically belongs to a *given* community'.[24] The ability to publicly contest, debate and rearticulate ethical claims allows those who were formerly subjected to the hegemony of a particular ethical vision to now *politicise* their Muslim identities. A religious community becomes a political community, hence changing the boundaries which have traditionally constituted the latter in Islam.

Consequently, we have seen marked differences in the ways some Muslim movements organise themselves in diaspora. 'Lay' Muslims sometimes feel more inclined to become involved in Muslim associations in translocality because debates about political interpretations often take on a greater significance here.[25] We also see a tendency towards more open and dispersed forms of leadership, such as the phenomenon of elected imams in the United States.[26] As we have noted above, the leaders or ideologues of a diasporic Muslim community might actually be based in settings far removed from those of their constituencies. The cases of the Sufi saint Zindapir (Pakistan) and the Naqshbandi Sheikh Nazim (Cyprus), both of whom possess sizeable numbers of adherents in the UK, illustrate this point well (see Chapter Four). It is not only the more conservative Sufi cults that have been affected by these translocal upheavals. The rise of the 'Islamist new intellectuals' (see Chapter Five) is also linked to the transnational circulation of books, pamphlets and media technologies. Indeed, the new intellectuals' versatility with these technologies, when contrasted with the relative 'backwardness' of traditional sources of religious authority, goes a long way towards explaining their popularity — especially among the younger generation of Muslims. Even the icons of traditionalism have been forced at times to pay credence to the efficacy of the new intellectuals. For example, echoes of popular ideologues such as Ali Shariati can be heard in the speeches of Imam Khomeini.[27] And the eminent faculty at al-Azhar has had to adjust to the fact that many young Muslims today are more willing to take their political theory from Rashid Ghannoushi than from a venerable 'alim.

The critical reform of Islam is an ongoing project. It is by no means the dominant tendency in contemporary Islam, but it is growing rapidly and its results can be seen to some degree in every corner of the Muslim world, whether it be an Indonesian university student questioning the authority of his village imam, a British-Asian Muslim castigating the 'un-Islamic' practices of her parents, or Abdolkarim Soroush challenging the political legitimacy of the Iranian state. Critical Islam is also a gradual process. It is a slow (r)evolution, one working away quietly (but with occasional high-profile soundbites) at the grassroots of Muslim society. Obviously there is still considerable work to be done. As

Talal Asad points out, Muslims still have a lot of thinking to do before they can claim to possess a distinctive vision of polity. All too often, claims about an Islamic political theory turn out to be little more than anti-Western polemics, or else reaffirmations of the nation-state with a few 'Islamic' terms thrown in for good measure.[28] What *can* safely be said to be changing, however, are the boundaries of Muslim political community. In summary, then, I want to review the arguments I have made as to why translocality must be seen as a large part of these changes.

The first sense in which translocal space changes the boundaries of Muslim political community is related to the fact that in many of the cases we have dealt with community is constituted not in accordance with ethno-national identity, but rather in terms of one's identification with and, more crucially, rearticulation of a particular set of ethical claims (e.g. Islam as a 'good'). Muslims are disembedded from national contexts and resettled in interstitial spaces (i.e. 'in' a society but not 'of' it) such that Islam becomes invested with a new political relevance. 'The religious' rather than 'the national' becomes the focus of political identity. A second change relates to how the boundaries of political community are transformed in translocal spaces when 'other' cultures and new structural contexts are encountered. A good example of this is the recasting of classical concepts such as dar al-islam, dar al-harb, and dar al-'ahd (see Chapter Four), which was instigated by Islam's cognisance of its minority status in diaspora. Muslim notions of 'inside' and 'outside' have suddenly been inverted and traditional forms of hegemony (e.g. those seeking to label some Muslims as deviants or heretics) are forced to redraw the contours of their identity to account for the Muslim 'other'. A third and closely related change concerns the widening of the parameters which determine who is permitted to speak on behalf of Islam. What was religious becomes 'political' as soon as Muslims begin to question the authority of those who have previously been recognised as legitimate sources of knowledge (e.g. the ulama). New intellectuals, university students and lay Muslims – men *and* women – can to some degree all be seen as sources of ijtihad and purveyors of authentic Islam. Their debates and critiques, I want to argue, constitute a dramatic widening of the *Muslim public sphere*. Furthermore, its emergence can be explained to a large extent as a consequence of translocality – in other words, the travelling theories, hybrid/diasporic identities and media technologies which Muslims are increasingly embracing. This public sphere also fulfils a crucial political function insofar as it offers a discursive space in which Muslims can articulate their normative claims (i.e. 'Islam') from a multiplicity of subject positions. As we have seen, though, this is not a space devoid of hegemony. There are still those forces seeking to monopolise the political agenda and to denounce any Muslims who deviate from their vision. The nature of this arena is such, however, that dissenting voices will always be heard. And as we have seen above, there are those who are doing much more than arguing for a greater toleration of different opinions. A number of Muslim thinkers have been undertaking ambitious critiques of their religion's traditional conceptual lexicon, and producing innovative reformulations which help to construct an Islam for contemporary, translocal life.

Therefore, in seeking to answer the question of how Muslims today are reimagining the umma, we can identify two broad, and, in some senses, seemingly contradictory trends. I want to argue however that the apparent incompatibility of these tendencies is only an illusion because, in reality, they are both aspects of the same process. On the one hand, translocality brings together Muslims of diverse sociocultural, sectarian and theological backgrounds. By forcing Islam to hold a mirror up to itself, translocality makes it aware of the many differences (and disunities) within. On the other hand, however, translocality and globalisation are providing Muslims with a greater capacity to communicate, interact and otherwise bridge the distances between them. In this sense, translocality resonates with the Qur'anic injunction to Muslims of different nations to get to know one another (Qur'an 49: 13). It promises that the umma can become a social reality. Although these two forces are seemingly contradictory – one a drive to differentiate, the other a call to unity – they are both constitutive of a single process leading Muslims towards greater 'globality' (see Chapter One) in the sense of a new consciousness of the world as a single space. The Muslim urge to 'relate internationally' thus becomes an impetus to negotiate difference, and to reformulate Islam in the face of globality. I am not in any way arguing that the first tendency, that towards 'unity', will triumph. When I speak of reimagining the umma, I am talking about more than Muslims simply stressing their similarities, de-emphasising their differences and living together in a single global community. Rather, I am speaking about Muslims *reconceptualising* the umma; that is, revising their ideas about who, what and where political community can be. Understood in this way – as possessing a critical edge – the idiom of 'reimagination' potentially has far more radical consequences.

A new politics of translocal space?

Rob Walker has noted that most attempts to explore the conjunction of social movements and world politics have tended to operate within the normative codes of conventional statist politics. He goes on to make the following suggestion:

> An empirical exploration of this conjunction would more usefully begin by examining whether particular movements do or do not express these codes, in their explicit aspirations or their collective practices. It would ask about the articulations of identity and difference, self and other, space and time that constrain and inform their capacity to rearticulate their understanding of the political under contemporary conditions. It would ask about the connections between such rearticulations in different structural locations.[29]

My exploration of Muslim political community has been an attempt to do exactly this. I began by arguing that global sociocultural transformations are giving rise to new forms of transnational politics which conventional readings of the political – and especially the realist tradition in international relations – are incapable of accounting for. The nation-state model, I suggested, is under threat from a number of 'distanciating' processes which disembed peoples and cultures from particular territorial locales and spread their social relations across space and time. As a result, political identities no longer inhabit the exclusive container of the nation-state and must be seen as configured in and between multiple political spaces – a condition I termed *translocality*. I went on to argue that disciplinary projects outside international relations – namely, post-colonial studies, cultural studies and critical anthropology – have developed far more sophisticated ways of thinking about 'the international' in the present context, emphasising as they do the fact that 'locality' is now an increasingly difficult concept to apprehend given the volume of movement, travel and communication between spaces and places. '[T]he spatial extension of households and ethnic communities across national borders', writes Michael Peter Smith, 'is producing new patterns of cultural and political appropriation and resistance by transnational migrants and refugees who in some ways partake of two nation-states but in other ways *move beyond them*'.[30] The declining efficacy of the nation-state means therefore that 'the national' no longer possesses a monopoly over descriptions of political identity. This fact has allowed non- or post-national formulations of political organisation to enter the picture. As a result of this, some writers have been led to speculate about new forms of post-national cosmopolitan identity,[31] while others have followed Walker's suggestion and undertaken studies of particular movements whose discourses imagine non-statist forms of political community. The present study can be seen as an example of the latter. I chose to focus on Islam because it represents a prominent non-statist, non-national identity discourse which today claims widespread – in fact, one would almost be justified in saying truly 'global' – validity as an ethical construct. Furthermore, there exist today significant translocal Muslim communities which have been constituted by a variety of migratory and post-colonial flows. My claim is that many of the movements which have arisen out of these communities can be seen as a form of what Smith has called 'transnational grassroots politics'.

I began my portrayal of the Muslim translocality by arguing for a non-essentialist definition of Islam, focusing more on Muslim subjectivity and less on some objectified entity called Islam. This was necessary in order to allow for the multiple definitions, interpretations and articulations of Islam to be found in translocal space. I went on to examine the nature of Muslim discourse in relation to the debates on modernity, postmodernity and the West. I accepted Bobby Sayyid's thesis that the decentring of the West has eroded its totalisation of the discourse of political modernity, but argued that the same forces which have relativised Western hegemony are having the same effect on Muslim hegemony. The result of which is that we find multiple and varied articulations of Islam; a consequence of this is that we have to concentrate not only on the debate between Islam and the West, but also on conversations and contestations occurring *within* Islam. Next I examined two particular sociohistorical contexts in which the Muslim concept of the umma has been articulated as a political project. Both of them, I argued, are important in that they represent key points of reference for contemporary Muslim discourse. The first was the Prophet's community in Medina during the first years of Islam. I explained how this polity, born of travel (the hijra), represented a new idiom of political community in the context of seventh-century Arabia – a shift from tribal, kin-based relations to a confessional community based on a common religious faith. During this period, Muhammad maintained a total monopoly over the articulation of Islam, representing as he did the medium through which the religion was revealed. With his death, however, *Muslim politics*, in the sense of debates over who was authorised to speak for Islam, began. I then examined the use of a Pan-Islamic umma discourse by the anti-colonial reformers of the nineteenth and early twentieth centuries. I noted that the concept of the umma took on a particular resonance at that time because the vast majority of the Muslim world, from North Africa to Southeast Asia, was subject to the same Western hegemony. This represented the first time since Islam's enormous transnational expansion that virtually all Muslims were able to perceive a common 'other'. The processes arising from decolonisation, which I see as an important component of translocality, have given rise to new forms of post-colonial Islam, and I suggested that this is perhaps the best context in which to understand contemporary Islamist discourse.

I then returned to the concept of translocality which I had introduced in the first chapter. I outlined several qualities of translocal space – travelling theory, hybridity and diasporic identity – which I see as crucial to understanding the dynamics of cultural politics in translocality. I first examined a set of ideas surrounding the notion of 'travelling theory' as a means by which to understand how meanings change through movement from one social context to another. I then went on to look at various theoretical formulations of hybridity. This trope, I argued, can be useful in accounting for the transformation of ideas and cultures in translocal spaces, and also in understanding the interplay of competing interpretations and idioms *within* a culture. I suggested that a focus on hybridity is perhaps most meaningful when discussing encounters between variations of an ostensibly homogenous cultural system (e.g. Islam) within translocality. I then examined some of the discourses on migrant and diasporic identity and took issue with those metropolitan post-colonial theorists who celebrate the 'free-floating' nature of diasporic identity. I pointed out that such a perspective requires the adoption of an ironic stance which not all identities – and particularly not *politicised* identities (such as Islam) – possess. Travel, migrancy and hybridity, I therefore concluded, should not be celebrated as part of a postmodern carnival, or as an ontological fad.

Having analysed some of the key theoretical concepts related to translocality, I then began a detailed empirical portrait of the Muslim diaspora. In it, I sought to provide something like a 'case study' of what happens to Islam when it 'travels' into new contexts – and particularly when it enters into and settles amongst non-Muslim societies in the West. My discussion here was organised according to three themes, each of which illustrated a different aspect of the wider Muslim translocality: *debates within the Muslim community* provided examples of encounters and negotiations with the Muslim other; some of the ways in which Muslims are *rethinking Islam* were illustrated by examining contemporary discourses on politics, community and gender; and the final section on *Muslim transnationalism* reminded us of the wider global network of sociopolitical relations in which these various discourses are embedded. I argued that diasporic Islam represents a form of interstitial identity, or, to use Homi Bhabha's terminology, a 'third space', in which the majority society's conception of the political is not embraced, but neither is that of the 'homeland' – especially among the younger generation. This gives rise to forms of political identity which are somehow 'in-between'. Viewed from a translocal perspective, these travelling identities represent a new mode of 'relating internationally' in which the boundaries of political community are constantly open to rearticulation.

In the final chapter I used communications, media and information technologies as a contextual lens through which to read the hybridity of contemporary Islamist discourse. I first examined the historical salience of literacy and modern printing in eroding the traditional scholars' monopoly over legitimate articulations of Islam. I went on to argue that information technology today is intensifying this process by providing lay Muslims with resources such as the Internet and CD-ROM-based textual libraries that allow them to read, interpret and produce Islamic knowledge for themselves. I also looked at the ways in which broadcast, distributive and networked technologies are helping Muslims to forge and sustain distanciated links reminiscent of the umma concept. These forces are also giving voice to alternative sources of Islamic authority and contributing to the development of a wider Muslim public sphere. The case of the Internet in the Arab Gulf states illustrated the transformative potential (and state responses to it) of translocal technologies which become 're-localised' in specific sociopolitical contexts. These technologies are often perceived to represent a threat to established sources of political legitimacy, and hence the latter then seek (often with only mixed success) to circumscribe these new public spheres. A related development in other parts of the Muslim world, I pointed out, has been the emergence of a new breed of Islamist intellectual seeking to encourage and capitalise on this new populist spirit (e.g. 'a chemist, an engineer, an economist, or a jurist are all ulama'). The discourse of the new intellectual often seeks to question the legitimacy of both the state and the mosque (a symbol of traditional conservatism) as sources of 'authentic' Islam. In this sense the new Islamist positions himself in spaces which institutionalised forms of politics cannot reach. The new Islamist intellectual thus represents yet another form of interstitial political identity, inhabiting the borderzones of institutional forms. His anti-statist discourse, articulated via various media, serves as a form of authority (modern, post-traditional) through which an authentic message (Islam, ethicality) is transmitted.

As we have seen in this conclusion, translocality is also contributing to the emergence of new forms of 'critical Islam', by producing thinkers committed to the renewal and reform of religious dogma. Within translocality, these debates over authority in Islam constitute a new form of Muslim public sphere which, in turn, serves to widen the boundaries of Muslim political community. In a broad sense, then, we can conclude that the rethinking of political community is largely a result of Muslims living in translocal spaces which are themselves the product of wider migratory and globalising processes. The example of translocal Islam is therefore only one aspect of a much wider trend. Where Muslims are reimagining the umma, other identities have discrepant communal visions – their own forms of 'transnational grassroots politics'. The state and its 'international relations' are still with us, however, and will be for some time to come. The state will never go out with a bang, and IR will never spontaneously combust. Our ambivalent inclinations towards their normative visions will, however, most likely intensify over time and, eventually, the borders will overflow.

Notes

Introduction

1 Ataullah Siddiqui, 'Muslims in the Contemporary World: Dialogue in Perspective', *World Faiths Encounter*, No. 20, July 1998.
2 Chris Sulavik, 'Citicorp to Launch Islamic Banking Unit', *Reuters*, 9 April 1996.
3 Michael Peter Smith, 'Can You Imagine? Transnational Migration and the Globalization of Grassroots Politics', *Social Text*, No. 39, Summer 1994, p. 15.
4 John Eade, 'Reconstructing Places: Changing Images of Locality in Docklands and Spitalfields', in John Eade (ed.), *Living the Global City: Globalization as Local Process*, London: Routledge, 1997, p. 128.
5 *Ibid.*, p. 129.

1 Beyond disciplinary boundaries

1 Benedict Anderson, *Imagined Communities: Reflections on the Origin and Spread of Nationalism*, London: Verso, Revised Edition, 1991.
2 See Homi Bhabha (ed.), *Nation and Narration*, London: Routledge, 1990.
3 See John Vasquez, *The Power of Power Politics*, London: Pinter, 1983; and Justin Rosenberg, 'What's the Matter with Realism?', *Review of International Studies*, Vol. 16, No. 4, October 1990, pp. 285–303.
4 See John Burton, *World Society*, London: Cambridge University Press, 1972; and Richard Falk, *The Promise of World Order*, Brighton: Wheatsheaf, 1987.
5 See Robert O. Keohane and Joseph S. Nye Jr., *Power and Interdependence*, Boston: Little Brown, 1977; and Stephen Krasner (ed.), *International Regimes*, Ithaca, NY: Cornell University Press, 1983.
6 R.B.J. Walker, *Inside/Outside: International Relations as Political Theory*, Cambridge: Cambridge University Press, 1993, pp. ix–x.
7 Chantal Mouffe, 'For a Politics of Nomadic Identity', in George Robertson, Melinda Mash, Lisa Tickner, Jon Bird, Barry Curtis and Tim Putnam (eds), *Travellers' Tales: Narratives of Home and Displacement*, London: Routledge, 1994, p. 108.
8 *Ibid.*
9 Benedict Anderson, 'Exodus', *Critical Inquiry*, Vol. 20, Winter 1994, pp. 323–4.
10 See Andrew Linklater, *The Transformation of Political Community*, Cambridge: Polity Press, 1998. Linklater outlines what he terms a 'post-Westphalian' conception of the citizen.
11 See e.g. Mary Dietz, 'Context Is All: Feminism and Theories of Citizenship', in Chantal Mouffe (ed.), *Dimensions of Radical Democracy*, London: Verso, 1992.
12 See e.g. Mervyn Frost, *Ethics in International Relations: A Constitutive Theory*, Cambridge: Cambridge University Press, 1996; and Michael Walzer (ed.), *Toward A Global Civil Society*, Providence, RI: Berghahn Books, 1995.

13 See Cynthia Weber, *Simulating Sovereignty: Intervention, the State and Symbolic Exchange*, Cambridge: Cambridge University Press, 1995; Jens Bartelson, *A Genealogy of Sovereignty*, Cambridge: Cambridge University Press, 1995; and Thomas J. Biersteker and Cynthia Weber (eds), *State Sovereignty as Social Construct*, Cambridge: Cambridge University Press, 1996.

14 Arjun Appadurai, 'Sovereignty Without Territoriality: Notes for a Postnational Geography', in Patricia Yaeger, *The Geography of Identity*, Ann Arbor, MI: University of Michigan Press, 1996, p. 47.

15 Robin Cohen, 'Diasporas, the Nation-State, and Globalisation', in Wang Gungwu (ed.), *Global History and Migrations*, Boulder, CO: Westview Press, 1997, p. 135. Emphasis added.

16 See Doug McAdam, John D. McCarthy and Mayer N. Zald (eds), *Comparative Perspectives on Social Movements*, New York: Cambridge University Press, 1996; and Enrique Laraña, Hank Johnston and Joseph K. Gersfield (eds), *New Social Movements: From Ideology to Identity*, Philadelphia, PA: Temple University Press, 1994.

17 R.B.J. Walker, 'Social Movements/World Politics', *Millennium*, Vol. 23, No. 3, 1994, p. 673.

18 John Gerard Ruggie, 'Territoriality and Beyond: Problematizing Modernity in International Relations', *International Organization*, Vol. 47, No. 1, Winter 1993, p. 172.

19 Saskia Sassen, *The Global City*, Princeton, PA: Princeton University Press, 1991.

20 James Holston and Arjun Appadurai, 'Cities and Citizenship', *Public Culture*, Vol. 8, 1996, pp. 182–204.

21 Michael Peter Smith, 'Can You Imagine? Transnational Migration and the Globalization of Grassroots Politics', *Social Text*, No. 39, Summer 1994, pp. 15–33.

22 R.B.J. Walker, 'International Relations and the Concept of the Political', in Ken Booth and Steve Smith (eds), *International Relations Theory Today*, Cambridge: Polity Press, 1995, p. 324.

23 Ruggie, *op. cit.*.

24 James N. Rosenau, *Turbulence in World Politics: A Theory of Change and Continuity*, Princeton, PA: Princeton University Press, 1990.

25 Several recent examples of this genre can be found in the series *Borderlines*, edited by David Campbell and Michael Shapiro for the University of Minnesota Press. See for example Thom Kuehls, *Beyond Sovereign Territory: The Space of Ecopolitics*, Minneapolis, MN: University of Minnesota Press, 1996; and Michael J. Shapiro and Hayward R. Alker (eds), *Challenging Boundaries: Global Flows, Territorial Identities*, Minneapolis, MN: University of Minnesota Press, 1996.

26 Andrew Linklater, *Men and Citizens in the Theory of International Relations*, London: Macmillan, 1990; Andrew Linklater, *Beyond Realism and Marxism: Critical Theory and International Relations*, London: Macmillan, 1990; Andrew Linklater, *The Transformation of Political Community*, Cambridge: Polity Press, 1998.

27 Linklater, *The Transformation of Political Community*, p. 200.

28 Walker, *Inside/Outside*, p. 14.

29 *Ibid.*, p. 17.

30 Walker, 'International Relations and the Concept of the Political', p. 308.

31 R.B.J. Walker, *One World, Many Worlds*, Boulder, CO: Lynne Rienner, 1988, p. 102. Emphasis added.

32 Walker, *Inside/Outside*, p. 6.

33 *Ibid.*, p. 13.

34 *Ibid.*, p. 164.

35 *Ibid.*, p. 5.

36 Walker, 'Social Movements/World Politics', p. 672.

37 Walker, 'International Relations and the Concept of the Political', pp. 322–3.

38 Walker, 'Social Movements/World Politics', p. 684.

39 *Ibid.*, pp. 684–90.

40 *Ibid.*, p. 690.
41 Warren Magnusson, 'The Reification of Political Community', in R.B.J. Walker and Saul H. Mendlovitz (eds), *Contending Sovereignties: Redefining Political Community*, Boulder, CO: Lynne Rienner, 1990, p. 45.
42 *Ibid.*, p. 51.
43 *Ibid.*, p. 52. Emphasis added.
44 *Ibid.*
45 *Ibid.*, p. 55.
46 R.B.J. Walker, 'Sovereignty, Identity, and Community', in R.B.J. Walker and Saul H. Mendlovitz (eds), *Contending Sovereignties: Redefining Political Community*, Boulder, CO: Lynne Rienner, 1990, p. 181.
47 *Ibid.*
48 *Ibid.*
49 Walker, 'Social Movements/World Politics', p. 699.
50 Barry Buzan, 'The Levels of Analysis Problem in International Relations Reconsidered', in Ken Booth and Steve Smith (eds), *International Relations Theory Today*, Cambridge: Polity Press, 1995, p. 214.
51 Yosef Lapid, 'Culture's Ship: Returns and Departures in International Relations Theory', in Y. Lapid and F. Kratochwil (eds), *The Return of Culture and Identity in IR Theory*, Boulder, CO: Lynne Rienner, 1996, p. 10.
52 See Cynthia Enloe, *Bananas, Beaches and Bases: Making Feminist Sense of International Relations*, London: Pandora, 1989; and Christine Sylvester, *Feminist Theory and International Relations in a Postmodern Era*, Cambridge: Cambridge University Press, 1994.
53 See Edward Said, *Orientalism*, London: Penguin, 1995.
54 Michael Kearney, 'Borders and Boundaries of State and Self at the End of Empire', *Journal of Historical Sociology*, Vol. 4, No. 1, 1991, p. 53.
55 *Ibid.*, p. 64.
56 Kamala Visweswaran, *Fictions of Feminist Ethnography*, Minneapolis, MN: University of Minnesota Press, 1994.
57 Dale F. Eickelman, 'Anthropology and International Relations', in Walter Goldschmidt (ed.), *Anthropology and Public Policy: A Dialogue*, Washington, DC: American Anthropological Association, 1986, p. 35.
58 *Ibid.*, p. 40.
59 *Ibid.*, p. 37. Perhaps Eickelman's emphasis on Oman's 'communist fighting' prowess also had something to do with the book's intended audience which was presumably US State Department policy-makers.
60 *Ibid.*, p. 40.
61 James Clifford, 'Introduction: Partial Truths', in James Clifford and George E. Marcus (eds), *Writing Culture: The Poetics and Politics of Ethnography*, Berkeley, CA: University of California Press, 1986, p. 2.
62 *Ibid.*, p. 22.
63 Anthony Giddens, *The Consequences of Modernity*, Oxford: Polity Press, 1990, p. 64.
64 Anthony Giddens, *Modernity and Self-Identity*, Cambridge: Polity Press, 1991, p. 21.
65 Craig Calhoun, 'Indirect Relationships and Imagined Communities: Large-Scale Social Integration and the Transformation of Everyday Life', in Pierre Bourdieu and James S. Coleman (eds), *Social Theory for a Changing World*, Boulder, CO: Westview Press, 1991, p. 114.
66 Giddens, *The Consequences of Modernity*, p. 64. Emphasis added.
67 Roland Robertson, 'Glocalization: Time–Space and Homogeneity–Heterogeneity', in Mike Featherstone, Scott Lash and Roland Robertson (eds), *Global Modernities*, London: Sage, 1995.
68 Roland Robertson, *Globalization: Social Theory and Global Change*, London: Sage, 1992, p. 144.

69 *Ibid.*, p. 145.
70 Giddens, *Modernity and Self-Identity*, p. 18.
71 Robertson, *Globalization*, p. 145.
72 Malcolm Waters, *Globalization*, London: Routledge, 1995, p. 41.
73 Robertson, *Globalization*, p. 135. Emphasis added.
74 *Ibid.*, p. 132.
75 Ulrich Beck, *Risk Society: Towards a New Modernity*, London: Sage, 1992.
76 Robertson, 'Glocalization', p. 40.
77 Roland Robertson, 'Social Theory, Cultural Relativity and the Problem of Globality', in Anthony D. King (ed.), *Culture, Globalization and the World-System*, London: Macmillan, 1991, p. 73.
78 Arjun Appadurai, 'Disjuncture and Difference in the Global Cultural Economy', in Mike Featherstone (ed.), *Global Culture: Nationalism, Globalization and Modernity*, London: Sage, 1990, p. 307.
79 See e.g. Featherstone, *op. cit.*; Anthony D. King (ed.), *Culture, Globalization and the World-System*, London: Macmillan, 1991; Robertson, *Globalization*.
80 Robertson, *Globalization*, p. 141.
81 Janet Abu-Lughod, 'Going Beyond Global Babble', in Anthony D. King (ed.), *Culture, Globalization and the World-System: Contemporary Conditions for the Representation of Identity*, London: Macmillan, 1991.
82 *Ibid.*, p. 131.
83 Ulf Hannerz, *Cultural Complexity: Studies in the Social Organization of Meaning*, New York: Columbia University Press, 1992. For Hannerz, *forms of life* involve 'the everyday practicalities of production and reproduction, activities going on in work places, domestic settings, neighborhoods, and some variety of other places' (p. 47).
84 Clifford Geertz, *The Interpretation of Cultures*, London: Fontana Press, 1993, p. 89.
85 Hannerz, *Cultural Complexity*.
86 Arjun Appadurai, *Modernity at Large: Cultural Dimensions of Globalization*, Minneapolis, MN: University of Minnesota Press, 1996, p. 13.
87 *Ibid.*
88 Pnina Werbner, 'Essentialising Essentialism, Essentialising Silence: Ambivalence and Multiplicity in the Constructions of Racism and Ethnicity', in Pnina Werbner and Tariq Modood (eds), *Debating Cultural Hybridity: Multi-Cultural Identities and the Politics of Anti-Racism*, London: Zed Books, 1997, p. 228.
89 Gerd Baumann, 'Dominant and Demotic Discourses of Culture: Their Relevance to Multi-Ethnic Alliances', in Pnina Werbner and Tariq Modood (eds), *Debating Cultural Hybridity: Multi-Cultural Identities and the Politics of Anti-Racism*, London: Zed Books, 1997, p. 214.
90 Werbner, p. 230.
91 *Ibid.*, p. 239.
92 Mouffe, *op. cit.*.
93 Lila Abu-Lughod, 'Writing Against Culture', in Richard G. Fox (ed.), *Recapturing Anthropology: Working in the Present*, Santa Fe, NM: School of American Research Press, 1991, pp. 152–3.
94 Ayse S. Çaglar, 'Hyphenated Identities and the Limits of "Culture"', in Tariq Modood and Pnina Werbner (eds), *The Politics of Multiculturalism in the New Europe*, London: Zed Books, 1997, p. 176.
95 Abu-Lughod, 'Writing Against Culture', p. 154.
96 *Ibid.*, p. 151.
97 Karen Fog Olwig, 'Cultural Sites: Sustaining a Home in a Deterritorialized World', in Karen Fog Olwig and Kirsten Hastrup (eds), *Siting Culture: the Shifting Anthropological Object*, London: Routledge, 1991, pp. 32–3.
98 *Ibid.*, p. 35.
99 *Ibid.*, p. 19. Emphasis added.

196   *Notes*

100 *Ibid.*, p. 17.
101 Kearney, p. 58.
102 Ulf Hannerz, 'Scenarios for Peripheral Cultures', in Anthony D. King (ed.), *Culture, Globalization and the World-System: Contemporary Conditions for the Representation of Identity*, London: Macmillan, 1991, p. 118.
103 *Ibid.*, p. 117.
104 See e.g. Karen Fog Olwig, *Global Culture, Island Identity: Continuity and Change in the Afro-Caribbean Community of Nevis*, Reading, MA: Harwood Academic Publishers, 1993; and Linda Basch, Nina Glick Schiller and Cristina Szanton Blanc, *Nations Unbound: Transnational Projects, Postcolonial Predicaments, and Deterritorialized Nation-States*, Amsterdam: Gordon and Breach, 1994.
105 Ulf Hannerz, *Transnational Connections: Culture, People, Places*, London: Routledge, 1996, p. 88.
106 *Ibid.*, p. 89.
107 Khachig Tololyan, 'Rethinking *Diaspora*(s): Stateless Power in the Transnational Moment', *Diaspora*, Vol. 5, No. 1, 1996, p. 4.
108 Basch *et al.*, p. 268.
109 Thomas Faist, 'International Migrations and Transnational Social Spaces: The Bridging Functions of Social Capital in the Economic Realm', Paper presented at the Second International MigCities Conference, Liege, 6–8 November 1997.
110 Basch *et al.*, p. 7.
111 Abu-Lughod, 'Writing Against Culture'.
112 Kearney, p. 55.
113 Basch *et al.*, p. 290–1.
114 Faist, p. 26.
115 *Ibid.*
116 Appadurai, 'Sovereignty Without Territoriality', p. 47.
117 Appadurai, *Modernity at Large*, pp. 160–1.
118 *Ibid.*, p. 165.
119 *Ibid.*
120 *Ibid.*, p. 166.
121 *Ibid.*, p. 20.
122 *Ibid.*, p. 167.
123 *Ibid.*, p. 168.
124 *Ibid.*, p. 176.
125 *Ibid.*, pp. 176–7.
126 Basch *et al.*, p. 33.
127 Fog Olwig, 'Cultural Sites', p. 35.
128 Appadurai, *Modernity at Large*, p. 55.
129 *Ibid.*, p. 199.
130 Giddens, *The Consequences of Modernity*, p. 64.
131 William E. Connolly, *Identity/Difference: Democratic Negotiations of Political Paradox*, Ithaca, NY: Cornell University Press, 1991, p. 172.
132 James Clifford, *Routes: Travel and Translation in the Late Twentieth Century*, Cambridge, MA: Harvard University Press, 1997, p. 269.
133 Bhabha, Homi, 'The Third Space: Interview with Homi Bhabha', in Jonathan Rutherford (ed.), *Identity: Community, Culture, Difference*, London: Lawrence and Wishart, 1990, p. 211.
134 David Campbell, 'Political Prosaics, Transversal Politics, and the Anarchical World', in Michael J. Shapiro and Hayward R. Alker (eds), *Challenging Boundaries: Global Flows, Territorial Identities*, Minneapolis, MN: University of Minnesota Press, 1996, p. 9.
135 Mike Featherstone, *Undoing Culture: Globalization, Postmodernism and Identity*, London: Sage, 1995, p. 6.

2 Before, during and after the west

1 Edward Mortimer, *Faith and Power: The Politics of Islam*, London: Faber, 1982, p. 396.
2 Bobby S. Sayyid, *A Fundamental Fear: Eurocentrism and the Emergence of Islamism*, London: Zed Books, 1997, p. 47.
3 See e.g. Abdul Hamid M. el-Zein, 'Beyond Ideology and Theology: The Search for the Anthropology of Islam', *Annual Review of Anthropology*, Vol. 6, 1977, pp. 227–54; and Aziz al-Azmeh, *Islams and Modernities*, London: Verso, 2nd Edition, 1996.
4 Dale F. Eickelman, 'The Study of Islam in Local Contexts', *Contributions to Asian Studies*, Vol. 17, 1982, p. 1.
5 Talal Asad, *Genealogies of Religion*, Baltimore, MD: Johns Hopkins University Press, 1993, pp. 16–17.
6 Veena Das, 'For a Folk-Theology and Theological Anthropology of Islam', *Contributions to Indian Sociology*, Vol. 18, No. 2, 1984, p. 296.
7 Al-Azmeh, p. 65.
8 See Edward Said, *Orientalism*, London: Penguin, 1995.
9 Asad, *Genealogies of Religion*, p. 29.
10 Al-Azmeh, pp. 177–8.
11 Sayyid, p. 40.
12 James Piscatori, *Islam in a World of Nation-States*, Cambridge: Cambridge University Press, 1986, p. 11.
13 According to the research of Reinhard Schulze, for example, this set phrase is less than two hundred years old. See his 'Islam und Herrschaft. Zur politischen Instrumentalisierung einer Religion', in M. Lüders (ed.), *Der Islam im Aufbruch? Perspektive der arabischen Welt*, Munich: Piper, 1992.
14 Dale F. Eickelman and James Piscatori, *Muslim Politics*, Princeton, PA: Princeton University Press, 1996, p. 4.
15 Asad, *Genealogies of Religion*, p. 1.
16 Mahmut Mutman, 'Under the Sign of Orientalism: The West vs. Islam', *Cultural Critique*, Winter 1992 93, p. 165.
17 Stuart Hall, 'The West and the Rest: Discourse and Power', in Stuart Hall and Bram Gieben (eds), *Formations of Modernity*, Cambridge: Polity Press, 1992, p. 277.
18 *Ibid.*
19 *Ibid.*
20 Johannes Fabian, *Time and the Other: How Anthropology Makes its Object*, New York: Columbia University Press, 1983. Quoted in Mutman, *op. cit.*
21 Perhaps even quite literally 'named'. Citing Wilfred Cantwell Smith's remarks on the absence of the term 'Islam' in the titles of books written by Muslims in the late eighteenth and early nineteenth centuries, Armando Salvatore argues that 'through the consolidation of transcultural dynamics between the "West" and "Islam" the originally endogenous process of reification of the latter became ineluctably heteronomous and no longer in pace with its subjectification. As a side-effect, Western Orientalists gained increasing legitimation for their view according to which Islam *as such* is the vehicle of a communal ethos and a collective identity that are, nonetheless, virtually devoid of any subjective labour comparable to the modern Western one'. See Armando Salvatore, *Islam and the Political Discourse of Modernity*, Reading, MA: Ithaca Press, 1997, p. 76.
22 Talal Asad, 'Modern Power and the Reconfiguration of Religious Traditions', *Stanford Electronic Humanities Review*, Vol. 5, No. 1: Contested Politics, 1996, pp. 1, 4–5.
23 *Ibid.*, p. 1.
24 Sayyid, p. 103.
25 *Ibid.*, p. 105.
26 Interestingly, Reinhard Schulze argues that a variation on this theme can be found in certain breeds of Islamist thinking where 'modernity is seen not as the negation of Islam but as its predecessor. All that is not Islamic is necessarily modern, and on the

other hand, all that is truly Islamic perfects the Modern. Consequently, Islam and modernity did not form an antithesis, but rather a historical chain: modernity would inevitably flow into Islam.' This reads almost like an Islamist reformulation of Lenin's ideas on imperialism and capitalism: 'Islam, the highest form of modernity'. See Reinhard Schulze, 'How Medieval is Islam? Muslim Intellectuals and Modernity', in Jochen Hippler and Andrea Lueg (eds), *The Next Threat: Western Perceptions of Islam*, London: Pluto Press, 1995, p. 61.

27 Sayyid, p. 128.
28 Mehrzad Boroujerdi, 'Iranian Islam and the Faustian Bargain of Western Modernity', *Journal of Peace Research*, Vol. 34, No. 1, 1997, p. 2. Of course we also need to ask whether any of these presumptions can actually be linked to the downfall of the Soviet Union.
29 Sayyid, p. 148.
30 *Ibid.*, p. 149.
31 *Ibid.*, pp. 19–22.
32 *Ibid.*, p. 23.
33 T. Sunier, 'Islam and Ethnicity among Turks: The Changing Role of Islam and Muslim Organizations', in W.A.R. Shadid and P.S. van Koningsveld (eds), *Islam in Dutch Society*, Kampen: Kok Pharos, 1992, p. 144.
34 Revathi Krishnaswamy, 'Mythologies of Migrancy: Postcolonialism, Postmodernism and the Politics of (Dis)location', *ARIEL: A Review of International English Literature*, Vol. 26, No. 1, January 1995, p. 129.
35 My account of the early period in Medina relies heavily on the standard works by W. Montgomery Watt (*Muhammad at Medina*, Oxford: Clarendon Press, 1956) and Maxime Rodinson (*Muhammad*, London: Penguin, 2nd English Edition, 1996) as well as Al-Tabari's *Ta'rikh ar-Rusul wa'l-Muluk* (Cairo: Dar al-Marif, 1960–1977). The reader should also be aware of competing accounts of this early period of Islamic history, most notably Patricia Crone, *Slaves on Horses: the Evolution of the Islamic Polity*, London: Cambridge University Press, 1980; Michael Cook and Patricia Crone, *Hagarism: The Making of the Islamic World*, Cambridge: Cambridge University Press, 1977; and Fred M. Donner, 'The Formation of the Early Islamic State', *Journal of the American Oriental Society*, Vol. 56, 1986, pp. 283–96. The fact that we do not know for sure what life in Medina was like only serves to reinforce the importance of its discursive construction in contemporary accounts, Muslim and non-Muslim alike.
36 I use the 'scare quotes' here because Muhammad sought quite explicitly to link his religion with the two older Abrahamic faiths, Judaism and Christianity. For him, Islam was the culmination of this tradition rather than a new religion unto itself.
37 Ira Lapidus, *A History of Islamic Societies*, Cambridge: Cambridge University Press, 1988, p. 27; W. Montgomery Watt, *Muhammad at Medina*, p. 1.
38 Lapidus, p. 27. Another useful survey of the classical doctrine of *hijra* can be found in Muhammad Khalid Masud, 'The obligation to migrate: the doctrine of *hijra* in Islamic law', in Dale F. Eickelman and James Piscatori (eds), *Muslim Travellers: Pilgrimage, Migration, and the Religious Imagination*, Berkeley, CA: University of California Press, 1990.
39 H.A.R. Gibb and J.H. Kramers (eds), *Shorter Encyclopedia of Islam*, Leiden: E.J. Brill, 1991, p. 603; Watt, *Muhammad at Medina*, p. 240.
40 W. Montgomery Watt, *Islamic Political Thought*, Edinburgh: Edinburgh University Press, 1987, pp. 7–14, 49–50.
41 Sura ii. 43: 'We have made you a community [umma] in the middle so that you may bear witness against mankind.' Ali and Arberry render 'in the middle' as, respectively, 'justly balanced' and 'just', a translation which I find disatisfying since it ignores the spatial implications of the Arabic *wasat*, 'middle or center'. Various interpretations regard this as implying that Islam is to be seen as a religion in between Christianity

and Judaism (Montgomery Watt) or as the religion of Arabia which 'is in an intermediate position in the Old World' (Yusuf Ali). It may also refer to the mediatory position which Muhammad's community occupied in Medina.

42 Mohammed Arkoun, *Rethinking Islam*, Boulder, CO: Westview Press, 1994, p. 21.
43 Lapidus, p. 351. Emphasis added.
44 Richard Bulliet, *Islam: The View from the Edge*, New York: Columbia University Press, 1994.
45 See Benedict Anderson, *Imagined Communities: Reflections on the Origin and Spread of Nationalism*, London: Verso, Revised Edition, 1991, pp. 44–6 and *passim*.
46 Jacob Landau, *The Politics of Pan-Islam*, Oxford: Clarendon Press, 1994, p. 183.
47 Landau, pp. 183–5; Nikki Keddie, 'Sayyid Jamel al-Din "al-Afghani" ', in Ali Rahnema (ed.), *Pioneers of Islamic Revival*, London: Zed Books, 1994.
48 Yvonne Haddad, 'Muhammad Abduh: Pioneer of Islamic Reform', in Ali Rahnema (ed.), *Pioneers of Islamic Revival*, London: Zed Books, 1994, p. 31.
49 See Muhammad Abduh, *al-A'mal al-Kamila*, Beirut: al-Mu'assasa al-'Arabiya li'l-Dirasat wa'l-Nashr, 1972.
50 Albert Hourani, *Arabic Thought in the Liberal Age, 1798–1939*, Cambridge: Cambridge University Press, 1983, pp. 130–60.
51 Schulze, 'How Medieval is Islam?', p. 64.
52 Seyyed Vali Reza Nasr, 'Mawdudi and the Jama'at-i Islami: The Origins, Theory and Practice of Islamic Revivalism', in Ali Rahnema (ed.), *Pioneers of Islamic Revival*, London: Zed Books, 1994, p. 99.
53 *Ibid.*, p. 101.
54 Landau, pp. 271–2.
55 Abul A'la Mawdudi, *Unity of the Muslim World*, Lahore: Islamic Publications, Fifth Edition, 1992, pp. 19, 34.
56 Nasr, p. 108.
57 Abul A'la Mawdudi, *First Principles of the Islamic State*, Lahore: Islamic Publications, Third Edition, 1967, p. 26.
58 Abul A'la Mawdudi, *Political Theory of Islam*, Lahore: Islamic Publications, 1960, p. 35.
59 Charles J. Adams, 'Mawdudi and the Islamic State', in John L. Esposito (ed.), *Voices of Resurgent Islam*, New York: Oxford University Press, 1983, p. 117.
60 Mawdudi, *Political Theory of Islam*, p. 37. Emphasis in original.
61 *Ibid.*, p. 22.
62 See Mawdudi, *First Principles of the Islamic State*, p. 7.
63 *Ibid.*, p. 13.
64 Eickelman and Piscatori, *Muslim Politics*, p. 57. Emphasis added.

3 Modes of translocality

1 Abu Salim al-'Ayyashi, *Ma' al-Mawa'id*, Riyadh: Dar al-Rifa'i, 1984. See also Abderrahmane El-Moudden, 'The Ambivalence of *Rihla*: Community Integration and Self-Definition in Moroccan Travel Accounts: 1300–1800', in Dale F. Eickelman and James Piscatori (eds), *Muslim Travellers: Pilgrimage, Migration, and the Religious Imagination*, Berkeley, CA: University of California Press, 1990. My own account is largely derived from this latter source.
2 My comments on Shariati rely heavily on Ali Rahnema, 'Ali Shariati: Teacher, Preacher, Rebel', in Ali Rahnema (ed.), *Pioneers of Islamic Revival*, London: Zed Books, 1994. See also Rahnema's book-length study of Shariati, *An Islamic Utopian: a Political Biography of Ali Shari'ati*, London: I.B. Tauris, 1998.
3 Edward Said, *The World, the Text and the Critic*, London: Faber and Faber, 1984, p. 226.
4 *Ibid.*
5 *Ibid.*, p. 230.
6 James Clifford, 'Notes on Travel and Theory', *Inscriptions*, No. 5, 1989, p. 5.

7 Said, *The World, the Text and the Critic*, p. 239.
8 *Ibid.*, p. 247.
9 *Ibid.*, p. 241.
10 *Ibid.*
11 *Ibid.*, pp. 246–7.
12 Abdul R. JanMohamed, 'Worldliness-without-World, Homelessness-as-Home: Toward a Definition of the Specular Border Intellectual', in Michael Sprinker (ed.), *Edward Said: A Critical Reader*, Oxford: Blackwell, 1992, p. 100.
13 Clifford, 'Notes on Travel and Theory', p. 2.
14 Jan Nederveen Pieterse, 'Globalization as Hybridization', in Mike Featherstone, Scott Lash and Roland Robertson (eds), *Global Modernities*, London: Sage, 1995, p. 171.
15 M.M. Bakhtin, *The Dialogic Imagination*, Austin, TX: University of Texas Press, 1981, p. 358.
16 *Ibid.*, p. 360.
17 *Ibid.* Emphasis in original.
18 *Ibid.*
19 Nikos Papastergiadis, 'Tracing Hybridity in Theory', in P. Werbner and Tariq Modood (eds), *Debating Cultural Hybridity*, London: Zed Books, 1997, p. 259.
20 See Paul Gilroy, *The Black Atlantic: Modernity and Double Consciousness*, London: Verso, 1993; and M.M. Bakhtin, *op. cit.*.
21 Homi Bhabha, 'Culture's In-Between', in Stuart Hall and Paul du Gay (eds), *Questions of Cultural Identity*, London: Sage, 1996, p. 58.
22 Homi Bhabha, *The Location of Culture*, London: Routledge, 1994, p. 114.
23 *Ibid.*, pp. 113–14.
24 *Ibid.*, p. 219.
25 Jonathan Rutherford, 'The Third Space: Interview with Homi Bhabha', in Jonathan Rutherford (ed.), *Identity: Community, Culture, Difference*, London: Laurence and Wishart, 1990, p. 211.
26 Ulf Hannerz, *Cultural Complexity: Studies in the Social Organization of Meaning*, New York: Columbia University Press, 1992, p. 265.
27 Michael M.J. Fischer and Mehdi Abedi, *Debating Muslims: Cultural Dialogues in Postmodernity and Tradition*, Madison, WI: University of Wisconsin Press, 1990, p. 317.
28 William Rowe and Vivian Schelling, *Memory and Modernity: Popular Culture in Latin America*, London: Verso, 1991, p. 231.
29 *Ibid.*
30 Nederveen Pieterse, 'Globalization as Hybridization', p. 169. Emphasis added.
31 *Ibid.*, p. 179.
32 *Ibid.*, p. 168.
33 *Ibid.*, p. 171.
34 *Ibid.*, p. 172.
35 *Ibid.*, p. 180.
36 Susanne Hoeber Rudolph, 'Introduction: Religion, States, and Transnational Civil Society', in Susanne Hoeber Rudolph and James Piscatori (eds), *Transnational Religion and Fading States*, Boulder, CO: Westview Press, 1997, p. 1.
37 James Rosenau, *Along the Domestic-Foreign Frontier: Exploring Governance in a Turbulent World*, Cambridge: Cambridge University Press, 1997.
38 Michael Kearney, 'Borders and Boundaries of State and Self at the End of Empire', *Journal of Historical Sociology*, Vol. 4, No. 1, 1991; and Renato Rosaldo, *Culture and Truth: The Remaking of Social Analysis*, London: Routledge, 1993.
39 Bhabha, *The Location of Culture*, pp. 36–9.
40 Smadar Lavie and Ted Swedenburg, 'Introduction: Displacement, Diaspora, and Geographies of Identity', in Smadar Lavie and Ted Swedenburg, *Displacement, Diaspora, and Geographies of Identity*, Durham, NC: Duke University Press, 1996.
41 Rudolph, *op. cit.*.

42 Arjun Appadurai, *Modernity at Large: Cultural Dimensions of Globalization*, Minneapolis, MN: University of Minnesota Press, 1996.
43 Rudolph, p. 2.
44 Bhabha, *The Location of Culture*, pp. 216 7, 38 9.
45 Lavie and Swedenburg, p. 15.
46 Nederveen Pieterse, 'Globalization as Hybridization', p. 178.
47 Talal Asad, *Genealogies of Religion: Discipline and Reasons of Power in Christianity and Islam*, Baltimore, MD: Johns Hopkins University Press, 1993, pp. 263–4.
48 Lavie and Swedenburg, p. 10.
49 Jonathan Friedman, 'Global System, Globalization and the Parameters of Modernity', in Mike Featherstone, Scott Lash and Roland Robertson (eds), *Global Modernities*, London: Sage, 1995, p. 82.
50 Bakhtin, *The Dialogic Imagination*, p. 305.
51 Nederveen Pieterse, 'Globalization as Hybridization', p. 173.
52 Edward Said, 'Media, Margins and Modernity', Edward Said in conversation with Raymond Williams in Tony Pinkney (ed.), *The Politics of Modernism: Against the New Conformists*, London: Verso, 1989.
53 Hamid Naficy, *The Making of Exile Cultures: Iranian Television in Los Angeles*, Minneapolis, MN: University of Minnesota Press, 1993, p. 127.
54 Aijaz Ahmad, *In Theory: Classes, Nations, Literatures*, London: Verso, 1994, p. 128. Emphasis added.
55 *Ibid.*, p. 130. Emphasis added.
56 Pheng Cheah, 'Given Culture: Rethinking Cosmopolitical Freedom in Transnationalism', in Pheng Cheah and Bruce Robbins (eds), *Cosmopolitics: Thinking and Feeling beyond the Nation*, Minneapolis, MN: University of Minnesota Press, 1998, p. 302.
57 Bhabha, *The Location of Culture*, p. 225. Emphasis added.
58 Salman Rushdie, *Imaginary Homelands: Essays and Criticism 1981 1991*, London: Granta Books, 1992, pp. 124–5. Emphasis added.
59 James Clifford, *Routes: Travel and Translation in the Late Twentieth Century*, Cambridge, MA: Harvard University Press, 1997, p. 251.
60 *Ibid.*, p. 269.
61 R. Radhakrishnan, *Diasporic Mediations: Between Home and Location*, Minneapolis, MN: University of Minnesota Press, 1996, p. 161.
62 Ziauddin Sardar, *Postmodernism and the Other: The New Imperialism of Western Culture*, London: Pluto Press, 1998.
63 Revathi Krishnaswamy, 'Mythologies of Migrancy: Postcolonialism, Postmodernism and the Politics of (Dis)location', *ARIEL: A Review of International English Literature*, Vol. 26, No. 1, January 1995, p. 132.
64 Mike Featherstone, *Undoing Culture: Globalization, Postmodernism and Identity*, London: Sage, 1995, pp. 144–5.

4 The new political communities of the Muslim diaspora

1 See e.g. Robin Cohen, *Global Diasporas*, London: UCL Press, 1997; William Safran, 'Diasporas in Modern Societies: Myths of Homeland and Return', *Diaspora*, Vol. 1, No. 1, 1991, pp. 83–99; and James Clifford, 'Diasporas', *Cultural Anthropology*, Vol. 9, No. 3, 1994, pp. 302–38.
2 Dale F. Eickelman and James Piscatori (eds), *Muslim Travellers: Pilgrimage, Migration, and the Religious Imagination*, Berkeley, CA: University of California Press, 1990, p. xiii.
3 James Clifford: *Routes: Travel and Translation in the Late Twentieth Century*, Cambridge, MA: Harvard University Press, 1997, pp. 250–1.
4 Fatima Mernissi, *Women and Islam: An Historical and Theological Enquiry*, Oxford: Blackwell, 1991, p. 15.

5 Felice Dassetto and A. Bastenier, *L'Islam transplanté*, Antwerp: Editions EPO, 1984.
6 Steven Vertovec and Ceri Peach, 'Introduction: Islam in Europe and the Politics of Religion and Community', in Steven Vertovec and Ceri Peach (eds), *Islam in Europe: The Politics of Religion and Community*, London: Macmillan, 1997, p. 38.
7 An excellent bibliographic essay reviewing many country studies of Muslims in Europe can be found in Jørgen Nielsen, *Muslims in Western Europe*, Edinburgh: Edinburgh University Press, 2nd Edition, 1995, pp. 172–84; for the American context a useful introductory reader is Yvonne Yazbeck Haddad (ed.), *The Muslims of America*, Oxford: Oxford University Press, 1991.
8 Katy Gardner's work on Bangladeshi transmigrants has come perhaps the closest to the kind of analysis I am proposing; see Katy Gardner, *Global Migrants, Local Lives: Travel and Transformation in Rural Bangladesh*, Oxford: Clarendon Press, 1995.
9 Felice Dassetto, 'Islam and Europe', Paper presented at the International Conference on Muslim Minorities in Post-Bipolar Europe, Skopje, Macedonia, 1993.
10 Stuart Hall, 'Religious Cults and Social Movements in Jamaica', in R. Bocock and K. Thompson (eds), *Religion and Ideology*, Manchester: Manchester University Press, 1985, p. 272.
11 Eickelman and Piscatori, *Muslim Travellers*, p. xii.
12 *Ibid.*
13 Ismail R. Faruqi, 'The Path of Dawah in the West', *The Muslim World League Journal*, Vol. 14, Nos. 7–8, March–April, 1987, p. 56, quoted in John O. Voll, 'Islamic Issues for Muslims in the United States', in Yvonne Yazbeck Haddad (ed.), *The Muslims of America*, Oxford: Oxford University Press, 1991.
14 Muhammad Khalid Masud, 'The Obligation to Migrate: The Doctrine of *Hijra* in Islamic Law', in Dale F. Eickelman and James Piscatori (eds), *Muslim Travellers: Pilgrimage, Migration, and the Religious Imagination*, Berkeley, CA: University of California Press, 1990, pp. 42–3.
15 Akbar S. Ahmed and Hastings Donnan, 'Islam in the Age of Postmodernity', in Akbar S. Ahmed and Hastings Donnan (eds), *Islam, Globalization and Postmodernity*, London: Routledge, 1994, pp. 4–5.
16 Ross Dunn, 'International Migrations of Literate Muslims in the Later Middle Period: The Case of Ibn Battuta', in Ian Richard Netton (ed.), *Golden Roads: Migration, Pilgrimage, and Travel in Mediaeval and Modern Islam*, London: Curzon Press, 1993, p. 79. Emphasis added.
17 See e.g. the various chapters in Eickelman and Piscatori, *Muslim Travellers*; Netton, *op. cit.*; and also Patricia Risso, *Merchants and Faith: Muslim Commerce and Culture in the Indian Ocean*, Boulder, CO: Westview Press, 1995.
18 Dunn, p. 83.
19 Jan Nederveen Pieterse, 'Travelling Islam: Mosques without Minarets', in Ayse Öncü and Petra Wayland (eds), *Space, Culture and Power: New Identities in Globalizing Cities*, London: Zed Books, 1997, p. 181.
20 See Abderrahmane El-Moudden, 'The Ambivalence of *Rihla*: Community Integration and Self-definition in Moroccan Travel Accounts, 1300–1800', in Dale F. Eickelman and James Piscatori (eds), *Muslim Travellers: Pilgrimage, Migration, and the Religious Imagination*, Berkeley, CA: University of California Press, 1990, pp. 69–84.
21 *Ibid.*, p. 69.
22 Ali Rahnema, 'Ali Shariati: Teacher, Preacher, Rebel', in Ali Rahnema (ed.), *Pioneers of Islamic Revival*, London: Zed Books, 1994, p. 220.
23 *Ibid.*, pp. 220–222.
24 See S. Lash and J. Urry, *The End of Organized Capitalism*, Oxford: Polity Press, 1987, cited in Akbar S. Ahmed and Hastings Donnan, 'Islam in the Age of Postmodernity', in Akbar S. Ahmed and Hastings Donnan (eds), *Islam, Globalization and Postmodernity*, London: Routledge, 1994, p. 5.

25 Several anthropologists have undertaken studies of Islam in these 'local' contexts. See e.g. John R. Bowen, '*Salat* in Indonesia: The Social Meanings of an Islamic Ritual', *Man*, Vol. 24, 1989, pp. 600–19; Michael Lambek, 'Certain Knowledge, Contestable Authority: Power and Practice on the Islamic Periphery', *American Ethnologist*, Vol. 17, No. 1, February 1990, pp. 23–40; Robert W. Hefner and Patricia Horvatich (eds), *Islam in an Era of Nation-States: Politics and Religious Renewal in Muslim Southeast Asia*, Honolulu, HA: University of Hawai'i Press, 1997; and David Westerlund and Eva Evers Rosander (eds), *African Islam and Islam in Africa: Encounters between Sufis and Islamists*, London: Hurst and Company, 1997. A useful overview can be found in Dale F. Eickelman, 'The Study of Islam in Local Contexts', *Contributions to Asian Studies*, Vol. 17, 1982.

26 Nederveen Pieterse, 'Travelling Islam', p. 197.

27 Omar Khalidi, 'Muslim Minorities: Theory and Experience of Muslim Interaction in Non-Muslim Societies', *Journal of the Institute of Muslim Minority Affairs*, Vol. 10, No. 2, July 1989, p. 425.

28 *Ibid.*

29 Barbara D. Metcalf, 'Introduction: Sacred Words, Sanctioned Practice, New Communities', in Barbara D. Metcalf (ed.), *Making Muslim Space in North America and Europe*, Berkeley, CA: University of California Press, 1996, p. 7.

30 *Ibid.*

31 T. Sunier, 'Islam and Ethnicity Among Turks', in W.A.R. Shadid and P.S. van Koningsveld (eds), *Islam in Dutch Society*, Kampen: Kok Pharos, 1992, p. 145.

32 Although there are clearly situations in which religious politics in the homeland have played a key role in the constitution of identity (e.g. the Arab–Israeli conflict, Kashmir, Lebanon), my primary focus in this study is on the ways in which religion becomes politicised in diaspora.

33 A.K. Barkatulla, Director of the Islamic Computing Centre and *'alim*, Personal Interview, 21 July 1998.

34 Sunier, p. 155; H. van Ooijen, 'Religion and Emancipation: A Study of the Development of Moroccan Islamic Organizations in a Dutch Town', in W.A.R. Shadid and P.S. van Koningsveld (eds), *Islam in Dutch Society*, Kampen: Kok Pharos, 1992, corroborates this.

35 Hamid Naficy, *The Making of Exile Cultures: Iranian Television in Los Angeles*, Minneapolis, MN: University of Minnesota Press, 1993, p. 173.

36 Michael M.J. Fischer and Mehdi Abedi, *Debating Muslims: Cultural Dialogues in Postmodernity and Tradition*, Madison, WI: University of Wisconsin Press, 1990, p. 88.

37 *Ibid.*, pp. 318–32.

38 Dilwar Hussain, ex-member of the executive board of Young Muslims UK, Personal Interview, Leicester, 28 July 1998.

39 Felice Dassetto and Gerd Nonneman, 'Islam in Belgium and the Netherlands: Towards a Typology of "Transplanted" Islam', in G. Nonneman, T. Niblock and B. Szajkowski (eds), *Muslim Communities in the New Europe*, Reading: Ithaca Press, 1996, p. 194.

40 Metcalf, *Making Muslim Space*, p. 10; also Czarina Wilpert, 'Religion and Ethnicity: Orientations, Perceptions and Strategies among Turkish Alevi and Sunni Migrants in Berlin', in Tomas Gerholm and Yngve Georg Lithman, *The New Islamic Presence in Western Europe*, London: Mansell Publishing, 1988, p. 92.

41 Metcalf, *Making Muslim Space*, p. 6.

42 Nederveen Pieterse, 'Travelling Islam', p. 180.

43 Hanns Thomä-Venske, 'The Religious Life of Muslims in Berlin', in Tomas Gerholm and Yngve Georg Lithman, *The New Islamic Presence in Western Europe*, London: Mansell Publishing, 1988, p. 79.

44 Landman, Nico, 'The Islamic Broadcasting Foundation in the Netherlands: Platform or Arena?', in Steven Vertovec and Ceri Peach (eds), *Islam in Europe: The Politics of Religion and Community*, London: Macmillan, 1997, p. 35.

45 *Ibid.*, p. 38.
46 Dr Ataullah Siddiqui, Research Fellow, Islamic Foundation, Personal Interview, Leicester, 29 July 1998.
47 Fischer and Abedi, pp. 321–2.
48 Farhang Rajaee, 'Iranian Ideology and Worldview: The Cultural Export of the Revolution', in John L. Esposito (ed.), *The Iranian Revolution: Its Global Impact*, Miami, FL: Florida International University Press, 1990, pp. 76–7.
49 Thomä-Venske, p. 79.
50 Lale Yalçin-Heckman, 'Are Fireworks Islamic?: Towards an Understanding of Turkish Migrants and Islam in Germany', in Charles Stewart and Rosalind Shaw (eds), *Syncretism/Anti-Syncretism: The Politics of Religious Synthesis*, London: Routledge, 1994, p. 188.
51 Siddiqui, interview.
52 Dr S.M.I. Andrabi, exiled Kashmiri intellectual and activist, Personal Interview, London, 20 July 1998.
53 Phillip Lewis, *Islamic Britain: Religion, Politics and Identity among British Muslims*, London: I.B. Tauris, 1994, p. 15.
54 Jørgen Nielsen, 'A Muslim Agenda for Britain: Some Reflections', *New Community*, Vol. 17, No. 3, April 1991, p. 467.
55 Yalçin-Heckmann, p. 183.
56 *Ibid.*
57 Thomä-Venske, p. 79.
58 Elizabeth Scantlebury, 'Muslims in Manchester: The Depiction of a Religious Community', *New Community*, Vol. 21, No. 3, July 1995.
59 *Ibid.*, p. 430.
60 *Ibid.*
61 Akbar Ahmed, 'Mutiny in the Mosque', *The Guardian*, 10 March 1994.
62 Siddiqui, interview.
63 *Ibid.*
64 Hussain, interview. He is referring to debates between different schools of theological and jurisprudential interpretation.
65 Scantlebury, p. 431.
66 Siddiqui, interview.
67 Lewis, *Islamic Britain*, pp. 117–19.
68 S.M. Darsh, *Muslims in Europe*, London: Ta-Ha, 1980, p. 89, quoted in Nederveen Pieterse, 'Travelling Islam', p. 189.
69 Tariq Modood, 'British Asian Muslims and the Rushdie Affair', *The Political Quarterly*, Vol. 61, No. 2, April–June 1990, p. 145.
70 Nederveen Pieterse, 'Travelling Islam', p. 189.
71 Thomä-Venske, p. 86.
72 Scantlebury, pp. 430–1.
73 Gary Bunt, 'Decision-Making Concerns in British Islamic Environments', *Islam and Christian-Muslim Relations*, Vol. 9, No. 1, 1998, p. 104.
74 Dassetto and Nonneman, p. 216.
75 Fred Halliday notes for example that after the leading religious figure of the Yemeni community in the UK returned permanently to Yemen, the younger generation began to question traditional authority. This eventually led to the establishment of a number of secular nationalist organisations. Landman reports the problems for Sufi orders in The Netherlands accruing from their reliance on a religious leadership based in the home country. See Fred Halliday, *Arabs in Exile*, London: I.B. Tauris, 1992, p. 38; and Landman, p. 38.
76 Dassetto and Nonneman, p. 216.
77 Lewis, *Islamic Britain*, p. 190.
78 *Ibid.*

79 Hussain, interview.
80 Adam Lebor, *A Heart Turned East*, London: Little, Brown and Company, 1997, p. 153.
81 *Ibid.*, p. 154.
82 Lewis, *Islamic Britain*, p. 207.
83 Siddiqui, interview.
84 See for example Mustafa Yusuf McDermott and Muhammad Manazir Ahsan, *The Muslim Guide: For Teachers, Employers, Community and Social Administrators in Britain*, Leicester: The Islamic Foundation, 2nd Revised Edition, 1993.
85 Metcalf, *Making Muslim Space*, pp. xv–xix.
86 See 'Open letter to FOSIS', *Q-News*, Vol. 2, No. 17, 23–30 July 1993, for an example of how young Muslims are critiquing older student/mosque organisations and ideologies.
87 Lewis, *Islamic Britain*, p. 142.
88 Siddiqui, interview.
89 Eickelman and Piscatori, *Muslim Travellers*, p. xv.
90 Nielsen, *Muslims in Western Europe*, p. 116.
91 Dr Sa'ad al-Faqih, Movement for Islamic Reform in Arabia (MIRA), Personal Interview, London, 12 May 1998.
92 Metcalf, *Making Muslim Space*, p. 10.
93 Jean Ellis, 'Local Government and Community Needs: A Case Study of Muslims in Coventry', *New Community*, Vol. 17, No. 3, April 1991, p. 372. The term 'Wahhabi' refers to followers of the puritanical movement initiated by the Arabian religious reformer Muhammad ibn Abdul Wahhab in the eighteenth century. Various contemporary Muslims use it as a term of abuse.
94 Scantlebury, p. 428.
95 Nielsen, *Muslims in Western Europe*, p. 116.
96 Czarina Wilpert, 'Religion and Ethnicity: Orientations, Perceptions and Strategies among Turkish Alevi and Sunni Migrants in Berlin', in Tomas Gerholm and Yngve Georg Lithman, *The New Islamic Presence in Western Europe*, London: Mansell Publishing, 1988.
97 Shadid, W.A.R. and P.S. van Koningsveld, 'Legal Adjustments for Religious Minorities', in W.A.R. Shadid and P.S. van Koningsveld (eds), *Islam in Dutch Society*, Kampen: Kok Pharos, 1992, p. 15.
98 Dassetto and Nonneman, p. 215.
99 Bunt, pp. 105–6.
100 Siddiqui, interview.
101 For a useful self-description see *Hizb ut-Tahrir*, London: Al-Khilafah Publications, n.d.
102 Lebor, p. 141.
103 Hussain, interview.
104 Barkatulla, interview.
105 Al-Faqih, interview.
106 *Ibid.*
107 Pnina Werbner, 'Islamic Radicalism and the Gulf War: Lay Preachers and Political Dissent among British Pakistanis', in Bernard Lewis and Dominique Schnapper (eds), *Muslims in Europe*, London: Pinter, 1994, p. 114.
108 Scantlebury, p. 429.
109 Hussain, interview.
110 Phillip Lewis, 'The Bradford Council of Mosques and the Search for Muslim Unity', in Steven Vertovec and Ceri Peach (eds), *Islam in Europe: The Politics of Religion and Community*, London: Macmillan, 1997, p. 109.
111 Andrabi, interview.
112 Fischer and Abedi, p. 318.

113 Siddiqui, interview.
114 Barkatulla, interview.
115 Sunier, p. 157.
116 Pnina Werbner, 'The Making of Muslim Dissent: Hybridized Discourses, Lay Preachers, and Radical Rhetoric among British Pakistanis', *American Ethnologist*, Vol. 23, No. 1, 1996, p. 116.
117 This is not to claim, however, that Muslim responses to these events were wholly consistent. See James Piscatori (ed.), *Islamic Fundamentalisms and the Gulf Crisis*, Chicago, IL: American Academy of Arts and Sciences, 1991.
118 Werbner, 'The Making of Muslim Dissent', p. 108.
119 Dr Muhammad al-Mass'ari, Committee for the Defence of Legitimate Rights (CDLR), Personal Interview, London, 3 April 1997.
120 Al-Faqih, interview.
121 Andrabi, interview.
122 In institutional terms, an important step in this direction was taken with the formation of the Muslim Council of Britain in late 1997. It is as yet too early to determine the fate of this organisation but early signs are encouraging.
123 Shabbir Akhtar, *Be Careful with Muhammad!*, London: Bellew, 1989, pp. 76–7. Quoted in Lewis, *Islamic Britain*, p. 192.
124 Lewis, *Islamic Britain*, p. 192.
125 Dr Zaki Badawi, Chairman of the Imams and Mosques Council, Personal Interview, London, 15 September 1998.
126 Metcalf, *Making Muslim Space*, p. 19.
127 Hussain, interview.
128 James Piscatori, 'The Rushdie Affair and the Politics of Ambiguity', *International Affairs*, Vol. 66, No. 4, 1990, p. 778.
129 Shabbir Akhtar, *A Faith for All Seasons, Islam and Western Modernity*, London: Bellew, 1990, pp. 66–7. Cited in Lewis, *Islamic Britain*, p. 190.
130 Frederick Mathewson Denny, 'The Legacy of Fazlur Rahman', in Yvonne Yazbeck Haddad (ed.), *The Muslims of America*, Oxford: Oxford University Press, 1991, p. 104. See Fazlur Rahman, *Islam and Modernity: Transformation of an Intellectual Tradition*, Chicago, IL: University of Chicago Press, 1982, pp. 36–9.
131 Syed Abul Hasan Ali Nadwi, *Muslims in the West: The Message and Mission*, Leicester: The Islamic Foundation, 1983, p. 190. Emphasis added.
132 Nielsen, *Muslims in Western Europe*, p. 115.
133 Hussain, interview.
134 Nielsen, *Muslims in Western Europe*, p. 115.
135 There are those who would claim that ijtihad is not simply 'free thinking' but actually refers to a form of jurisprudential practice with very specific methodologies and boundaries. It is a testament, however, to the development of what Barbara Metcalf has called a diasporic 'Islamic English' that this term is usually translated as, and associated with, notions of free, independent thinking.
136 Hussain, interview.
137 Werbner, 'The Making of Muslim Dissent', p. 115.
138 Fischer and Abedi, p. 323.
139 Lewis, *Islamic Britain*, p. 208.
140 Lebor, pp. 101–2.
141 Dominique Schnapper, 'Muslim Communities, Ethnic Minorities and Citizens', in Bernard Lewis and Dominique Schnapper (eds), *Muslims in Europe*, London: Pinter, 1994, p. 149.
142 *Ibid.*, p. 148.
143 Nielsen, *Muslims in Western Europe*, pp. 116–17.
144 Hussain, interview.

145 H.A.R. Gibb and J.H. Kramers (eds), *Shorter Encyclopaedia of Islam*, Leiden: E.J. Brill, 1991, pp. 68–9.
146 See Sayyid 'Abd al-'Aziz b. Muhammad al-Siddiq, *Hukm al-iqama bi-bilad al-kufr wa-bayan wujuhiha fi-ba'd al-Ahwal*, Tangier: Bughaz, 1985, quoted in Masud, *op. cit.*.
147 Hussain, interview.
148 Ataullah Siddiqui, 'Muslims in the Contemporary World: Dialogue in Perspective', *World Faiths Encounter*, No. 20, July 1998, p. 26.
149 Jacques Waardenburg, 'Muslims as Dhimmis: The Emancipation of Muslim Immigrants in Europe: The Case of Switzerland', in W.A.R. Shadid and P.S. van Koningsveld, *Muslims in the Margin: Political Responses to the Presence of Islam in Western Europe*, Kampen: Kok Pharos, 1996.
150 Siddiqui, 'Muslims in the Contemporary World', p. 27.
151 Waardenburg, *op. cit.*.
152 Siddiqui, 'Muslims in the Contemporary World', p. 27.
153 Jocelyn Cesari, 'Islam in France: Social Challenge or Challenge of Secularism?', Paper presented at the Middle East Studies Association Annual Conference, November, 1997, p. 8. Emphasis added.
154 *Ibid.*, p. 10.
155 Dassetto and Nonneman, p. 194.
156 Werbner, 'The Making of Muslim Dissent', p. 115.
157 *Ibid.*, pp. 103, 115.
158 Fischer and Abedi, p. 317, quoting a young African-American Muslim woman.
159 Hussain, interview.
160 Vertovec and Peach, p. 41.
161 See Qur'an 16: 93 and 49: 13.
162 Anwar Ibrahim, 'The *Ummah* and Tomorrow's World', *Futures*, Vol. 26, 1991, pp. 302–10.
163 See Jurgen Habermas, *Moral Consciousness and Communicative Action*, Cambridge: Polity Press, 1990; and *The Structural Transformation of the Public Sphere: An Inquiry into a Category of Bourgeois Society*, Cambridge: Polity Press, 1992.
164 See e.g. Bobby S. Sayyid, *A Fundamental Fear: Eurocentrism and the Emergence of Islamism*, London: Zed Books, 1997; and Ziauddin Sardar, *Postmodernism and the Other. The New Imperialism of Western Culture*, London: Pluto Press, 1998.
165 Lewis, *Islamic Britain*, p. 185.
166 *Ibid.*, p. 184.
167 Vertovec and Peach, p. 40.
168 Jørgen Nielsen, 'Muslims in Britain: Searching for an Identity?' *New Community*, Vol. 13, No. 3, Spring 1987, p. 392.
169 Yasmin Alibhai-Brown, 'A New Islam for the West', *The Independent*, 14 February 1994, quoted in Vertovec and Peach, p. 40. At least one author also points to ways in which diaspora can actually *exclude* some women from religious life. Landman points out that the shrines of certain Sufi saints constitute the spaces of women's Islam in certain countries of origin. These sites are obviously absent in diaspora, and women are often excluded from the mosques – usually an unfamiliar institution to them in any case – with which they are replaced in Europe.
170 Nico Landman, 'The Islamic Broadcasting Foundation in the Netherlands: Platform or Arena?', in Steven Vertovec and Ceri Peach (eds), *Islam in Europe: The Politics of Religion and Community*, London: Macmillan, 1997, p. 238.
171 Fischer and Abedi, p. 320.
172 Lewis, *Islamic Britain*, p. 195.
173 Fatima Mernissi, *Women and Islam: An Historical and Theological Enquiry*, Oxford: Blackwell, 1991, p. 11; see also Fatima Mernissi, *Women's Rebellion and Islamic Memory*, London: Zed Books, 1996.

174 Lewis, *Islamic Britain*, p. 196.
175 *Ibid.*, p. 188.
176 Barbara D. Metcalf, 'Islam and Women: The Case of the Tablighi Jama'at', *Stanford Electronic Humanities Review*, Vol. 5, No. 1: Contested Polities, 1996, p. 5.
177 Dale F. Eickelman and James Piscatori, *Muslim Politics*, Princeton, PA: Princeton University Press, 1996, p. 150.
178 Yahya Sadowski, '"Just" a Religion: For the Tablighi Jama'at, Islam is not totalitarian', *The Brookings Review*, Vol. 14, No. 3, Summer 1996, p. 3.
179 Felice Dassetto, 'The Tabligh Organization in Belgium', in Tomas Gerholm and Yngve Georg Lithman, *The New Islamic Presence in Western Europe*, London: Mansell Publishing, 1988, p. 162.
180 Metcalf, 'Islam and Women', p. 4.
181 Dassetto, 'The Tabligh Organization in Belgium', p. 160.
182 Metcalf, *Making Muslim Space*, p. xv.
183 See Hamid Naficy, *The Making of Exile Cultures: Iranian Television in Los Angeles*, Minneapolis, MN: University of Minnesota Press, 1993.
184 Metcalf, *Making Muslim Space*, p. 11.
185 Lebor, pp. 101–2.
186 Barbara D. Metcalf, '"Remaking Ourselves": Islamic Self-Fashioning in a Global Movement of Spiritual Renewal', in Martin E. Marty and R. Scott Appleby (eds), *Accounting for Fundamentalisms*, Chicago, IL: University of Chicago Press, 1994, p. 721.
187 Van Bommel, , pp. 129–30.
188 *Ibid.*, p. 128.
189 Thomä-Venske, pp. 80–2.
190 Lebor, p. 103.
191 '"Hamas charity" funds frozen', *The Guardian*, 9 March 1996.
192 Piscatori, 'The Rushdie Affair', p. 787.
193 *Ibid.*, p. 785.
194 Sunier, p. 160.
195 Landman, p. 34.
196 Ahmed and Donnan, p. 5.
197 *Ibid.*, pp. 6–7.
198 Barkatulla, interview.
199 Nelly van Doorn, 'Portrait of a Female Preacher', *Inside Indonesia*, No. 52, October–December 1997, pp. 8–9.
200 Siddiqui, interview.
201 Rosalind Shaw and Charles Stewart, 'Introduction: Problematizing Syncretism', in Charles Stewart and Rosalind Shaw (eds), *Syncretism/Anti-Syncretism: The Politics of Religious Synthesis*, London: Routledge, 1994, p. 12.
202 Hussain, interview.
203 Salman Rushdie, *Imaginary Homelands: Essays and Criticism 1981–1991*, London: Granta, 1992, pp. 124–5.
204 Nederveen Pieterse, 'Travelling Islam', pp. 186, 198.
205 Eickelman and Piscatori, *Muslim Politics*, p. 153.
206 Clifford, *Routes*, p. 277.

5 Transnational public spheres

1 Abdul Hamid el-Zein, 'Beyond Ideology and Theology: The Search for the Anthropology of Islam', *Annual Review of Anthropology*, Vol. 6, 1977, pp. 227–54; Aziz al-Azmeh, *Islams and Modernities*, London: Verso, 2nd Edition, 1996.
2 John Richard Bowen, *Muslims Through Discourse*, Princeton, PA: Princeton University Press, 1993.

3   William R. Roff (ed.), *Islam and the Political Economy of Meaning*, London: Croom Helm, 1987.
4   Dale F. Eickelman, 'Changing Interpretations of Islamic Movements', in William R. Roff (ed.), *Islam and the Political Economy of Meaning*, London: Croom Helm, 1987, p. 18.
5   In my usage of the term 'information technology' (IT), I am casting the net widely to include all electronic media from the telegraph and radio through to the Internet. There is also a sense in which sources of 'populist' Islamic literature (see main text) and desktop publishing should also be considered an aspect of this phenomenon since they rely heavily on advances in design and print technology for their wide dissemination.
6   David Morley and Kevin Robins, *Spaces of Identity: Global Media, Electronic Landscapes and Cultural Boundaries*, London: Routledge, 1995, p. 1.
7   See Edward Said, *Covering Islam: How the Media and the Experts Determine How We See the Rest of the World*, London: Vintage, Revised Edition, 1997; and Akbar S. Ahmed, *Postmodernism and Islam: Predicament and Promise*, London: Routledge, 1992 (see especially Chapter 6).
8   Susan S. Davis and Douglas A. Davis, ' "The Mosque and the Satellite": Media and Adolescence in a Moroccan Town', *Journal of Youth and Adolescence*, Vol. 24, No. 5, 1995, pp. 577–93.
9   Lila Abu-Lughod, 'Bedouins, Cassettes and Technologies of Public Culture', *Middle East Report*, July–August 1989, pp. 7–11, 47; 'Finding a Place for Islam: Egyptian Television and the National Interest', *Public Culture*, Vol. 5, No. 3, 1993, pp. 493–513.
10   Steven Barraclough, 'Satellite Television and Islamists in Pakistan, Iran and Egypt', Paper presented at the British Society for Middle East Studies Conference on 'Rethinking Islam', Oxford, July 1997.
11   A notable exception is the special issue of *Media, Culture and Society* on 'Islam and Communication' (Vol. 15, No. 1, 1993). This is a collection of essays of varied quality; an excellent critique of this special issue was offered by Annabelle Sreberny-Mohammadi in the same journal later that year (Annabelle Sreberny-Mohammadi, 'On reading "Islam and Communication" ', *Media, Culture and Society*, Vol. 15, No. 4, 1993, pp. 661–8).
12   See e.g. Richard Cole, 'Islamic Terrorists Organize, Raise Funds in U.S. while Plotting Attacks', *Associated Press*, 24 May 1997; 'Intelligence Battle in Cyberspace', *Intelligence Newsletter*, 27 April 1995; and Mike Mokrzycki, 'Battleground of Bits and Bytes', *The Jerusalem Post*, 19 April 1995.
13   See Francis Robinson, 'Islam and the Impact of Print', *Modern Asian Studies*, Vol. 27, No. 1, 1993, pp. 229–51; the various chapters in George N. Atiyeh (ed.), *The Book in the Islamic World: The Written Word and Communication in the Middle East*, Albany, NY: SUNY Press, 1995; and Dale F. Eickelman and James Piscatori, *Muslim Politics*, Princeton, PA: Princeton University Press, 1996, pp. 122–4.
14   *al-qur'ān* = 'the recitation'.
15   See Brinkley Messick, *The Calligraphic State: Textual Domination and History in a Muslim Society*, Berkeley, CA: University of California Press, 1993.
16   Dale F. Eickelman, 'The Study of Islam in Local Contexts', *Contributions to Asian Studies*, Vol. 17, 1982, p. 10.
17   Robinson, 'Islam and the Impact of Print', p. 245.
18   Geoffrey Roper, 'Faris al-Shidyaq and the Transition from Scribal to Print Culture in the Middle East', in George N. Atiyeh (ed.), *The Book in the Islamic World: The Written Word and Communication in the Middle East*, Albany, NY: SUNY Press, 1995, p. 210.
19   Dale F. Eickelman, *Knowledge and Power in Morocco: The Education of a Twentieth Century Notable*, Princeton, PA: Princeton University Press, 1985, pp. 168–9; see also Dale F. Eickelman, 'The Art of Memory: Islamic Education and its Social Reproduction', *Comparative Studies in Society and History*, Vol. 20, No. 4, October 1978, pp. 485–516.

20 Dale F. Eickelman, 'National Identity and Religious Discourse in Contemporary Islam', *International Journal of Islamic and Arabic Studies*, Vol. 6, No. 1, pp. 1–20.
21 Olivier Roy, *The Failure of Political Islam*, London: I.B. Tauris, 1994, pp. 89–106.
22 *Ibid.*, pp. 96–7.
23 Serif Mardin, *Religion and Social Change in Modern Turkey: The Case of Bediüzzaman Saïd Nursi*, Albany, NY: SUNY Press, 1989, p. 24.
24 Several anthropologists have undertaken studies of Islam in these 'local' contexts. See e.g. John R. Bowen, '*Salat* in Indonesia: The Social Meanings of an Islamic Ritual', *Man*, Vol. 24, 1989, pp. 600–19; Michael Lambek, 'Certain Knowledge, Contestable Authority: Power and Practice on the Islamic Periphery', *American Ethnologist*, Vol. 17, No. 1, February 1990, pp. 23–40; Robert W. Hefner and Patricia Horvatich (eds), *Islam in an Era of Nation-States: Politics and Religious Renewal in Muslim Southeast Asia*, Honolulu, HA: University of Hawai'i Press, 1997; and David Westerlund and Eva Evers Rosander (eds), *African Islam and Islam in Africa: Encounters between Sufis and Islamists*, London: Hurst and Company, 1997.
25 Victoria Bernal, 'Gender, Culture, and Capitalism: Women and the Remaking of Islamic "Tradition" in a Sudanese Village', *Comparative Studies of Society and History*, Vol. 36, 1994, p. 40.
26 Barbara D. Metcalf, 'The Pilgrimage Remembered: South Asian Accounts of the *Hajj*', in Dale F. Eickelman and James Piscatori (eds), *Muslim Travellers: Pilgrimage, Migration, and the Religious Imagination*, Berkeley, CA: University of California Press, 1990, p. 87.
27 Patricia Horvatich, 'Ways of Knowing Islam', *American Ethnologist*, Vol. 21, No. 4, 1994, p. 817.
28 Although these students usually have no formal connection to the Ahmaddiya movement, and do not subscribe to their beliefs, this is still a fitting testimony to the translocal nature of derogatory labels!
29 *Ibid.*, p. 818.
30 *Ibid.*, pp. 821–2.
31 Bernal, p. 41.
32 Abdelwahab El-Affendi, 'Eclipse of Reason: The Media in the Muslim World', *Journal of International Affairs*, Vol. 47, Summer 1993, pp. 163–93.
33 Richard Bulliet, *Islam: The View from the Edge*, New York: Columbia University Press, 1994, p. 200.
34 Robert D. Crane, 'Premise and Promise in the Islamization of Knowledge: A Contribution Toward Unity in Diversity', in Robert D. Crane (ed.), *Preparing to Islamize America*, Reston, VA: International Institute of Islamic Thought, 1987; Ziauddin Sardar, *Information and the Muslim World*, London: Mansell, 1988.
35 Larry A. Poston, 'Da'wa in the West', in Yvonne Yazbeck Haddad (ed.), *The Muslims of America*, New York: Oxford University Press, 1991, p. 133.
36 A.K. Barkatulla, personal interview, London, 21 July, 1998.
37 *Ibid.*
38 *Ibid.*
39 Dr Sa'ad al-Faqih, Personal Interview, London, 14 August 1998.
40 Ziauddin Sardar, 'Paper, Printing and Compact Disks: The Making and Unmaking of Islamic Culture', *Media, Culture and Society*, Vol. 15, No. 1, January 1993, pp. 55–6.
41 This is a program which contains rules and guidelines which tell a computer how to process, 'think' and make decisions with particular sets of data. It is usually written in an artificial intelligence language such as PROLOG.
42 Sardar, 'Paper, Printing and Compact Disks', p. 56.
43 Al-Faqih, interview.
44 Barkatulla, interview.
45 Abdul Kadir Barkatulla, 'Information Technology and Islamic Studies', Unpublished MPhil dissertation, University of Wales at Lampeter, 1992.

46 Barkatulla, interview.
47 Neil MacFarquhar, 'With Mixed Feelings, Iran Tiptoes to the Internet', *New York Times*, 8 October 1996.
48 Eickelman, 'National Identity and Religious Discourse in Contemporary Islam'.
49 Benedict Anderson, *Imagined Communities: Reflections on the Origin and Spread of Nationalism*, London: Verso, Revised Edition, 1991.
50 Eickelman and Piscatori, *Muslim Politics*, p. 122.
51 Mardin, *op. cit.*.
52 Yves Gonzalez-Quijano, 'Les Livres Islamiques: Histoires ou Mythes?', *Peuples méditerranéens*, Nos. 56–7, July–December 1991, pp. 283–92.
53 David Edwards, 'Print Islam: Media and religious revolution in Afghanistan', *Anthropological Quarterly*, Vol. 68, July 1995, pp. 171–84.
54 Muhsin Mahdi, 'From the Manuscript Age to the Age of Printed Books', in George N. Atiyeh (ed.), *The Book in the Islamic World: The Written Word and Communication in the Middle East*, Albany, NY: SUNY Press, 1995, p. 13.
55 Robinson, 'Islam and the Impact of Print', p. 250; cf. Eickelman and Piscatori, *Muslim Politics*, p. 125.
56 Edwards, p. 13; also Eickelman and Piscatori, *Muslim Politics*, p. 125.
57 See http://www.miraserve.com/
58 Ulf Hannerz, *Transnational Connections: Culture, People, Places*, London: Routledge, 1996, p. 21.
59 Sardar, 'Paper, Printing and Compact Disks', p. 55.
60 Eickelman and Piscatori, *Muslim Politics*, p. 122.
61 *Ibid.*, pp. 121–2.
62 Morley and Robins, pp. 1–2.
63 Various authors, 'Region joins the global revolution', *MEED Special Report*, 1 March 1996.
64 See http://www.IANAnet.org/fatwa/
65 Prof. Muhammad al-Massari, Personal Interviews, London, June 1995 and March 1997.
66 'Bin Baz calls on Muslims to ignore bulletins seeking to split their ranks', *Saudi Gazette*, 12 November 1994.
67 Lila Abu-Lughod, 'Dramatic Reversals: Political Islam and Egyptian Television', in Joel Beinin and Joe Stark (eds), *Political Islam*, London: I.B. Tauris, 1997; Eickelman, 'National Identity and Religious Discourse in Contemporary Islam'.
68 See Barraclough, 'Satellite Television and Islamists'.
69 Malise Ruthven, 'The West's Secret Weapon against Islam', *The Sunday Times*, 1 January 1995.
70 Andrew Rathmell, 'Netwar in the Gulf', *Jane's Intelligence Review*, January 1997, pp. 29–32.
71 *Reuters* (Rome), 4 September 1996.
72 Dr Sa'ad al-Faqih, Personal Interview, London, March 1997.
73 Hannerz, *Transnational Connections*, p. 101.
74 Phillip Lewis, *Islamic Britain: Religion, Politics and Identity among British Muslims*, London: I.B. Tauris, 1994, pp. 206–7.
75 A brief survey of diasporic Muslim uses of the Internet in Europe has been undertaken by Felice Dassetto. See his *La Construction de L'Islam Européen*, Paris: L'Harmattan, 1996, pp. 291–94.
76 Arjun Appadurai, *Modernity at Large: Cultural Dimensions of Globalization*, Minneapolis, MN: University of Minnesota Press, 1996, pp. 195, 197.
77 Anderson, *Imagined Communities*.
78 Jon Anderson, ' "Cybarites", Knowledge Workers, and New Creoles on the Superhighway', *Anthropology Today*, Vol. 11, No. 4, August 1995, pp. 13–15.
79 Jon Anderson, 'Cybernauts of the Arab Diaspora: Electronic Mediation in Transnational Cultural Identities', Paper presented at the Couch-Stone Symposium on 'Postmodern Culture, Global Capitalism and Democratic Action', University of Maryland, April 1997.

80 Jon Anderson, 'Islam and the Globalization of Politics', Paper presented to the Council on Foreign Relations Muslim Politics Study Group, New York City, 25 June 1996, p. 1.
81 *Ibid.*
82 Margot Cohen, 'Modern Times: Islam on the Information Highway', *Far Eastern Economic Review*, 29 August 1996.
83 Kathy Evans, 'Thoroughly Modern Mullahs', *The Guardian*, 16 March 1996.
84 See e.g. Michael Wine, 'Islamist Organisations on the Internet', available on-line at http://www.ict.org.il/articles/islamnet.htm; a critical response to this article by a Muslim organisation on the Internet can be found at http://msanews.mynet.net/MSANEWS/199808/19980816.0.html
85 Richard Cole, 'Islamic Terrorists Organize'; 'Intelligence Battle in Cyberspace'.
86 Benedict Anderson, 'Exodus', *Critical Inquiry*, Vol. 20, Winter 1994, p. 327.
87 See, for example, http://www.ou.edu/cyermuslim/cy_jihad.html
88 Al-Faqih, interview.
89 Anderson, 'Cybernauts of the Arab Diaspora', p. 2.
90 Anderson, 'Islam and the Globalization of Politics', p. 1.
91 Al-Faqih, interview.
92 Anderson, 'Cybernauts of the Arab Diaspora', p. 3.
93 Several representative sites are as follows: The Islamic Gateway (www.ummah.org.uk); IslamiCity (www.islam.org); and the Muslim Students Association News Network (msanews.mynet.net).
94 http://acc6.its.brooklyn.cuny.edu/~jabedi/
95 http://acc6.its.brooklyn.cuny.edu/~jabedi/tabligh.html
96 'British mosques on the superhighway', 30 June 1996, at http://www.malaysia.net/muslimedia
97 Anderson, *Imagined Communities*, p. 6.
98 Hamid Naficy, *The Making of Exile Cultures: Iranian Television in Los Angeles*, Minneapolis, MN: University of Minnesota Press, 1993.
99 Al-Faqih, interview.
100 *Ibid.*
101 *IPS*, 4 April 1997.
102 Habib Trabelsi, 'Saudis Near End of Seven-Year Wait to Surf the Net', *Agence France Presse*, 15 July 1998.
103 *Reuters*, 18 June 1996.
104 *IPS*, 4 April 1997.
105 *Reuters*, 28 August 1996.
106 *Xinhua Press Agency*, 4 November 1996.
107 Carroll Bogert, 'Chat Rooms and Chadors', *Newsweek*, 21 August 1995.
108 *Reuters*, 4 April 1996.
109 Al-Faqih, interview.
110 Appadurai, *Modernity at Large*, pp. 195–6.
111 Roy, p. 95.
112 Hassan al-Turabi, 'The Islamic State', in John L. Esposito, *Voices of Resurgent Islam*, New York: Oxford University Press, 1983, p. 245.
113 Muhammad Al-Mass'ari, 'Ruling by Kufr is Haram', Unpublished manuscript, n.d.
114 Eickelman, 'Changing Interpretations of Islamic Movements', p. 27.
115 Anderson, ' "Cybarites" ', p. 13.
116 Roy, p. 95.
117 Eickelman, *Knowledge and Power in Morocco*, p. 169.
118 Roy, p. 95. Emphasis added.
119 For an account of how diasporic movements are using information technology to challenge state borders see Amir Hassanpour, 'Satellite Footprints as National

Borders: MED-TV and the Extraterritoriality of State Sovereignty', *Journal of Muslim Minority Affairs*, Vol. 18, No. 1, 1998, pp. 53–72.
120 James Clifford, *Routes: Travel and Translation in the Late Twentieth Century*, Cambridge, MA: Harvard University Press, 1997, p. 276.

6 Reimagining the umma?

1 Dale F. Eickelman, 'Inside the Islamic Reformation', *Wilson Quarterly*, Vol. 22, No. 1, Winter 1998, pp. 80–9.
2 Talal Asad, *Genealogies of Religion: Discipline and Reasons of Power in Christianity and Islam*, Baltimore, MD: Johns Hopkins University Press, 1993, p. 17.
3 Fazlur Rahman, *Islam and Modernity: Transformation of an Intellectual Tradition*, Chicago, IL: University of Chicago Press, 1982, p. 141.
4 Rosalind Shaw and Charles Stewart, 'Introduction: Problematizing Syncretism', in Charles Stewart and Rosalind Shaw (eds), *Syncretism/Anti-Syncretism: The Politics of Religious Synthesis*, London: Routledge, 1994, p. 7.
5 *Ibid.*, p. 8.
6 R. Radhakrishnan, *Diasporic Mediations: Between Home and Location*, Minneapolis, MN: University of Minnesota Press, 1996, p. 162.
7 Dr Ataullah Siddiqui, Personal Interview, Leicester, 29 July 1998.
8 Bobby S. Sayyid, *A Fundamental Fear: Eurocentrism and the Emergence of Islamism*, London: Zed Books, 1997, p. 114.
9 Akeel Bilgrami, 'What Is a Muslim? Fundamental Commitment and Cultural Identity', in Kwame Anthony Appiah and Henry Louis Gates (eds), *Identities*, Chicago, IL: University of Chicago Press, 1995, p. 218.
10 Sayyid, p. 118.
11 Pnina Werbner, 'The Making of Muslim Dissent: Hybridized Discourses, Lay Preachers, and Radical Rhetoric among British Pakistanis', *American Ethnologist*, Vol. 23, No. 1, 1996, p. 116.
12 Rahman, *op. cit.*.
13 *Ibid.*, p. 141.
14 H.A.R. Gibb and J.H. Kramers (eds), *Shorter Encyclopedia of Islam*, Leiden: E.J. Brill, 1991, p. 185.
15 *Ibid.*, p. 160.
16 Talal Asad, 'Modern Power and the Reconfiguration of Religious Traditions', *Stanford Electronic Humanities Review*, Vol. 5, No. 1: Contested Politics, 1996, p. 5.
17 Hassan Hanafi, *Min al-'aqida ila l-thawra*, Cairo: Maktaba Mabduli, 5 Volumes, 1987.
18 See Richard C. Martin and Mark R. Woodward with Dwi S. Atmaja, *Defenders of Reason in Islam: Mu'tazilism from Medieval School to Modern Symbol*, Oxford: Oneworld, 1997.
19 Rahman, p. 140.
20 Ruhallah Khomeini, *Islam and Revolution*, Translated by Hamid Algar, Berkeley, CA: Mizan, 1981. For a critique of *wilayat al-faqih* see Sami Zubaida, *Islam, the People and the State: Essays on Political Ideas and Movements in the Middle East*, London: I.B. Tauris, Revised edition, 1993.
21 See Valla Vakili, 'Debating Religion and Politics in Iran: The Political Thought of Abdolkarim Soroush', Council on Foreign Relations Studies Department Occasional Paper No. 2, 1996.
22 See e.g. Mohammed Arkoun, *Pour une critique de la raison islamique*, Paris: Maisonneuve et Larose, 1984; *Essais sur la pensée islamique*, Paris: Maisonneuve et Larose, 3rd Edition, 1984; and 'The Concept of Authority in Islamic Thought', in Klaus Ferdinand and Mehdi Mozaffari (eds), *Islam: State and Society*, London: Curzon Press, 1988.
23 Mohammed Arkoun, *Rethinking Islam*, Boulder, CO: Westview Press, 1994, p. 22.

24 Werner Schiffauer, 'Migration and Religiousness', in Tomas Gerholm and Yngve Georg Lithman, *The New Islamic Presence in Western Europe*, London: Mansell Publishing, 1988, p. 154. Emphasis added.

25 Hanns Thomä-Venske, 'The Religious Life of Muslims in Berlin', in Tomas Gerholm and Yngve Georg Lithman, *The New Islamic Presence in Western Europe*, London: Mansell Publishing, 1988, p. 80.

26 Barbara D. Metcalf, 'Introduction: Sacred Words, Sanctioned Practice, New Communities', in Barbara D. Metcalf (ed.), *Making Muslim Space in North America and Europe*, Berkeley, CA: University of California Press, 1996, p. 11.

27 James Piscatori, 'The Rushdie Affair and the Politics of Ambiguity', *International Affairs*, Vol. 66, No. 4, 1990, p. 775.

28 One representative example of this genre is Kalim Siddiqui, 'Beyond the Muslim Nation-States', in Isma'il R. Al-Faruqi and Abdullah Omar Nasseef (eds), *Social and Natural Sciences: The Islamic Perspective*, Sevenoaks: Hodder and Stoughton, 1981.

29 R.B.J. Walker, 'Social Movements/World Politics', *Millennium*, Vol. 23, No. 3, 1994, p. 700.

30 Michael Peter Smith, 'Can You Imagine? Transnational Migration and the Globalization of Grassroots Politics', *Social Text*, No. 39, Summer 1994, p. 15. Emphasis added.

31 See e.g. Pheng Cheah and Bruce Robbins (eds), *Cosmopolitics: Thinking and Feeling Beyond the Nation*, Minneapolis, MN: University of Minnesota Press, 1998.

Bibliography

Abduh, Muhammad, *al-A'mal al-Kamila*, Beirut: al-Mu'assasa al-'Arabiya li'l-Dirasat wa'l-Nashr, 1972.

Abu-Lughod, Janet, 'Going Beyond Global Babble', in Anthony D. King (ed.), *Culture, Globalization and the World-System: Contemporary Conditions for the Representation of Identity*, London: Macmillan, 1991.

Abu-Lughod, Lila, 'Bedouins, Cassettes and Technologies of Public Culture', *Middle East Report*, July–August 1989, pp. 7–11, 47.

—— 'Writing Against Culture', in Richard G. Fox (ed.), *Recapturing Anthropology: Working in the Present*, Santa Fe, NM: School of American Research Press, 1991.

—— 'Dramatic Reversals: Political Islam and Egyptian Television', in Joel Beinin and Joe Stark (eds), *Political Islam*, London: I.B. Tauris, 1997.

Adams, Charles J., 'Mawdudi and the Islamic State', in John L. Esposito (ed.), *Voices of Resurgent Islam*, New York: Oxford University Press, 1983.

Ahmad, Aijaz, *In Theory: Classes, Nations, Literatures*, London: Verso, 1994.

Ahmed, Akbar S., *Postmodernism and Islam: Predicament and Promise*, London: Routledge, 1992.

—— 'Mutiny in the Mosque', *The Guardian*, March 10, 1994.

Ahmed, Akbar S. and Hastings Donnan, 'Islam in the Age of Postmodernity', in Akbar S. Ahmed and Hastings Donnan (eds), *Islam, Globalization and Postmodernity*, London: Routledge, 1994.

Akhtar, Shabbir, *Be Careful with Muhammad!*, London: Bellew, 1989.

Akhtar, Shabbir, *A Faith for All Seasons, Islam and Western Modernity*, London: Bellew, 1990.

Al-Ayyashi, Abu Salim, *Ma' al-Mawa'id*, Riyadh: Dar al-Rifa'i, 1984.

Al-Azmeh, Aziz, *Islams and Modernities*, London: Verso, 2nd Edition, 1996.

Alibhai-Brown, Yasmin, 'A New Islam for the West', *The Independent*, 14 February 1994.

Al-Mass'ari, Muhammad, 'Ruling by Kufr is Haram', Unpublished manuscript, n.d.

Al-Siddiq, Sayyid 'Abd al-'Aziz b. Muhammad, *Hukm al-iqama bi-bilad al-kufr wa-bayan wujubiha fi-ba'd al-Ahwal*, Tangier: Bughaz, 1985.

Al-Tabari, *Ta'rikh ar-Rusul wa'l-Muluk*, Cairo: Dar al-Marif, 1960–1977.

Al-Turabi, Hassan, 'The Islamic State', in John L. Esposito, *Voices of Resurgent Islam*, New York: Oxford University Press, 1983.

Anderson, Benedict, *Imagined Communities: Reflections on the Origin and Spread of Nationalism*, London: Verso, Revised Edition, 1991.

—— 'Exodus', *Critical Inquiry*, Vol. 20, Winter 1994

Anderson, Jon, ' "Cybarites", Knowledge Workers, and New Creoles on the Super-highway', *Anthropology Today*, Vol. 11, No. 4, August 1995.

—— 'Islam and the Globalization of Politics', Paper presented to the Council on Foreign Relations Muslim Politics Study Group, New York City, 25 June 1996.

—— 'Cybernauts of the Arab Diaspora: Electronic Mediation in Transnational Cultural Identities', Paper presented at the Couch-Stone Symposium on 'Postmodern Culture, Global Capitalism and Democratic Action', University of Maryland, April 1997.

Appadurai, Arjun, 'Disjuncture and Difference in the Global Cultural Economy', in Mike Featherstone (ed.), *Global Culture: Nationalism, Globalization and Modernity*, London: Sage, 1990.

—— *Modernity at Large: Cultural Dimensions of Globalization*, Minneapolis, MN: University of Minnesota Press, 1996.

—— 'Sovereignty Without Territoriality: Notes for a Postnational Geography', in Patricia Yaeger, *The Geography of Identity*, Ann Arbor, MI: University of Michigan Press, 1996.

Arkoun, Mohammed, *Pour une critique de la raison islamique*, Paris: Maisonneuve et Larose, 1984.

—— *Essais sur la pensée islamique*, Paris: Maisonneuve et Larose, 3rd Edition, 1984.

—— 'The Concept of Authority in Islamic Thought', in Klaus Ferdinand and Mehdi Mozaffari (eds), *Islam: State and Society*, London: Curzon Press, 1988.

—— *Rethinking Islam*, Boulder, CO: Westview Press, 1994.

Asad, Talal, 'Modern Power and the Reconfiguration of Religious Traditions', *Stanford Electronic Humanities Review*, Vol. 5, No. 1: Contested Politics, 1996.

—— *Genealogies of Religion: Discipline and Reasons of Power in Christianity and Islam*, Baltimore, MD: Johns Hopkins University Press, 1993.

Atiyeh, George N. (ed.), *The Book in the Islamic World: The Written Word and Communication in the Middle East*, Albany, NY: SUNY Press, 1995.

Ayatollah Ahmad Jannati, Sermon at Tehran University, 20 December 1996.

Bakhtin, M.M., *The Dialogic Imagination*, Austin, TX: University of Texas Press, 1981.

Barkatulla, Abdul Kadir, 'Information Technology and Islamic Studies', Unpublished MPhil Book, University of Wales at Lampeter, 1992.

Barraclough, Steven, 'Satellite Television and Islamists in Pakistan, Iran and Egypt', Paper presented at the British Society for Middle East Studies Conference on 'Re-thinking Islam', Oxford, July 1997.

Bartelson, Jens, *A Genealogy of Sovereignty*, Cambridge: Cambridge University Press, 1995.

Basch, Linda, Nina Glick Schiller and Cristina Szanton Blanc, *Nations Unbound: Transnational Projects, Postcolonial Predicaments, and Deterritorialized Nation-States*, Amsterdam: Gordon and Breach, 1994.

Baumann, Gerd, 'Dominant and Demotic Discourses of Culture: Their Relevance to Multi-Ethnic Alliances', in Pnina Werbner and Tariq Modood (eds), *Debating Cultural Hybridity: Multi-Cultural Identities and the Politics of Anti-Racism*, London: Zed Books, 1997.

Beck, Ulrich, *Risk Society: Towards a New Modernity*, London: Sage, 1992.

Bernal, Victoria, 'Gender, Culture, and Capitalism: Women and the Remaking of Islamic "Tradition" in a Sudanese Village', *Comparative Studies of Society and History*, Vol. 36, 1994.

Bhabha, Homi, *The Location of Culture*, London: Routledge, 1994.

—— 'Culture's In-Between', in Stuart Hall and Paul du Gay (eds), *Questions of Cultural Identity*, London: Sage, 1996.

—— (ed.), *Nation and Narration*, London: Routledge, 1990.

Biersteker, Thomas J. and Cynthia Weber (eds), *State Sovereignty as Social Construct*, Cambridge: Cambridge University Press, 1996.

Bilgrami, Akeel, 'What Is a Muslim? Fundamental Commitment and Cultural Identity', in Kwama Anthony Appiah and Henry Louis Gates (eds), *Identities*, Chicago, IL: University of Chicago Press, 1995.

'Bin Baz calls on Muslims to Ignore Bulletins Seeking to Split their Ranks', *Saudi Gazette*, 12 November 1994.

Bogert, Carroll, 'Chat Rooms and Chadors', *Newsweek*, 21 August 1995.

Boroujerdi, Mehrzad, 'Iranian Islam and the Faustian Bargain of Western Modernity', *Journal of Peace Research*, Vol. 34, No. 1, 1997.

Bowen, John R., '*Salat* in Indonesia: The Social Meanings of an Islamic Ritual', *Man*, Vol. 24, 1989.

—— *Muslims Through Discourse*, Princeton, PA: Princeton University Press, 1993.

Bulliet, Richard, *Islam: The View from the Edge*, New York: Columbia University Press, 1994.

Bunt, Gary, 'Decision-Making Concerns in British Islamic Environments', *Islam and Christian-Muslim Relations*, Vol. 9, No. 1, 1998.

Burton, John, *World Society*, London: Cambridge University Press, 1972.

Buzan, Barry, 'The Levels of Analysis Problem in International Relations Reconsidered', in Ken Booth and Steve Smith (eds), *International Relations Theory Today*, Cambridge: Polity Press, 1995.

Caglar, Ayse S., 'Hyphenated Identities and the Limits of "Culture"', in Tariq Modood and Pnina Werbner (eds), *The Politics of Multiculturalism in the New Europe*, London: Zed Books, 1997

Calhoun, Craig, 'Indirect Relationships and Imagined Communities: Large-Scale Social Integration and the Transformation of Everyday Life', in Pierre Bourdieu and James S. Coleman (eds), *Social Theory for a Changing World*, Boulder, CO: Westview Press, 1991.

Campbell, David, 'Political Prosaics, Transversal Politics, and the Anarchical World', in Michael J. Shapiro and Hayward R. Alker (eds), *Challenging Boundaries: Global Flows, Territorial Identities*, Minneapolis, MN: University of Minnesota Press, 1996

Cesari, Jocelyn, 'Islam in France: Social Challenge or Challenge of Secularism?', Paper presented at the Middle East Studies Association Annual Conference, November, 1997.

Cheah, Pheng, 'Given Culture: Rethinking Cosmopolitical Freedom in Transnationalism', in Pheng Cheah and Bruce Robbins (eds), *Cosmopolitics: Thinking and Feeling beyond the Nation*, Minneapolis, MN: University of Minnesota Press, 1998.

Cheah, Pheng and Bruce Robbins (eds), *Cosmopolitics: Thinking and Feeling beyond the Nation*, Minneapolis, MN: University of Minnesota Press, 1998.

Clifford, James, 'Diasporas', *Cultural Anthropology*, Vol. 9, No. 3, 1994.

—— 'Traveling Cultures', in L. Grossberg, C. Nelson and P. Treichler (eds), *Cultural Studies*, London: Routledge, 1992.

—— 'Introduction: Partial Truths', in James Clifford and George E. Marcus (eds), *Writing Culture: The Poetics and Politics of Ethnography*, Berkeley, CA: University of California Press, 1986.

—— 'Notes on Travel and Theory', *Inscriptions*, No. 5, 1989.

—— *Routes: Travel and Translation in the Late Twentieth Century*, Cambridge, MA: Harvard University Press, 1997.

Cohen, Margot, 'Modern Times: Islam on the Information Highway', *Far Eastern Economic Review*, 29 August 1996.

Cohen, Robin, 'Diasporas, the Nation-State, and Globalisation', in Wang Gungwu (ed.), *Global History and Migrations*, Boulder, CO: Westview Press, 1997.

—— *Global Diasporas*, London: UCL Press, 1997.

Cole, Richard, 'Islamic Terrorists Organize, Raise Funds in U.S. while Plotting Attacks', *Associated Press*, 24 May 1997.

Connolly, William E., *Identity/Difference: Democratic Negotiations of Political Paradox*, Ithaca, NY: Cornell University Press, 1991.

Cook, Michael and Patricia Crone, *Hagarism: The Making of the Islamic World*, Cambridge: Cambridge University Press, 1977.

Crane, Robert D., 'Premise and Promise in the Islamization of Knowledge: A Contribution Toward Unity in Diversity', in Robert D. Crane (ed.), *Preparing to Islamize America*, Reston, VA: International Institute of Islamic Thought, 1987.

Crone, Patricia, *Slaves on Horses: the Evolution of the Islamic Polity*, London: Cambridge University Press, 1980.

Darsh, S.M., *Muslims in Europe*, London: Ta-Ha, 1980.

Das, Veena, 'For a Folk-Theology and Theological Anthropology of Islam', *Contributions to Indian Sociology*, Vol. 18, No. 2, 1984.

Dassetto, Felice, 'The Tabligh Organization in Belgium', in Tomas Gerholm and Yngve Georg Lithman, *The New Islamic Presence in Western Europe*, London: Mansell Publishing, 1988.

—— 'Islam and Europe', Paper presented at the International Conference on Muslim Minorities in Post-Bipolar Europe, Skopje, Macedonia, 1993.

—— *La Construction de L'Islam Européen*, Paris: L'Harmattan, 1996.

Dassetto, Felice and A. Bastenier, *L'Islam transplanté*, Antwerp: Editions EPO, 1984.

Dassetto, Felice and Gerd Nonneman, 'Islam in Belgium and the Netherlands: Towards a Typology of "Transplanted" Islam', in G. Nonneman, T. Niblock and B. Szajkowski (eds), *Muslim Communities in the New Europe*, Reading: Ithaca Press, 1996

Davis, Susan S. and Douglas A. Davis, '"The Mosque and the Satellite": Media and Adolescence in a Moroccan Town', *Journal of Youth and Adolescence*, Vol. 24, No. 5, 1995.

Denny, Frederick Mathewson, 'The Legacy of Fazlur Rahman', in Yvonne Yazbeck Haddad (ed.), *The Muslims of America*, Oxford: Oxford University Press, 1991.

Dietz, Mary, 'Context Is All: Feminism and Theories of Citizenship', in Chantal Mouffe (ed.), *Dimensions of Radical Democracy*, London: Verso, 1992.

Donner, Fred M., 'The Formation of the Early Islamic State', *Journal of the American Oriental Society*, Vol. 56, 1986.

Dunn, Ross, 'International Migrations of Literate Muslims in the Later Middle Period: The Case of Ibn Battuta', in Ian Richard Netton (ed.), *Golden Roads: Migration, Pilgrimage, and Travel in Mediaeval and Modern Islam*, London: Curzon Press, 1993.

Eade, John, 'Reconstructing Places: Changing Images of Locality in Docklands and Spitalfields', in John Eade (ed.), *Living the Global City: Globalization as Local Process*, London: Routledge, 1997.

Edwards, David, 'Print Islam: Media and religious revolution in Afghanistan', *Anthropological Quarterly*, Vol. 68, July 1995.

Eickelman, Dale F., 'National Identity and Religious Discourse in Contemporary Islam', *International Journal of Islamic and Arabic Studies*, Vol. 6, No. 1, 1989.

—— 'The Art of Memory: Islamic Education and its Social Reproduction', *Comparative Studies in Society and History*, Vol. 20, No. 4, October 1978.

—— 'The Study of Islam in Local Contexts', *Contributions to Asian Studies*, Vol. 17, 1982.

—— *Knowledge and Power in Morocco: The Education of a Twentieth Century Notable*, Princeton: Princeton University Press, 1985.

—— 'Anthropology and International Relations', in Walter Goldschmidt (ed.), *Anthropology and Public Policy: A Dialogue*, Washington: American Anthropological Association, 1986.

—— 'Changing Intepretations of Islamic Movements', in William R. Roff (ed.), *Islam and the Political Economy of Meaning*, London: Croom Helm, 1987.

—— 'Inside the Islamic Reformation', *Wilson Quarterly*, Vol. 22, No. 1, Winter 1998.

Eickelman, Dale F. and James Piscatori, *Muslim Politics*, Princeton, PA: Princeton University Press, 1996.

—— (eds), *Muslim Travellers: Pilgrimage, Migration, and the Religious Imagination*, Berkeley, CA: University of California Press, 1990.

El-Affendi, Abdelwahab, 'Eclipse of Reason: The Media in the Muslim World', *Journal of International Affairs*, Vol. 47, Summer 1993.

El-Moudden, Abderrahmane, 'The Ambivalence of *Rihla*: Community Integration and Self-definition in Moroccan Travel Accounts: 1300–1800', in Dale F. Eickelman and James Piscatori (eds), *Muslim Travellers: Pilgrimage, Migration, and the Religious Imagination*, Berkeley, CA: University of California Press, 1990.

El-Zein, Abdul Hamid M., 'Beyond Ideology and Theology: The Search for the Anthropology of Islam', *Annual Review of Anthropology*, Vol. 6, 1977.

Ellis Jean, 'Local Government and Community Needs: A Case Study of Muslims in Coventry', *New Community*, Vol. 17, No. 3, April 1991.

Enloe, Cynthia, *Bananas, Beaches and Bases: Making Feminist Sense of International Relations*, London: Pandora, 1989.

Evans, Kathy, 'Thoroughly Modern Mullahs', *The Guardian*, 16 March 1996.

Fabian, Johannes, *Time and the Other: How Anthropology Makes its Object*, New York: Columbia University Press, 1983.

Faist, Thomas, 'International Migrations and Transnational Social Spaces: The Bridging Functions of Social Capital in the Economic Realm', Paper presented at the Second International MigCities Conference, Liege, 6–8 November 1997.

Falk, Richard, *The Promise of World Order*, Brighton: Wheatsheaf, 1987.

Faruqi, Ismail R., 'The Path of Dawah in the West', *The Muslim World League Journal*, Vol. 14, Nos. 7–8, March–April, 1987.

Featherstone, Mike, *Undoing Culture: Globalization, Postmodernism and Identity*, London: Sage, 1995.

'Finding a Place for Islam: Egyptian Television and the National Interest', *Public Culture*, Vol. 5, No. 3, 1993.

Fischer, Michael M.J. and Mehdi Abedi, *Debating Muslims: Cultural Dialogues in Postmodernity and Tradition*, Madison, WI: University of Wisconsin Press, 1990.

Fog Olwig, Karen, 'Cultural sites: Sustaining a Home in a Deterritorialized World', in Karen Fog Olwig and Kirsten Hastrup (eds), *Siting Culture: The Shifting Anthropological Object*, London: Routledge, 1991.

—— *Global Culture, Island Identity: Continuity and Change in the Afro-Caribbean Community of Nevis*, Reading: Harwood Academic Publishers, 1993.

Friedman, Jonathan, 'Global System, Globalization and the Parameters of Modernity', in Mike Featherstone, Scott Lash and Roland Robertson (eds), *Global Modernities*, London: Sage, 1995.

Frost, Mervyn, *Ethics in International Relations: A Constitutive Theory*, Cambridge: Cambridge University Press, 1996.

Gardner, Katy, *Global Migrants, Local Lives: Travel and Transformation in Rural Bangladesh*, Oxford: Clarendon Press, 1995.

Geertz, Clifford, *The Interpretation of Cultures*, London: Fontana Press, 1993.

Gibb, H.A.R. and J.H. Kramers (eds), *Shorter Encyclopedia of Islam*, Leiden: E.J. Brill, 1991.

Giddens, Anthony, *The Consequences of Modernity*, Oxford: Polity Press, 1990.

—— *Modernity and Self-Identity*, Cambridge: Polity Press, 1991.

Gilroy, Paul, *The Black Atlantic: Modernity and Double Consciousness*, London: Verso, 1993.

Gonzalez-Quijano, Yves, 'Les Livres Islamiques: Histoires ou Mythes?' *Peuples méditerranéens*, Nos. 56–7, July–December 1991.

Habermas, Jurgen, *Moral Consciousness and Communicative Action*, Cambridge: Polity Press, 1990.

—— *The Structural Transformation of the Public Sphere: An Inquiry into a Category of Bourgeois Society*, Cambridge: Polity Press, 1992.

Haddad, Yvonne, 'Muhammad Abduh: Pioneer of Islamic Reform', in Ali Rahnema (ed.), *Pioneers of Islamic Revival*, London: Zed Books, 1994.

Haddad, Yvonne Yazbeck (ed.), *The Muslims of America*, Oxford: Oxford University Press, 1991.

Hall, Stuart, 'Religious Cults and Social Movements in Jamaica', in R. Bocock and K. Thompson (eds), *Religion and Ideology*, Manchester: Manchester University Press, 1985.

—— 'The West and the Rest: Discourse and Power', in Stuart Hall and Bram Gieben (eds), *Formations of Modernity*, Cambridge: Polity Press, 1992.

Halliday, Fred, *Arabs in Exile*, London: I.B. Tauris, 1992.

' "Hamas charity" funds frozen', *The Guardian*, 9 March 1996.

Hanafi, Hassan, *Min al-'aqida ila l-thawra*, Cairo: Maktaba Mabduli, 5 Volumes, 1987.

Hannerz, Ulf, 'Scenarios for Peripheral Cultures', in Anthony D. King (ed.), *Culture, Globalization and the World-System*, London: Macmillan, 1991.

—— *Cultural Complexity: Studies in the Social Organization of Meaning*, New York: Columbia University Press, 1992.

—— *Transnational Connections: Culture, People, Places*, London: Routledge, 1996.

Hassanpour, Amir, 'Satellite Footprints as National Borders: MED-TV and the Extraterritoriality of State Sovereignty', *Journal of Muslim Minority Affairs*, Vol. 18, No. 1, 1998.

Hefner, Robert W. and Patricia Horvatich (eds), *Islam in an Era of Nation-States: Politics and Religious Renewal in Muslim Southeast Asia*, Honolulu, HA: University of Hawai'i Press, 1997.

Hizb ut-Tahrir, London: Al-Khilafah Publications, n.d.

Holston, James and Arjun Appadurai, 'Cities and Citizenship', *Public Culture*, Vol. 8, 1996.

Horvatich, Patricia, 'Ways of Knowing Islam', *American Ethnologist*, Vol. 21, No. 4, 1994.

Hourani, Albert, *Arabic Thought in the Liberal Age, 1798–1939*, Cambridge: Cambridge University Press, 1983.

Ibrahim, Anwar, 'The *Ummah* and Tomorrow's World', *Futures*, Vol. 26, 1991.

'Intelligence Battle in Cyberspace', *Intelligence Newsletter*, 27 April 1995.

JanMohamed, Abdul R., 'Worldliness-without-World, Homelessness-as-Home: Toward a Definition of the Specular Border Intellectual', in Michael Sprinker (ed.), *Edward Said: A Critical Reader*, Oxford: Blackwell, 1992.

Kearney, Michael, 'Borders and Boundaries of State and Self at the End of Empire', *Journal of Historical Sociology*, Vol. 4, No. 1, 1991.

Keddie, Nikki, 'Sayyid Jamel al-Din "al-Afghani" ', in Ali Rahnema (ed.), *Pioneers of Islamic Revival*, London: Zed Books, 1994.

Keohane, Robert O. and Joseph S. Nye Jr., *Power and Interdependence*, Boston, MA: Little Brown, 1977.

Khalidi, Omar, 'Muslim Minorities: Theory and Experience of Muslim Interaction in Non-Muslim Societies', *Journal of the Institute of Muslim Minority Affairs*, Vol. 10, No. 2, July 1989.

Khomeini, Ruhallah, *Islam and Revolution*, trans. Hamid Algar, Berkeley, CA: Mizan, 1981.

King, Anthony D. (ed.) *Culture, Globalization and the World-System*, London: Macmillan, 1991.

Krasner, Stephen (ed.), *International Regimes*, Ithaca, NY: Cornell University Press, 1983.

Krishnaswamy, Revathi, 'Mythologies of Migrancy: Postcolonialism, Postmodernism and the Politics of (Dis)location', *ARIEL: A Review of International English Literature*, Vol. 26, No. 1, January 1995.

Kristeva, Julia, *Strangers to Ourselves*, New York: Columbia University Press, 1994.

Kuehls, Thom, *Beyond Sovereign Territory: The Space of Ecopolitics*, Minneapolis, MN: University of Minnesota Press, 1996.

Laclau, Ernesto (ed.), *The Making of Political Identities*, London: Verso, 1994.

Lambek, Michael, 'Certain Knowledge, Contestable Authority: Power and Practice on the Islamic Periphery', *American Ethnologist*, Vol. 17, No. 1, February 1990.

Landau, Jacob, *The Politics of Pan-Islam*, Oxford: Clarendon Press, 1994.

Landman, Nico, 'The Islamic Broadcasting Foundation in the Netherlands: Platform or Arena?', in Steven Vertovec and Ceri Peach (eds), *Islam in Europe: The Politics of Religion and Community*, London: Macmillan, 1997.

Lapid, Yosef, 'Culture's Ship: Returns and Departures in International Relations Theory', in Y. Lapid and F. Kratochwil (eds), *The Return of Culture and Identity in IR Theory*, Boulder, CO: Lynne Rienner, 1996.

Lapidus, Ira, *A History of Islamic Societies*, Cambridge: Cambridge University Press, 1988.

Laraña, Enrique, Hank Johnston and Joseph K. Gersfield (eds), *New Social Movements: From Ideology to Identity*, Philadelphia, PA: Temple University Press, 1994.

Lash, S. and J. Urry, *The End of Organized Capitalism*, Oxford: Polity Press, 1987.

Lavie, Smadar and Ted Swedenburg, 'Introduction: Displacement, Diaspora, and Geographies of Identity', in Smadar Lavie and Ted Swedenburg, *Displacement, Diaspora, and Geographies of Identity*, Durham, NC: Duke University Press, 1996.

Lebor, Adam, *A Heart Turned East*, London: Little, Brown and Company, 1997.

Lewis, Phillip, *Islamic Britain: Religion, Politics and Identity among British Muslims*, London: I.B. Tauris, 1994.

—— 'The Bradford Council of Mosques and the Search for Muslim Unity', in Steven Vertovec and Ceri Peach (eds), *Islam in Europe: The Politics of Religion and Community*, London: Macmillan, 1997.

Linklater, Andrew, *Beyond Realism and Marxism: Critical Theory and International Relations*, London: Macmillan, 1990.

—— *Men and Citizens in the Theory of International Relations*, London: Macmillan, 1990.

—— *The Transformation of Political Community*, Cambridge: Polity Press, 1998.

McAdam, Doug, John D. McCarthy and Mayer N. Zald (eds), *Comparative Perspectives on Social Movements*, New York: Cambridge University Press, 1996.

McDermott, Mustafa Yusuf and Muhammad Manazir Ahsan, *The Muslim Guide: For Teachers, Employers, Community and Social Administrators in Britain*, Leicester: The Islamic Foundation, 2nd Revised Edition, 1993.

MacFarquhar, Neil, 'With Mixed Feelings, Iran Tiptoes to the Internet', *New York Times*, 8 October 1996.

Magnusson, Warren, 'The Reification of Political Community', in R.B.J. Walker and Saul H. Mendlovitz (eds), *Contending Sovereignties: Redefining Political Community*, Boulder, CO: Lynne Rienner, 1990.

Mahdi, Muhsin, 'From the Manuscript Age to the Age of Printed Books', in George N. Atiyeh (ed.), *The Book in the Islamic World: The Written Word and Communication in the Middle East*, Albany, NY: SUNY Press, 1995.

Mahfouz, Naguib, *The Journey of Ibn Fattouma*, London: Doubleday, 1993.

Mardin, Serif, *Religion and Social Change in Modern Turkey: The Case of Bediüzzaman Saïd Nursi*, Albany, NY: SUNY Press, 1989.

Martin, Richard C. and Mark R. Woodward with Dwi S. Atmaja, *Defenders of Reason in Islam: Mu'tazilism from Medieval School to Modern Symbol*, Oxford: Oneworld, 1997.

Masud, Muhammad Khalid, 'The Obligation to Migrate: The Doctrine of *Hijra* in Islamic Law', in Dale F. Eickelman and James Piscatori (eds), *Muslim Travellers: Pilgrimage, Migration, and the Religious Imagination*, Berkeley, CA: University of California Press, 1990.

Mattelart, Armand, *Mapping World Communication: War, Progress, Culture*, Minneapolis, MN: University of Minnesota Press, 1994.

Mawdudi, Abul A'la, *Political Theory of Islam*, Lahore: Islamic Publications, 1960.

—— *First Principles of the Islamic State*, Lahore: Islamic Publications, 3rd Edition, 1967.

——*Unity of the Muslim World*, Lahore: Islamic Publications, 5th Edition, 1992.

Mernissi, Fatima, *Women and Islam: An Historical and Theological Enquiry*, Oxford: Blackwell, 1991.

—— *Women's Rebellion and Islamic Memory*, London: Zed Books, 1996.

Messick, Brinkley, *The Calligraphic State: Textual Domination and History in a Muslim Society*, Berkeley, CA: University of California Press, 1993.

Metcalf, Barbara D., 'Islam and Women: The Case of the Tablighi Jama'at', *Stanford Electronic Humanities Review*, Vol. 5, No. 1: Contested Polities, 1996.

—— 'The Pilgrimage Remembered: South Asian Accounts of the *Hajj*', in Dale F. Eickelman and James Piscatori (eds), *Muslim Travellers: Pilgrimage, Migration, and the Religious Imagination*, Berkeley, CA: University of California Press, 1990.

—— ' "Remaking Ourselves": Islamic Self-Fashioning in a Global Movement of Spiritual Renewal', in Martin E. Marty and R. Scott Appleby (eds), *Accounting for Fundamentalisms*, Chicago, IL: University of Chicago Press, 1994.

—— 'Introduction: Sacred Words, Sanctioned Practice, New Communities', in Barbara D. Metcalf (ed.), *Making Muslim Space in North America and Europe*, Berkeley, CA: University of California Press, 1996.

Modood, Tariq, 'British Asian Muslims and the Rushdie Affair', *The Political Quarterly*, Vol. 61, No. 2, April–June 1990.

Mokrzycki, Mike, 'Battleground of Bits and Bytes', *The Jerusalem Post*, 19 April 1995.

Morley, David and Kevin Robins, *Spaces of Identity: Global Media, Electronic Landscapes and Cultural Boundaries*, London: Routledge, 1995.

Mortimer, Edward, *Faith and Power: The Politics of Islam*, London: Faber, 1982.

Mouffe, Chantal, 'For a Politics of Nomadic Identity', in George Robertson, Melinda Mash, Lisa Tickner, Jon Bird, Barry Curtis and Tim Putnam (eds), *Travellers' Tales: Narratives of Home and Displacement*, London: Routledge, 1994.

Mutman, Mahmut, 'Under the Sign of Orientalism: The West vs. Islam', *Cultural Critique*, Winter 1992–93.

Nadwi, Syed Abul Hasan Ali, *Muslims in the West: The Message and Mission*, Leicester: The Islamic Foundation, 1983.

Naficy, Hamid, *The Making of Exile Cultures: Iranian Television in Los Angeles*, Minneapolis, MN: University of Minnesota Press, 1993.

Nasr, Seyyed Vali Reza, 'Mawdudi and the Jama'at-i Islami: The Origins, Theory and Practice of Islamic Revivalism', in Ali Rahnema (ed.), *Pioneers of Islamic Revival*, London: Zed Books, 1994.

Nederveen Pieterse, Jan, 'Globalization as Hybridization', in Mike Featherstone, Scott Lash and Roland Robertson (eds), *Global Modernities*, London: Sage, 1995.

—— 'Travelling Islam: Mosques without Minarets', in Ayse Öncü and Petra Wayland (eds), *Space, Culture and Power: New Identities in Globalizing Cities*, London: Zed Books, 1997.

Nielsen, Jørgen, 'Muslims in Britain: Searching for an Identity?' *New Community*, Vol. 13, No. 3, Spring 1987.

—— 'A Muslim Agenda for Britain: Some Reflections', *New Community*, Vol. 17, No. 3, April 1991.

—— *Muslims in Western Europe*, Edinburgh: Edinburgh University Press, 2nd Edition, 1995.

'Open letter to FOSIS', *Q-News*, Vol. 2, No. 17, 23–30 July 1993.

Papastergiadis, Nikos, 'Tracing Hybridity in Theory', in P. Werbner and Tariq Modood (eds), *Debating Cultural Hybridity*, London: Zed Books, 1997.

Piscatori, James, *Islam in a World of Nation-States*, Cambridge: Cambridge University Press, 1986.

—— 'The Rushdie Affair and the Politics of Ambiguity', *International Affairs*, Vol. 66, No. 4, 1990.

—— (ed.), *Islamic Fundamentalisms and the Gulf Crisis*, Chicago, IL: American Academy of Arts and Sciences, 1991.

Poston, Larry A., 'Da'wa in the West', in Yvonne Yazbeck Haddad (ed.), *The Muslims of America*, New York: Oxford University Press, 1991.

Radhakrishnan, R., *Diasporic Mediations: Between Home and Location*, Minneapolis, MN: University of Minnesota Press, 1996.

Rahman, Fazlur, *Islam and Modernity: Transformation of an Intellectual Tradition*, Chicago, IL: University of Chicago Press, 1982.

Rahnema, Ali, 'Ali Shariati: Teacher, Preacher, Rebel', in Ali Rahnema (ed.), *Pioneers of Islamic Revival*, London: Zed Books, 1994.

—— *An Islamic Utopian: A Political Biography of Ali Shari'ati*, London: I.B. Tauris, 1998.

Rajaee, Farhang, 'Iranian Ideology and Worldview: The Cultural Export of the Revolution', in John L. Esposito (ed.), *The Iranian Revolution: Its Global Impact*, Miami, FL: Florida International University Press, 1990.

Rathmell, Andrew, 'Netwar in the Gulf', *Jane's Intelligence Review*, January 1997.

Risso, Patricia, *Merchants and Faith: Muslim Commerce and Culture in the Indian Ocean*, Boulder, CO: Westview Press, 1995.

Robertson, Roland, 'Social Theory, Cultural Relativity and the Problem of Globality', in Anthony D. King (ed.), *Culture, Globalization and the World-System*, London: Macmillan, 1991.

—— *Globalization: Social Theory and Global Change*, London: Sage, 1992.

—— 'Glocalization: Time-Space and Homogeneity-Heterogeneity', in Mike Featherstone, Scott Lash and Roland Robertson (eds), *Global Modernities*, London: Sage, 1995.

Robinson, Francis, 'Islam and the Impact of Print', *Modern Asian Studies*, Vol. 27, No. 1, 1993.

Rodinson, Maxime, *Muhammad*, London: Penguin, 2nd English Edition, 1996.

Roff, William R. (ed.), *Islam and the Political Economy of Meaning*, London: Croom Helm, 1987.

Roper, Geoffrey, 'Faris al-Shidyaq and the Transition from Scribal to Print Culture in the Middle East', in George N. Atiyeh (ed.), *The Book in the Islamic World: The Written Word and Communication in the Middle East*, Albany, NY: SUNY Press, 1995.

Rosaldo, Renato, *Culture and Truth: The Remaking of Social Analysis*, London: Routledge, 1993.

Rosenau, James N., *Turbulence in World Politics: A Theory of Change and Continuity*, Princeton, PA: Princeton University Press, 1990.

—— *Along the Domestic-Foreign Frontier: Exploring Governance in a Turbulent World*, Cambridge: Cambridge University Press, 1997.

Rosenberg, Justin, 'What's the Matter with Realism?' *Review of International Studies*, Vol. 16, No. 4, October 1990.

Rowe, William and Vivian Schelling, *Memory and Modernity: Popular Culture in Latin America*, London: Verso, 1991.

Roy, Olivier, *The Failure of Political Islam*, London: I.B. Tauris, 1994.

Rudolph, Susanne Hoeber, 'Introduction: Religion, States, and Transnational Civil Society', in Susanne Hoeber Rudolph and James Piscatori (eds), *Transnational Religion and Fading States*, Boulder, CO: Westview Press, 1997.

Ruggie, John Gerard, 'Territoriality and Beyond: Problematizing Modernity in International Relations', *International Organization*, Vol. 47, No. 1, Winter 1993.

Rushdie, Salman, *Imaginary Homelands: Essays and Criticism 1981–1991*, London: Granta Books, 1992.

Rutherford, Jonathan, 'The Third Space: Interview with Homi Bhabha', in Jonathan Rutherford (ed.), *Identity: Community, Culture, Difference*, London: Lawrence and Wishart, 1990.

Ruthven, Malise, 'The West's Secret Weapon against Islam', *The Sunday Times*, 1 January 1995.

Sadowski, Yahya, ' "Just" a Religion: For the Tablighi Jama'at, Islam is not totalitarian', *The Brookings Review*, Vol. 14, No. 3, Summer 1996.

Safran, William, 'Diasporas in Modern Societies: Myths of Homeland and Return', *Diaspora*, Vol. 1, No. 1, 1991.

Said, Edward, 'Media, Margins and Modernity', Edward Said in conversation with Raymond Williams in Tony Pinkney (ed.), *The Politics of Modernism: Against the New Conformists*, London: Verso, 1989.

—— *The World, the Text and the Critic*, London: Faber and Faber, 1984.

—— *Orientalism*, London: Penguin, 1995.

—— *Covering Islam: How the Media and the Experts Determine How We See the Rest of the World*, London: Vintage, Revised Edition, 1997.

Salvatore, Armando, *Islam and the Political Discourse of Modernity*, Reading, MA: Ithaca Press, 1997.

Sardar, Ziauddin, *Information and the Muslim World*, London: Mansell, 1988.

—— 'Paper, Printing and Compact Disks: The Making and Unmaking of Islamic Culture', *Media, Culture and Society*, Vol. 15, No. 1, January 1993.

—— *Postmodernism and the Other: The New Imperialism of Western Culture*, London: Pluto Press, 1998.

Sassen, Saskia, *The Global City*, Princeton, PA: Princeton University Press, 1991.

Sayyid, Bobby S., *A Fundamental Fear: Eurocentrism and the Emergence of Islamism*, London: Zed Books, 1997.

Scantlebury, Elizabeth, 'Muslims in Manchester: The Depiction of a Religious Community', *New Community*, Vol. 21, No. 3, July 1995.

Schiffauer, Werner, 'Migration and Religiousness', in Tomas Gerholm and Yngve Georg Lithman, *The New Islamic Presence in Western Europe*, London: Mansell Publishing, 1988.

Schnapper, Dominique, 'Muslim Communities, Ethnic Minorities and Citizens', in Bernard Lewis and Dominique Schnapper (eds), *Muslims in Europe*, London: Pinter, 1994.

Schulze, Reinhard, 'Islam und Herrschaft. Zur politischen Instrumentalisierung einer Religion', in M. Lüders (ed.), *Der Islam im Aufbruch? Perspektive der arabischen Welt*, Munich: Piper Publ., 1992.

—— 'How Medieval is Islam? Muslim Intellectuals and Modernity', in Jochen Hippler and Andrea Lueg (eds), *The Next Threat: Western Perceptions of Islam*, London: Pluto Press, 1995.

Shadid, W.A.R. and P.S. van Koningsveld, 'Legal Adjustments for Religious Minorities', in W.A.R. Shadid and P.S. van Koningsveld (eds), *Islam in Dutch Society*, Kampen: Kok Pharos, 1992.

Shapiro, Michael J. and Hayward R. Alker (eds), *Challenging Boundaries: Global Flows, Territorial Identities*, Minneapolis, MN: University of Minnesota Press, 1996.

Shaw, Rosalind and Charles Stewart, 'Introduction: Problematizing Syncretism', in Charles Stewart and Rosalind Shaw (eds), *Syncretism/Anti-Syncretism: The Politics of Religious Synthesis*, London: Routledge, 1994.

Siddiqui, Ataullah, 'Muslims in the Contemporary World: Dialogue in Perspective', *World Faiths Encounter*, No. 20, July 1998.

Siddiqui, Kalim, 'Beyond the Muslim Nation-States', in Isma'il R. Al-Faruqi and Abdullah Omar Nasseef (eds), *Social and Natural Sciences: The Islamic Perspective*, Sevenoaks: Hodder and Stoughton, 1981.

Smith, Michael Peter, 'Can You Imagine? Transnational Migration and the Globalization of Grassroots Politics', *Social Text*, No. 39, Summer 1994.

Sreberny-Mohammadi, Annabelle, 'On reading "Islam and Communication"', *Media, Culture and Society*, Vol. 15, No. 4, 1993.

Sulavik, Chris, 'Citicorp to Launch Islamic Banking Unit', *Reuters*, 9 April 1996.

Sunier, T., 'Islam and Ethnicity Among Turks', in W.A.R. Shadid and P.S. van Koningsveld (eds), *Islam in Dutch Society*, Kampen: Kok Pharos, 1992.

Sylvester, Christine, *Feminist Theory and International Relations in a Postmodern Era*, Cambridge: Cambridge University Press, 1994.

Thomä-Venske, Hanns, 'The Religious Life of Muslims in Berlin', in Tomas Gerholm and Yngve Georg Lithman, *The New Islamic Presence in Western Europe*, London: Mansell Publishing, 1988.

Tololyan, Khachig, 'Rethinking *Diaspora*(s): Stateless Power in the Transnational Moment', *Diaspora*, Vol. 5, No. 1, 1996.

Trabelsi, Habib, 'Saudis Near End of Seven-Year Wait to Surf the Net', *Agence France Presse*, 15 July 1998.

Vakili, Valla, 'Debating Religion and Politics in Iran: The Political Thought of Abdolkarim Soroush', Council on Foreign Relations Studies Department Occasional Paper No. 2, 1996.

van Bommel, A., 'The History of Muslim Umbrella Organizations', in W.A.R. Shadid and P.S. van Koningsveld (eds), *Islam in Dutch Society*, Kampen: Kok Pharos, 1992.

van Doorn, Nelly, 'Portrait of a Female Preacher', *Inside Indonesia*, No. 52, October–December 1997.

van Ooijen, H., 'Religion and Emancipation: A Study of the Development of Moroccan Islamic Organizations in a Dutch Town', in W.A.R. Shadid and P.S. van Koningsveld (eds), *Islam in Dutch Society*, Kampen: Kok Pharos, 1992.

Various authors, 'Region joins the global revolution', *MEED Special Report*, 1 March 1996.

Vasquez, John, *The Power of Power Politics*, London: Pinter, 1983.

Vertovec, Steven and Ceri Peach, 'Introduction: Islam in Europe and the Politics of Religion and Community', in Steven Vertovec and Ceri Peach (eds), *Islam in Europe: The
Politics of Religion and Community*, London: Macmillan, 1997.

Viswesvaran, Kamala, *Fictions of Feminist Ethnography*, Minneapolis, MN: University of
Minnesota Press, 1994.

Voll, John O., 'Islamic Issues for Muslims in the United States', in Yvonne Yazbeck
Haddad (ed.), *The Muslims of America*, Oxford: Oxford University Press, 1991.

Waardenburg, Jacques, 'Muslims as Dhimmis: The Emancipation of Muslim Immigrants
in Europe: The Case of Switzerland', in W.A.R. Shadid and P.S. van Koningsveld,
Muslims in the Margin: Political Responses to the Presence of Islam in Western Europe, Kampen:
Kok Pharos, 1996.

Walker, R.B.J., *One World, Many Worlds*, Boulder, CO: Lynne Rienner, 1988.

—— 'Sovereignty, Identity, and Community', in R.B.J. Walker and Saul H. Mendlovitz
(eds), *Contending Sovereignties: Redefining Political Community*, Boulder, CO: Lynne Rienner,
1990.

—— *Inside/Outside: International Relations as Political Theory*, Cambridge: Cambridge University Press, 1993.

—— 'Social Movements/World Politics', *Millennium*, Vol. 23, No. 3, 1994.

—— 'International Relations and the Concept of the Political', in Ken Booth and Steve
Smith (eds), *International Relations Theory Today*, Cambridge: Polity Press, 1995.

Walzer, Michael (ed.), *Toward A Global Civil Society*, Providence, RI: Berghahn Books, 1995.

Waters, Malcolm, *Globalization*, London: Routledge, 1995.

Watt, W. Montgomery, *Muhammad at Medina*, Oxford: Clarendon Press, 1956.

—— *Islamic Political Thought*, Edinburgh: Edinburgh University Press, 1987.

Weber, Cynthia, *Simulating Sovereignty: Intervention, the State and Symbolic Exchange*, Cambridge:
Cambridge University Press, 1995.

Werbner, Pnina, 'Islamic Radicalism and the Gulf War: Lay Preachers and Political
Dissent among British Pakistanis', in Bernard Lewis and Dominique Schnapper (eds),
Muslims in Europe, London: Pinter, 1994.

—— 'The Making of Muslim Dissent: Hybridized Discourses, Lay Preachers and
Radical Rhetoric among British Pakistanis', *American Ethnologist*, Vol. 23, No. 1, 1996.

—— 'Essentialising Essentialism, Essentialising Silence: Ambivalence and Multiplicity in
the Constructions of Racism and Ethnicity', in Pnina Werbner and Tariq Modood
(eds), *Debating Cultural Hybridity: Multi-Cultural Identities and the Politics of Anti-Racism*,
London: Zed Books, 1997.

Westerlund, David and Eva Evers Rosander (eds), *African Islam and Islam in Africa: Encounters
between Sufis and Islamists*, London: Hurst and Company, 1997.

Wilpert, Czarina, 'Religion and Ethnicity: Orientations, Perceptions and Strategies
among Turkish Alevi and Sunni Migrants in Berlin', in Tomas Gerholm and Yngve
Georg Lithman, *The New Islamic Presence in Western Europe*, London: Mansell Publishing,
1988.

Yalçin-Heckman, Lale, 'Are Fireworks Islamic?: Towards an Understanding of Turkish
Migrants and Islam in Germany', in Charles Stewart and Rosalind Shaw (eds),
Syncretism/Anti-Syncretism: The Politics of Religious Synthesis, London: Routledge, 1994.

Zubaida, Sami, *Islam, the People and the State: Essays on Political Ideas and Movements in the
Middle East*, London: I.B. Tauris, Revised Edition, 1993.

Glossary of Arabic/Islamic terms

'alim Religious scholar (singular of *ulama*)
dar al-'ahd 'Land of Treaty'
dar al-harb 'Land of War'
dar al-islam 'Land of Islam'
da'wa Propagation of the religion
darura 'Imperative need'
din wa dawla 'Religion and state'
faqih Legal scholar or jurist
fatwa Opinion or edict of a legal scholar (plural: *fatawa*)
fiqh Islamic legal science
hadith Historically transmitted report about the Prophet Muhammad
hajj Pilgrimage to Mecca
halal Permissible
haram Forbidden
hijra Migration
ijaza License to transmit/teach religious knowledge (esp. *hadith*)
ijma Consensus
ijtihad Independent reasoning or judgement
ikhtilaf Differences of opinion as regards *fiqh*
isra The Prophet's night journey to Jerusalem
istihsan Legal methodology employed in the absence of textual precedent
istislah Reasoning based on a "search for the good" (or for *maslaha*)
jahiliya Pre- or non-Islamic ignorance
kalam Scholastic theology
khilafa The institution of rule by the Caliph
khutba The sermon given at a Friday congregational prayer
madhhab School of Islamic law (plural: *madhahib*)
madrasa Religious school
majlis al-shura Consultative council
maslaha Common good
qiyas A legal methodology based on analogical deduction
rihla Travel
shari'a Religious law

shura   Consultation

sira   Biographical literature about the Prophet.

sunna   'Orthodox' traditions of the Prophet

tafsir   Qur'anic exegesis

tawhid   Unity of God

ulama   Religious scholars (singular: *'alim*)

umma   The world community of Muslims

usul al-fiqh   Principles of legal science

wilayat al-faqih   Sovereignty or guardianship of the legal scholar (Khomeini's doctrine of governance)

Index

post-national politics 26
post-Westphalian politics 20, 26
postmodernity 2, 60, 66, 67
postnationality 48
Poston, L.A. 158
power 88, 100, 179
power/knowledge 27, 39, 84, 88, 90
print-capitalism 75, 155, 161, 169
print-Islam 161, 162
problematising the political 19-26
public space 11-12
Punjab 47

Q-News 125, 126, 141, 165
Qatar 171, 172
Qom 161, 167
Qur'an 182, 183, 184; diaspora 103, 104; media and information technology 155, 158, 159, 160, 161, 169; political community 110, 119, 123, 132-5, 140, 142-4, 150; umma 70, 71, 72, 78
Qutb, S. 79, 137, 162

Radhakrishnan, R. 104, 180-1
Rahman, F. 133, 182, 183, 184
rashidun (rightly-guided caliphs) 72
realism 7, 8; classic 6; political 14
reason/dogma 61
reductionism 67
Refah party 128, 147
religion 57, 58-9, 77, 80-1, 111-14, 141
Renan, E. 75
resistance 88
rihla (travel for education) 112, 113-14
Robertson, R. 33-4, 35, 36
Robins, K. 153-4
Robinson, F. 168
Rosaldo, R. 97
Rosenau, J.N. 19-20, 97
Rowe, W. 95
Roy, O. 156, 176
Rudolph, S.H. 97
Ruggie, J.G. 19-20
Rushdie, S.: Imaginary Homelands 183; Satanic Verses 103, 104, 111, 130, 131, 135, 147-8

Sadat, A. 80
Said, E. 27, 54, 85-6, 87-8, 89, 101-2
SalatBase 161, 165
Sardar, Z. 105, 160
Sartre, J.-P. 114
Saudi Arabia 185; King Abdul Aziz City for Science and Technology 172; media

and information technology 157-8, 162, 164, 171, 174-5; political community 128, 146, 147-8; *see also* Committee for the Defence of Legitimate Rights
Sayyid, S. 113, 181, 188; umma 54, 55, 59, 64-5, 66-9, 81
Scantlebury, E. 122
Schelling, V. 95
Schiffauer, W. 185
Schnapper, D. 135
Schulze, R. 76-7
sectarian conflict 127
self-identity 32
Serbia 47
Shapiro, M.J. 26
Shari'a (Islamic Law) 70, 72, 76
Shariati, A. 83-4, 114, 118, 162
Shaw, R. 180
Shi'a 73, 118, 130, 131
shura (consultation) 78-9
Siddiqui, A. 119, 131, 138-9
Simmel, G. 33
Singapore 18, 173
situated difference 39
Smith, A. 31
Smith, M.P. 178, 188
social movements 16-17, 19, 22-4
sociology 26, 30, 53; of globalisation 30-8
Soroush, A. 183, 184, 185
South Asia 90, 105, 141, 148, 165
Southeast Asia 73, 137, 153, 157
sovereignty 14, 17, 20, 21, 22, 25
space 97-8; *see also* political spaces; third space; time-space
Sri Lanka 47
state 8, 22, 43; sovereignty 14, 17, 25
state-centrism 6
Stewart, C. 180
subject/order 27
Sudan 176
Sufi 119, 127, 131, 139, 185
Sunier, T. 117
Sunni 70, 73, 118, 127, 146, 160, 161, 179, 183
supranational political forms 17-18, 19
Swadhyaya movement 23
Swedenburg, T. 97, 98, 99, 106
Sylvester, C. 26
syncretism 102
Syria 74, 118, 163

Ta-Ha 125